Problem Solving in Data Structures & Algorithms Using C

First Edition

By Hemant Jain

ACKNOWLEDGEMENT

The author is very grateful to GOD ALMIGHTY for his grace and blessing.

Deepest gratitude for the help and support of my brother Dr. Sumant Jain. This book would not have been possible without the support and encouragement he provided.

I would like to express profound gratitude to my guide/ my friend Naveen Kaushik for his invaluable encouragement, supervision and useful suggestion throughout this book writing work. His support and continuous guidance enable me to complete my work successfully.

Last but not least, I am thankful to Anil Berry and Others who helped me directly or indirectly in completing this book.

Hemant Jain

TABLE OF CONTENTS

TABLE OF CONTENTS 5

TABLE OF CONTENTS 7

CHAPTER 0: HOW TO USE THIS BOOK 13

CHAPTER 1: INTRODUCTION - PROGRAMMING OVERVIEW 17

CHAPTER 2: ALGORITHMS ANALYSIS 38

CHAPTER 3: APPROACH TO SOLVE ALGORITHM DESIGN PROBLEMS 50

CHAPTER 4: ABSTRACT DATA TYPE 55

CHAPTER 5: SEARCHING 69

CHAPTER 6: SORTING 100

CHAPTER 7: LINKED LIST 119

CHAPTER 8: STACK 169

CHAPTER 9: QUEUE 191

CHAPTER 10: TREE 201

CHAPTER 11: PRIORITY QUEUE 248

CHAPTER 12: HASH-TABLE 272

CHAPTER 13: GRAPHS 286

CHAPTER 14: STRING ALGORITHMS 305

CHAPTER 15: ALGORITHM DESIGN TECHNIQUES 335

CHAPTER 16: BRUTE FORCE ALGORITHM 341

CHAPTER 17: GREEDY ALGORITHM 347

CHAPTER 18: DIVIDE-AND-CONQUER, DECREASE-AND-CONQUER 356

CHAPTER 19: DYNAMIC PROGRAMMING 368

CHAPTER 20: BACKTRACKING AND BRANCH-AND-BOUND 377

CHAPTER 21: COMPLEXITY THEORY AND NP COMPLETENESS 380

CHAPTER 22: INTERVIEW STRATEGY 389

CHAPTER 23: SYSTEM DESIGN 391

APPENDIX 423

INDEX **424**

TABLE OF CONTENTS

TABLE OF CONTENTS 5

TABLE OF CONTENTS 7

CHAPTER 0: HOW TO USE THIS BOOK 13

    WHAT THIS BOOK IS ABOUT 13

    PREPARATION PLANS 13

    SUMMARY 16

CHAPTER 1: INTRODUCTION - PROGRAMMING OVERVIEW 17

    INTRODUCTION 17

    VARIABLE 17

    POINTERS 17

    ARRAY 18

    TWO DIMENSIONAL ARRAY 20

    ARRAY INTERVIEW QUESTIONS 21

    STRUCTURE 24

    POINTER TO STRUCTURE 25

    DYNAMIC MEMORY ALLOCATION 26

    FUNCTION 27

    CONCEPT OF STACK 27

    SYSTEM STACK AND FUNCTION CALLS 28

    PARAMETER PASSING, CALL BY VALUE 29

    PARAMETER PASSING, CALL BY REFERENCE 30

    RECURSIVE FUNCTION 31

    EXERCISES 36

CHAPTER 2: ALGORITHMS ANALYSIS 38

    INTRODUCTION 38

    ASYMPTOTIC ANALYSIS 38

    BIG-O NOTATION 38

    OMEGA-Ω NOTATION 39

    THETA-Θ NOTATION 40

    COMPLEXITY ANALYSIS OF ALGORITHMS 40

    TIME COMPLEXITY ORDER 41

    DERIVING THE RUNTIME FUNCTION OF AN ALGORITHM 42

    TIME COMPLEXITY EXAMPLES 42

    MASTER THEOREM 46

    MODIFIED MASTER THEOREM 48

    EXERCISE 49

CHAPTER 3: APPROACH TO SOLVE ALGORITHM DESIGN PROBLEMS 50

    INTRODUCTION 50

    CONSTRAINTS 50

    IDEA GENERATION 51

    COMPLEXITIES 52

    CODING 52

Testing 53

Example 53

Summary 54

CHAPTER 4: ABSTRACT DATA TYPE **55**

Abstract data type (ADT) 55

Data-Structure 55

Array 56

Linked List 57

Stack 58

Queue 58

Trees 59

Binary Tree 59

Binary Search Trees (BST) 60

Priority Queue (Heap) 61

Hash-Table 62

Dictionary / Symbol Table 63

Graphs 65

Graph Algorithms 66

Sorting Algorithms 67

Counting Sort 67

End note 68

CHAPTER 5: SEARCHING **69**

Introduction 69

Why Searching? 69

Different Searching Algorithms 69

Linear Search – Unsorted Input 69

Linear Search – Sorted 70

Binary Search 70

String Searching Algorithms 71

Hashing and Symbol Tables 71

How sorting is useful in Selection Algorithm? 71

Problems in Searching 72

Exercise 98

CHAPTER 6: SORTING **100**

Introduction 100

Type of Sorting 101

Bubble-Sort 101

Modified (improved) Bubble-Sort 103

Insertion-Sort 104

Selection-Sort 105

Merge-Sort 107

Quick-Sort 109

Quick Select 111

Bucket Sort 113

Generalized Bucket Sort 114

Heap-Sort 114

TREE SORTING 115

EXTERNAL SORT (EXTERNAL MERGE-SORT) 115

COMPARISONS OF THE VARIOUS SORTING ALGORITHMS 116

SELECTION OF BEST SORTING ALGORITHM 116

EXERCISE 117

CHAPTER 7: LINKED LIST **119**

INTRODUCTION 119

LINKED LIST 119

TYPES OF LINKED LIST 119

SINGLY LINKED LIST 120

DOUBLY LINKED LIST 144

CIRCULAR LINKED LIST 154

DOUBLY CIRCULAR LIST 162

EXERCISE 167

CHAPTER 8: STACK **169**

INTRODUCTION 169

THE STACK ABSTRACT DATA TYPE 169

STACK USING ARRAY (MACRO) 171

STACK USING ARRAY (DYNAMIC MEMORY) 173

STACK USING ARRAY (GROWING CAPACITY IMPLEMENTATION) 174

STACK USING ARRAY (GROWING-REDUCING CAPACITY IMPLEMENTATION) 174

STACK USING LINKED LIST 176

PROBLEMS IN STACK 177

PROS AND CONS OF ARRAY AND LINKED LIST IMPLEMENTATION OF STACK 190

USES OF STACK 190

EXERCISE 190

CHAPTER 9: QUEUE **191**

INTRODUCTION 191

THE QUEUE ABSTRACT DATA TYPE 191

QUEUE USING ARRAY 192

QUEUE USING LINKED LIST 194

PROBLEMS IN QUEUE 197

EXERCISE 199

CHAPTER 10: TREE **201**

INTRODUCTION 201

TERMINOLOGY IN TREE 202

BINARY TREE 203

TYPES OF BINARY TREES 205

PROBLEMS IN BINARY TREE 207

BINARY SEARCH TREE (BST) 227

PROBLEMS IN BINARY SEARCH TREE (BST) 228

EXERCISE 244

CHAPTER 11: PRIORITY QUEUE **248**

INTRODUCTION 248

TYPES OF HEAP 249

Heap ADT Operations...250

Operation on Heap...250

Heap-Sort...260

Uses of Heap..264

Problems in Heap...264

Exercise...270

CHAPTER 12: HASH-TABLE...272

Introduction..272

Hash-Table..273

Hashing with Open Addressing...274

Hashing with Separate chaining...278

Problems in Hashing...281

Exercise...284

CHAPTER 13: GRAPHS...286

Introduction..286

Graph Representation...288

Adjacency Matrix...288

Adjacency List...289

Graph traversals...291

Depth First Traversal..291

Breadth First Traversal...293

Problems in Graph..295

Directed Acyclic Graph...296

Topological Sort..296

Minimum Spanning Trees (MST)...297

Shortest Path Algorithms in Graph...299

Exercise...304

CHAPTER 14: STRING ALGORITHMS...305

Introduction..305

String Matching...305

Dictionary / Symbol Table..309

Problems in String..320

Memmove Function...329

Exercise...333

CHAPTER 15: ALGORITHM DESIGN TECHNIQUES...335

Introduction..335

Brute Force Algorithm..335

Greedy Algorithm...335

Divide-and-Conquer, Decrease-and-Conquer...336

Dynamic Programming..337

Reduction / Transform-and-Conquer..338

Backtracking...338

Branch-and-bound..339

A* Algorithm...340

Conclusion..340

CHAPTER 16: BRUTE FORCE ALGORITHM **341**

INTRODUCTION 341

PROBLEMS IN BRUTE FORCE ALGORITHM 341

CONCLUSION 346

CHAPTER 17: GREEDY ALGORITHM **347**

INTRODUCTION 347

PROBLEMS ON GREEDY ALGORITHM 347

CHAPTER 18: DIVIDE-AND-CONQUER, DECREASE-AND-CONQUER **356**

INTRODUCTION 356

GENERAL DIVIDE-AND-CONQUER RECURRENCE 357

MASTER THEOREM 357

PROBLEMS ON DIVIDE-AND-CONQUER ALGORITHM 359

CHAPTER 19: DYNAMIC PROGRAMMING **368**

INTRODUCTION 368

PROBLEMS ON DYNAMIC PROGRAMMING ALGORITHM 368

CHAPTER 20: BACKTRACKING AND BRANCH-AND-BOUND **377**

INTRODUCTION 377

PROBLEMS ON BACKTRACKING ALGORITHM 377

CHAPTER 21: COMPLEXITY THEORY AND NP COMPLETENESS **380**

INTRODUCTION 380

DECISION PROBLEM 380

COMPLEXITY CLASSES 380

CLASS P PROBLEMS 380

CLASS NP PROBLEMS 381

CLASS CO-NP 383

NP–HARD: 384

NP–COMPLETE PROBLEMS 384

REDUCTION 385

END NOTE 388

CHAPTER 22: INTERVIEW STRATEGY **389**

INTRODUCTION 389

RESUME 389

NONTECHNICAL QUESTIONS 389

TECHNICAL QUESTIONS 389

CHAPTER 23: SYSTEM DESIGN **391**

SYSTEM DESIGN 391

SYSTEM DESIGN PROCESS 391

SCALABILITY THEORY 392

DESIGN SIMPLIFIED FACEBOOK 396

DESIGN A SHORTENING SERVICE LIKE BITLY 402

STOCK QUERY SERVER 404

DESIGN A BASIC SEARCH ENGINE DATABASE 405

DUPLICATE INTEGER IN MILLIONS OF DOCUMENTS 407

ZOMATO 409

YOUTUBE 410

DESIGN IRCTC 411

OBJECT ORIENTED CLASS DIAGRAM 412

THE ABOVE RELATION ARE AS FOLLOWS: 412

ALARM CLOCK 413

DESIGN FOR ELEVATOR OF A BUILDING 414

VALET PARKING SYSTEM 416

OO DESIGN FOR A MCDONALDS SHOP 417

OBJECT ORIENTED DESIGN FOR A RESTAURANT 418

OBJECT ORIENTED DESIGN FOR A LIBRARY SYSTEM 419

SUGGEST A SHORTEST PATH 420

EXERCISE 421

APPENDIX **423**

APPENDIX A 423

INDEX..**424**

CHAPTER 0: HOW TO USE THIS BOOK

What this book is about

This book is about usage of data structures and algorithms in computer programming. Data structures are the ways in which data is arranged in computers memory. Algorithms are set of instructions to solve some problem by manipulating these data structures.

Designing an efficient algorithm to solve a computer science problem is a skill of Computer programmer. This is the skill which tech companies like Google, Amazon, Microsoft, Facebook, Adobe and many others are looking for in an interview. Once we are comfortable with a programming language, the next step is to learn how to write efficient algorithms.

This book assumes that you are a C language developer. You are not an expert in C language, but you are well familiar with concepts of pointers, functions, arrays and recursion. At the start of this book, we will be revising the C language fundamentals that will be used throughout this book. We will be looking into some of the problems in arrays and recursion too.

Then in the coming chapter we will be looking into Complexity Analysis:. Followed by the various data structures and their algorithms. Will look into a linked list, stack, queue, trees, heap, Hash-Table and graphs. We will also be looking into sorting, searching techniques.

And we will be looking into algorithm analysis of various algorithm techniques, we will be looking into brute force algorithms, greedy algorithms, divide and conquer algorithms, dynamic scheduling, reduction and back tracking.

In the end, we will be looking into system design that will give a systematic approach to solve the design problems in an Interview.

Preparation Plans

Given the limited time you have before your next interview, it is important to have a solid preparation plan. The preparation plan depends upon the time and which companies you are planning to target. Below are the three-preparation plan for 1 Month, 3 Month and 5 Month durations.

1 Month Preparation Plans

Below is a list of topics and approximate time user need to take to finish these topics. These are the most important chapters that must to be prepared before appearing for an interview.

This plan should be used when you have a small time before an interview. These chapters cover 90% of data structures and algorithm interview questions. In this plan since we are reading about the various ADT in chapter 4 so we can use these datatype easily without knowing the internal details how they are implemented.

Chapter 24 is for system design, you must read this chapter if you are three or more years of experienced. Anyway, reading this chapter will give the reader a broader perspective of various designs.

Time	Chapters	Explanation
Week 1	Chapter 1: Introduction - Programming Overview Chapter 2: Algorithms Analysis Chapter 3: Approach To Solve Algorithm Design Problems Chapter 4: Abstract Data Type	You will get a basic understanding of how to find complexity of a solution. You will know how to handle new problems. You will read about a variety of datatypes and their uses.
Week 2	Chapter 5: Searching Chapter 6: Sorting Chapter 14: String Algorithms	Searching, Sorting and String algorithm consists of a major portion of the interviews.
Week 3	Chapter 7: Linked List Chapter 8: Stack Chapter 9: Queue	Linked lists are one of the favorites in an interview.
Week 4	Chapter 10: Tree Chapter 23: Interview Strategy Chapter 24: System Design	This portion you will read about Trees and System Design. You are good to go for interviews. Best of luck.

3 Month Preparation Plan

This plan should be used when you have some time to prepare for an interview. This preparation plan includes nearly everything in this book except various algorithm techniques. Algorithm problems that are based on dynamic programming divide & conquer etc. Which are asked in vary specific companies like Google, Facebook, etc. Therefore, until you are planning to face interview with them you can park these topics for some time and focus on the rest of the topics.

Again, same thing here with system design problems, the more experience you are, the more important this chapter becomes. However, if you are a fresher from college, then also you should read this chapter.

Time	Chapters	Explanation
Week 1	Chapter 1: Introduction - Programming Overview Chapter 2: Algorithms Analysis Chapter 3: Approach To Solve Algorithm Design Problems Chapter 4: Abstract Data Type	You will get a basic understanding of how to find complexity of a solution. You will know how to handle new problems. You will read about a variety of datatypes and their uses.
Week 2 & Week 3	Chapter 5: Searching Chapter 6: Sorting Chapter 14: String Algorithms	Searching, sorting and string algorithm consists of a major portion of the interviews.
Week 4 & Week 5	Chapter 7: Linked List Chapter 8: Stack Chapter 9: Queue	Linked lists are one of the favorites in an interview.
Week 6 & Week 7	Chapter 10: Tree Chapter 11: Heap	This portion you will read about trees and heap data structures.
Week 8 & Week 9	Chapter 12: Hash-Table Chapter 13: Graphs	Hash-Table are used thorough the book in various places but now it's time to understand how Hash-Table are actually implemented. Graphs are used to propose a solution many real life problems.
Week 10	Chapter 23: Interview Strategy Chapter 24: System Design	Interview strategy and system design chapter are the final chapters of this course.

Week 11 & Week 12	Revision of the chapters listed above.	At this time, you need to revise all the chapters that we have seen in this book. Whatever is left needs to be completed and the exercise that may be left needing to be solved in this period of time.

5 Month Preparation Plan

In this preparation plan is made on top of 3-month plan. In this plan, the students should look for algorithm design chapters. In addition, in the rest of the time they need to practice more and more from www.topcoder.com and other resources. If you are targeting google, Facebook, etc., then it is highly recommended to join topcoder and practice as much as possible.

Time	Chapters	Explanation
Week 1 Week 2	Chapter 1: Introduction - Programming Overview Chapter 2: Algorithms Analysis Chapter 3: Approach To Solve Algorithm Design Problems Chapter 4: Abstract Data Type	You will get a basic understanding of how to find complexity of a solution. You will know how to handle new problems. You will read about a variety of datatypes and their uses.
Week 3 Week 4 Week 5	Chapter 5: Searching Chapter 6: Sorting Chapter 14: String Algorithms	Searching, sorting and string algorithm consists of a major portion of the interviews.
Week 6 Week 7 Week 8	Chapter 7: Linked List Chapter 8: Stack Chapter 9: Queue	Linked lists are one of the favorites in an interview.
Week 9 Week 10	Chapter 10: Tree Chapter 11: Heap	This portion you will read about trees
Week 11 Week 12	Chapter 12: Hash-Table Chapter 13: Graphs	Hash-Table are used thorough the book in various places but now it's time to understand how Hash-Table are actually implemented. Graphs are used to propose a solution many real life problems.
Week 13 Week 14 Week 15 Week 16	Chapter 15: Algorithm Design Techniques Chapter 16: Brute Force Chapter 17: Greedy Algorithm Chapter 18: Divide-And-Conquer, Decrease-And-Conquer Chapter 19: Dynamic Programming Chapter 20: Backtracking And Branch-And-Bound Chapter 21: Complexity Theory And Np Completeness	These chapters contain various algorithms types and their usage. Once the user is familiar with most of this algorithm. Then the next step is to start solving topcoder problems from https://www.topcoder.com/
Week 17 Week 18	Chapter 22: Interview Strategy Chapter 23: System Design	Interview strategy and system design chapter are the final chapters of this course.
Week 19 Week 20	Revision of the chapters listed above.	At this time, you need to revise all the chapters that we have seen in this book. Whatever is left needs to be completed and the exercise that may be left needing to be solved in this period.

Summary

These are few preparation plans that can be followed to complete this book there by preparing for the interview. It is highly recommended that the user should read the problem statement first, then he should try to solve the problems by himself and then only he should look into the solution to find the approach of the book practicing more and more problems open our thinking capacity and you will be able to handle new problems in an interview. System design is a topic that is not asked much from a fresher from college, but as you gain experience its importance increase. We will recommend practicing all the problems given in this book, then solve more and more problems from online resources like www.topcoder.com, www.careercup.com, www.geekforgeek.com etc.

CHAPTER 1: INTRODUCTION - PROGRAMMING OVERVIEW

Introduction

This chapter emphasizes on the fundamentals of C Programming language. It will talk about variables, pointers, recursion, arrays etc.

Variable

For every variable, some memory is allocated. The size of this memory depends on the type of the variable. For example, 2 bytes are allocated for *integer* type, 4 bytes are allocated for *float* type, etc.

Program 1.1

```
1.      #include <stdio.h>
2.
3.      int main()
4.      {
5.              int var1,var2,var3;
6.              var1=100;
7.              var2=200;
8.              var3=var1+var2;
9.              printf("Adding %d and %d will give %d", var1,var2,var3);
10.             return 0;
11.     }
```

Analysis:
Line 5: Memory is allocated for variables var1, var2 and var3. Whenever we declare a variable, then memory is allocated for storing the value in the variable. In our example, 2 bytes are allocated for each of the variable.
Line 6 & 7: Value 100 is stored in variable var1 and value 200 is stored in variable var2.
Line 8: Value of var1 and var2 is added and stored in var3.
Line 9: Finally, the value of var1, var2 and var3 is printed to screen.

Pointers

Pointers are nothing more than variables that store memory addresses of a variable and can be used to access the value stored at those addresses. Various operators such as *, &, and [], enable us to use pointers.

Address - The numeric location of a place in memory. An address of a memory is used by the computer to identify data stored in it quickly. Just as the postal address of a house is used to identify a house by the postman.

Dereference - A pointer stores an address of a location in the memory. To get what value it contains, we need to dereference the pointer, meaning we need to go to that location and get the value stored there.

Program 1.2

```
1.      int main()
2.      {
3.              int var;
4.              int* ptr;
5.              var = 10;
6.              ptr = &var;
7.
8.              printf("Value stored at variable var is %d\n",var);
9.              printf("Value stored at variable var is %d\n", *ptr);
10.
11.             printf("The address of variable var is %p \n", &var);
12.             printf("The address of variable var is %p \n", ptr);
13.             return 0;
14.     }
```

Analysis:

Line 3: An *integer* type variable var is created.

Line 4: A pointer to int ptr is created.

Line 6: Address of var is stored in ptr.

Line 8 & 9: Value stored in variable var is printed to screen. * Operator is used to get the value stored at the pointer location.

Line 11 & 12: Memory address of var is printed to the screen. & operator is used to get the address of a variable.

Point to Remember:

1. You can define a pointer by including a * before the name of the variable. (Pointer declaration)
2. You can get the value stored at address by adding * before the variable name. (Pointer use)
3. You can get the address of a variable by using & operator.

Array

Arrays are the most basic data structures used to store information. An array is a data structure used to store multiple data elements of the same data type. All the data is stored sequentially. The value stored at any index can be accessed in constant time.

Program 1.3

```
1.      int main()
2.      {
3.              int arr[10];
4.              for (int i = 0; i < 10; i++)
5.              {
6.                      arr[i] = i;
7.              }
8.              printArray(arr,10);
9.      }
```

Analysis:

Line 3: Defines an array of *integer*s. The array is of size 10 - which means that it can store 10 *integer*s inside it.

Line 6: Array elements are accessed using subscript operator []. Lowest subscript is 0 and highest subscript is (size of array – 1). Value 0 to 9 is stored in the array at index 0 to 9.

Line 8: Array and its size are passed to printArray() function.

Program 1.4

```
1.      void printArray(int arr[], int count)
2.      {
3.              printf("Values stored in array are : ");
4.              for (int i = 0; i < count; i++)
5.              {
6.                      printf(" [ %d ] ", arr[i]);
7.              }
8.      }
```

Analysis:

Line 1: Array variable arr and its variable count are passed as arguments to printArray() function.
Line 4-7: Finally array values are printed to screen using the printf function in a for loop.

Point to Remember:
1. Array index always starts from 0 index and highest index is size -1.
2. The subscript operator has highest precedence if you write arr[2]++. Then the value of arr[2] will be incremented.

Each element of the array has a memory address. The following program will print the value stored in an array and their address.

Program 1.5

```
1.      void printArrayAddress(int arr[], int count)
2.      {
3.              printf("Values stored in array are : ");
4.              for (int i = 0; i < count; i++)
5.              {
6.                      printf("Data: [%d] has Address: [%p] \n", arr[i],arr+ i);
7.              }
8.      }
```

Analysis:

Line 6: Value stored in an array is printed. The address of the various elements in the array is also printed.

Point to Remember: For array elements, consecutive memory location is allocated.

Program 1.6

```
1.      void printArrayUsingPointer(int arr[], int count)
2.      {
3.              printf("Values stored in array are : ");
4.              int* ptr = arr;
5.              for (int i = 0; i < count; i++)
6.              {
7.                      printf("Data: [%d] has Address: [%p] \n", *ptr, ptr);
8.                      ptr++;
9.              }
10.     }
```

Analysis:

Line 4: A pointer to an int is created and it will point to the array.

Line 7: value stored in pointer is printed to scree.

Line 8: Pointer is incremented.

Two Dimensional Array

We can define two dimensional or multidimensional array. It is an array of array.

Program 1.7

```
1.      int main()
2.      {
3.              int arr[4][2];
4.              int count = 0;
5.              for (int i = 0; i < 4; i++)
6.                      for (int j = 0; j < 2; j++)
7.                              arr[i][j] = count++;
8.
9.              print2DArray((int**)arr, 4, 2);
10.             print2DArrayAddress((int**)arr, 4, 2);
11.     }
```

```
1.      void print2DArray(int* arr[], int row, int col)
2.      {
3.              for (int i = 0; i < row; i++)
4.                      for (int j = 0; j < col; j++)
5.                              printf("[ %d ]", *(arr + i * col + j ));
6.
7.      }
```

```
1.      void print2DArrayAddress(int* arr[], int row, int col)
2.      {
3.              for (int i = 0; i < row; i++)
4.                      for (int j = 0; j < col; j++)
5.                              printf("Value: %d, Address: %p\n", *(arr+i*col+j),
(arr+i*col+j));
6.      }
```

Analysis:
- An array is created with dimension 4 x 2. The array will have 4 rows and 2 columns.
- Value is assigned to the array
- Finally the value stored in array is printed to screen and also the address used to store values is printed by using print2DArray() and print2DarrayAddress() function.

We can define a *pointer* array similar to an array of *integer.* The array element will store a *pointer* inside it.

Program 1.8

```
1.      void printArray(int* arr[], int count)
2.      {
3.              int *ptr;
4.              for (int i = 0; i < count; i++)
5.              {
6.                      ptr = arr[i];
7.                      printf("[ %d ]", *ptr);
8.              }
9.      }
```

```
1.      void printArrayAddress(int* arr[], int count)
2.      {
3.              int *ptr;
4.              for (int i = 0; i < count; i++)
5.              {
6.                      ptr = arr[i];
7.                      printf("Value is: %d, Address is: %p\n", *ptr,ptr);
8.              }
9.      }
```

```
1.      int main()
2.      {
3.              int one = 1, two = 2, three = 3;
4.              int* arr[3];
5.              arr[0] = &one;
6.              arr[1] = &two;
7.              arr[2] = &three;
8.              printArray(arr, 3);
9.              printArrayAddress(arr, 3);
10.     }
```

Analysis:
- Three variables, one, two and three are defined.
- Pointer array arr is defied.
- The address of one, two and three is stored inside array arr.
- printArray() and printArrayAddress() functions are used to print value stored in the array.

Array Interview Questions

The following section will discuss the various algorithms that are applicable to arrays and will follow by list of practice problems with similar approaches.

Sum Array

Program: Write a function that will return the sum of all the elements of the *integer* array given array and its size as an argument.

Program 1.9

```
int SumArray(int arr[], int size)
{
        int total=0;
        int index=0;
        for(index=0;index<size;index++)
        {
                total = total + arr[index];
        }
        return total;
}
```

Sequential Search

Program 1.10: Write a function which will search in an array that some value is present in the array or not.

```
int SequentialSearch(int arr[], int size, int value)
{
        int i = 0;
        for(i = 0; i < size; i++) {
                if(value == arr[i] )
                        return i;
        }
        return -1;
}
```

Analysis:
- Since we have no idea about the data sotred in array or if the data is not sorted then we have to search tha array in sequential manner one by one.
- If we find the value we are looking for we return that index.
- Else we return -1 index as we didn't found the value we are looking for.

In the above example, the data are not sorted. If the data is sorted, a binary search may be done. We examine the middle position at each step. Depending upon the data that we are searching is greater or smaller than the middle value. We will search either the left or the right portion of the array. At each step, we are eliminating half of the search space there by making this algorithm very efficient the linear search.

Binary Search

Program 1.11: Binary search in a sorted array.

```
/* Binary Search Algorithm – Iterative Way */
int BinarySearch (int arr[], int size, int value)
{
        int low = 0, mid;
        int high = size-1;
        while (low <= high)
        {
                mid = low + (high-low)/2;        /* To avoid the overflow */
```

```
            if (arr[mid] == value)
                    return mid;
            else if (arr[mid] < value)
                    low = mid + 1;
            else
                    high = mid - 1;
    }
    return -1;
}
```

Analysis:
- Since we have data sorted in increasing / decreasing order we can apply more efficient binary search. At each step we reduce our search space by half.
- At each step we compare the middle value with the value we are searching for. If mid value is equal to the value we are searching for then we return the middle index.
- If the value is smaller then the middle value we search the left half of the array.
- If the value is grater then the middle value then we search the right half of the array.
- If we find the value we are looking for then its indes is returned or -1 is returned otherwise.

Rotating an Array by K positions.

For example, an array [10,20,30,40,50,60] rotate by 2 positions to [30,40,50,60,10,20]

Program 1.12

```
void rotateArray(int *a,int n,int k)
{
        reverseArray(a,k);
        reverseArray(&a[k],n-k);
        reverseArray(a,n);
}
```

```
void reverseArray(int *a,int n)
{
        for(int i=0,j=n-1;i<j;i++,j--)
        {
                a[i]^=a[j]^=a[i]^=a[j];
        }
}
```

```
1,2,3,4,5,6,7,8,9,10          =>          5,6,7,8,9,10,1,2,3,4
1,2,3,4,5,6,7,8,9,10   =>   4,3,2,1,10,9,8,7,6,5   => 5,6,7,8,9,10,1,2,3,4
```

Analysis:
- Rotating array is basically done in two parts trick. In the first part we first reverse elements of array first half and then second half.
- Then we reverse the whole array there by completing the whole rotation.

Find the largest sum contiguous subarray.

Given an array of positive and negative *integer* s, find a contiguous subarray whose sum (sum of elements) is maximized.

Program 1.13

```
int maxSubArraySum(int a[], int size)
{
        int maxSoFar = 0, maxEndingHere = 0;

        for (int i = 0; i < size; i++)
        {
                maxEndingHere = maxEndingHere + a[i];
                if (maxEndingHere < 0)
                        maxEndingHere = 0;
                if (maxSoFar < maxEndingHere)
                        maxSoFar = maxEndingHere;
        }
        return maxSoFar;
}
```

Analysis:

- Maximum subarray in an array is found in a single scan. We keep track of globle maximum sum so far and the maximum sum which include the current element.
- When we find globle maximum value so far is less then the maximu value containing current value we update the globle maximum value.
- Finally return the globle maximum value.

Structure

Structures are used when we want to process data of multiple data types as a single entity.

Program 1.14: Demonstrating Structure

```
1. struct coord{
2.        int x;
3.        int y;
4. };
5. int main()
6. {
7.        struct coord point;
8.        point.x=10;
9.        point.y=10;
10.       printf("X axis coord value is %d \n", point.x);
11.       printf("Y axis coord value is %d \n", point.y);
12.       printf("Size of structure is %d bytes\n", sizeof(point));
13.       return 0;
14. }
```

Output:

```
X axis coord value is 10
Y axis coord value is 10
Size of structure is 8 bytes
```

Analysis:

Line 1-4: We have declared structure "coord", which contain two elements inside it. The two elements x and y corresponding to x-axis and y-axis coordinates.

Line 8: We have declared a variable "point" of type "struct coord".

Line 9-10: We have assigned coordinate (10, 10), to x and y element of the "point". Various elements of a structure are assessed using the dot(.) operator.

Line 11-12: We are printing the value stored in the x and y elements of the point that is of type struct coord.

Line 13: We are printing the size of struct point. Since structure consists of more than one element, then the size of a structure is the sum of all the elements inside it.

Pointer to structure

Pointers can be used to access the various elements of a structure. The various elements of a structure are accessed by pointer using -> operator.

Program 1.15: Pointer to structure

```
1.      #include<stdio.h>
2.      struct student {
3.              int rollNo;
4.              char* firstName;
5.              char* lastName;
6.      };
7.      int main()
8.      {
9.              int i=0;
10.             struct student stud;
11.             struct student* ptrStud;
12.             ptrStud= &stud;
13.             ptrStud->rollNo=1;
14.             ptrStud->firstName ="john";
15.             ptrStud->lastName ="smith";
16.             printf("Roll No: %d  Student Name: %s %s ", ptrStud->rollNo,
ptrStud->firstName, ptrStud->lastName);
17.
18.             return 0;
19.     }
```

Analysis:

Line 2-6: We have declared a struct student that contain roll no, first and last name of a student.

Line 12: We have declared a pointer to struct student.

Line 13-15: Pointer ptrStud is pointing to stud. We have used ptrStud to assign a value to struct stud. We have used -> operator to access the various elements of the structure pointed by ptrStud.
Note: If we have used the stud to assign we would have used "." operator. The same structure when accessed using pointer we use indirection operator "->".
Line 16: We have finally printed all the various elements of structure variable stud.

Note: In the same way you can use -> operator to access elements of the Union.

Dynamic Memory Allocation

In c language, dynamic memory is allocated using the malloc(), calloc() and realloc() functions. The dynamic memory required to be freed using the free() function.

Malloc function

Definition of the malloc function is as below.

```
void *malloc (size_t size);
```

It allocates a memory block of length "size" bytes and return a pointer to the block. It will return NULL if the system does not have enough memory.

The C standard defines void* is a generic pointer that is required to be casted to the required type. Most C compilers need this casting. However, the latest ANSI C standard does not require.
E.g.

```
int* p = (int *) malloc (sizeof(int));
```

Calloc function

Definition of calloc function is as below.

```
void *calloc (size_t num, size_t size);
```

It allocates a memory block of length "num * size" bytes and return a pointer to the block. It will return NULL if the system does not have enough memory. One thing more it does that, it initializes every byte to zero.

Realloc function

Definition of realloc function is as below.

```
void *realloc (void *ptr, size_t newSize);
```

It is used to change the memory block size of a previously allocated block of memory pointed by ptr. It returns a memory block of the newSize. If the block size if increased, then the content of the old memory block is copied to a newly allocated region. If the pointer returned by the function is different from the old pointer ptr. Then ptr will no longer point to a valid location. So in general you should not use ptr once it is passed to realloc() function. If ptr is NULL, realloc works same as malloc().
Note: Again, you need to cast the return value of malloc/calloc/realloc before using it. int *i = (int *) malloc(size);

Free Function

The memory that is allocated using malloc/calloc/realloc need to be freed using a free() function. The syntax of the free() function is as below.

```
void free (void *pointer);
```

A pointer to previously allocated memory is passed to free() function. The free() function will put the allocated memory block back to heap section.

Function

Functions are used to provide modularity to the program. By using function, we can divide complex tasks into smaller manageable tasks. The use of the function is also to avoid duplicate code. For example, we can define a function sum() which take two *integer* s and return their sum. Then we can use this function multiple times whenever we want sum of two *integer* s.

Program 1.16: Demonstrating Function Calls

```
1.      #include <stdio.h>
2.      /* function declaration */
3.      int sum(int num1, int num2);
4.      int main()
5.      {
6.              /* local variable definition */
7.              int x = 10;
8.              int y = 20;
9.              int result;
10.             /* calling a function to find sum */
11.             result = sum(x, y);
12.             printf( "Sum is : %d\n", result );
13.             return 0;
14.     }
15.     /* function returning the sum of two numbers */
16.     int sum(int num1, int num2)
17.     {
18.             /* local variable declaration */
19.             int result;
20.             result= num1+num2;
21.             return result;
22.     }
```

Output:

```
Sum is:30
```

Analysis:

Line 3: function declaration of sum() function

Line 11: sum function is called from this main by passing variable x and y with value 10 and 20 at this point control flow will go to *Line 16*.

Line 16: variables passed to sum function are copied into num1 and num2 local variables.

Line 20 & 21: the sum is calculated and saved in a variable result. And the result is returned. Control flow comes back to line number 11.

Line 11-12: return value of the sum function is saved in a local variable result and printed to the screen.

Concept of Stack

A stack is a memory in which values are stored and retrieved in "last in first out" manner. Data is added to stack using push operation and data is taken out of stack using pop operation.

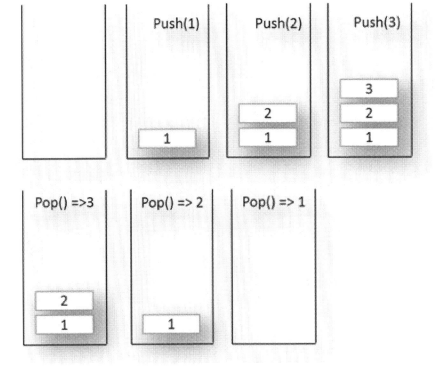

1. Initially the stack was empty. Then we have added value 1 to stack using push(1) operator.
2. Similarly, push(2) and push(3)
3. Pop operation take the top of the stack. Stack data is added and deleted in "last in, first out" manner.
4. First pop() operation will take 3 out of the stack.
5. Similarly, other pop operation will take 2 then 1 out of the stack
6. In the end, the stack is empty when all the elements are taken out of the stack.

System stack and Function Calls

When the function is called, the current execution is stopped and the control goes to the called function. After the called function exits / returns, the execution resumes from the point at which the execution was stopped.

To get the exact point at which execution should be resumed, the address of the next instruction is stored in the stack. When the function call complete the address at the top of the stack is taken out.

Program 1.17

```
1.      void fun2()
2.      {
3.              printf("fun2 line 1\n");
4.      }
5.
6.      void fun1()
7.      {
8.              printf("fun1 line 1\n");
9.              fun2();
10.             printf("fun1 line 2\n");
11.     }
12.
```

```
13.     int main()
14.     {
15.             printf("main line 1\n");
16.             fun1();
17.             printf("main line 2\n");
18.     }
```

Output:

```
main line 1
fun1 line 1
fun2 line 1
fun1 line 2
main line 2
```

Analysis:

Line 13: Every program starts with main() function.

Line 15: This is the first statement that will be executed. And we will get "main line 1" as output.

Line 16: fun1() is called. Before control goes to fun1() then next instruction that is address of line 17 is stored in the system stack.

Line 6: Control goes to fun1() function.

Line 8: This is the first statement inside fun1(), this will print "fun1 line 1" to output.

Line 9: fun2() is called from fun1(). Before control goes to fun2() address of the next instruction that is address of line 10 is added to the system stack.

Line 1: Control goes to fun2() function.

Line 3: "fun2 line 1" is printed to screen.

Line 10: When fun2 exits, control come back to fun1. And the program reads the next instruction from the stack, and line 10 is executed. And print "fun1 line 2" to screen.

Line 17: When fun1 exits, control comes back to the main function. And program reads the next instruction from the stack and line number 17 is executed and finally "main line 2" is printed to screen.

Points to remember:
1. Functions are implemented using a stack.
2. When a function is called the address of the next instruction is pushed into the stack.
3. When a function is finished the address of the execution is taken out of the stack.

Parameter passing, Call by value

Arguments can be passed from one function to other using parameters. By default, all the parameters are passed by value. That means a separate copy is created inside the called function and the variable in the calling function remains unchanged.

Program 1.18

```
1.      void increment(int var)
2.      {
3.              var++;
4.      }
5.
```

```
6.      int main()
7.      {
8.              int i = 10;
9.              printf("Value of i before increment is : %d \n", i);
10.             increment(i);
11.             printf("Value of i before increment is : %d \n", i);
12.     }
```

Output:

```
Value of i before increment is : 10
Value of i before increment is : 10
```

Analysis:

Line 8: variable "i" is declared and value 10 is initialized to it.

Line 9: value if "i" is printed.

Line 10: increment function is called. When a function is called the value of the parameter is copied into another variable of the called function. Flow of control goes to line no 1.

Line 3: value of var is incremented by 1. But remember, it is just a copy inside the increment function.

Line 11: When the function exits, the value of "i" is still 10.

Points to remember:
1. Pass by value just creates a copy of variable.
2. Pass by value, value before and after the function call remain same.

Parameter passing, Call by Reference

If you need to change the value of the parameter inside the function, then you should use call by reference. C language by default passes by value. Therefore, to make it happen, you need to pass the address of a variable and changing the value of the variable using this address inside the called function.

Program 1.19

```
1.      void increment(int *ptr)
2.      {
3.              (*ptr)++;
4.      }
5.      int main()
6.      {
7.              int i = 10;
8.              printf("Value of i before increment is : %d \n", i);
9.              increment(&i);
10.             printf("Value of i before increment is : %d \n", i);
11.     }
```

Output:

```
Value of i before increment is : 10
Value of i before increment is : 11
```

Analysis:

Line 9: Address of "i" is passed to the function increment. Function increment takes a pointer to int as argument.

Line 3: Variable at the address ptr is accessed and its value is incremented.

Line 10: Finally, incremented value is printed to screen.

Points to remember:

1. Call by reference is implemented indirectly by passing the address of a variable to the function.

Recursive Function

A recursive function is a function that calls itself, directly or indirectly.

A recursive function consists of two parts: Termination Condition and Body (which include recursive expansion).

1. Termination Condition: A recursive function always contains one or more terminating condition. A condition in which recursive function is processing a simple case and will not call itself.

2. Body (including recursive expansion): The main logic of the recursive function contained in the body of the function. It also contains the recursion expansion statement that in turn calls the function itself.

Three important properties of recursive algorithm are:
1) A recursive algorithm must have a termination condition.
2) A recursive algorithm must change its state, and move towards the termination condition.
3) A recursive algorithm must call itself.

Note: The speed of a recursive program is slower because of stack overheads. If the same task can be done using an iterative solution (loops), then we should prefer an iterative solution (loops) in place of recursion to avoid stack overhead.

Note: Without termination condition, the recursive function may run forever and will finally consume all the stack memory.

Factorial

Program 1.20: Factorial Calculation. N! = N* (N-1).... 2*1.

```
1.      int factorial(unsigned int i)
2.      {
3.              /* Termination Condition */
4.              if(i <= 1)
5.                      return 1;
6.              /* Body, Recursive Expansion */
7.              return i * factorial(i - 1);
8.      }
```

Analysis:

Each time function fn is calling fn-1. *Time Complexity* is *O(N)*

Print Base 10 *Integer* s

Program 1.21

```
1.      void printInt(unsigned int number)
2.      {
3.              char digit = number % 10 + '0';
4.              if (number /= 10)
5.                      printInt(number/10);
6.              printf("%c", digit);
7.      }
```

Analysis:

Line 3: Each time remainder is calculated and stored its char equivalent in digit.

Line 4-5: if the number is greater than 10 then the number divided by 10 is passed to printInt() function.

Line 6: Number will be printed with higher order first than the lower order digits.

Time Complexity is **O(N)**

Print Base 16 *Integer* s

Program 1.22: Generic print to some specific base function.

```
1.      void printInt(unsigned int number, const int base)
2.      {
3.              char* conversion = "0123456789ABCDEF";
4.              char digit = number % base ;
5.              if (number /= base)
6.                      printInt(number,base);
7.              printf("%c", conversion[digit]);
8.      }
```

Analysis:

Line 1: base value is also provided along with the number.

Line 4: remainder of the number is calculated and stored in digit.

Line 5-6: if the number is greater than base then, number divided by base is passed as an argument to the printInt() function recursively.

Line 7: Number will be printed with higher order first than the lower order digits.

Time Complexity is **O(N)**

Integer to String

Program 1.23

```
1.      char * intToStr(char *p, unsigned int number)
2.      {
3.              char digit = number % 10 + '0';
4.              if (number /= 10)
5.                      p = intToStr(p, number);
6.              *p++ = digit;
7.              return (p);
8.      }
```

Analysis:

Line 1: character buffer p is passed as argument and number is passed, which need to be converted to string.

Line 3: least significant digit of the number is converted into corresponding character.

Line 4-5: if the number is greater than 10 then, number divided by 10 is passed as an argument to the intToStr () function recursively.

Line 6: The character is stored in the buffer p higher order first, then the lower order digits.

Time Complexity is **O(N)**

Tower of Hanoi

The **Tower of Hanoi** (also called the **Tower of Brahma**) We are given three rods and N number of disks, initially all the disks are added to first rod (the leftmost one) in decreasing size order. The objective is to transfer the entire stack of disks from first tower to third tower (the rightmost one), moving only one disk at a time and never a larger one onto a smaller.

Program 1.24

```
1.      void towerOfHanoi(int num, char src, char dst, char temp)
2.      {
3.              if (num < 1)
4.                      return;
5.
6.              towerOfHanoi(num - 1, src, temp, dst);
7.              printf("\n Move disk %d from peg %c to peg %c", num, src, dst);
8.              towerOfHanoi(num - 1, temp, dst, src);
9.      }
```

```
1.      int main()
2.      {
3.              int num = 4;
4.              printf("The sequence of moves involved in the Tower of Hanoi are :\n");
5.              towerOfHanoi(num, 'A', 'C', 'B');
6.              return 0;
7.      }
```

Analysis: TowerOfHanoi problem if we want to move N disks from source to destination, then we first move N-1 disks from source to temp, then move the lowest Nth disk from source to destination. Then will move N-1 disks from temp to destination.

Greatest common divisor (GCD)

Program 1.25

```
1.      int GCD(int m, int n)
2.      {
3.          if(m<n)
4.              return (GCD(n, m));
5.          if(m%n == 0)
6.              return (n);
7.          return(GCD(n, m%n));
8.      }
```

Analysis: Euclid's algorithm is used to find gcd. GCD(n,m) == GCD(m, n mod m)

Fibonacci Number

Program 1.26

```
1.      int fibonacci(int n)
2.      {
3.          if (n <= 1)
4.              return n;
5.          return fibonacci(n - 1) + fibonacci(n - 2);
6.      }
```

Analysis: Fibonacci number are calculated by adding sum of the previous two number.
There is an unefficiency in the solution we will look better solution in coming chapters.

All permutations of an *integer* array

Program 1.27

```
1.      void printArray(int arr[], int count)
2.      {
3.          printf("Values stored in array are : ");
4.          for (int i = 0; i < count; i++)
5.          {
6.              printf(" %d ", arr[i]);
7.          }
8.          printf("\n");
9.      }
10.     void swap(int* arr, int x, int y){
11.         int temp = arr[x];
12.         arr[x] = arr[y];
13.         arr[y] = temp;
14.         return;
15.     }
```

```
16.      void permutation(int *arr, int i, int length) {
17.           if (length == i){
18.                printArray(arr, length);
19.                return;
20.           }
21.           int j = i;
22.           for (j = i; j < length; j++) {
23.                swap(arr, i, j);
24.                permutation(arr, i + 1, length);
25.                swap(arr, i, j);
26.           }
27.           return;
28.      }
29. int main()
30. {
31.      int arr[5];
32.      for (int i = 0; i < 5; i++)
33.      {
34.           arr[i] = i;
35.      }
36.      permutation(arr, 0, 5);
37. }
```

Analysis:

In permutation function at each recursive call number at index, "i" is swapped with all the numbers that are right of it. Since the number is swapped with all the numbers in its right one by one it will produce all the permutation possible.

Binary search using recursion

Program 1.28

```
1.   /* Binary Search Algorithm – Recursive Way */
2.   int BinarySearchRecursive(int arr[ ], int low, int high, int value)
3.   {
4.        int mid = low + (high-low)/2;       /* To avoid the overflow */
5.        if (arr[mid] == value)
6.             return mid;
7.        else if (arr[mid] < value)
8.             return BinarySearchRecursive (arr, mid + 1, high, value);
9.        else
10.            return BinarySearchRecursive (arr, low, mid - 1 , value);
11.       return -1;
12.  }
```

Analysis:

Similar iterative solution we had already seen. Now lets look into the recursive solution of the same problem in this solution also we are diving the search space into half and doing the same what we had done in the iterative solution.

1. Find average of all the elements in an array.

2. Find the sum of all the elements of a two dimensional array.

3. Find the largest element in the array.

4. Find the smallest element in the array.

5. Find the second largest number in the array.

6. Print all the maxima's in an array. (A value is a maximum if the value before and after its index are smaller than it is or does not exist.)
   Hint:
   a) Start traversing array from the end and keep track of the max element.
   b) If we encounter an element > max, print the element and update max.

7. Print alternate elements in an array.

8. Given an array with value 0 or 1, write a program to segregate 0 on the left side and 1 on the right side.

9. Given a list of intervals, merge all overlapping intervals.
   Input: {[1, 4], [3, 6], [8, 10]}
   Output: {[1, 6], [8, 10]}

10. Write a function that will take intervals as input and takes care of overlapping intervals.

11. Reverse an array in-place. (You cannot use any additional array in other wards *Space Complexity* should be *O(1).*)
    Hint: Use two variable, start and end. Start set to 0 and end set to (n-1). Increment start and decrement end. Swap the values stored at arr[start] and arr[end]. Stop when start is equal to end or start is greater than end.

12. Given an array of 0s and 1s. We need to sort it so that all the 0s are before all the 1s.
    Hint: Use two variable, start and end. Start set to 0 and end set to (n-1). Increment start and decrement end. Swap the values stored at arr[start] and arr[end] only when arr[start] == 1 and arr[end]==0. Stop when start is equal to end or start is greater than end.

13. Given an array of 0s, 1s and 2s. We need to sort it so that all the 0s are before all the 1s. And all the 1s are before 2s.
    Hint: Same as above first think 0s and 1s as one group and move all the 2s on the right side. Then do a second pass over the array to sort 0s and 1s.

14. Find the duplicate elements in an array of size n where each element is in the range 0 to n-1.

    Hint:
    Approach 1: Compare each element with all the elements of the array (using two loops) $O(n^2)$ solution
    Approach 2: Maintain a Hash-Table. Set the hash value to 1 if we encounter the element for the first time. When we same value again we can see that the hash value is already 1 so we can print that value. *O(n)* solution, but additional space is required.
    Approach 3: We will exploit the constraint "every element is in the range 0 to n-1".
    We can take an array arr[] of size n and set all the elements to 0. Whenever we get a value say val1. We will increment the value at arr[var1] index by 1. In the end, we can traverse the array arr and print

the repeated values. Additional *Space Complexity* will be **O(n)** which will be less then Hash-Table approach.

15. Find the maximum element in a sorted and rotated array. Complexity: **O(logn)**
    Hint: Use binary search algorithm.

16. Given an array with 'n' elements & a value 'x', find two elements in the array that sums to 'x'.

    Hint:
    Approach 1: Sort the array.
    Approach 2: Using a Hash-Table.

17. Write a function to find the sum of every number in an int number. Example: input= 1984, output should be 32 (1+9+8+4).

18. Write a function to compute Sum(N) = 1+2+3+...+N.

CHAPTER 2: ALGORITHMS ANALYSIS

Introduction

Computer programmer learn by experience. We learn by seeing solved problems and solving new problems by ourselves. Studying various problem-solving techniques and by understanding how different algorithms are designed helps us to solve the next problem that is given to us. By considering a number of different algorithms, we can begin to develop pattern so that the next time a similar problem arises, we are better able to solve it.

When an interviewer asks to develop a program in an interviewer, what are the steps that an interviewee should follow. We will be taking a systematic approach to handle the problem and finally reaching to the solution.

Algorithm

An algorithm is a set of steps to accomplish a task.
An algorithm in a computer program is a set of steps applied over a set of input to produce a set of output.

Knowledge of algorithm helps us to get our desired result faster by applying the right algorithm.

The most important properties of an algorithm are:
1. Correctness: The algorithm should be correct. It should be able to process all the given inputs and provide correct output.
2. Efficiency: The algorithm should be efficient in solving problems.

Algorithmic complexity is defined as how fast a particular algorithm performs. Complexity is represented by function $T(n)$ - time versus the input size n.

Asymptotic analysis

Asymptotic analysis is used to compare the efficiency of algorithm independently of any particular data set or programming language.

We are generally interested in the order of growth of some algorithm and not interested in the exact time required for running an algorithm. This time is also called Asymptotic-running time.

Big-O Notation

Definition: "f(n) is big-O of g(n)" or $f(n) = O(g(n))$, if there are two +ve constants c and n0 such that
$f(n) \leq c\, g(n)$ for all $n \geq n0$,

In other words, c g(n) is an upper bound for f(n) for all $n \geq n0$

The function f(n) growth is slower than c g(n)

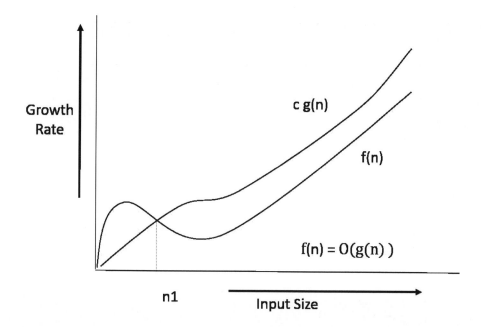

Example: $n^2 + n = O(n^2)$

Omega-Ω Notation

Definition: "f(n) is omega of g(n)." or f(n) = Ω(g(n)) if there are two +ve constants c and n0 such that
c g(n) ≤ f(n) for all n ≥ n0

In other words, c g(n) is lower bound for f(n)
Function f(n) growth is faster than c g(n)

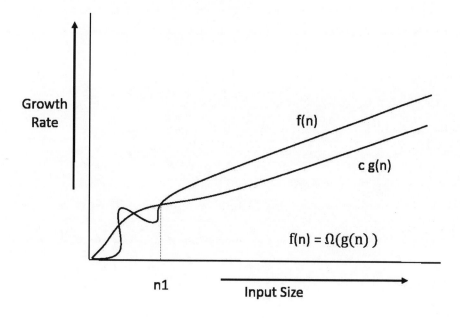

Find relationship of $f(n) = n^c$ and $g(n) = c^n$
$f(n) = \Omega\,(g(n))$

Theta-Θ Notation

Definition: "f(n) is theta of g(n)." or f(n) = Θ(g(n)) if there are three +ve constants c1, c2 and n0 such that c1 g(n) ≤ f(n) ≤ c2 g(n) for all n ≥ n0

g(n) is an asymptotically tight bound on f(n).
Function f(n) grows at the same rate as g(n).

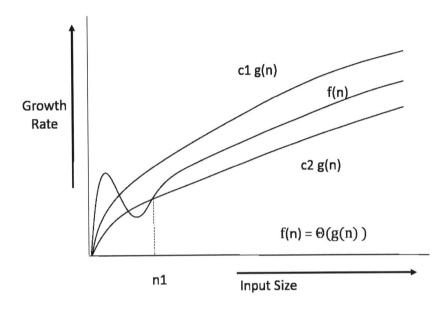

Example: $n^3 + n^2 + n = Θ(n^2)$

Example: $n^2 + n = Θ(n^2)$
Find relationship of $f(n) = 2n^2 + n$ and $g(n) = n^2$
$f(n) = O(g(n))$
$f(n) = Θ(g(n))$
$f(n) = Ω(g(n))$

Note:- Asymptotic Analysis is not perfect, but that is the best way available for analysing algorithms.

For example, say there are two sorting algorithms first take $f(n) = 10000n\,log\,n$ and $f(n) = n^2$ time. The asymptotic analysis says that the first algorithm is better (as it ignores constants) but actually for a small set of data when n is small then 10000, the second algorithm will perform better. To consider this drawback of asymptotic analysis case analysis of the algorithm is introduced.

Complexity analysis of algorithms

1) Worst Case complexity: It is the complexity of solving the problem for the worst input of size n. It provides the upper bound for the algorithm. This is the most common analysis done.

2) Average Case complexity: It is the complexity of solving the problem on an average. We calculate the time for all the possible inputs and then take an average of it.

3) Best Case complexity: It is the complexity of solving the problem for the best input of size n.

Time Complexity Order

A list of commonly occurring algorithm *Time Complexity* in increasing order:

Name	Notation	
Constant	$O(1)$	
Logarithmic	$O(\log n)$	
Linear	$O(n)$	
N-LogN	$O(n \log n)$	
Quadratic	$O(n^2)$	
Polynomial	$O(n^c)$	c is a constant & c>1
Exponential	$O(c^m)$	c is a constant & c>1
Factorial or N-power-N	$O(n!)$ or $O(n^n)$	

Constant Time: *O(1)*

An algorithm is said to run in constant time regardless of the input size.
Examples:
1. Accessing n^{th} element of an array
2. Push and pop of a stack.
3. Enqueue and dequeue of a queue.
4. Accessing an element of Hash-Table.
5. Bucket sort

Linear Time: *O(n)*

An algorithm is said to run in linear time if the execution time of the algorithm is directly proportional to the input size.
Examples:
1. Array operations like search element, find min, find max etc.
2. Linked list operations like traversal, find min, find max etc.

Note: when we need to see/ traverse all the nodes of a data-structure for some task then complexity is no less than *O(n)*

Logarithmic Time: *O(logn)*

An algorithm is said to run in logarithmic time if the execution time of the algorithm is proportional to the logarithm of the input size. Each step of an algorithm, a significant portion of the input is pruned out without traversing it.
Example:
1. Binary search

Note: We will read about these algorithms in this book.

N-LogN Time: *O(nlog(n))*

An algorithm is said to run in logarithmic time if the execution time of an algorithm is proportional to the product of input size and logarithm of the input size.
Example:
1. Merge-Sort
2. Quick-Sort (Average case)
3. Heap-Sort

Note: Quicksort is a special kind of algorithm to sort a list of numbers. Its worst-case complexity is $O(n^2)$ and average case complexity is $O(n \log n)$.

Quadratic Time: *O(n2)*

An algorithm is said to run in logarithmic time if the execution time of an algorithm is proportional to the square of the input size.
Examples:
1. Bubble-Sort
2. Selection-Sort
3. Insertion-Sort

Deriving the Runtime Function of an Algorithm

Constants

Each statement takes a constant time to run. *Time Complexity* is $O(1)$

Loops

The running time of a loop is a product of running time of the statement inside a loop and number of iterations in the loop. *Time Complexity* is $O(n)$

Nested Loop

The running time of a nested loop is a product of running time of the statements inside loop multiplied by a product of the size of all the loops. *Time Complexity* is $O(n^c)$
Where c is a number of loops. For two loops, it will be $O(n^2)$

Consecutive Statements

Just add the running times of all the consecutive statements

If-Else Statement

Consider the running time of the larger of if block or else block. And ignore the other one.

Logarithmic statement

If each iteration the input size of decreases by a constant multiple factors.
$O(\log n)$.

Time Complexity Examples

Example 1

```
int fun(int n)
{
        int m = 0;
        for (int i = 0; i<n; i++)
                m += 1;
        return m;
}
```

Time Complexity: **O(n)**

Example 2

```
int fun(int n)
{
        int i=0, j=0, m = 0;
        for (i = 0; i<n; i++)
                for (j = 0; j<n; j++)
                        m += 1;
        return m;
}
```

Time Complexity: $O(n^2)$

Example 3

```
int fun(int n)
{
        int i=0, j=0, m = 0;
        for (i = 0; i<n; i++)
                for (j = 0; j<i; j++)
                        m += 1;
        return m;
}
```

Time Complexity: O(N+(N-1)+(N-2)+...) == O(N(N+1)/2) == $O(n^2)$

Example 4

```
int fun(int n)
{
        int i = 0, m = 0;
        i = 1;
        while (i < n) {
                m += 1;
                i = i * 2;
        }
        return m;
}
```

Each time problem space is divided into half. Time Complexity: **O(log(n))**

Example 5

```
int fun(int n)
{
        int i = 0, m = 0;
        i = n;
        while (i > 0) {
                m += 1;
                i = i / 2;
        }
        return m;
}
```

Same as above each time problem space is divided into half.
Time Complexity: **O(log(n))**

Example 6

```
int fun(int n)
{
        int i = 0, j = 0, k = 0, m = 0;
        i = n;
        for (i = 0; i<n; i++)
                for (j = 0; j<n; j++)
                        for (k = 0; k<n; k++)
                                m += 1;
        return m;
}
```

Outer loop will run for n number of iterations. In each iteration of the outer loop, inner loop will run for n iterations of their own. Final complexity will be n*n*n
Time Complexity: $O(n^3)$

Example 7

```
int fun(int n)
{
        int i = 0, j = 0, k = 0, m = 0;
        i = n;
        for (i = 0; i<n; i++)
                for (j = 0; j<n; j++)
                        m += 1;

        for (i = 0; i<n; i++)
                for (k = 0; k<n; k++)
                        m += 1;

        return m;
}
```

These two groups of for loop are in consecutive so their complexity will add up to form the final complexity of the program.
Time Complexity: T(n) = $O(n^2) + O(n^2) = O(n^2)$

Example 8

```
int fun(int n)
{
        int i = 0, j = 0, m = 0;

        for (i = 0; i<n; i++)
                for (j = 0; j< sqrt(n); j++)
                        m += 1;
        return m;
}
```

Time Complexity: $O(n * \sqrt{n}) = O(n^{3/2})$

44

Example 9

```
int fun(int n)
{
        int i = 0, j = 0, m = 0;

        for (i = n; i > 0; i /= 2)
                for (j = 0; j < i; j++)
                        m += 1;
        return m;
}
```

Each time problem space is divided into half.
Time Complexity: **O(log(n))**

Example 10

```
int fun(int n)
{
        int i = 0, j = 0, m = 0;

        for (i = 0; i < n; i++)
                for (j = i; j > 0; j--)
                        m += 1;
        return m;
}
```

O(N+(N-1)+(N-2)+...) = O(N(N+1)/2) // arithmetic progression.
Time Complexity:$O(n^2)$

Example 11

```
int fun(int n)
{
        int i = 0, j = 0, k = 0, m = 0;

        for (i = 0; i<n; i++)
                for (j = i; j<n; j++)
                        for (k = j+1; k<n; k++)
                                m += 1;

        return m;
}
```

Time Complexity: $O(n^3)$

Example 12

```
int fun(int n)
{
        int i = 0, j = 0, m = 0;

        for (i = 0; i<n; i++)
                for (; j<n; j++)
                        m += 1;
        return m;
}
```

Think carefully once again before finding a solution, j value is not reset at each iteration.
Time Complexity: **O(n)**

Example 13

```
int fun(int n)
{
        int i = 1, j = 0, m = 0;

        for (i = 1; i<=n; i *= 2)
                for (j = 0; j<=i; j++)
                        m += 1;

        return m;
}
```

The inner loop will run for 1, 2, 4, 8,... n times in successive iteration of the outer loop.
Time Complexity: T(n) = O(1+ 2+ 4+ ....+n/2+n) = *O(n)*

Master Theorem

The master theorem solves recurrence relations of the form:
$T(n)$ = a T(n/b) + f(n)

Where a ≥ 1 and b > 1.
"n" is the size of the problem.
"a" is a number of sub problem in the recursion.
"n/b" is the size of each sub-problem.
"f(n)" is the cost of the division of the problem into sub problem or merge of results of sub problems to get the final result.

It is possible to determine an asymptotic tight bound in these three cases:
Case 1: when f(n)=O $(n^{log_b a - \epsilon})$ and constant ϵ > 1, than the final *Time Complexity* will be:
T(n) =$\theta(n^{log_b a})$

Case 2: when f(n) = $\theta(n^{log_b a} log^k n)$ and constant k ≥ 0, than the final *Time Complexity* will be:
T(n)= $\theta(n^{log_b a} log^{k+1} n)$

Case 3: when f(n) = $\Omega(n^{log_b a+\epsilon})$ and constant ϵ > 1, Then the final *Time Complexity* will be:
T(n) =$\theta(f(n))$

46

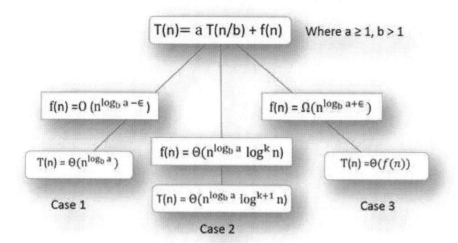

Example 14: Take an example of Merge-Sort, $T(n) = 2\ T(n/2) + n$

Sol:-

$log_b\ a = log_2\ 2 = 1$

$f(n) = n = \Theta(n^{log_2 2}\ log^0\ n)$

Case 2 applies and $T(n) = \Theta(n^{log_2 2}\ log^{0+1}\ n)$

$T(n) = \Theta(n\ log(n))$

Example 15: Binary Search $T(n) = T(n/2) + O(1)$

Sol:-

$log_b\ a = log_2\ 1 = 0$

$f(n) = 1 = \Theta(n^{log_2 1}\ log^0\ n)$

Case 2 applies and $T(n) = \Theta(n^{log_2 1}\ log^{0+1}\ n)$

$T(n) = \Theta(log(n))$

Example 16: Binary tree traversal $T(n) = 2T(n/2) + O(1)$

Sol:-

$log_b\ a = log_2\ 2 = 1$

$f(n) = 1 = O(n^{log_2 2-1})$

Case 1 applies and $T(n) = \Theta(n^{log_2 2})$

$T(n) = \Theta(n)$

Example 17: Take an example $T(n) = 2\ T(n/2) + n^2$

Sol:-

$log_b\ a = log_2\ 2 = 1$

$f(n) = n^2\ = \Omega(n^{log_2 2+1})$

Case 3 applies and $T(n) = \Theta(f(n))$

$T(n) = \Theta(n^2)$

Example 18: Take an example $T(n) = 4\ T(n/2) + n^2$

Sol:-

$log_b\ a = log_2\ 4 = 2$

$f(n) = n^2\ = \Theta(n^{log_2 4}\ log^0\ n)$

Case 2 applies and $T(n) = \Theta(n^{log_2 4}\ log^{0+1}\ n)$

$T(n) = \Theta(n^2\ log\ n)$

Modified Master theorem

This is a shortcut to solving the same problem easily and fast. If the recurrence relation is in the form of T(n)= a T(n/b) + dx^s

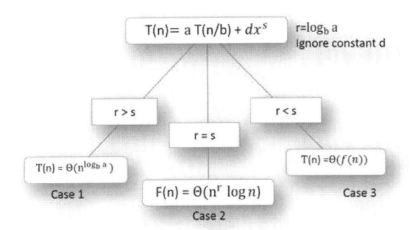

Example 19: $T(n) = 2\ T(n/2) + n^2$
Sol:-
$r = log_2\ 2$
$s = 2$
Case 3: $log_2\ 2 < s$
T(n) =Θ(f(n)) = Θ(n^2)

Example 20: T (n) = T (n/2) + 2n
Sol:-
$r = log_2\ 1 = 0$
$s = 1$
Case 3
T(n)= Θ(n)

Example 21: T (n) = 16T (n/4) + n
Sol:-
$r = 2$
$s = 1$
Case 1
T(n)= Θ(n^2)

Example 22: T (n) = 2T (n/2) + n log n
Sol:-
There is logn in f(n) so use master theorem shortcut will not word.
f(n) = n log(n) = $\Theta(n^{log_2\ 2}\ log^1\ n)$
T(n) = $\Theta(n^{log_2\ 2}\ log^{0+1}\ n) = \Theta(n\ log(n))$

Example 23: $T(n) = 2\ T(n/4) + n^{0.5}$
Sol:-
$r = log_4\ 2 = 0.5 = s$
Case 2:
T(n) = $\Theta(n^{log_4\ 2}\ log^{0.5+1}\ n) = \Theta(n^{0.5}\ log^{1.5}\ n)$

48

Example 24: $T(n) = 2\,T(n/4) + n^{0.49}$
Sol:-
Case 1:
$T(n) = \Theta(n^{log_4 2}) = \Theta(n^{0.5})$

Example 25: $T(n) = 3T(n/3) + \sqrt{n}$
Sol:-
$r = log_3 3 = 1$
$s = \frac{1}{2}$
Case 1
$T(n) = \Theta(n)$

Example 26: $T(n) = 3T(n/4) + n \log n$
Sol:-
There is logn in f(n) so see if master theorem.
$f(n) = n \log n = \Omega(n^{log_4 3} \log^1 n)$
Case 3:
$T(n) = \Theta(nlog(n))$

Example 27: $T(n) = 3T(n/3) + n/2$
Sol:-
r=1=s
Case 2:
$T(n) = \Theta(nlog(n))$

Exercise

1. True or false
    a. $5n + 10\,n^2 = O(n^2)$
    b. $n \log n + 4n = O(n)$
    c. $\log(n^2) + 4 \log(\log n) = O(logn)$
    d. $12\,n^{1/2} + 3 = O(n^2)$
    e. $3^n + 11\,n^2 + n^{20} = O(2^n)$

2. What is the best-case run *Time Complexity* of searching an array?

3. What is the average-case run *Time Complexity* of searching an array?

CHAPTER 3: APPROACH TO SOLVE ALGORITHM DESIGN PROBLEMS

Introduction

Know the theoretical knowledge of the algorithm is essential, but it is not sufficient. You need to have a systematic approach to solve a problem. Our approach is fundamentally different to solve any algorithm design question. We will follow a systematic five-step approach to reach to our solution. Master this approach and you will be better than most of the candidates in interviews.

Five steps for solving algorithm design questions are:
1. Constraints
2. Ideas Generation
3. Complexities
4. Coding
5. Testing

Constraints

Solving a technical question is not just about knowing the algorithms and designing a good software system. The interviewer wants to know you approach towards any given problem. May people make mistakes like they do not ask clarifying questions about a given problem? They assume a lot of things and begin working with that. There are a lot of data that is missing that you need to collect from your interviewer before beginning to solve a problem.

In this step, you will capture all the constraints about the problem. We should never try to solve a problem that is not completely defined. Interview questions are not like exam paper where all the details about a problem are well defined. In the interview, the interviewer actually expects you to ask questions and clarify the problem.

For example : When the problem statement says that write an algorithm to sort numbers.

The first information you need to capture is what king of data. Let us suppose interviewer respond with the answer *Integer*.
The second information that you need to know what is the size of data. Your algorithm differs if the input data size if 100 *integer*s or 1 billion *integers*.

Basic guideline for the Constraints for an array of numbers:
1. How many numbers of elements in the array?
2. What is the range of value in each element? What is the min and max value?
3. What is the kind of data in each element is it an *integer* or a *floating* point?
4. Does the array contain unique data or not?

Basic guideline for the Constraints for an array of string:
1. How many numbers of elements in the array?
2. What is the length of each string? What is the min and max length?
3. Does the array contain unique data or not?

Basic guideline for the Constraints for a Graph
1. How many nodes are there in the graph?
2. How many edges are there in the graph?
3. Is it a weighted graph? What is the range of weights?
4. Is the graph directed or undirected?
5. Is there is a loop in the graph?
6. Is there negative sum loop in the graph?
7. Does the graph have self-loops?

We have already seen this in graph chapter that depending upon the constraints the algorithm applied changes and so is the complexity of the solution.

Idea Generation

We have covered a lot of theoretical knowledge in this book. It is impossible to cover all the questions as new ones are created every day. So we should know how to handle new problems. Even if you know the solution of a problem asked by the interviewer then also you need to have a discussion with the interviewer and reach to the solution. You need to analyze the problem also because the interviewer may modify a question a little bit and the approach to solve it will vary.

Well, how to solve a new problem? The solution to this problem is that you need to do a lot of practice and the more you practice the more you will be able to solve any new question, which come in front of you. When you have solved enough problems, you will be able to see a pattern in the questions and able to solve new problems easily.

Following is the strategy that you need to follow to solve an unknown problem:
1. Try to simplify the task in hand.
2. Try a few examples
3. Think of a suitable data-structure.
4. Think about similar problems you have already solved.

Try to simplify the task in hand

Let us look into the following problem:
Husbands and their wives are standing in random in a line. They have been numbered for husbands H1, H2, H3 and so on. And their corresponding wives have number W1, W2, W3 and so on. You need to arrange them so that H1 will stand first, followed by W1, then H2 followed by W2 and so on.

At the first look, it looks difficult, but it is a simple problem. Try to find a relation of the final position.

$P(Hi) = i*2 - 1$
$P(Wi) = i*2$

The rest of the algorithm we are leaving you to do something like Insertion-Sort and you are done.

Try a few examples

In the same above problem if you have tried it with some example for 3 husband and wife pair then you may have reached to the same formula that we have shown in the previous section. Some time thinking some more examples try to solve the problem at hand.

Think of a suitable data-structure

For some problems, it is straight forward which data structure will be most suitable for. For example, if we have a problem finding min/max of some given value, then probably heap is the data structure we are looking for. We have seen a number of data structure throughout this book. And we have to figure out which data-structure will suite our need.

Let's look into a problem: We are given a stream of data at any time we can be asked to tell the median value of the data and maybe we can be asked to pop median data.

We can think about some sort of tree, may be balanced tree where the root is the median. Wait but it is not so easy to make sure the tree root to be a median.
A heap can give us minimum or maximum so we cannot get the desired result from it too. However, what if we use two heap one max heap and one min heap. The smaller values will go to min heap and the bigger values will go to max heap. In addition, we can keep the count of how many elements are there in the heap. The rest of the algorithm you can think yourself.

For every new problem think about the data structure, you know and may be one of them or some combination of them will solve your problem.

Think about similar problems you have already solved
Let us suppose you are given two linked list head pointer and they meet at some point and need to find the point of intersection. However, in place of the end of both the linked list to be a null pointer there is a loop.
You know how to find intersection point of two intersecting linked list, you know how to find if a linked list have a loop (three-pointer solution). Therefore, you can apply both of these solutions to find the solution of the problem in hand.

Complexities

Solving a problem is not just finding a correct solution. The solution should be fast and should have reasonable memory requirement. You have already read about Big-O notation in the previous chapters. You should be able to do Big-O analysis. In case you think the solution you have provided is not that optimal and there is some more efficient solution, then think again and try to figure out this information.

Most interviewers expect that you should be able to find the time and *Space Complexity* of the algorithms. You should be able to compute the time and *Space Complexity* instantly. Whenever you are solving some problem, you should find the complexity associated with it from this you would be able to choose the best solutions. In some problems there is some trade-offs between space and *Time Complexity*, so you should know these trade-offs. Sometime taking some bit more space saves a lot of time and make your algorithm much faster.

Coding

At this point, you have already captured all the constraints of the problem, proposed few solutions, evaluated the complexities of the various solutions and picked the one solution to do final coding. Never ever, jump into coding before discussing constraints, Idea generation and complexity with the interviewer.

We are accustomed to coding in an IDE like visual studio. So many people struggle when asked to write code on a whiteboard or some blank sheet. Therefore, we should have a little practice to the coding on a sheet of paper. You should think before coding because there is no back button in sheet of paper. Always try to write modular code. Small functions need to be created so that the code is clean and managed. If there is a swap function so just use this function and tell the interviewer that you will write it later. Everybody knows that you can write swap code.

Testing

Once the code is written, you are not done. It is most important that you test your code with several small test cases. It shows that you understand the importance of testing. It also gives confidence to your interviewer that you are not going to write a buggy code.

Once you are done with, your coding it is a good practice that you go through your code line by line with some small test case. This is just to make sure your code is working as it is supposed to work.

You should test few test cases.
Normal test cases: These are the positive test cases, which contain the most common scenario, and focus is on the working of the base logic of the code. For example, if we` are going to write some algorithm for linked list, then this may contain what will happen when a linked list with 3 or 4 nodes is given as input. These test cases you should always run in your head before saying the code is done.

Edge cases: These are the test cases, which are going to test the boundaries of the code. For the same linked list algorithm, edge cases may be how the code behaves when an empty list is passed or just one node is passed. These test cases you should always run in your head before saying the code is done. Edge cases may help to make your code more robust. Just few checks need to be added to the code to take care of the condition.

Load testing: In this kind of test, your code will be tested with a huge data. This will allow us to test if your code is slow or too much memory intensive.

Always follow these five steps never jump to coding before doing constraint analysis, idea generation, and Complexity Analysis:. At least never, miss the testing phase.

Example

Let us suppose the interviewer ask you to give a best sorting algorithm.
Some interviewee will directly jump to Quick-Sort **O(nlogn)**. Oops, mistake you need to ask many questions before beginning to solve this problem.

Questions 1: What kind of data we are talking about? Are they *integer* s?
Answer: Yes, they are *integer* s.

Questions 2: How much data are we going to sort?
Answer: May be thousands.

Questions 3: What exactly is this data about?
Answer: They store a person's age

Questions 4: What kind of data-structure used to hold this data?
Answer: Data are given in the form of some array

Questions 5: Can we modify the given data-structure? In addition, many, many more…?
Answer: No, you cannot modify the data structure provided

Ok from the first answer, we will deduce that the data is *integer* . The data is not so big it just contains a few thousand entries. The third answer is interesting from this we deduce that the range of data is 1-150. Data is provided in an array. From fifths answer we deduce that we have to create our own data structure and we cannot modify the array provided. So finally, we conclude, we can just use bucket sort to sort the data. The range is just 1-150 so we need just 151-capacity integral array. Data is under thousands so we do not have to worry about data overflow and we get the solution in linear time $O(N)$.

Note: We will read sorting in the coming chapters.

Summary

At this point, you know the process of handling new problems very well. In the coming chapter we will be looking into a lot of various data structure and the problems they solve. A huge number of problems are solved in this book. But is recommended so first try to solve them by yourself, then look for the solution. Always think about the complexity of the problem. In the interview interaction is the key to get problem described completely and discuss your approach with the interviewer.

CHAPTER 4: ABSTRACT DATA TYPE

Abstract data type (ADT)

An abstract data type (ADT) is a logical description of how we view the data and the operations that are allowed on it. ADT is defined as a user point of view of a data type. ADT concerns about the possible values of the data and what are interface exposed by it.

ADT does not concern about the actual implementation of the data structure.

For example, a user wants to store some *integer* s and find a mean of it. Does not talk about how exactly it will be implemented.

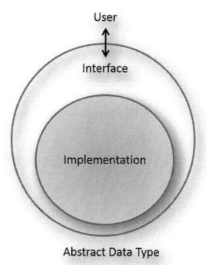

Data-Structure

Data structures are concrete representations of data and are defined as a programmer point of view. Data-structure represents how data will be stored in memory. All data-structures have their own pros and cons. And depending upon the problem at hand, we pick a data-structure that is best suited for it.

For example, we can store data in an array, a linked-list, stack, queue, tree, etc.

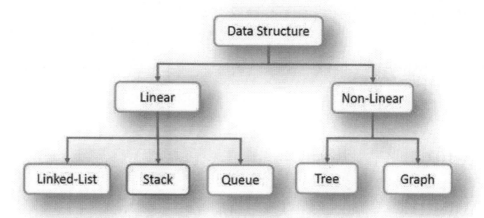

Array

0	1	2	3	4	5	6	7	8	9
1	2	3	4	5	6	7			

Array represent a collection of multiple elements of the same datatype. Arrays are fixed size data structure, the size of this data structure must be known at compile time and cannot be changed after that. Arrays are the most common data structure used to store data.

As we cannot change the size of an array, we generally declare large size array to handle any future data expansion. This ends up in creating large size array, where most of the space is unused.

Array ADT Operations

Below is the API of array:

Insert(x, k): adds an element at kth position
If we want to just store value k at index x, and we do not care about the value already stored in that location than this operation is done in **O(1)** constant time.
However, if we care about the previous values stored in an array, so insertions and deletions of an element is time consuming as we have to shift other elements by one position respectively. In this case, insertion and deletion take **O(n)** time.

Delete(k): delete element at kth position
If we want to just mark that there is no value stored at index k, this operation is done in **O(1)** constant time.
However, if we care about the other values stored in an array, so deletions of an element are time consuming as we have to shift other elements by one position respectively. In this case, deletion takes **O(n)** time.

FindKth(k): find element at position k
The biggest advantage of the array is that if we know index of an element then it can be accessed in **O(1)** *Time Complexity*. We just need to return A[k].

Find(x): find position of element
If the array is unsorted, then find(x) an element will take **O(n)** *Time Complexity*.
If the array is sorted, then find(x) is fast using binary search and will take **O(logn)** *Time Complexity*.

PrintList(): display all the elements in the list
PrintList Just run through the array and print one element at a time. Uses one loop. Linear time **O(n)**.

IsEmpty(): check if number of elements are zero
Searching if there is no element stored in array also take linear time **O(n)**.

Linked List

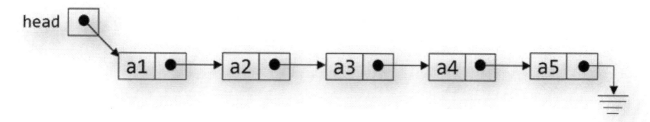

Linked lists are dynamic data structure and memory is allocated at run time. The concept of linked list is not to store data contiguously. Use links that point to the next elements.

Performance wise linked lists are slower than arrays because there is no direct access to linked list elements. The linked list is a useful data structure when we don't know the number of elements to be stored ahead of time.

There are many flavors of linked list that you will see: linear, circular, doubly, and doubly circular.

Linked List ADT Operations

Below is the API of Linked list.

Insert(k): adds k to the start of the list
Insert an element at the start of the list. Just create a new element and move pointers. So that this new element becomes the new element of the list. This operation will take $O(1)$ constant time.

Delete(): delete element at the start of the list
Delete an element at the start of the list. We just need to move one pointer. This operation will also take $O(1)$ constant time.

PrintList(): display all the elements of the list.
Start with the first element and then follow the pointers. This operation will take $O(N)$ time.

Find(k): find the position of element with value k
Start with the first element and follow the pointer until we get the value we are looking for or reach the end of the list. This operation will take $O(N)$ time.
Note: binary search does not work on linked lists.

FindKth(k): find element at position k
Start from the first element and follow the links until you reach the kth element. This operation will take $O(N)$ time.

IsEmpty(): check if the number of elements in the list are zero.
Just check the head pointer of the list it should be Null. Which means list is empty. This operation will take $O(1)$ time.

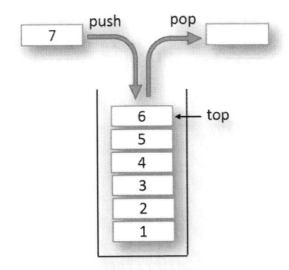

Stack is a special kind of data structure that follows Last-In-First-Out (LIFO) strategy. This means that the element that is added to stack last will be the first to be removed.

The various applications of stack are:
1. Recursion: recursive calls are preformed using system stack.
2. Postfix evaluation of expression.
3. Backtracking
4. Depth-first search of trees and graphs.
5. Converting a decimal number into a binary number etc.

Stack ADT Operations

Push(k): Adds a new item to the top of the stack

Pop(): Remove an element from the top of the stack and return its value.

Top(): Returns the value of the element at the top of the stack

Size(): Returns the number of elements in the stack

IsEmpty(): determines whether the stack is empty. It returns 1 if the stack is empty or return 0.

Note: All the above Stack operations are implemented in *O(1) Time Complexity*.

Queue

A queue is a First-In-First-Out (FIFO) kind of data structure. The element that is added to the queue first will be the first to be removed from the queue and so on.

Queue has the following application uses:
1. Access to shared resources (e.g., printer)
2. Multiprogramming
3. Message queue

Queue ADT Operations:

Enqueue(): Add a new element to the back of the queue.

Dequeue(): remove an element from the front of the queue and return its value.

Front(): return the value of the element at the front of the queue.

Size(): returns the number of elements inside the queue.

IsEmpty(): returns 1 if the queue is empty otherwise return 0

Note: All the above Queue operations are implemented in **O(1)** *Time Complexity*.

Trees

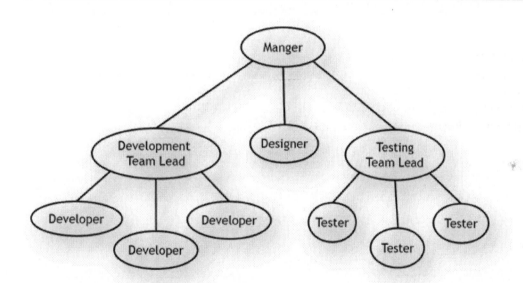

Tree is a hierarchical data structure. The top element of a tree is called the root of the tree. Except the root element, every element in a tree has a parent element, and zero or more child elements. The tree is the most useful data structure when you have hierarchical information to store.

There are many types of trees, for example, binary-tree, Red-black tree, AVL tree, etc.

Binary Tree

A binary tree is a type of tree in which each node has at most two children (0, 1 or 2) which are referred as left child and right child.

Binary Search Trees (BST)

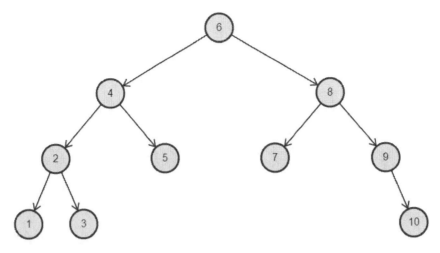

A binary search tree (BST) is a binary tree on which nodes are ordered in the following way:
1. The key in the left subtree is less than the key in its parent node.
2. The key in the right subtree is greater or equal the key in its parent node.

Binary Search Tree ADT Operations

Insert(k): Insert an element k into the tree.

Delete(k): Delete an element k from the tree.

Search(k): Search a particular value k into the tree if it is present or not.

FindMax(): Find the maximum value stored in the tree.

FindMin(): Find the minimum value stored in the tree.

The average *Time Complexity* of all the above operations on a binary search tree is O(log n), the case when the tree is balanced.

The worst-case *Time Complexity* will be **O(n)** when the tree is skewed. A binary tree is skewed when tree is not balanced.
There are two types of skewed tree.
1. Right Skewed binary tree: A binary tree in which each node is having either only a right child or no child at all.
2. Left Skewed binary tree: A binary tree in which each node is having either only a left child or no child at all.

Balanced Binary search tree

There are few binary search tree, which always keeps themselves balanced. Most important among them are Red-Black Tree (RB-Tree) and AVL tree.

The standard template library (STL) is implemented using this Red-Black Tree (RB-Tree).

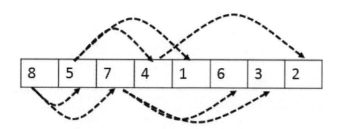

Priority queue is implemented using a binary heap data structure. In a heap, the records are stored in an array so that each key is larger than its two children keys. Each node in the heap follow the same rule that the parent value is greater than its two child.

There are two types of the heap data structure:
1. Max heap: each node should be greater than or equal to each of its children.
2. Min heap: each node should be smaller than or equal to each of its children.

A heap is a useful data structure when you want to get max/min one by one from data. Heap-Sort uses max heap to sort data in increasing/decreasing order.

Heap ADT Operations

Insert() - Adding a new element to the heap. The *Time Complexity* of this operation is O(log(n))

Extract() - Extracting max for max heap case (or min for min heap case). The *Time Complexity* of this operation is O(log(n))

Heapify() – To convert a list of numbers in an array into a heap. This operation has a *Time Complexity O(n)*

Delete() – Delete an element from the heap. The *Time Complexity* of this operation is O(log(n))

Hash Function

Object ---------------------------------------> Index

A Hash-Table is a data structure that maps keys to values. Each position of the Hash-Table is called a slot. The Hash-Table uses a hash function to calculate an index of an array of slots. We use the Hash-Table when the number of keys actually stored is small relatively to the number of possible keys.

The process of storing objects using a hash function is as follows:
1. Create an array of size M to store objects, this array is called Hash-Table.
2. Find a hash code of an object by passing it through the hash function.
3. Take module of hash code by the size of Hash-Table to get the index of the table where objects will be stored.
4. Finally store these objects in the designated index.

The process of searching objects in Hash-Table using a hash function is as follows:
1. Find a hash code of the object we are searching for by passing it through the hash function.
2. Take module of hash code by the size of Hash-Table to get the index of the table where objects are stored.
3. Finally, retrieve the object from the designated index.

Hash-Table Abstract Data Type (ADT)

ADT of Hash-Table contains the following functions:
Insert(x): Add object x to the data set.
Delete(x): Delete object x from the data set.
Search(x): Search object x in data set.

The Hash-Table is a useful data structure for implementing dictionary. The average time to search for an element in a Hash-Table is $O(1)$. A Hash Table generalizes the notion of an array.

Dictionary / Symbol Table

A symbol table is a mapping between a string(key) and a value, which can be of any dta type. A value can be an *integer* such as occurrence count, dictionary meaning of a word and so on.

Binary Search Tree (BST) for Strings

Binary Search Tree (BST) is the simplest way to implement symbol table. Simple string compare function can be used to compare two strings. If all the keys are random, and the tree is balanced. Then on an average key lookup can be done in logarithmic time.

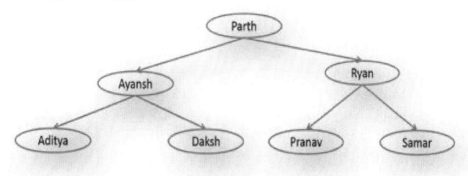

BINARY SEARCH TREE AS DICTIONARY

Hash-Table

The Hash-Table is another data structure, which can be used for symbol table implementation. Below Hash-Table diagram, we can see the name of that person is taken as the key, and their meaning is the value of the search. The first key is converted into a hash code by passing it to appropriate hash function. Inside hash function the size of Hash-Table is also passed, which is used to find the actual index where values will be stored. Finally, the value that is meaning of name is stored in the Hash-Table, or you can store a reference to the string which store meaning can be stored into the Hash-Table.

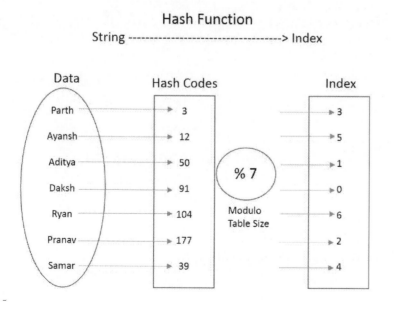

Hash-Table has an excellent lookup of constant time.

Let us suppose we want to implement autocomplete the box feature of Google search. When you type some string to search in google search, it propose some complete string even before you have done typing. BST cannot solve this problem as related strings can be in both right and left subtree.

The Hash-Table is also not suited for this job. One cannot perform a partial match or range query on a Hash-Table. Hash function transforms string to a number. Moreover, a good hash function will give a distributed hash bode even for partial string and there is no way to relate two strings in a Hash-Table.

Trie and Ternary Search tree are a special kind of tree, which solves partial match, and range query problem well.

Trie

Trie is a tree, in which we store only one character at each node. This final key value pair is stored in the leaves. Each node has K children, one for each possible character. For simplicity purpose, let us consider that the character set is 26, corresponds to different characters of English alphabets.

Trie is an efficient data structure. Using Trie, we can search the key in O(M) time. Where M is the maximum string length. Trie is also suitable for solving partial match and range query problems.

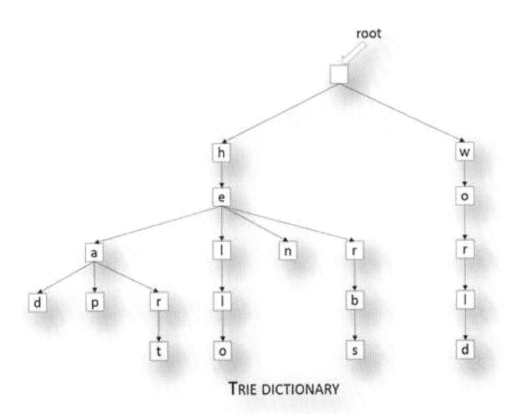

TRIE DICTIONARY

Ternary Search Trie/ Ternary Search Tree

Tries having a very good search performance of O(M) where M is the maximum size of the search string. However, tries having very high space requirement. Every node Trie contain references to multiple nodes, each reference corresponds to possible characters of the key. To avoid this high space requirement Ternary Search Trie (TST) is used.

A TST avoid the heavy space requirement of the traditional Trie while still keeping many of its advantages. In a TST, each node contains a character, an end of key indicator, and three pointers. The three pointers are corresponding to current char hold by the node(equal), characters less than and character greater than.

The *Time Complexity* of ternary search tree operation is proportional to the height of the ternary search tree. In the worst case, we need to traverse up to 3 times that many links. However, this case is rare.

Therefore, TST is a very good solution for implementing Symbol Table, Partial match and range query.

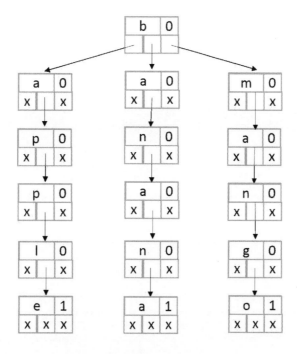

TERNARY Search Tree

Graphs

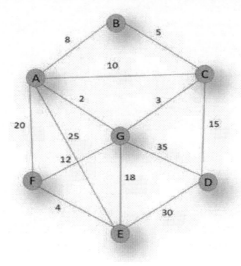

A graph is a data structure which represents a network, that connects a collection of nodes called vertices, and there connections, called edges. An edge can be seen as a path between two nodes. These edges can be either directed or undirected. If a path is directed then you can move only in one direction, while in an undirected path you can move in both the directions.

Graph Algorithms

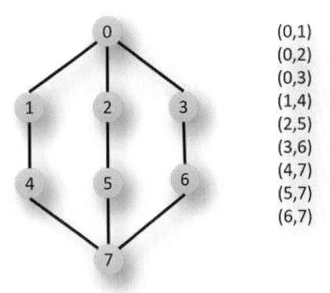

(0,1)
(0,2)
(0,3)
(1,4)
(2,5)
(3,6)
(4,7)
(5,7)
(6,7)

Depth-First Search (DFS)

The DFS algorithm we start from starting point and go into depth of graph until we reach a dead end and then move up to parent node (Backtrack). In DFS, we use stack to get the next vertex to start a search. Alternatively, we can use recursion (system stack) to do the same.

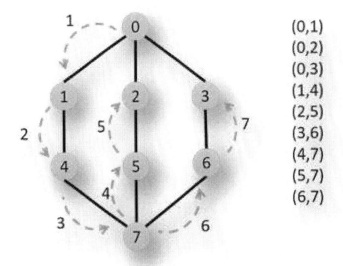

(0,1)
(0,2)
(0,3)
(1,4)
(2,5)
(3,6)
(4,7)
(5,7)
(6,7)

Depth First Traversal
0, 1, 4, 7 , 5, 2, 6, 3

Breadth-First Search (BFS)

In BFS algorithm, a graph is traversed in layer-by-layer fashion. The graph is traversed closer to the starting point. The queue is used to implement BFS.

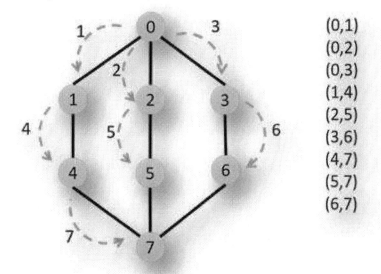

(0,1)
(0,2)
(0,3)
(1,4)
(2,5)
(3,6)
(4,7)
(5,7)
(6,7)

Breadth First Traversal
0, 1, 2, 3, 4, 5, 6, 7

Sorting Algorithms

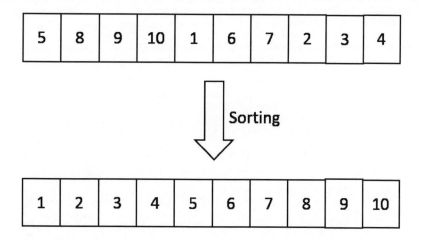

Sorting is the process of placing elements from a collection into ascending or descending order.
Sorting arranges data elements in order so that searching become easier.
There are good sorting functions available which does sorting in $O(nlogn)$ time, so in this book when we need sorting we will use sort() function and will assume that the sorting is done in $O(nlogn)$ time.

Counting Sort

Counting sort is the simplest and most efficient type of sorting. Counting sort has a strict requirement of a predefined range of data.

Like, sort how many people are in which age group. We know that the age of people can vary between 1 and 130.

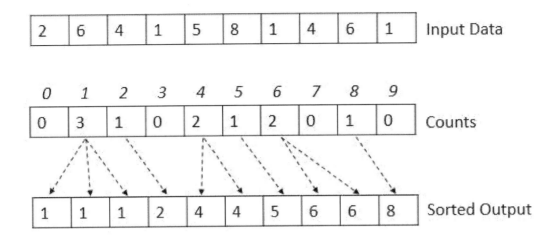

If we know the range of input, then sorting can be done using counting in O(n+k).

End note

This chapter have provided a brief introduction of the various data structures, algorithms and their complexities. In the coming chapters we will look into all these data structure in details. If you know the interface of the various data structures, then you can use them while solving other problems without knowing the internal details how they are implemented.

CHAPTER 5: SEARCHING

Introduction

In Computer Science, Searching is the algorithmic process of finding a particular item in a collection of items. The item may be a keyword in a file, a record in a database, a node in a tree or a value in an array etc.

Why Searching?

Imagine you are in a library with millions of books. You want to get a specific book with specific title. How will you find? You will just start searching by initial letter of the book title. Then you continue matching with a whole book title until you find your desired book. (By doing this small heuristic you have reduced the search space by a factor of 26, consider we have an equal number of books whose title begin with particular char.)

Similarly, computer stores lots of information and to retrieve this information efficiently, we need very efficient searching algorithms. To make searching efficient, we keep the data in some proper order. There are certain ways of organizing the data. If you keep the data in proper order, it is easy to search required element. For example, Sorting is one of the process for making data organized.

Different Searching Algorithms

- Linear Search – Unsorted Input
- Linear Search – Sorted Input
- Binary Search (Sorted Input)
- String Search: Tries, Suffix Trees, Ternary Search.
- Hashing and Symbol Tables

Linear Search – Unsorted Input

When elements of an array are not ordered or sorted and we want to search for a particular value, we need to scan the full array unless we find the desired value. This kind of algorithm known as unordered linear search. The major problem with this algorithm is less performance or high *Time Complexity* in worst case.

Example 5.1

```
int linearSearchUnsorted(int arr[], int size, int value) {
int i = 0;
        for(i = 0 ; i < size ; i++) {
                if(value == arr[i] )
                        return i;
        }
        return -1;
}
```

Time Complexity: *O(n)*. As we need to traverse the complete array in worst case. Worst case is when your desired element is at the last position of the array. Here, 'n' is the size of the array.
Space Complexity: *O(1)*. No extra memory is used to allocate the array.

Linear Search – Sorted

If elements of the array are sorted either in increasing order or in decreasing order, searching for a desired element will be much more efficient than unordered linear search. In many cases, we do not need to traverse the complete array. Following example explains when you encounter a greater element from the increasing sorted array, you stop searching further. This is how this algorithm saves the time and improves the performance.

Example 5.2

```
int linearSearchSorted(int arr[], int size, int value)
{
        int i = 0;
        for(i = 0 ; i < size ; i++)
        {
                if(value == arr[i] )
                        return i;
                else if( value < arr[i] )
                        return -1;
        }
        return -1;
}
```

Time Complexity: *O(n)*. As we need to traverse the complete array in worst case. Worst case is when your desired element is at the last position of the sorted array. However, in the average case this algorithm is more efficient even though the growth rate is same as unsorted.
Space Complexity: *O(1)*. No extra memory is used to allocate the array.

Binary Search

How do we search a word in a dictionary? In general, we go to some approximate page (mostly middle) and start searching from that point. If we see the word that we are searching is same then we are done with the search. Else, if we see the page is before the selected pages, then apply the same procedure for the first half otherwise to the second half. Binary Search also works in the same way. We get the middle point from the sorted array and start comparing with the desired value.

Note: Binary search requires the array to be sorted otherwise binary search cannot be applied.

Example 5.3

```
/* Binary Search Algorithm – Iterative Way */
int Binarysearch(int arr[], int size, int value)
{
        int low = 0;
        int high = size-1;
        int mid;
        while (low <= high)
        {
                mid = low + (high-low)/2;       /* To avoid the overflow */
                if (arr[mid] == value)
                        return mid;
```

```
                        else if (arr[mid] < value)
                                low = mid + 1;
                        else
                                high = mid - 1;
                }
        return -1;
}
```

Time Complexity: *O(logn)*. We always take half input and throwing out the other half. So the recurrence relation for binary search is T(n) = T(n/2) + c. Using master theorem (divide and conquer), we get T(n) = *O(logn)*
Space Complexity: O(1)

Example 5.4

```
/* Binary Search Algorithm – Recursive Way */
int BinarySearchRecursive(int arr[], int low, int high, int value)
{
        if(low > high)
                return -1;
        int mid = low + (high-low)/2;        /* To avoid the overflow */
        if (arr[mid] == value)
                return mid;
        else if (arr[mid] < value)
                return BinarySearchRecursive (arr, mid + 1, high, value);
        else
                return BinarySearchRecursive (arr, low, mid - 1 , value);
}
```

Time Complexity: O(logn).
Space Complexity: O(logn) For system stack in recursion

String Searching Algorithms

Refer String chapter.

Hashing and Symbol Tables

Refer Hash-Table chapter.

How sorting is useful in Selection Algorithm?

Selection problems can be converted to sorting problems. Once the array is sorted, it is easy to find the minimum/maximum (or desired element) from the sorted array. The method 'Sorting and then Selecting' is inefficient for selecting a single element, but it is efficient when many selections need to be made from the array. It is because only one initial expensive sort is needed, followed by many cheap selection operations.

For example, if we want to get the maximum element from an array. After sorting the array, we can simply return the last element from the array. What if we want to get second maximum. Now, we do not have to sort the array again and we can return the second last element from the sorted array. Similarly, we can return the kth maximum element by just one scan of the sorted list.

So with the above discussion, sorting is used to improve the performance. In general this method requires **O(nlogn)** (for sorting) time. With the initial sorting, we can answer any query in one scan, **O(n)**.

Problems in Searching

Print Duplicates in Array

Given an array of n numbers, print the duplicate elements in the array.

First approach: Exhaustive search or Brute force, for each element in array find if there is some other element with the same value. This is done using two for loop, first loop to select the element and second loop to find its duplicate entry.

Example 5.5

```
void printRepeating(int arr[], int size)
{
        int i, j;
        printf(" Repeating elements are ");
        for(i = 0; i < size; i++)
                for(j = i+1; j < size; j++)
                        if(arr[i] == arr[j])
                                printf(" %d ", arr[i]);
}
```

The Time Complexity is $O(n^2)$ and Space Complexity is $O(1)$

Second approach: Sorting, Sort all the elements in the array and after this in a single scan, we can find the duplicates.

Example 5.6

```
void printRepeating(int arr[], int size)
{
        int i;
        Sort(arr, size);
        printf(" Repeating elements are ");
        for(i = 1; i < size; i++)
        {
                if(arr[i] == arr[i-1])
                        printf(" %d ", arr[i]);
        }
}
```

Sorting algorithms take $O(n . log\, n)$ time and single scan take $O(n)$ time.
The *Time Complexity* of an algorithm is $O(n . log\, n)$ and *Space Complexity* is $O(1)$

Third approach: Hash-Table, using Hash-Table, we can keep track of the elements we have already seen and we can find the duplicates in just one scan.

Example 5.7

```
void printRepeating(int arr[], int size)
{
        HashTable h;
        int i;

        printf(" Repeating elements are ");
        for(i = 0; i < size; i++)
        {
                if(findValue (h, arr[i]) )
                        printf(" %d ", arr[i]);
                else
                        addValue(h, arr[i]);
        }
}
```

Hash-Table insert and find take constant time $O(1)$ so the total *Time Complexity* of the algorithm is $O(n)$ time. *Space Complexity* is also $O(n)$.

Forth approach: Counting, this approach is only possible if we know the range of the input. If we know that, the elements in the array are in the range 0 to n-1. We can reserve and array of length n and when we see an element we can increase its count. In just one single scan, we know the duplicates. If we know the range of the elements, then this is the fastest way to find the duplicates.

Example 5.8

```
void printRepeating(int arr[], int size)
{
        int *count = (int *)calloc(sizeof(int), size);
        int i;

        printf(" Repeating elements are ");
        for(i = 0; i < size; i++)
        {
                if(count[arr[i]] == 1)
                        printf(" %d ", arr[i]);
                else
                        count[arr[i]]++;
        }
}
```

Counting approach just uses an array so insert and find take constant time $O(1)$ so the total *Time Complexity* of the algorithm is $O(n)$ time. *Space Complexity* for creating count array is also $O(n)$.

Find max, appearing element in an array

Given an array of n numbers, find the element, which appears maximum number of times.

First approach: Exhaustive search or Brute force, for each element in array find how many times this particular value appears in array. Keep track of the maxCount and when some element count is greater than it then update the maxCount. This is done using two for loop, first loop to select the element and second loop to count the occurrence of that element.

The Time Complexity is $O(n^2)$ and Space Complexity is $O(1)$

Example 5.9

```
int getMax(int arr[], int size)
{
        int i, j;
        int max = arr[0], count = 1, maxCount = 1;

        for (i = 0; i < size; i++)
        {
                count = 1;
                for (j = i + 1; j < size; j++)
                        if (arr[i] == arr[j])
                                count++;
                if (count > maxCount)
                {
                        max = arr[i];
                        maxCount = count;
                }
        }
        return max;
}
```

Second approach: Sorting, Sort all the elements in the array and after this in a single scan, we can find the counts. Sorting algorithms take $O(n . log\ n)$ time and single scan take $O(n)$ time. The *Time Complexity* of an algorithm is $O(n . log\ n)$ and *Space Complexity* is $O(1)$

Example 5.10

```
int getMax(int arr[], int size)
{
        int max = arr[0], maxCount = 1,  curr = arr[0], currCount = 1;
        int i;
        Sort(arr, size);
        for (i = 1; i < size; i++)
        {
                if (arr[i] == arr[i - 1])
                        currCount++;
                else
                {
                        currCount = 1;
                        curr = arr[i];
                }
                if (currCount > maxCount)
                {
                        maxCount = currCount;
                        max = curr;
                }
        }
        return max;
}
```

Third approach: Counting, This approach is only possible if we know the range of the input. If we know that, the elements in the array are in the range 0 to n-1. We can reserve and array of length n and when we see an element we can increase its count. In just one single scan, we know the duplicates. If we know the range of the elements, then this is the fastest way to find the max count.

Counting approach just uses array so to increase count take constant time $O(1)$ so the total *Time Complexity* of the algorithm is $O(n)$ time. *Space Complexity* for creating count array is also $O(n)$.

Example 5.11

```
#define N 100
int getMax(int arr[], int size)
{
        int max = arr[0], maxCount = 1;
        int *count = (int *)calloc(sizeof(int), N);
        int i;

        for (i = 0; i < size; i++)
        {
                count[arr[i]]++;
                if (count[arr[i]] > maxCount)
                {
                        maxCount = count[arr[i]];
                        max = arr[i];
                }
        }
        return max;
}
```

Majority element in an Array

Given an array of n elements. Find the majority element, which appears more than n/2 times. Return 0 in case there is no majority element.

First approach: Exhaustive search or Brute force, for each element in array find how many times this particular value appears in array. Keep track of the maxCount and when some element count is greater than it then update the maxCount. This is done using two for loop, first loop to select the element and second loop to count the occurrence of that element.

Once we have the final, maxCount we can see if it is greater than n/2, if it is greater than we have a majority if not we do not have any majority.

The Time Complexity is $O(n^2) + O(1) = O(n^2)$ and Space Complexity is $O(1)$

Example 5.12

```
int getMajority(int arr[], int size)
{
        int i, j;
        int max=0, count=0 , maxCount=0;
        for(i = 0; i < size; i++)
        {
                for(j = i+1; j < size; j++)
                        if(arr[i] == arr[j])
                                count++;
                if(count > maxCount)
                {
                        max = arr[i];
                        maxCount = count;
                }
        }
        if (maxCount > size/2)
                return max;
        else
                return 0;
}
```

Second approach: Sorting, Sort all the elements in the array. If there is a majority than the middle element at the index n/2 must be the majority number. So just single scan can be used to find its count and see if the majority is there or not.

Sorting algorithms take $O(n.\log n)$ time and single scan take $O(n)$ time.
The *Time Complexity* of an algorithm is $O(n.\log n)$ and *Space Complexity* is $O(1)$

Example 5.13

```
int getMajority(int arr[], int size)
{
        int majIndex = size/2, count = 1;
        int i;
        int candidate;
        Sort(arr,size);
        candidate = arr[majIndex];
        count = 0;
        for (i = 0; i < size; i++)
                if(arr[i] == candidate)
                        count++;
        if (count > size/2)
                return arr[majIndex];
        else
                return 0;
}
```

Third approach: This is a cancelation approach (Moore's Voting Algorithm), if all the elements stand against the majority and each element is cancelled with one element of majority if there is majority then majority prevails.

- Set the first element of the array as majority candidate and initialize the count to be 1.
- Start scanning the array.
    - If we get some element whose value same as a majority candidate, then we increase the count.
    - If we get an element whose value is different than the majority candidate, then we decrement the count.
    - If count become 0, that means we have a new majority candidate. Make the current candidate as majority candidate and reset count to 1.
    - At the end, we will have the only probable majority candidate.
- Now scan through the array once again to see if that candidate we found above have appeared more then n/2 times.

Counting approach just scans throw array two times. The _Time Complexity_ of the algorithm is $O(n)$ time. _Space Complexity_ for creating count array is also $O(1)$.

Example 5.14

```
int getMajority(int arr[], int size)
{
        int majIndex = 0, count = 1;
        int i;
        int candidate;
        for(i = 1; i < size; i++)
        {
                if(arr[majIndex] == arr[i])
                        count++;
                else
                        count--;
                if(count == 0)
                {
                        majIndex = i;
                        count = 1;
                }
        }
        candidate = arr[majIndex];
        count = 0;
        for (i = 0; i < size; i++)
                if(arr[i] == candidate)
                        count++;
        if (count > size/2)
                return arr[majIndex];
        else
                return 0;
}
```

Find the missing number in an Array

Given an array of n-1 elements, which are in the range of 1 to n. There are no duplicates in the array. One of the *integer* is missing. Find the missing element.

First approach: Exhaustive search or Brute force, for each value in the range 1 to n, find if there is some element in array which have the same value. This is done using two for loop, first loop to select value in the range 1 to n and the second loop to find if this element is in the array or not.

The Time Complexity is $O(n^2)$ and Space Complexity is $O(1)$

Example 5.15

```
int findMissingNumber(int arr[], int size)
{
        int i, j, found = 0;
        for (i = 1; i <= size; i++)
        {
                found = 0;
                for (j = 0; j < size; j++)
                {
                        if (arr[j] == i)
                        {
                                found = 1;
                                break;
                        }
                }
                if (found == 0)
                        return i;
        }
}
```

Second approach: Sorting, Sort all the elements in the array and after this in a single scan, we can find the duplicates.

Sorting algorithms take $O(n . log\ n)$ time and single scan take $O(n)$ time.
The *Time Complexity* of an algorithm is $O(n . log\ n)$ and *Space Complexity* is $O(1)$

Third approach: Hash-Table, using Hash-Table, we can keep track of the elements we have already seen and we can find the missing element in just one scan.

Hash-Table insert and find take constant time $O(1)$ so the total *Time Complexity* of the algorithm is $O(n)$ time. *Space Complexity* is also $O(n)$.

Forth approach: Counting, we know the range of the input so counting will work. As we know that, the elements in the array are in the range 0 to n-1. We can reserve and array of length n and when we see an element we can increase its count. In just one single scan, we know the missing element.

Counting approach just uses an array so insert and find take constant time $O(1)$ so the total *Time Complexity* of the algorithm is $O(n)$ time. *Space Complexity* for creating count array is also $O(n)$.

Fifth approach: You are allowed to modify the given input array. Modify the given input array in such a way that in the next scan you can find the missing element.

When you scan through the array. When at index "index", the value stored in the array will be arr[index] so add the number "n + 1" to arr[arr[index]]. Always read the value from the array using a reminder operator "%". When you scan the array for the first time and modified all the values, then one single scan you can see if there is some value in the array which is smaller than "n+1" that index is the missing number.

In this approach, the array is scanned two times and the *Time Complexity* of this algorithm is $O(n)$. *Space Complexity* is $O(1)$.

Sixth approach: Summation formula to find the sum of n numbers from 1 to n. Subtract the values stored in the array and you will have your missing number.
The *Time Complexity* of this algorithm is $O(n)$. *Space Complexity* is $O(1)$.

Seventh approach: XOR approach to find the sum of n numbers from 1 to n. XOR the values stored in the array and you will have your missing number.
The *Time Complexity* of this algorithm is $O(n)$. *Space Complexity* is $O(1)$.

Example 5.16

```
int findMissingNumber(int arr[], int size, int range)
{
        int i;
        int xorSum = 0;
        //get the XOR of all the numbers from 1 to range
        for (i = 1; i <= range; i++)
                xorSum ^= i;

        //loop through the array and get the XOR of elements
        for (i = 0; i<size; i++)
                xorSum ^= arr[i];

        return xorSum;
}
```

Note: Same problem can be asked in many forms (sometimes you have to do the xor of the range sometime you do not):
1. There are numbers in the range of 1-n out of which all appears single time but one that appear two times.
2. All the elements in the range 1-n are appearing 16 times and one element appear 17 times. Find the element that appears 17 times.

Find Pair in an Array

Given an array of n numbers, find two elements such that their sum is equal to "value"

First approach: Exhaustive search or Brute force, for each element in array find if there is some other element, which sum up to the desired value. This is done using two for loop, first loop to select the element and second loop to find another element.

The Time Complexity is $O(n^2)$ and Space Complexity is $O(1)$

Example 5.17

```
int FindPair(int* arr, int size, int value)
{
        int i, j;
        for (i = 0; i < size; i++)
                for (j = i + 1; j < size; j++)
                        if ((arr[i] + arr[j] ) == value)
                        {
                                printf("The pair is %d, %d",arr[i],arr[j]);
                                return 1;
                        }
        return 0;
}
```

Second approach: Sorting, Steps are as follows:
1. Sort all the elements in the array.
2. Take two variable first and second. Variable first= 0 and second = size -1
3. Compute sum = arr[first]+arr[second]
4. If the sum is equal to the desired value, then we have the solution
5. If the sum is less than the desired value, then we will increase first
6. If the sum is greater than the desired value, then we will decrease the second
7. We repeat the above process till we get the desired pair or we get first >= second (don't have a pair)

Sorting algorithms take $O(n \cdot \log n)$ time and single scan take $O(n)$ time.
The *Time Complexity* of an algorithm is $O(n \cdot \log n)$ and *Space Complexity* is $O(1)$

Example 5.18

```
int FindPair(int* arr, int size, int value)
{
        int first = 0, second = size - 1;
        int curr;
        Sort(arr, size);

        while (first < second)
        {
                curr = arr[first] + arr[second];
                if (curr == value)
                {
                        printf("The pair is %d, %d", arr[first], arr[second]);
                        return 1;
                }
                else if (curr < value)
                        first++;
                else
                        second--;
        }
        return 0;
}
```

Third approach: Hash-Table, using Hash-Table, we can keep track of the elements we have already seen and we can find the pair in just one scan.

1. For each element, insert the value in Hashtable. Let say current value is arr[index]
2. And see if the value - arr[index] is already in a Hashtable.
3. If value - arr[index] is in the Hashtable then we have the desired pair.
4. Else, proceed to the next entry in the array.

Hash-Table insert and find take constant time $O(1)$ so the total _Time Complexity_ of the algorithm is $O(n)$ time. _Space Complexity_ is also $O(n)$.

Example 5.19

```
int FindPair(int* arr, int size, int value)
{
        HashTable h;
        int i;
        for (i = 0; i < size; i++)
        {
                if (findValue(h, value - arr[i]))
                {
                        printf("The pair is %d, %d", arr[i], value - arr[i]);
                        return 1;
                }
                addValue(h, arr[i]);
        }
        return 0;
}
```

Forth approach: Counting, This approach is only possible if we know the range of the input. If we know that, the elements in the array are in the range 0 to n-1. We can reserve and array of length n and when we see an element we can increase its count. In place of the Hashtable in the above approach, we will use this array and will find out the pair.

Counting approach just uses an array so insert and find take constant time $O(1)$ so the total _Time Complexity_ of the algorithm is $O(n)$ time. _Space Complexity_ for creating count array is also $O(n)$.

Find the Pair in two Arrays

Given two array X and Y. Find a pair of elements (x_i, y_i) such that $x_i \in X$ and $y_i \in Y$ where $x_i + y_i = value$.

First approach: Exhaustive search or Brute force, loop through element xi of X and see if you can find (value – xi) in Y. Two for loop.
The Time Complexity is $O(n^2)$ and Space Complexity is $O(1)$

Second approach: Sorting, Sort all the elements in the second array Y. For each element if X you can see if that element is there in Y by using binary search.

Sorting algorithms take $O(m . log\ m)$ and searching will take $O(n . log\ m)$ time.
The Time Complexity of an algorithm is $O(n . log\ m)\ or\ O(m . log\ m)$ and Space Complexity is $O(1)$

Third approach: Sorting, Steps are as follows:
1. Sort the elements of both X and Y in increasing order.
2. Take the sum of the smallest element of X and the largest element of Y.
3. If the sum is equal to value, we got our pair.
4. If the sum is smaller than value, take next element of X
5. If the sum is greater than value, take the previous element of Y

Sorting algorithms take $O(n.\log n) + O(m.\log m)$ for sorting and searching will take $O(n+m)$ time. The Time Complexity of an algorithm is $O(n.\log n)$ Space Complexity is $O(1)$

Forth approach: Hash-Table, Steps are as follows:
1. Scan through all the elements in the array Y and insert them into Hashtable.
2. Now scan through all the elements of array X, let us suppose the current element is xi see if you can find (value - xi) in the Hashtable.
3. If you find the value, you got your pair.
4. If not, then go to the next value in the array X.

Hash-Table insert and find take constant time $O(1)$ so the total *Time Complexity* of the algorithm is $O(n)$ time. *Space Complexity* is also $O(n)$.

Fifth approach: Counting, This approach is only possible if we know the range of the input. Same as Hashtable implementation just use a simple array in place of Hashtable and you are done.

Counting approach just uses an array so insert and find take constant time $O(1)$ so the total *Time Complexity* of the algorithm is $O(n)$ time. *Space Complexity* for creating count array is also $O(n)$.

Two elements whose sum is closest to zero

Given an Array of *integer* s, both +ve and -ve. You need to find the two elements such that their sum is closest to zero.

First approach: Exhaustive search or Brute force, for each element in array find the other element whose value when added will give minimum absolute value. This is done using two for loop, first loop to select the element and second loop to find the element that should be added to it so that the absolute of the sum will be minimum or close to zero.

The Time Complexity is $O(n^2)$ and Space Complexity is $O(1)$

Example 5.20

```
void minAbsSumPair(int arr[], int size)
{
        int l, r, minSum, sum, minFirst, minSecond;

        /* Array should have at least two elements*/
        if(size < 2)
        {
                printf("Invalid Input");
                return;
        }
}
```

```
            /* Initialization of values */
            minFirst = 0;
            minSecond = 1;
            minSum = abs(arr[0] + arr[1]);
            for(l = 0; l < size - 1; l++)
            {
                    for(r = l+1; r < size; r++)
                    {
                            sum = abs(arr[l] + arr[r]);
                            if(sum < minSum)
                            {
                                    minSum = sum;
                                    minFirst = l;
                                    minSecond = r;
                            }
                    }
            }
            printf(" The two elements with minimum sum are %d & %d", arr[minFirst],
arr[minSecond]);
}
```

Second approach: Sorting

Steps are as follows:

1. Sort all the elements in the array.
2. Take two variable firstIndex = 0 and secondIndex = size -1
3. Compute sum = arr[firstIndex]+arr[secondIndex]
4. If the sum is equal to the 0 then we have the solution
5. If the sum is less than the 0 then we will increase first
6. If the sum is greater then the 0 then we will decrease the second
7. We repeat the above process 3 to 6, till we get the desired pair or we get first >= second

Example 5.21

```
void minAbsSumPair(int arr[], int size)
{
        int l, r, minSum, sum, minFirst, minSecond;
        /* Array should have at least two elements*/
        if (size < 2)
        {
                printf("Invalid Input");
                return;
        }
        Sort(arr, size);
        /* Initialization of values */

        minFirst = 0;
        minSecond = size - 1;
        minSum = abs(arr[minFirst] + arr[minSecond]);
```

```
            for (l = 0, r = size - 1; l < r;)
            {
                    sum = (arr[l] + arr[r]);
                    if (abs(sum) < minSum)
                    {
                            minSum = abs(sum);
                            minFirst = l;
                            minSecond = r;
                    }
                    if (sum < 0)
                            l++;
                    else if (sum > 0)
                            r++;
                    else
                            break;
            }
            printf(" The two elements with minimum sum are %d & %d", arr[minFirst],
arr[minSecond]);
}
```

Find maxima in a bitonic array

A bitonic array comprises of an increasing sequence of *integer* s immediately followed by a decreasing sequence of *integer* s. Since the elements are sorted in some order, we should go for algorithm similar to binary search. The steps are as follows:

1. Take two variable for storing start and end index. Variable start=0 and end=size-1
2. Find the middle element of the array.
3. See if the middle element is the maxima. If yes, return the middle element.
4. Alternatively, If the middle element in increasing part, then we need to look for in mid+1 and end.
5. Alternatively, if the middle element is in the decreasing part, then we need to look in the start and mid-1.
6. Repeat step 2 to 5 till we get the maxima.

Example 5.22

```
int SearchBotinicArrayMax(int arr[], int size)
{
        int start = 0, end = size - 1, mid;
        int maximaFound = 0;
        if (size < 3)
        {
                printf("error");
                return 0;
        }
        while (start <= end)
        {
                mid = (start + end) / 2;
                if (arr[mid - 1] < arr[mid] && arr[mid + 1] < arr[mid])//maxima
                {
                        maximaFound = 1;
                        break;
                }
```

84

```
                else if (arr[mid - 1] < arr[mid] && arr[mid] < arr[mid + 1])//increasing
                {
                        start = mid + 1;
                }
                else if (arr[mid - 1] > arr[mid] && arr[mid] > arr[mid + 1])//decreasing
                {
                        end = mid - 1;
                }
                else
                {
                        break;
                }
        }
        if (maximaFound == 0)
        {
                printf("error");
                return 0;
        }
        return arr[mid];
}
```

Search element in a bitonic array

A bitonic array comprises of an increasing sequence of *integer* s immediately followed by a decreasing sequence of *integer* s. To search an element in a bitonic array :

1. Find the index or maximum element in the array. By finding the end of increasing part of the array, using modified binary search.
2. Once we have the maximum element, search the given value in increasing part of the array using binary search.
3. If the value is not found in increasing part, search the same value in decreasing part of the array using binary search.

Example 5.23

```
int SearchBitonicArray(int arr[], int size, int key)
{
        int  max = FindMaxBitonicArray(arr, size);

        int k = BinarySearch(arr, 0, max, key, true);
        if (k != -1)
                return k;
        else
                return BinarySearch(arr, max + 1, size - 1, key, false);
}
```

```c
int FindMaxBitonicArray(int arr[], int size)
{
        int start = 0, end = size - 1, mid;
        if (size < 3)
        {
                printf("error");
                return 0;
        }
        while (start <= end)
        {
                mid = (start + end) / 2;
                if (arr[mid - 1] < arr[mid] && arr[mid + 1] < arr[mid])//maxima
                {
                        return mid;
                }
                else if (arr[mid - 1] < arr[mid] && arr[mid] < arr[mid + 1])//increasing
                {
                        start = mid + 1;
                }
                else if (arr[mid - 1] > arr[mid] && arr[mid] > arr[mid + 1])//increasing
                {
                        end = mid - 1;
                }
                else
                {
                        break;
                }
        }
        printf("error");
        return 0;
}
```

```c
int BinarySearch(int arr[], int start, int end, int key, int isInc)
{
        int mid;
        if (end < start)
                return -1;
        mid = (start + end) / 2;
        if (key == arr[mid])
                return mid;
        if (isInc && key < arr[mid] ||
                !isInc && key > arr[mid])
        {
                return BinarySearch(arr, start, mid - 1, key, isInc);
        }
        else
        {
                return BinarySearch(arr, mid + 1, end, key, isInc);
        }
}
```

Occurrence counts in sorted Array

Given a sorted array arr[] find the number of occurrences of a number.

First approach: Brute force, Traverse the array and in linear time we will get the occurrence count of the number. This is done using one loop.

The Time Complexity is $O(n)$ and Space Complexity is $O(1)$

Example 5.24

```
int findKeyCount(int arr[], int size, int key)
{
        int i, count = 0;
        for (i = 0; i < size ; i++)
        {
                if (arr[i] == key)
                        count++;
        }
        return count;
}
```

Second approach: Since we have sorted array, we should think about some binary search.
1. First, we should find the first occurrence of the key.
2. Then we should find the last occurrence of the key.
3. Take the difference of these two values and you will have the solution.

Example 5.25

```
int findKeyCount(int arr[], int size, int key)
{
        int firstIndex, lastIndex;
        firstIndex = findFirstIndex(arr, 0, size -1, key);
        lastIndex = findLastIndex(arr, 0, size - 1, key);
        return (lastIndex - firstIndex + 1);
}
```

```
int findFirstIndex(int arr[], int start, int end, int key)
{
        int mid;
        if (end < start)
                return -1;

        mid = (start + end) / 2;

        if (key == arr[mid] && (mid == start || arr[mid - 1] != key))
                return mid;
        if (key <= arr[mid])// <= is us the number.t in sorted array.
        {
                return findFirstIndex(arr, start, mid - 1, key);
        }
```

```
        else
        {
                return findFirstIndex(arr, mid + 1, end, key);
        }
}
```

```
int findLastIndex(int arr[], int start, int end, int key)
{
        int mid;
        if (end < start)
                return -1;

        mid = (start + end) / 2;

        if (key == arr[mid] && (mid == end || arr[mid + 1] != key))
                return mid;

        if (key < arr[mid])//  <
        {
                return findLastIndex(arr, start, mid - 1, key);
        }
        else
        {
                return findLastIndex(arr, mid + 1, end, key);
        }
}
```

Separate even and odd numbers in Array

Given an array of even and odd numbers, write a program to separate even numbers from the odd numbers.

First approach: allocate a separate array, then scan through the given array, and fill even numbers from the start and odd numbers from the end.

Second approach: Algorithm is as follows.
1. Initialize the two variable left and right. Variable left=0 and right= size-1.
2. Keep increasing the left index until the element at that index is even.
3. Keep decreasing the right index until the element at that index is odd.
4. Swap the number at left and right index.
5. Repeat steps 2 to 4 until left is less than right.

Example 5.26

```
void swap(int *first, int *second)
{
        int temp = *first;
        *first = *second;
        *second = temp;
}
```

```
void seperateEvenAndOdd(int arr[], int size)
{
        int left = 0, right = size - 1;

        while (left < right)
        {
                if (arr[left] % 2 == 0 )
                {
                        left++;
                }
                else if(arr[right] % 2 == 1)
                {
                        right--;
                }
                else
                {
                        swap(&arr[left], &arr[right]);
                        left++;
                        right--;
                }
        }
}
```

Stock purchase-sell problem

Given an array, whose nth element is the price of the stock on nth day. You are asked to buy once and sell once, on what date you will be buying and at what date you will be selling to get maximum profit.
Or
Given an array of numbers, you need to maximize the difference between two numbers, such that you can subtract the number, which appear before form the number that appear after it.

First approach: Brute force, for each element in array find if there is some other element whose difference is maximum. This is done using two for loop, first loop to select, buy date index and the second loop to find its selling date entry.
The Time Complexity is $O(n^2)$ and Space Complexity is $O(1)$

Second approach: Another clever solution is to keep track of the smallest value seen so far from the start. At each point, we can find the difference and keep track of the maximum profit. This is a linear solution.

The *Time Complexity* of the algorithm is $O(n)$ time. *Space Complexity* for creating count array is also $O(1)$.

Example 5.27

```c
void maxProfit(int stocks[], int size)
{
        int buy = 0, sell = 0;
        int curMin = 0;
        int currProfit=0;
        int maxProfit = 0;
        int i;

        for (i = 0; i < size; i++)
        {
                if (stocks[i] < stocks[curMin])
                        curMin = i;

                currProfit = stocks[i] - stocks[curMin];

                if (currProfit > maxProfit)
                {
                        buy = curMin;
                        sell = i;
                        maxProfit = currProfit;
                }
        }

        printf("\nPurchase day is- %d at price %d", buy, stocks[buy]);
        printf("\nSell day is- %d at price %d", sell, stocks[sell]);
}
```

Find a median of an array

Given an array of numbers of size n, if all the elements of the array are sorted then find the element, which lie at the index n/2.

First approach: Sort the array and return the element in the middle.

Sorting algorithms take $O(n . \log n)$.
The *Time Complexity* of an algorithm is $O(n . \log n)$ and *Space Complexity* is $O(1)$

Example 5.28

```c
int getMedian(int arr[], int size)
{
        sort(arr, size);
        return arr[size / 2];
}
```

Second approach: Use QuickSelect algorithm. This algorithm we will look into the next chapter. In QuickSort algorithm just skip the recursive call that we do not need.

The average *Time Complexity* of this algorithm will be $O(1)$

Find median of two sorted arrays.

First approach: Keep track of the index of both the array, say the index are i and j. keep increasing the index of the array which ever have a smaller value. Use a counter to keep track of the elements that we have already traced.

The *Time Complexity* of an algorithm is $O(n)$ and *Space Complexity* is $O(1)$

Example 5.29

```
int findMedian(int arrFirst[], int sizeFirst, int arrSecond[], int sizeSecond)
{
        //cealing function.
        int medianIndex = ((sizeFirst + sizeSecond) + (sizeFirst + sizeSecond) % 2) / 2;
        int i = 0, j = 0;
        int count = 0;
        while (count < medianIndex - 1)
        {
                if (i < sizeFirst - 1 && arrFirst[i] < arrSecond[j])
                        i++;
                else
                        j++;

                count++;
        }

        if (arrFirst[i] < arrSecond[j])
                return arrFirst[i];
        else
                return arrSecond[j];
}
```

Find kth element of two sorted arrays.

Find kth Smallest Element in the Union of Two Sorted Arrays

Example 5.30

```
1.      #define ERROR -999;
2.      int min(int a, int b)
3.      {
4.              return a > b ? b : a;
5.      }
```

```
6.        int find_kth(int first[], int second[], int sizeFirst, int sizeSecond, int k)
7.        {
8.                if (sizeFirst + sizeSecond < k)
9.                        return ERROR;
10.
11.               if (sizeFirst == 0)
12.                       return second[k - 1];
13.
14.               if (sizeSecond == 0)
15.                       return first[k - 1];
16.
17.               if (k == 1)
18.                       return min(first[0], second[0]);
19.
20.               /* Now divide and conquer */
21.               int i = min(sizeFirst, k / 2);
22.               int j = min(sizeSecond, k / 2);
23.
24.               if (first[i - 1] > second[j - 1])
25.                       return find_kth(first, second + j, i, sizeSecond - j, k - j);
26.               else
27.                       return find_kth(first + i, second, sizeFirst - i, j, k - i);
28.       }
```

Search 01 Array

Given an array of 0's and 1's. All the 0's come before 1's. Write an algorithm to find the index of the first 1.
Or
You are given an array which contains either 0 or 1, and they are in sorted order Ex. a [] = { 1,1,1,1,0,0,0} How will you count no of 1's and 0's?

First approach: Binary Search, since the array is sorted using binary search to find the desired index.
The Time Complexity of an algorithm is $O(log\ n)$ and Space Complexity is $O(1)$

Example 5.31

```
int BinarySearch01Wrapper(int arr[], int size)
{
        if (size == 1 && arr[0] == 1)
                return 0;

        return BinarySearch01(arr, 0, size - 1);
}
```

```
int BinarySearch01(int arr[], int start, int end)
{
        int mid;
        if (end < start)
                return -1;

        mid = (start + end) / 2;

        if (1 == arr[mid] && 0 == arr[mid - 1])
                return mid;

        if (0 == arr[mid])
        {
                return BinarySearch01(arr, mid + 1, end);
        }
        else
        {
                return BinarySearch01(arr, start, mid - 1);
        }
}
```

Search in sorted rotated Array

Given a sorted array of n *integer* s which is rotated an unknown number of times. Find an element in the array.

First approach: Since the array is sorted, we can use modified binary search to find the element.
The Time Complexity of an algorithm is $O(\log n)$ and Space Complexity is $O(1)$
Example 5.32

```
int BinarySearchRotateArray(int arr[], int start, int end, int key)
{
        int mid;
        if (end < start)
                return -1;

        mid = (start + end) / 2;

        if (key == arr[mid])
                return mid;
        if (arr[mid] > arr[start])
        {
                if (arr[start] <= key && key < arr[mid])
                {
                        return BinarySearchRotateArray(arr, start, mid - 1, key);
                }
                else
                {
                        return BinarySearchRotateArray(arr, mid + 1, end, key);
                }
        }
}
```

```
            else
            {
                    if (arr[mid] < key && key <= arr[end])
                    {
                            return BinarySearchRotateArray(arr, mid + 1, end, key);
                    }
                    else
                    {
                            return BinarySearchRotateArray(arr, start, mid - 1, key);
                    }
            }
    }

    int BinarySearchRotateArrayWrapper(int arr[], int size, int key)
    {
            return BinarySearchRotateArray(arr, 0, size - 1, key);
    }
```

First Repeated element in the array

Given an unsorted array of n elements, find the first element, which is repeated.

First approach: Exhaustive search or Brute force, for each element in array find if there is some other element with the same value. This is done using two for loop, first loop to select the element and second loop to find its duplicate entry.

The Time Complexity is $O(n^2)$ and Space Complexity is $O(1)$

Example 5.33

```
int FirstRepeated(int* arr, int size)
{
        int i, j;
        for (i = 0; i < size; i++)
                for (j = i + 1; j < size; j++)
                        if (arr[i] == arr[j])
                                return arr[i];

        return 0;
}
```

Second approach: Hash-Table, using Hash-Table, we can keep track of the number of times a particular element came in the array. First scan just populate the Hashtable. In the second, scan just look the occurrence of the elements in the Hashtable. If occurrence is more for some element, then we have our solution and the first repeated element.

Hash-Table insert and find take constant time $O(1)$ so the total *Time Complexity* of the algorithm is $O(n)$ time. *Space Complexity* is also $O(n)$ for maintaining hash.

Transform Array

How would you swap elements of an array like [a1 a2 a3 a4 b1 b2 b3 b4] to convert it into [a1 b1 a2 b2 a3 b3 a4 b4]?

Approach:
- First swap elements in the middle pair
- Next swap elements in the middle two pairs
- Next swap elements in the middle three pairs
- Iterate n-1 steps.

Ex: with n = 4.
a1 a2 a3 a4 b1 b2 b3 b4
a1 a2 a3 b1 a4 b2 b3 b4
a1 a2 b1 a3 b2 a4 b3 b4
a1 b1 a2 b2 a3 b3 a4 b4

Example 5.34

```
void transformArrayAB1(int arr[], int size)
{
        int N = size/2, i, j;
        for (i = 1; i < N; i++)
        {
                for (j = 0; j < i; j++)
                {
                        swap(&arr[N-i+2*j], &arr[N-i+2*j+1]);
                }
        }
}
void swap(int *a,int *b)
{
        int t=*a;
        *a=*b;
        *b=t;
}
```

Find 2nd largest number in an array with minimum comparisons

Suppose you are given an unsorted array of n distinct elements. How will you identify the second largest element with minimum number of comparisons?

First approach: Find the largest element in the array. Then replace the last element with the largest element. Then search the second largest element int the remaining n-1 elements.
The total number of comparisons is: (n-1) + (n-2)

Second approach: Sort the array and then give the (n-1) element. This approach is still more inefficient.

Third approach: Using priority queue / Heap. This approach we will look into heap chapter. Use buildHeap() function to build heap from the array. This is done in n comparisons. Arr[0] is the largest number , and the grater among arr[1] and arr[2] is the second largest.
The total number of comparisons are: (n-1) + 1 = n

Check if two arrays are permutation of each other

Given two *integer* arrays. You have to check whether they are permutation of each other.

First approach: Sorting, Sort all the elements of both the arrays and Compare each element of both the arrays from beginning to end. If there is no mismatch, return true. Otherwise, false.
Sorting algorithms take $O(n.\log n)$ time and comparison take $O(n)$ time.
The *Time Complexity* of an algorithm is $O(n.\log n)$ and *Space Complexity* is $O(1)$

Example 5.35

```
int checkPermutation(int array1[], int size1, int array2[], int size2)
{
        if (size1 != size2)
                return 0;

        sort(array1, size1);
        sort(array2, size2);

        for (int i = 0; i < size1; i++){
                if (array1[i] != array2[i])
                        return 0;
        }
        return 1;
}
```

Second approach: Hash-Table (Assumption: No duplicates).
Steps are:
1. Create a Hash-Table for all the elements of the first array.
2. Traverse the other array from beginning to the end and search for each element in the Hash-Table.
3. If all the elements are found in, the Hash-Table return true otherwise return false.

Hash-Table insert and find take constant time $O(1)$ so the total *Time Complexity* of the algorithm is $O(n)$ time. *Space Complexity* is also $O(n)$.

Time Complexity = *O(n)* (For creation of Hash-Table and look-up), *Space Complexity* = *O(n)* (For creation of Hash-Table).

Example 5.36

```
int checkPermutation(int array1[], int size1, int array2[], int size2)
{
        int i;
        if (size1 != size2)
                return 0;
        Hashtable h;

        for (i = 0; i < size1; i++)
                insert(h, array1[i]);
```

```
        for (i = 0; i < size2; i++)
        {
                if (!containsValue(h, array2[i]))
                        return false;
        }
        return true;
}
```

Remove duplicates in an *integer* array

First approach: Sorting

Steps are as follows:

1. Sort the array.
2. Take two pointers. A subarray will be created with all unique elements starting from 0 to the first pointer (The first pointer points to the last index of the subarray). The second pointer iterates through the array from 1 to the end. Unique numbers will be copied from the second pointer location to first pointer location and the same elements are ignored.

Time Complexity calculation :

Time to sort the array = **O(nlogn)**.

Time to remove duplicates = **O(n)**. Overall *Time Complexity* = **O(nlogn)**.

No additional space is required so *Space Complexity* is **O(1)**.

Example 5.37

```
int removeDuplicates(int array[], int size)
{
        int j = 0;
        int i;

        if (size == 0)
                return 0;

        sort(array, size);

        for (i = 1; i < size; i++) {
                if (array[i] != array[j]) {
                        j++;
                        array[j] = array[i];
                }
        }
        return j + 1;
}
```

Searching for an element in a 2-d sorted array

Given a 2 dimensional array. Each row and column are sorted in ascending order. How would you find an element in it?

The algorithm works as:
1. Start with element at last column and first row
2. If the element is the value we are looking for, return true.
3. If the element is greater than the value we are looking for, go to the element at previous column but same row.
4. If the element is less than the value we are looking for, go to the element at next row but same column.
5. Return false, if the element is not found after reaching the element of the last row of the first column. Condition row < r && column >= 0 is false.

Running time = **O(N)**.

Example 5.38

```
int FindElementIn2DArray(int* arr[], int r, int c, int value)
{
        int row = 0;
        int column = c - 1;

        while (row < r && column >= 0){
                if (arr[row][column] == value)
                        return 1;
                else if (arr[row][column] > value)
                        column--;
                else
                        row++;
        }
        return 0;
}
```

Exercise

1. Given an array of n elements, find the first repeated element. Which of the following methods will work for us. And which, if the method will not work for us. If a method work, then implements it.
   - Brute force exhaustive search.
   - Use Hash-Table to keep an index of the elements and use the second scan to find the element.
   - Sorting the elements.
   - If we know the range of the element then we can use counting technique.

Hint: When order in which elements appear in input is important, we cannot use sorting.

2. Given an array of n elements, write an algorithm to find three elements in an array whose sum is a given value.

Hint: Try to do this problem using a brute force approach. Then try to apply the sorting approach along with a brute force approach. The *Time Complexity* will be $O(n^2)$

3. Given an array of −ve and +ve numbers, write a program to separate −ve numbers from the +ve numbers.

4. Given an array of 1's and 0's, write a program to separate 0's from 1's.
   Hint: QuickSelect, counting

5. Given an array of 0's, 1's and 2's, write a program to separate 0's , 1's and 2's.

6. Given an array whose elements is monotonically increasing with both negative and positive numbers. Write an algorithm to find the point at which list becomes positive.

7. Given a sorted array, find a given number. If found return the index if not, find the index of that number if it is inserted into the array.

8. Find max in sorted rotated array.

9. Find min in the sorted rotated array.

CHAPTER 6: SORTING

Introduction

Sorting is the process of placing elements from a collection into ascending or descending order. For example, when we play cards, sort cards, according to their value so that we can find the required card easily.

When we go to some library, the books are arranged according to streams (Algorithm, Operating systems, Networking etc.). Sorting arranges data elements in order so that searching become easier. When books are arranged in proper indexing order, then it is easy to find a book we are looking for.

This chapter discusses algorithms for sorting a set of N items. Understanding sorting algorithms are the first step towards understanding algorithm analysis. Many sorting algorithms are developed and analysed.

A sorting algorithm like *Bubble-Sort*, *Insertion-Sort* and *Selection-Sort* are easy to implement and are suitable for the small input set. However, for large dataset they are slow.

A sorting algorithm like *Merge-Sort*, *Quick-Sort* and *Heap-Sort* are some of the algorithms that are suitable for sorting large dataset. However, they are overkill if we want to sort the small dataset.

Some algorithm, which is suitable when we have some range information on input data.

Some other algorithm is there to sort a huge data set that cannot be stored in memory completely, for which external sorting technique is developed.

Before we start a discussion of the various algorithms one by one. First, we should look at comparison function that is used to compare two values.

Less function will return 1 if value1 is less than value2 otherwise, it will return 0.

```
int less(int value1, int value2)
{
        return value1 < value2;
}
```

More function will return 1 if value1 is more than value2 otherwise it will return 0.

```
int more(int value1, int value2)
{
        return value1 > value2;
}
```

The value in various sorting algorithms is compared using one of the above functions and it will be swapped depending upon the return value of these functions. If more() comparison function is used, then sorted output will be increasing in order and if less() is used than resulting output will be in descending order.

Type of Sorting

Internal Sorting: All the elements can be read into memory at the same time and sorting is performed in memory.
1. Selection-Sort
2. Insertion-Sort
3. Bubble-Sort
4. Quick-Sort

External Sorting: In this, the dataset is so big that it is impossible to load the whole dataset into memory so sorting is done in chunks.
1. Merge-Sort

Three things to consider in choosing, sorting algorithms for application:
1. Number of elements in list
2. A number of different orders of list required
3. The amount of time required to move the data or not move the data

Bubble-Sort

Bubble-Sort is the slowest algorithm for sorting, but it is heavily used, as it is easy to implement.

In Bubble-Sort, we compare each pair of adjacent values. We want to sort values in increasing order so if the second value is less than the first value then we swap these two values. Otherwise, we will go to the next pair. Thus, smaller values bubble to the start of the array.

We will have N number of passes to get the array completely sorted.
After the first pass, the largest value will be in the rightmost position.

First Pass

5	1	2	4	3	7	6	Swap
1	5	2	4	3	7	6	Swap
1	2	5	4	3	7	6	Swap
1	2	4	5	3	7	6	Swap
1	2	4	3	5	7	6	No Swap
1	2	4	3	5	7	6	Swap
1	2	4	3	5	6	7	

Example 6.1

```
1.        void BubbleSort(int* arr, int size)
2.        {
3.              int i, j, temp;
4.              for (i = 0 ; i < ( size - 1 ); i++)
5.              {
6.                    for (j = 0 ; j < size - i - 1; j++)
7.                    {
8.                          if (more(arr[j], arr[j+1]))
9.                          {
10.                                /* Swapping */
11.                                temp= arr[j];
12.                                arr[j]= arr[j+1];
13.                                arr[j+1] = temp;
14.                          }
15.                    }
16.              }
17.       .}
```

Analysis:

Line 4: The outer for loops represents the number of swaps that are done for comparison of data.

Line 6: The inner loop is actually used to do the comparison of data. At the end of each inner loop iteration, the largest value is moved to the end of the array. In the first iteration the largest value, in the second iteration the second largest and so on.

Line 8: more() function is used for comparison which means when the value of the first argument is greater than the value of the second argument then perform a swap. By this we are sorting in increasing order if we have, the *less()* function in place of more() than we will get decreasing order sorting.

Have a look into *more()* function in case you forgot

```
int more(int value1, int value2)
{
        return value1 > value2;
}
```

Complexity Analysis:

Each time the inner loop execute for (n-1), (n-2), (n-3)...
(n-1) + (n-2) + (n-3) + ... + 3 + 2 + 1 = n(n-1)/2

Worst case performance	$O(n^2)$
Average case performance	$O(n^2)$
Space Complexity	*O(1)* as we need only one temp variable
Stable Sorting	Yes

When there is no more swap in one pass of the outer loop. It indicates that all the elements are already in order so we should stop sorting. This sorting improvement in Bubble-Sort is extremely useful when we know that, except few elements rest of the array is already sorted.

Example 6.2

```
1.      void BubbleSort(int* arr, int size)
2.      {
3.              int i, j, temp, swapped=1;
4.              for (i = 0; i < (size - 1) && swapped; i++)
5.              {
6.                      swapped = 0;
7.                      for (j = 0; j < size - i - 1; j++)
8.                      {
9.                              if (more(arr[j], arr[j + 1]))
10.                             {
11.                                     /* Swapping */
12.                                     temp = arr[j];
13.                                     arr[j] = arr[j + 1];
14.                                     arr[j + 1] = temp;
15.                                     swapped = 1;
16.                             }
17.                     }
18.             }
19.     }
```

By applying this improvement, best case of this algorithm, when an array is nearly sorted, is improved. Best case is *O(n)*

Complexity Analysis:

Worst case performance	$O(n^2)$
Average case performance	$O(n^2)$
Space Complexity	O(1)
Adaptive: When array is nearly sorted	O(n)
Stable Sorting	Yes

Insertion-Sort *Time Complexity* is $O(n^2)$ which is same as *Bubble-Sort* but perform a bit better than it. It is the way we arrange our playing cards. We keep a sorted subarray. Each value is inserted into its proper position in the sorted sub-array in the left of it.

5	6	2	4	7	3	1	Insert 5
5	6	2	4	7	3	1	Insert 6
2	5	6	4	7	3	1	Insert 2
2	4	5	6	7	3	1	Insert 4
2	4	5	6	7	3	1	Insert 7
2	3	4	5	6	7	1	Insert 3
1	2	3	4	5	6	7	Insert 1

Example 6.3

```
1.      void insertion(int *arr, int size)
2.      {
3.             int temp,j;
4.             for(int i=1; i<size; i++)
5.             {
6.                    temp=arr[i];
7.                    for(j=i; j>0 && more(arr[j-1], temp)); j--)
8.                    {
9.                           arr[j]=arr[j-1];
10.                   }
11.                   arr[j]=temp;
12.            }
13.     }
```

Analysis:

Line 4: The outer loop is used to pick the value we want to insert into the sorted left array.

Line 6: The value we want to insert we have picked and saved in a temp variable.

Line 7-10: These are the lines which are implementing the inner loop and also doing the comparison using the more() function. The values are shifted to the right until we find the proper position of the temp value for which we are doing this iteration.

Line 11: This is the line in which we are actually placing the temp value into the proper position.

Line 4-12: In each iteration of the outer loop, the length of the sorted array increase by one. When we exit the outer loop the whole array is sorted.

Complexity Analysis:

Worst case Time Complexity	$O(n^2)$
Best case Time Complexity	$O(n)$
Average case Time Complexity	$O(n^2)$
Space Complexity	$O(1)$
Stable sorting	Yes

Selection-Sort

Selection-Sort searches the whole unsorted array and put the largest value at the end of it. This algorithm is having the same *Time Complexity*, but performs better than both bubble and Insertion-Sort as less number of comparisons required. The sorted array is created backward in Selection-Sort.

5	6	2	4	7	3	1	Swap
5	6	2	4	1	3	7	Swap
5	3	2	4	1	6	7	Swap
1	3	2	4	5	6	7	No Swap
1	3	2	4	5	6	7	Swap
1	2	3	4	5	6	7	No Swap
1	2	3	4	5	6	7	

Example 6.4:

```
1.      void SelectionSort(int* arr, int size)
2.      {
3.              int i, j, max, temp;
4.              for (i = 0; i < size - 1; i++)
5.              {
6.                      max = 0;
7.                      for (j = 1; j < size -1 - i ; j++)
8.                      {
9.                              if (arr[j] > arr[max])
10.                             {
11.                                     max = j;
12.                             }
13.                     }
14.                     temp = arr[size - 1 - i];
15.                     arr[size - 1 - i] = arr[max];
16.                     arr[max] = temp;
17.             }
18.     }
```

Analysis:

Line 4-17: It is the outer loop which is used to pick the largest value from the unsorted array. In each iteration, the largest value will be placed at the end of the array.

Line 6: The index of the max value is always set to the beginning of the array and we will iterate through the array to find the proper index.

Line 7-10: These are the inner loop lines to find the proper index of the maximum.

Line 14-17: This is the final replacement of the maximum value to the proper location. The sorted array is created backward.

Complexity Analysis:

Worst Case Time Complexity	$O(n^2)$
Best Case Time Complexity	$O(n^2)$
Average case Time Complexity	$O(n^2)$
Space Complexity	$O(1)$
Stable Sorting	No

The same algorithm can be implemented by creating the sorted array in the front of the array.

Example 6.5:

```
1.      void SelectionSort(int* arr, int size)
2.      {
3.              int i, j, min, temp;
4.              for (i = 0; i < size - 1; i++)
5.              {
6.                      min = i;
7.                      for (j = i + 1; j < size; j++)
8.                      {
9.                              if (arr[j] < arr[min])
10.                             {
11.                                     min = j;
12.                             }
13.                     }
14.                     temp = arr[i];
15.                     arr[i] = arr[min];
16.                     arr[min] = temp;
17.             }
18.     }
```

Merge-Sort

Example 6.6:

```c
1.      #include<stdio.h>
2
3.      void merge(int* arr,int* tempArray, int lowerIndex, int middleIndex, int upperIndex)
4.      {
5.              int lowerStart=lowerIndex;
6.              int lowerStop=middleIndex;
7.              int upperStart=middleIndex+1;
8.              int upperStop=upperIndex;
9.              int count=lowerIndex;
10.             while(lowerStart<=lowerStop && upperStart<=upperStop)
11.             {
12.                     if(arr[lowerStart]<arr[upperStart])
13.                             tempArray[count++]=arr[lowerStart++];
14.                     else
15.                             tempArray[count++]=arr[upperStart++];
16.             }
17.             while(lowerStart<=lowerStop)
18.             {
19.                     tempArray[count++]=arr[lowerStart++];
20.             }
21.             while( upperStart<=upperStop)
22.             {
23.                     tempArray[count++]=arr[upperStart++];
24.             }
25.             for(int i=lowerIndex;i<=upperIndex;i++)
26.                     arr[i]=tempArray[i];
27.     }
```

```c
1.      void mergeSrt(int *arr,int* tempArray, int lowerIndex, int upperIndex)
2.      {
3.              if(lowerIndex >= upperIndex)
4.                      return;
5.              int middleIndex=(lowerIndex+upperIndex)/2;
6.              mergeSrt(arr,tempArray,lowerIndex,middleIndex);
7.              mergeSrt(arr,tempArray,middleIndex+1,upperIndex);
8.              merge(arr,tempArray,lowerIndex,middleIndex,upperIndex);
9.      }
```

```c
1.      void mergeSort(int *arr, int size)
2.      {
3.              int *tempArray=(int*)malloc(size*sizeof(int));
4.              mergeSrt(arr,tempArray,0,size-1);
5.      }
```

```
1.      void printArray(int* arr, int size)
2.      {
3.              for(int i=0;i<size;i++)
4.                      printf(" %d ",arr[i]);
5.      }
```

```
1.      int main()
2.      {
3.              int arr[10]={3,4,2,1,6,5,7,8,1,1};
4.              mergeSort(arr,10);
5.              printArray(arr,10);
6.      }
```

- The *Time Complexity* of Merge-Sort is **O(nlogn)** in all 3 cases (best, average and worst) as Merge-Sort always divides the array into two halves and take linear time to merge two halves.
- It requires the equal amount of additional space as the unsorted list. Hence, it is not at all recommended for searching large unsorted lists.
- It is the best Sorting technique for sorting Linked Lists.

Complexity Analysis:

Worst Case Time Complexity	O(nlogn)
Best Case Time Complexity	O(nlogn)
Average Time Complexity	O(nlogn)
Space Complexity	O(n)
Stable Sorting	Yes

Quick-Sort

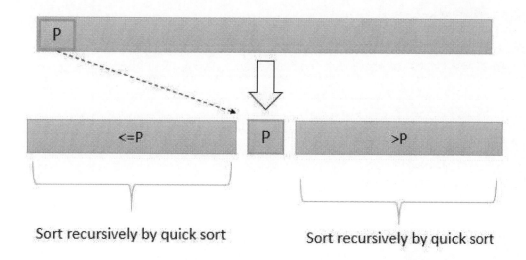

Sort recursively by quick sort   Sort recursively by quick sort

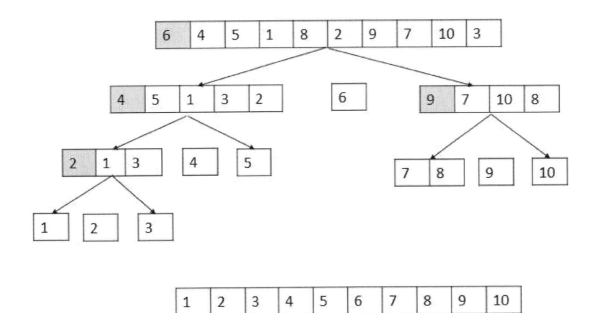

Example 6.7:

```
1.      int main()
2.      {
3.              int arr[10] = { 4, 5, 3, 2, 6, 7, 1, 8, 9, 10 };
4.              printArray(arr, sizeof(arr) / sizeof(int));
5.              quickSort(arr, sizeof(arr) / sizeof(int));
6.              printArray(arr, sizeof(arr) / sizeof(int));
7.      }
```

```
1.      void swap(int arr[], int first, int second)
2.      {
3.              int temp = arr[first];
4.              arr[first] = arr[second];
5.              arr[second] = temp;
6.      }
```

```
1.      void printArray(int arr[], int size)
2.      {
3.              for (int i = 0; i<size; i++)
4.                      printf(" %d ", arr[i]);
5.              printf("\n");
6.      }
```

```
1.      void quickSort(int arr[], int size)
2.      {
3.              quickSortUtil (arr, 0, size - 1);
4.      }
```

110

```
1.    void quickSortUtil (int arr[], int lower, int upper)
2.    {
3.            if (upper<=lower)
4.                return;
5.
6.            int pivot = arr[lower];
7.
8.            int start = lower;
9.            int stop = upper;
10.
11.           while ( lower < upper)
12.           {
13.                   while (arr[lower] <= pivot)
14.                   {
15.                           lower++;
16.                   }
17.                   while (arr[upper] > pivot)
18.                   {
19.                           upper--;
20.                   }
21.                   if (lower < upper)
22.                   {
23.                           swap(arr,upper,lower);
24.                   }
25.           }
26.           swap(arr, upper, start); //upper is the pivot position
27.
28.           quickSortUtil (arr, start, upper - 1); //pivot -1 is the upper for left sub array.
29.           quickSortUtil (arr, upper + 1, stop); // pivot + 1 is the lower for right sub array.
30.    }
```

- The space required by Quick-Sort is very less, only **O(nlogn)** additional space is required.
- Quicksort is not a stable sorting technique, so it might change the occurrence of two similar elements in the list while sorting.

Complexity Analysis:

Worst Case Time Complexity	$O(n^2)$
Best Case Time Complexity	O(nlogn)
Average Time Complexity	O(nlogn)
Space Complexity	O(nlogn)
Stable Sorting	No

Quick Select

Quick select is very similar to Quick-Sort in place of sorting the whole array we just ignore the one-half of the array at each step of Quick-Sort and just focus on the region of array on which we are interested.

Example 6.8:

```
1.      void quickSelect(int arr[], int lower, int upper,int k)
2.      {
3.              if (upper <= lower)
4.                      return;
5.
6.              int pivot = arr[lower];
7.
8.              int start = lower;
9.              int stop = upper;
10.
11.             while (lower < upper)
12.             {
13.                     while (arr[lower] <= pivot)
14.                     {
15.                             lower++;
16.                     }
17.                     while (arr[upper] > pivot)
18.                     {
19.                             upper--;
20.                     }
21.                     if (lower < upper)
22.                     {
23.                             swap(arr, upper, lower);
24.                     }
25.             }
26.
27.             swap(arr, upper, start); //upper is the pivot position
28.             if (k<upper)
29.                     quickSelect(arr, start, upper - 1, k); //pivot -1 is the upper for
left sub array.
30.             if (k>upper)
31.                     quickSelect(arr, upper + 1, stop, k); // pivot + 1 is the lower for
right sub array.
32.     }
```

```
1.      int quickSelect(int *a, int count, int index)
2.      {
3.              quickSelect(a, 0, count - 1, index - 1);
4.              return a[index - 1];
5.      }
```

Complexity Analysis:

Worst Case Time Complexity	$O(n^2)$
Best Case Time Complexity	$O(logn)$
Average Time Complexity	$O(logn)$
Space Complexity	$O(nlogn)$

Bucket Sort

Bucket sort is the simplest and most efficient type of sorting. Bucket sort has a strict requirement of a predefined range of data.

Like, sort how many people are in which age group. We know that the age of people can vary between 1 and 130.

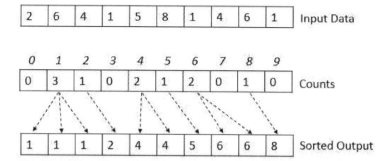

| 2 | 6 | 4 | 1 | 5 | 8 | 1 | 4 | 6 | 1 | Input Data |

0	1	2	3	4	5	6	7	8	9	
0	3	1	0	2	1	2	0	1	0	Counts

| 1 | 1 | 1 | 2 | 4 | 4 | 5 | 6 | 6 | 8 | Sorted Output |

Example 6.9:

```
1.      void BucketSort(int array[], int n, int range)
2.      {
3.              int i, j;
4.              int* count = (int*)malloc(range * sizeof(int));
5.
6.              for (i = 0; i < range; i++)
7.              {
8.                      count[i] = 0;
9.              }
10.
11.             for (i = 0; i < n; i++)
12.             {
13.                     count[array[i]]++;
14.             }
15.
16.             j = 0;
17.
18.             for (i = 0; i < range; i++)
19.             {
20.                     for (; count[i]>0; (count[i])--)
21.                     {
22.                             array[j++] = i;
23.                     }
24.             }
25.      free(count);
26.     }
```

Analysis:

Line 4: We have created a count array to store counts.

Line 6-9: count array elements are initialized to zero.

Line 11-14: Index corresponding to input array is incremented.

Line: 18-24: Finally, the information stored in count array is saved in the array.

Complexity Analysis:

Data structure	Array
Worst case performance	O(n+k)
Average case performance	O(n+k)
Worst case Space Complexity	O(k)

Where k - is number of distinct elements.
n – is the total number of elements in array.

Generalized Bucket Sort

There are cases when the element falling into a bucket are not unique but are in the same range. When we want to sort an index of a name, we can use the pointer bucket to store names.

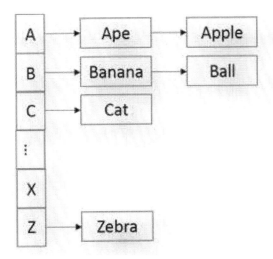

The buckets are already sorted and the elements inside each bucket can be kept sorted by using an Insertion-Sort algorithm. We are leaving this generalized bucket sort implementation to the reader of this book. The similar data structure will be defined in the coming chapter of Hash-Table using separate chaining.

Heap-Sort

Heap-Sort we have already studied in the Heap chapter.

Complexity Analysis:

Data structure	Array
Worst case performance	O(nlogn)
Average case performance	O(nlogn)
Worst case Space Complexity	O(1)

Tree Sorting

In-order traversal of the binary search tree can also be seen as a sorting algorithm. We will see this in binary search tree section of tree chapter.

Complexity Analysis:

Worst Case Time Complexity	$O(n^2)$
Best Case Time Complexity	O(nlogn)
Average Time Complexity	O(nlogn)
Space Complexity	O(n)
Stable Sorting	Yes

External Sort (External Merge-Sort)

When data need to be sorted is huge. Moreover, it is not possible to load it completely in memory (RAM) for such a dataset we use external sorting. Specific data is sorted using external Merge-Sort algorithm. First data are picked in chunks and it is sorted in memory. Then this sorted data is written back to disk. Whole data are sorted in chunks using *Merge-Sort*. Now we need to combine these sorted chunks into final sorted data.

Then we create queues for the data, which will read from the sorted chunks. Each chunk will have its own queue. We will pop from this queue and these queues are responsible for reading from the sorted chunks. Let us suppose we have K different chunks of sorted data each of length M.

The third step is using a Min-Heap, which will take input data from each of this queue. It will take one element from each queue. The minimum value is taken from the Heap and added to the final sorted element output. Then queue from which this min element is inserted in the heap will again popped and one more element from that queue is added to the Heap. Finally, when the data is exhausted from some queue that queue is removed from the input list. Finally, we will get a sorted data came out from the heap.

We can optimize this process further by adding an output buffer, which will store data coming out of Heap and will do a limited number of the write operation in the final Disk space.

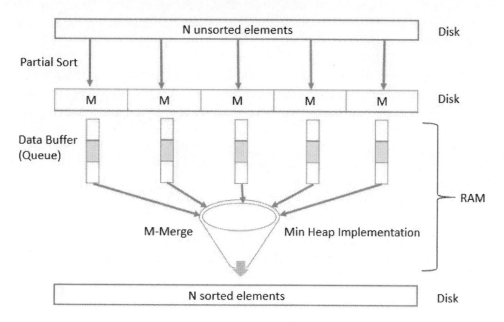

Note: No one will be asking to implement external sorting in an interview, but it is good to know about it.

Comparisons of the various sorting algorithms.

Sort	Average Time	Best Time	Worst Time	Space	Stability
Bubble-Sort	O(n²)	O(n²)	O(n²)	O(1)	Stable
Modified Bubble-Sort	O(n²)	O(n)	O(n²)	O(1)	Stable
Selection-Sort	O(n²)	O(n²)	O(n²)	O(1)	Unstable
Insertion-Sort	O(n²)	O(n)	O(n²)	O(1)	Stable
Heap-Sort	O(n*log(n))	O(n*log(n))	O(n*log(n))	O(1)	UnStable
Merge-Sort	O(n*log(n))	O(n*log(n))	O(n*log(n))	O(n)	Stable
Quick-Sort	O(n*log(n))	O(n*log(n))	O(n²)	O(n) worst case O(log(n)) average case	Unstable
Bucket Sort	O(n k)	O(n k)	O(n k)	O(n k)	Stable

Selection of Best Sorting Algorithm

No sorting algorithm is perfect. Each of them has their own pros and cons. Let us read one by one:

Quick-Sort: When you do not need a stable sort and average case performance matters more than worst-case performance. When data is random, we prefer the Quick-Sort. Average case *Time Complexity* of Quick-Sort is *O(nlogn)* and worst-case *Time Complexity* is *O(n²)*. *Space Complexity* of Quick-Sort is *O(logn)* auxiliary storage, which is stack space used in recursion.

Merge-Sort: When you need a stable sort and *Time Complexity* of *O(nlogn)*, Merge-Sort is used. In general, Merge-Sort is slower than Quick-Sort because of lot of copy happening in the merge phase. There are two uses of Merge-Sort when we want to merge two sorted linked lists and Merge-Sort is used in external sorting.

Heap-Sort: When you do not need a stable sort and you care more about worst-case performance than average case performance. It has guaranteed to be *O(nlogn)*, and uses *O(1)* auxiliary space, meaning that you will not unexpectedly run out of memory on very large inputs.

Insertion-Sort: When we need a stable sort, When N is guaranteed to be small, including as the base case of a Quick-Sort or Merge-Sort. Worst-case *Time Complexity* is *O(n²)*, it has a very small constant, so for smaller input size it performs better than Merge-Sort or Quick-Sort. It is also useful when the data is already pre-sorted in this case its best case running time is *O(N)*.

Bubble-Sort: Where we know the data is very nearly sorted. Say only two elements are out of place. Then in one pass, Bubble Sort will make the data sorted and in the second pass, it will see everything is sorted and then exit. Only takes 2 passes of the array.

Selection-Sort: Best Worst Average Case running time all *O(n²)*. It is only useful when you want to do something quick. They can be used when you are just doing some prototyping.

Counting-Sort: When you are sorting data within a limited range.

Radix-Sort: When log(N) is significantly larger than K, where K is the number of radix digits.

Bucket-Sort: When your input is more or less uniformly distributed.

Note: A stable sort is one that has guaranteed not to reorder elements with identical keys.

Exercise

1. Given a text file, print the words with their frequency. Now print the kth word in term of frequency.

   > 1. *First approach* may be you can use the sorting and return the kth element.
   > 2. *Second approach*: You can use the kth element quick select algorithm.
   > 3. *Third approach* You can use Hashtable or Trie to keep track of the frequency. Use Heap to get the Kth element.

2. Given K input streams of number in sorted order. You need to make a single output stream, which contains all the elements of the K streams in sorted order. The input streams support ReadNumber() operation and output stream support WriteNumber() operation.

   > 1. Read the first number from all the K input streams and add them to a Priority Queue. (Nodes should keep track of the input stream)
   > 2. Dequeue one element at a time from PQ, Put this element value to the output stream, Read the input stream number and from the same input stream add another element to PQ.
   > 3. If the stream is empty, just continue
   > 4. Repeat till PQ is empty.

3. Given K sorted arrays of fixed length M. Also, given a final output array of length M*K. Give an efficient algorithm to merge all the arrays into the final array, without using any extra space.
   Hint: you can use the end of the final array to make PQ.

4. How will you sort 1 PB numbers? 1 PB = 1000 TB.

5. What will be the complexity of the above solution?

6. Any other improvement on question 3 solution if the number of cores is eight.

7. Given an *integer* array that support three function findMin, findMax, findMedian. Sort the array.

8. Given a pile of patient files of High, mid and low priority. Sort these files such that higher priority comes first, then mid and last low priority.
   Hint: Bucket sort.

9. Write pros and cons of Heap-Sort, Merge-Sort and Quick-Sort.

10. Given a rotated - sorted array of N *integer* s. (The array was sorted then it was rotated some arbitrary number of times.) If all the elements in the array were unique the find the index of some value.
    Hint: Modified binary search

11. In the problem 9, what if there are repetitions allowed and you need to find the index of the first occurrence of the element in the rotated-sorted array.

12. Merge two sorted arrays into a single sorted array.
    Hint: Use merge method of Merge-Sort.

13. Given an array contain 0's and 1's, sort the array such that all the 0's come before 1's.

14. Given an array of English characters, sort the array in linear time.

15. Write a method to sort an array of strings so that all the anagrams are next to each other.

---

1. Loop through the array.
2. For each word, sort the characters and add it to the hash map with keys as sorted word and value as the original word. At the end of the loop, you will get all anagrams as the value to a key (which is sorted by its constituent chars).
3. Iterate over the hashmap, print all values of a key together and then move to the next key.
   Space Complexity: O(n), *Time Complexity:* O(n)

CHAPTER 7: LINKED LIST

Introduction

Let us suppose we have an array that contains following five elements 1, 2, 4, 5, 6. We want to insert an element with value "3" in between "2" and "4". In the array, we cannot do so easily. We need to create another array that is long enough to store the current values and one more space for "3". Then we need to copy these elements in the new space. This copy operation is inefficient.

To remove this fixed length constraint linked list is used.

Linked List

The linked list is a list of items, called nodes. Nodes have two parts, value part and link part. Value part is used to stores the data. The value part of the node can be either a basic data-type like an *integer* or it can be some other data-type like structure.
The link part is a pointer which is used to store addresses of the next element in the list.

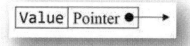

Types of Linked list

There are different types of linked lists. The main difference among them is how their nodes refer to each other.

Singly Linked List

Each node (Except the last node) has a reference to the next node in the linked list. The link portion of node contains the address of the next node. The link portion of the last node contains the value NULL.

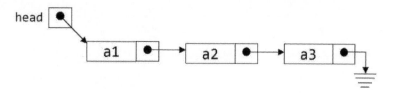

Doubly Linked list

The node in this type of linked list has reference to both previous and the next node in the list.

Circular Linked List

This type is similar to the singly linked list except that the last element points to the first node of the list. The link portion of the last node contains the address of the first node.

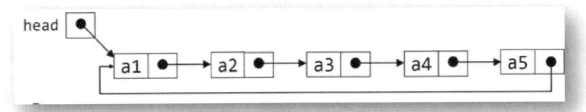

The various parts of linked list

1. Head: Head is a pointer that holds the address of the first node in the linked list.
2. Nodes: Items in the linked list are called nodes.
3. Value: The data that is stored in each node of the linked list.
4. Link: Link part of the node is used to store the address of the node.
   a. We will use "next" and "prev" to store address of next or previous node.

Singly Linked List

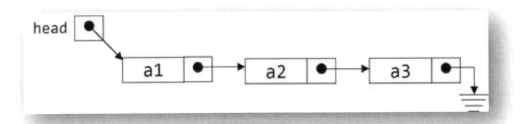

Let us look an example of Node, in this example, the value is of type int, but it can be of some other data-type. The link is nemed as next in the below structure. We have typedef the Node* to NodePtr so that our code looks clean.

```
struct Node {
int value;
Node *next;
};
typedef Node* NodePtr;
```

Note: For a singly linked, we should always test these three test cases before saying that the code is good to go. This one node and zero node case is used to catch boundary cases. It is always to take care of these cases before submitting code to the reviewer.
- Zero element / Empty linked list.
- One element / Just single node case.
- General case.

Note: Any program that is likely to change the head pointer is to be passed as a double pointer.

Basic operation of a linked list requires traversing a linked list. The various operations that we can perform on linked lists, many of these operations require list traversal:
- Insert an element in the list, this operation is used to create a linked list.
- Print various elements of the list.
- Search an element in the list.
- Delete an element from the list.
- Reverse a linked list.

You cannot use Head to traverse a linked list because if we use the head, then we lose the nodes of the list. We have to use another pointer variable of same data-type as the head.

Insert element in linked list

An element can be inserted into a linked list in various orders. Some of the example cases are mentioned below:
1. Insertion of an element at the start of linked list
2. Insertion of an element at the end of linked list
3. Insertion of an element at the 2nd position in linked list
4. Insert element in sorted order in linked list

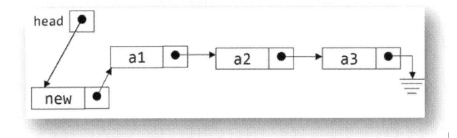

Example 7.1

1.	struct Node {
2.	int value;
3.	Node *next;
4.	};
5.	typedef Node* NodePtr;

```
1.      int InsertNode(NodePtr* ptrHead, int value)
2.      {
3.          printf("Insert Node: %d", value);
4.          NodePtr tempPtr = (NodePtr) malloc (sizeof (Node));
5.          if(!tempPtr)
6.              return -1;
7.          tempPtr->value=value;
8.          tempPtr->next=*ptrHead;
9.          *ptrHead=tempPtr;
10.         return 1;
11.     }
```

Analysis:

Line 1: Double pointer ptrHead is passed to the function as argument, as we want to assign the new node to the head of the linked list.

Line 3: Value passed as argument is printed to standard output.

Line 4: Memory is allocated for the new node of the list and is pointed by trmpPtr.

Line 5-6: Here it is checked if the system is able to allocate memory if malloc() succeeded in allocating memory it returns the address of that memory location. Moreover, if malloc() fails to allocate memory, then it returns NULL.

Line 7: The value passed as argument is stored in the memory pointed by tempPtr

Line 8: The new node next pointer will point to the head of the original list.

Line 9: The head of the original list will now start pointing to tempPtr. There by adding a node at the beginning of the linked list is done.

Traversing Linked List

Example 7.2: Print various elements of a linked list

```
1.      void PrintList(NodePtr head)
2.      {
3.              while(head)
4.              {
5.                      printf("value %d \n", head->value);
6.                      head=head->next;
7.              }
8.      }
```

Analysis:

Line 1: This function takes the head of the list as input argument.

Line 3: On this line, we are checking if the head is not NULL. If the head is not null then while block will execute.

Line 5: It prints value stored as the value of the current node.

Line 6: At this line, we are incrementing the head pointer, so that it will point to the next element of the linked list.

Complete code for list creation and printing the list.

Example 7.3:

```
1.      int main()
2.      {
3.              NodePtr head = NULL;
4.              int arr[5] = { 1, 2, 3, 4, 5 };
5.              int i;
6.              for (i = 0; i<5; i++)
7.              {
8.                      InsertNode(&head, arr[i]);
9.              }
10.             return 0;
11.     }
```

Analysis:

Line 3: Head pointer of the list is created and it is assigned the value NULL. Head pointing to NULL means the list is empty.

Line 4: In this, we have created an array of 5 elements. These elements will be sorted in the list.

Line 6-9: Value stored in array are stored in list by calling InsertNode function.

Sorted Insert

Insert an element in sorted order in linked list given Head pointer

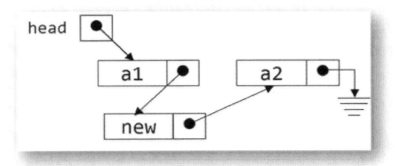

Example 7.4:

```
1.      int SortedInsert(NodePtr* ptrHead, int value)
2.      {
3.              NodePtr curr=*ptrHead;
4.              NodePtr tempNode = (NodePtr) malloc(sizeof(Node));
5.              printf("Insert element %d \n", value);
6.              if(!tempNode)
7.                      return -1;
8.              tempNode->value=value;
9.              tempNode->next=NULL;
10.             if(curr==NULL || curr->value>value)
11.             {
12.                     tempNode->next=*ptrHead;
13.                     *ptrHead=tempNode;
14.                     return 1;
15.             }
16.             while(curr->next != NULL &&
17.                     curr->next->value < value)
18.             {
19.                     curr=curr->next;
20.             }
21.             tempNode->next=curr->next;
22.             curr->next=tempNode;
23.             return 1;
24.     }
```

Analysis:

Line 3: Head of the list is stored in curr pointer.

Line 4-9: A new empty node of the linked list is created. And initialized by storing an argument value into its value. Next of the node will point to null.

Line 10-15: It checks if the list was empty or if the value stored in the first node is greater than the current value. Then this new created node will be added to the start of the list.

Line 16-20: We iterate through the list to find the proper position to insert the node.

Line 21-23: Finally, the node will be added to the list.

Insertion of an element at the end

Insertion of an element at the end of linked list (given head pointer, and tail pointer)

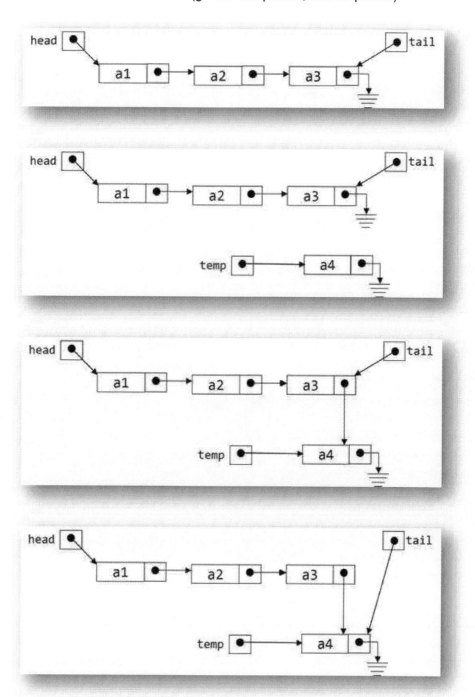

Example 7.5:

```
1.      int InsertNode(NodePtr* ptrHead, NodePtr* ptrTail, int value)
2.      {
3.          printf("Insert Node:: %d",value);
4.          NodePtr tempPtr= (NodePtr)malloc(sizeof(Node));
5.          if(!tempPtr)
6.              return -1;
7.          tempPtr->value=value;
8.          tempPtr->next=NULL;
9.          if(*ptrHead == NULL)
10.             {
11.                 *ptrTail=*ptrHead=tempPtr;
12.             }
13.         else
14.         {
15.             NodePtr tail = *ptrTail;
16.             tail->next=tempPtr;
17.             *ptrTail=tempPtr;
18.         }
19.         return 1;
20.     }
```

Analysis:

Line 4-8: New linked list node is created and the value stored inside it and its next points to NULL.

Line 9-12: If the linked list is empty. Then the new node will be pointed by ptrTail and ptrHead.

Line 15-17: If linked list is not empty, then list ptrHead will not change. Only the ptrTail will be changed and it will point to this new node.

Insert an element at the end of linked list given Head pointer

Example 7.6: Insert an element at the end of linked list given Head pointer

```
1.      int InsertAtEnd(NodePtr* ptrHead, int value)
2.      {
3.              printf("insert element %d \n", value);
4.              NodePtr head=*ptrHead;
5.              NodePtr tempNode = (NodePtr) malloc(sizeof(Node));
6.              if(!tempNode)
7.                      return -1;
8.              tempNode->value=value;
9.              tempNode->next=NULL;
10.             if(head==NULL)
11.             {
12.                     tempNode->next=*ptrHead;
13.                     *ptrHead=tempNode;
14.                     return 1;
15.             }
```

```
16.              while(head->next != NULL)
17.              {
18.                      head=head->next;
19.              }
20.              tempNode->next=head->next;
21.              head->next=tempNode;
22.              return 1;
23.      }
```

Analysis:

Line 3-14: New node is created and the value is stored inside it. If the list is empty, then it will be pointed by the head pointer ptrHead.

Line 16-19: Will traverse until the end of the list.

Line 20-21: Finally, new node is added to the end of the list.

Note: This operation is un-efficient as each time you want to insert an element you have to traverse to the end of the list. Therefore, the complexity of creation of the list is n^2. So how to make it efficient we have to keep track of the last element by keeping a tail pointer. Therefore, if it is required to always insert element at the end of linked list, then we will keep track of the tail pointer also.

Search Element in a Linked-List

Search element in linked list. Given a head pointer and value. Returns 1 if value found in list else returns 0.

Search in a single linked list can be only done in one direction. Since all elements in the list has reference to the next item in the list. Therefore, traversal of linked list is linear in nature.

Example 7.7:

```
1.      int SearchList(NodePtr head, int value)
2.      {
3.              while(head)
4.              {
5.                      If(head->value == value)
6.                      {
7.                              printf("The value is found");
8.                              return 1;
9.                      }
10.                     head=head->next;
11.             }
12.             return 0;
13.     }
```

Analysis:

Line 1: We do not need to modify the list so pointer to the head is passed (we do not need a double pointer).

Line 3: While loop will iterate through the list and will.

Line 5: Value of each element of list is compared with the given value if found, then "The value is found" will be printed to the screen. In addition, function will return 1.

Line 12: If the value is not found, then 0 will be returned from the function.

Delete element from the linked list

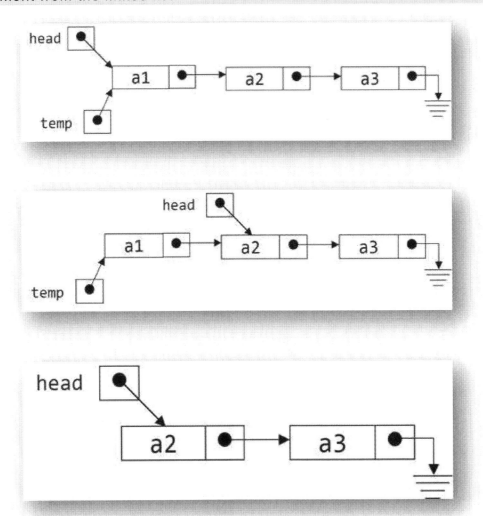

Delete First element in a linked list.

Example 7.8:

```
1.      void DeleteFirstNodes(NodePtr* ptrHead)
2.      {
3.              printf("\nDelete First Node \n");
4.              NodePtr tempNode=*ptrHead;
5.              if(tempNode==NULL)
6.                      return;
7.              *ptrHead = tempNode->next;
8.              free(tempNode);
9.      }
```

Analysis:

- We need to find the second element of the list and assign it as head of the linked list.
- If the list has at least one element, its first element will be deleted and the head of the list will point to the second element.

128

Delete node from the linked list given its value.

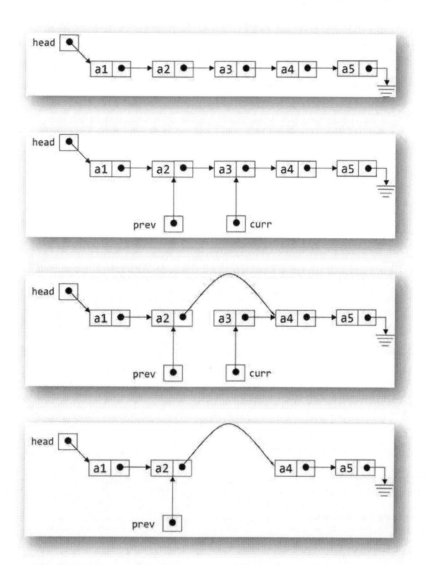

Example 7.9:

```
1.      void DeleteNode(NodePtr* ptrHead, int delValue)
2.      {
3.              printf("\nDelete Node \n");
4.              NodePtr currNode=*ptrHead;
5.              NodePtr nextNode;
6.
7.              if(currNode->value==delValue)/*first node */
8.              {
9.                      *ptrHead=currNode->next;
10.                     free(currNode);
11.                     return;
12.             }
13.
14.             while(currNode!=NULL)
15.             {
16.                     nextNode=currNode->next;
```

```
17.                    if(nextNode && nextNode->value == delValue)
18.                    {
19.                            currNode->next = nextNode->next;
20.                            free(nextNode);
21.                            return;
22.                    }
23.                    else
24.                    {
25.                            currNode=nextNode;
26.                    }
27.            }
28.    }
```

Analysis:

Line 7-12: If the value stored in first node is the value that need to deleted, so the head of the list will change so this case is handled separately. Else, in no other case head of linked list will change.

Line 14-27: In a for loop we will traverse the link list and try to find the node that need to be deleted. We are keeping nextNode as the next of currNode. We always compare nextNode value with the delValue and currNode's next pointer will point to the nextNode's next pointer. Then nextNode is the node that needs to be deleted which is finally free at line 20.

Delete all the occurrence of particular value in linked list.

Example 7.10:

```
1.      void DeleteNodes(NodePtr* ptrHead, int delValue)
2.      {
3.              printf("\nDelete Node \n");
4.              NodePtr currNode=*ptrHead;
5.              NodePtr nextNode;
6.              NodePtr delNode;
7.
8.              while(currNode!=NULL && currNode->value==delValue)/*first node */
9.              {
10.                     *ptrHead=currNode->next;
11.                     delNode=currNode;
12.                     currNode=currNode->next;
13.                     free(delNode);
14.             }
15.
16.             while(currNode!=NULL)
17.             {
18.                     nextNode=currNode->next;
19.                     if(nextNode && nextNode->value == delValue)
20.                     {
21.                             currNode->next = nextNode->next;
22.                             free(nextNode);
23.                     }
```

```
24.                else
25.                {
26.                        currNode=nextNode;
27.                }
28.            }
29.        }
```

Analysis:

Line 8-14: While loop will delete all the nodes that are at the front of the list, which have valued equal to delValue.

Line 16-28: In this while loop, we will be deleting all the nodes that are having value equal to the delValue.

Delete node from the linked list given its pointer

Example 7.11:

```
1.      void DeleteNodePtr(NodePtr* ptrHead, NodePtr ptrDel)
2.      {
3.              printf("\ndeleteNode\n");
4.              NodePtr currNode=*ptrHead;
5.              NodePtr nextNode;
6.
7.              if(ptrDel==NULL)
8.                      return;
9.
10.             if(currNode==ptrDel)//first node
11.             {
12.                     *ptrHead=currNode->next;
13.                     free(currNode);
14.             }
15.             while(currNode!=NULL)
16.             {
17.                     nextNode=currNode->next;
18.                     if(nextNode==ptrDel)//node to be deleated
19.                     {
20.                             currNode->next=nextNode->next;
21.                             free(nextNode); return;
22.                     }
23.                     else
24.                     {
25.                             currNode=nextNode;
26.                     }
27.             }
28.     }
```

Analysis:

Line 10-14: If the node that need to be deleted is the first node, then the head of the linked list will change and will point to the next element of the linked list.

Line 15-27: In this while, loop the node that is supposed to be deleted will be removed from the list.

Delete a single linked list

Delete all the elements of a linked list, given a pointer to head of linked list.

Example 7.12:

```
1.      void DeleteList(NodePtr* ptrHead)
2.      {
3.              printf("\nDelete List\n");
4.              NodePtr deleteMe=*ptrHead;
5.              NodePtr nextNode;
6.              while(deleteMe!=NULL)
7.              {
8.                      nextNode=deleteMe->next;
9.                      free(deleteMe);
10.                     deleteMe=nextNode;
11.             }
12.             *ptrHead=NULL;
13.     }
```

Analysis:
Line 6-11: In this while loop each node is deleted one by one. Until whole list is deleted.
Line 12: In this line head of linked list is assigned the value NULL there by making the list empty.

Reverse a linked list.

Reverse a singly linked List iteratively using three Pointers

Example 7.13:

```
1.      void ReverseList(NodePtr* ptrHead)
2.      {
3.              NodePtr currNode=*ptrHead;
4.              NodePtr prevNode;
5.              NodePtr nextNode;
6.              if(!currNode)
7.              {
8.                      return;
9.              }
10.             if(!currNode->next)
11.             {
12.                     return;
13.             }
14.             prevNode=currNode;
15.             currNode=currNode->next;
16.             prevNode->next=NULL;
17.             while(tempNode)
18.             {
19.                     nextNode= currNode ->next;
20.                     currNode ->next=prevNode;
21.                     prevNode= currNode;
22.                     currNode =nextNode;
```

```
23.
24.              }
25.              *ptrHead=prevNode;
26.      }
```

Analysis:

Line 17-24: The list is iterated. Make nextNode equal to the next node of the currNode. Make currNode node's next will point to prevNode. Then iterate the list by making prevNode point to currNode and currNode point to nextNode.

Recursively Reverse a singly linked List

Example 7.14: Recursively Reverse a singly linked List Arguments are current node and its next value.

```
1.       NodePtr reverseRecurseUtil (NodePtr currentNode, NodePtr nextNode)
2.       {
3.               NodePtr ret;
4.               if(!currentNode)
5.                       return NULL;
6.
7.               if(!currentNode->next)
8.               {
9.                       currentNode->next=nextNode;
10.                      return    currentNode;
11.              }
12.
13.              ret= reverseRecurseUtil (currentNode->next, currentNode);
14.              currentNode->next=nextNode;
15.
16.              return ret;
17.      }
18.
19.      void reverseRecurse(NodePtr* ptrHead)
20.      {
21.              *ptrHead=reverseRecurseUtil(*ptrHead,NULL);
22.      }
```

Analysis: *Line 19-22*: reverseRecurse function will call a reverseRecurseUtil function to reverse the list and the pointer returned by the reverseRecurseUtil will be the head of the reversed list.
Line 9 & 14: the current node will point to the nextNode that is previous node of the old list.

Note: A linked list can be reversed using two approaches the one approach is by using three pointers. The *Second approach* is using recursion both are linear solution, but three-pointer solution is more efficient.

Remove duplicates from the linked list

Remove duplicate values from the linked list. The linked list is sorted and it contains some duplicate values, you need to remove those duplicate values. (You can create the required linked list using SortedInsert() function)

Example 7.15:

```
1.      void RemoveDuplicate(NodePtr head)
2.      {
3.         NodePtr deleteMe;
4.         while(head)
5.         {
6.            if((head->next) && head->value == head->next->value)
7.            {
8.               deleteMe=head->next;
9.               head->next=deleteMe->next;
10.              free(deleteMe);
11.           }
12.           else
13.           {
14.              head=head->next;
15.           }
16.        }
17.     }
```

Analysis: *Line 4-16*: While loop is used to traverse the list. Whenever there is a node whose value is equal to the next node's value, that node will be removed from the list and delete that node.

Copy List Reversed

Copy the content of linked list in another linked list in reverse order. If the original linked list contains elements in order 1,2,3,4, the new list should contain the elements in order 4,3,2,1.

Example 7.16:

```
1.      void CopyListReversed(NodePtr head, NodePtr* ptrHead2)
2.      {
3.            printf("copy list");
4.            NodePtr tempNode=NULL;
5.            NodePtr tempNode2=NULL;
6.            while(head)
7.            {
8.                   tempNode2 = (NodePtr)malloc( sizeof(Node));
9.                   tempNode2->value=head->value;
10.                  tempNode2->next=tempNode;
11.                  tempNode=tempNode2;
12.                  head=head->next;
13.            }
14.           *ptrHead2=tempNode;
15.     }
```

Analysis: Traverse the list and add the node's value to the new list. Since the list is traversed in the forward direction and each node's value is added to another list so the formed list is reverse of the given list.

Copy the content of given linked list into another linked list

Copy the content of given linked list into another linked list. If the original linked list contains elements in order 1,2,3,4, the new list should contain the elements in order 1,2,3,4.

Example 7.17:

```
1.      void CopyList(NodePtr head, NodePtr* ptrHead2)
2.      {
3.         printf("copy list");
4.         NodePtr headNode=NULL;
5.         NodePtr tailNode=NULL;
6.         NodePtr tempNode=NULL;
7.
8.         if(head==NULL)
9.            return;
10.        headNode=(NodePtr)malloc(sizeof(Node));
11.        tailNode=headNode;
12.        headNode->value=head->value;
13.        headNode->next=NULL;
14.        head=head->next;
15.
16.        while(head)
17.        {
18.           tempNode=(NodePtr)malloc( sizeof(Node));
19.           tempNode->value=head->value;
20.           tempNode->next=NULL;
21.           tailNode->next=tempNode;
22.           tailNode=tailNode->next;
23.           head=head->next;
24.        }
25.        *ptrHead2=headNode;
26.      }
```

Analysis:

Traverse the list and add the node's value to new list, but this time always at the end of the list. Since the list is traversed in the forward direction and each node's value is added to the end of another list. Therefore, the formed list is same as the given list.

Compare List

Example 7.18:

```
1.      int compareList(NodePtr head1, NodePtr head2)
2.      {
3.             printf("compare list");
4.             if( head1==NULL && head2==NULL )
5.                    return 1;
6.             else if( (head1==NULL) ||(head2==NULL) || (head1->value!=head2->value) )
7.                    return 0;
8.             else
9.                    return compareList(head1->next,head2->next);
10.      }
```

Analysis:

Line 4-5: List is compared recursively. Moreover, if we reach the end of the list and both the lists are null. Then both the lists are equal and so return 1.

Line 6-7: List is compared recursively. If either one of the list is empty or the value of corresponding nodes is unequal, then this function will return 0.

Line 9: Recursively calls compare list function for the next node of the current nodes.

Compare List

Example 7.19:

```
1.      int compareList2(NodePtr head1, NodePtr head2)
2.      {
3.              while( head1!=NULL && head2!=NULL )
4.              {
5.                      if(head1->value!=head2->value)
6.                          return 0;
7.                      head1=head1->next;
8.                      head2=head2->next;
9.              }
10.             if(head1==head2)
11.             {
12.                     return 1;
13.             }
14.             else
15.             {
16.                     return 0;
17.             }
18.     }
```

Analysis:

Line 3-9: Both the lists are traversed till one list is empty or there value of the corresponding node is unequal.

Line 11-17: If both the list are reached to the end, which means both the list are equal so return 1 else return 0.

Find Length

Example 7.20: Find the length of given linked list.

```
1.      int findLength(NodePtr head)
2.      {
3.              int count = 0;
4.              while (head)
5.              {
6.                      count++;
7.                      head = head->next;
8.              }
9.              return count;
10.     }
```

Analysis: Length of linked list is found by traversing the list till we reach the end of list.

Nth Node from Beginning

Example 7.21:

```
1.      NodePtr nthNodeFromBegining(NodePtr head, int index)
2.      {
3.              int count = 0;
4.              while (head && count < index-1)
5.              {
6.                      count++;
7.                      head = head->next;
8.              }
9.
10.             if (head)
11.                     return head;
12.             else
13.                     return NULL;
14.     }
```

Analysis: Nth node can be found by traversing the list N-1 nuber of time and then return the node if it is not NULL else return NULL.

Nth Node from End

Example 7.22:

```
1.      NodePtr nthNodeFromEnd(NodePtr head, int index)
2.      {
3.              int size = findLength(head);
4.              int startIndex;
5.              if (size && size < index)
6.              {
7.                      printf("list does not have % elements", index);
8.                      return NULL;
9.              }
10.             startIndex = size - index + 1;
11.             return nthNodeFromBegining(head, startIndex);
12.     }
```

Analysis: First find the lentht of list, then nth node from end will be (length – nth +1) node from the beginning.

Example 7.23:

```
1.      NodePtr nthNodeFromEnd(NodePtr head, int index)
2.      {
3.              int count = 0;
4.              NodePtr temp = NULL;
5.              NodePtr curr = head;
6.              while (curr && count < index - 1)
7.              {
8.                      count++;
9.                      curr = curr->next;
10.             }
11.
12.             if (!curr)
13.                     return NULL;
14.
15.             temp = head;
16.
17.             while (curr)
18.             {
19.                     temp = temp->next;
20.                     curr = curr->next;
21.             }
22.             return temp;
23.     }
```

Analysis: Second approach is to use two pointers one is N steps / nodes ahead of the other when forward pointer reach the end of the list then the backward pointer will point to the desired node.

Example 7.24

```
1.      NodePtr nthNodeFromEnd(NodePtr head, int index)
2.      {
3.              static int count=0;
4.              NodePtr retval;
5.
6.              if (!head)
7.                      return NULL;
8.
9.              retval = nthNodeFromEnd3(head->next, index);
10.             if (retval)
11.                     return retval;
12.
13.             count++;
14.             if (count == index)
15.                     return head;
16.             else
17.                     return NULL;
18.     }
```

Loop Detect

1. Traverse through the list.
2. If the current node is not there in the Hash-Table then insert it into the Hash-Table.
3. If the current node is already in the hashtable then we have a loop.

Loop Detect

We have to find if there is a loop in the linked list. There are basically two ways to find if there is a loop in a linked list. One way is called "Slow pointer and fast pointer approach (SPFP)" the other is called "Reverse list approach". Both approaches are linear in nature, but still in SPFP approach we don't require to modify the linked list so it is preferred.

Find if there is a loop in a linked list. If there is a loop, then return 1 if not, then return 0. Use slow pointer fast pointer approach.

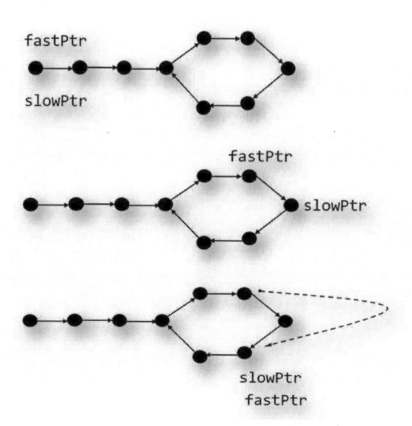

Example 7.25:

```
1.      int LoopDetect(NodePtr head)
2.      {
3.        printf("loop detect");
4.        NodePtr slowPtr;
5.        NodePtr fastPtr;
6.        slowPtr=fastPtr=head;
7.
8.        while(fastPtr->next&&fastPtr->next->next)
9.        {
10.         slowPtr=slowPtr->next;
11.         fastPtr=fastPtr->next->next;
12.         if(slowPtr==fastPtr)
13.         {
14.           return 1;
15.         }
16.       }
17.       return 0;
18.     }
```

Analysis:

Line 8-16: The list is traversed with two pointers, one is slow pointer and another is fast pointer. Slow pointer always moves one step. Fast pointer always moves two steps. If there is no loop, then control will come out of while loop. So return 0.

Line 12-15: If there is a loop, then there came a point in a loop where the fast pointer will come and try to pass slow pointer. When this point arrives, we come to know that there is a loop in the list. So return 1.

Reverse List Loop Detect

Find if there is a loop in a linked list. If there is a loop, then return 1 if not, then return 0. Use reverse list approach.

Example 7.26:

```
1.      int ReverseListLoopDetect(NodePtr head)
2.      {
3.            NodePtr* ptrHead=&head;
4.            NodePtr head2=head;
5.            reverseList(ptrHead);
6.            if(*ptrHead==head2)
7.            {
8.                  reverseList(ptrHead);
9.                  return 1;
10.           }
11.           else
12.           {
13.                 reverseList(ptrHead);
14.                 return 0;
15.           }
16.     }
```

Analysis:

Line 5: reverse the list at this line.

Line 6: compare the reversed list head pointer to the current node list head pointer.

Line 8-9: If the head of reversed list and the original list, are same then reverse the list back and return 1.

Line 13-14: If the head of the reversed list and the original list are not same then reverse the list back and return 0. Which means there is no loop.

Loop Type Detect

Find if there is a loop in a linked list. If there is no loop, then return 0, if there is loop return 1, if the list is circular then 2. Use slow pointer fast pointer approach.

Example 7.27:

```
1.      int LoopTypeDetect(NodePtr const head)
2.      {
3.              printf("loop detect");
4.              NodePtr slowPtr;
5.              NodePtr fastPtr;
6.
7.              slowPtr=fastPtr=head;
8.              while(fastPtr->next && fastPtr->next->next)
9.              {
10.
11.                     slowPtr=slowPtr->next;
12.                     fastPtr=fastPtr->next->next;
13.
14.                     if(head==fastPtr->next || head==fastPtr->next->next)
15.                     {
16.                             return 2;
17.                     }
18.                     if(slowPtr==fastPtr)
19.                     {
20.                             return 1;
21.                     }
22.             }
23.             return 0;
24.     }
```

Analysis: This program is same as the loop detect program except *Line 14-17.*

Line 14-17: If fast pointer reaches to the head of the list, then this means that there is a loop at the beginning of the list.

Example 7.28:

```
1.      void RemoveLoop(NodePtr* ptrHead)
2.      {
3.              int loopLength;
4.              NodePtr slowPtr,fastPtr, head;
5.              slowPtr=fastPtr=head=*ptrHead;
6.              NodePtr loopNode=NULL;
7.              while(fastPtr->next && fastPtr->next->next )
8.              {
9.                      fastPtr=fastPtr->next->next;
10.                     slowPtr=slowPtr->next;
11.
12.                     if(fastPtr==slowPtr || fastPtr->next==slowPtr)
13.                     {
14.                             loopNode=slowPtr;
15.                             break;
16.                     }
17.             }
18.             if(loopNode)
19.             {
20.                     NodePtr temp=loopNode->next;
21.                     loopLength=1;
22.                     while(temp!=loopNode)
23.                     {
24.                             loopLength++;
25.                             temp=temp->next;
26.                     }
27.                     temp=head;
28.                     NodePtr breakNode=head;
29.
30.                     for(int i=1;i<loopLength;i++)
31.                     {
32.                             breakNode=breakNode->next;
33.                     }
34.
35.                     while(temp != breakNode->next)
36.                     {
37.                             temp=temp->next;
38.                             breakNode=breakNode->next;
39.                     }
40.                     breakNode->next=NULL;
41.             }
42.     }
```

Analysis:
Loop through the list by two pointer, one fast pointer and one slow pointer. Fast pointer jumps two nodes at a time and slow pointer jump one node at a time. The point where these two pointer intersect is a pointer in the loop.
Then since we have a pointer in a loop we can find the length of the loop.

Take a pointer breakNode which point to the head of the linked list. Increment the list by loop length and then increment the head and breakNode pointer till both are equal. When you have a breakNode then assign its next to NULL.

There is one more solution possible to find the break point. The point where slow pointer and fast pointer meets in loop, call it loop point. Start one pointer from head and other from loop point increment both one step at a time they will meet at the loop point. Mark the next of loop point null and you are done. (This can be proved mathematically)

Find Intersection

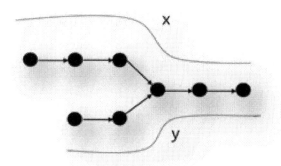

Example 7.29:

```
1.      NodePtr findIntersection(NodePtr head, NodePtr head2)
2.      {
3.              int l1=0;
4.              int l2=0;
5.              NodePtr tempHead=head;
6.              NodePtr tempHead2=head2;
7.
8.              while(tempHead)
9.              {
10.                     l1++;
11.                     tempHead=tempHead->next;
12.             }
13.             while(tempHead2)
14.             {
15.                     l2++;
16.                     tempHead2=tempHead2->next;
17.             }
18.
19.             int diff;
20.             if(l1<l2)
21.             {
22.                     NodePtr temp=head;
23.                     head=head2;
24.                     head2=temp;
25.                     diff=l2-l1;
26.             }
```

143

```
27.          else
28.          {
29.                  diff=l1-l2;
30.          }
31.
32.          for(;diff>0;diff--)
33.          {
34.                  head=head->next;
35.          }
36.          while(head!=head2)
37.          {
38.                  head=head->next;
39.                  head2=head2->next;
40.          }
41.
42.          return head;
43.  }
```

Analysis: Find length of both the lists. Find the difference of length of both the lists. Increment the longer list by diff steps, then increment both the lists and get the intersection point.

Doubly Linked List

In a Doubly-Linked list basically there are two pointers in each node. These pointers are called prev and next. The prev pointer of the node will point to the node previous to it and the next pointer will point to the node next to the given node.

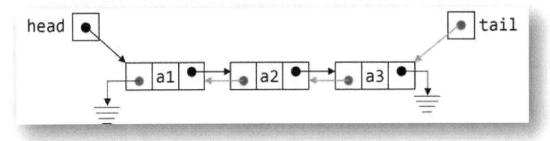

Let's look an example of Node, in this example the value is of type int, but it can be of some other data-type. The two link pointers are prev and next. We have typedef the Node* to NodePtr so that our code looks clean.

```
struct Node{
    int value;
    struct Node *next;
    struct Node *prev;
};

typedef Node* NodePtr;
```

144

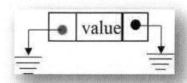

Search in a single linked list can be only done in one direction. Since all elements in the list has reference to the next item in the list. So traversal of linked list is linear in nature.

In a doubly linked list we keep track of both head of the linked list and tail of linked list.

Note: For a doubly linked list linked list there are few cases that we need to keep in mind while coding:
- Zero element case (head and tail both can be modified)
- Only element case (head and tail both can be modified)
- First element (head can be modified)
- General case
- The last element (tail can be modified)

Note: Any program which is likely to change head pointer or tail pointer is to be passed as a double pointer, which is pointing to head or tail pointer.

Traversing Linked List

Basic operation of a linked list requires traversing a linked list. The various operations that we can perform on linked lists, many of these operations require list traversal:
- Insert an element in the list, this operation is used to create a linked list.
- Print various elements of the list.
- Search an element in the list.
- Delete an element from the list.
- Reverse a linked list.

You cannot use Head to traverse a linked list because if we use the head, then we lose the nodes of the list. We have to use another pointer variable of same data-type as the head.

The list traversal code is mentioned next.

```
NodePtr current = head;

while (current != NULL) {
    /* Process current node */
    current = current->next;
}
```

For any linked list there are only three cases zero element, one element, and generally
Any program which is likely to change the head pointer is to be passed a double pointer

For doubly linked list we have a few more things
1. NULL values (head and tail both can be modified)
2. Only element (head and tail both can be modified)
3. First element (head can be modified)
4. General case

5. Last element (tail can be modified)

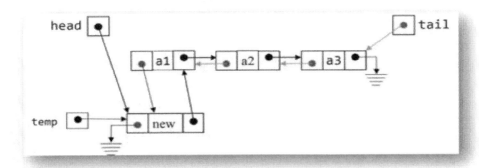

1.	#include<stdio.h>
2.	#include<stdlib.h>
3.	struct Node{
4.	int value;
5.	struct Node *next;
6.	struct Node *prev;
7.	};
8.	typedef Node* NodePtr;

Example 7.30:

```
1.      /* INSERT VALUE IN FRONT */
2.      int insertNode(NodePtr* ptrHead, NodePtr* ptrTail, int value)
3.      {
4.              printf("\n INSERT NODE\n");
5.              NodePtr temp=(NodePtr)malloc(sizeof(Node));
6.              if(!temp)
7.              return 0;
8.              NodePtr head=*ptrHead;
9.              if(!head)
10.             {
11.                     temp->value=value;
12.                     temp->next=NULL;
13.                     temp->prev=NULL;
14.                     *ptrTail=temp;
15.                     *ptrHead=temp;
16.             }
17.             else
18.             {
19.                     temp->value=value;
20.                     temp->next=head;
21.                     temp->prev=NULL;
22.                     head->prev=temp;
23.                     *ptrHead=temp;
24.             }
25.             return 1;
26.     }
```

Analysis: Insert in double linked list is same as insert in a singly linked list. Create a node assign NULL to prev pointer of the node. Then point next to the start of the list. If the list is empty then ptrTail will point to the node.

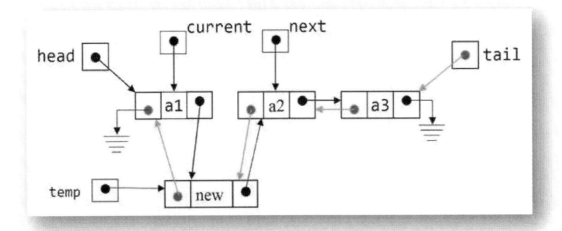

Example 7.31:

```
1.      //SORTED INSERT DECREASING
2.      int sortedInsert(NodePtr* ptrHead, NodePtr* ptrTail, int value)
3.      {
4.              printf("\nsorted insert\n");
5.              NodePtr temp=(NodePtr)malloc(sizeof(Node));
6.              if(!temp)
7.                      return 0;
8.              temp->value=value;
9.              NodePtr head=*ptrHead;
10.             if(!head)//first element
11.             {
12.                     temp->next=NULL;
13.                     temp->prev=NULL;
14.                     *ptrHead=temp;
15.                     *ptrTail=temp;
16.                     return 1;
17.             }
18.             if(head->value <= value)//at the begining
19.             {
20.                     temp->next=head;
21.                     temp->prev=NULL;
22.                     head->prev=temp;
23.                     *ptrHead=temp;
24.                     return 1;
25.             }
26.             while(head->next && head->next->value > value)//treversal
27.             {
28.                     head=head->next;
29.             }
30.             if(!head->next)//at the end
31.             {
32.                     *ptrTail=temp;
33.                     temp->next=NULL;
34.                     temp->prev=head;
35.                     head->next=temp;
36.             }
37.             else///all other
38.             {
39.                     temp->next=head->next;
40.                     temp->prev=head;
41.                     head->next=temp;
42.                     temp->next->prev=temp;
43.             }
44.             return 1;
45.     }
```

Analysis:

Find the proper location of the node and add it to the list. Manage next and prev pointer of the node so that list always remain double linked list.

Example 7.32:

```
1.      /*
2.      Print A singly linked list
3.      */
4.      void printList(NodePtr head)
5.      {
6.              printf("List is :: ");
7.              while(head!=NULL)
8.              {
9.                      printf(" %d  ",head->value);
10.                     head=head->next;
11.             }
12.             printf("\n");
13.     }
```

Analysis:
Print list is same as just traversing the list and printing the values of the nodes.

Reverse a doubly linked List iteratively

Example 7.33:

```
1.      /*
2.      Reverse a doubly linked List iteratively
3.      */
4.
5.      void reverseList(Node **ptrHead, Node **ptrTail)
6.      {
7.              NodePtr head=*ptrHead;
8.              NodePtr tempNode;
9.              while(head)
10.             {
11.                     tempNode=head->next;
12.                     head->next=head->prev;
13.                     head->prev=tempNode;
14.                     if(!head->prev)
15.                     {
16.                             *ptrTail=*ptrHead;
17.                             *ptrHead=head;
18.                             return;
19.                     }
20.                     head=head->prev;
21.             }
22.             return;
23.     }
```

Analysis:
Traverse the list and swap next and prev pointer of each node. When you have reached to the end of the list swap ptrTail and ptrHead pointers.

150

Example 7.34: Delete a singly linked list

```
1.       void deleteList(NodePtr* ptrHead, NodePtr* ptrTail)
2.       {
3.               printf("\ndeleteList\n");
4.               NodePtr deleteMe=*ptrHead;
5.               NodePtr nextNode;
6.               while(deleteMe!=NULL)
7.               {
8.                       nextNode=deleteMe->next;
9.                       free(deleteMe);
10.                      deleteMe=nextNode;
11.              }
12.              *ptrTail=ptrHead=NULL;
13.      }
```

Analysis:

Traverse the list and delete each node of the list one by one.

Delete a node given its pointer

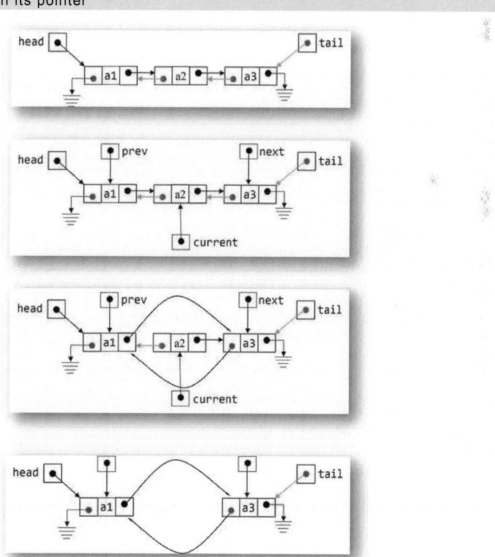

Example 7.35:

```
1.      void deleteNodePtr(NodePtr* ptrHead, NodePtr* ptrTail, NodePtr ptrDel)
2.      {
3.              printf("\ndeleteNode\n");
4.              NodePtr currNode=*ptrHead;
5.              NodePtr nextNode;
6.
7.              if(ptrDel==NULL || currNode ==NULL)
8.                      return;
9.
10.             if(currNode==ptrDel)//first node
11.             {
12.                     deleteMe = currNode;
13.                     currNode=currNode->next;
14.                     free(deleteMe);
15.                     *ptrHead = currNode;
16.                     if( currNode)
17.                             currNode->prev=NULL;
18.                     else
19.                             *ptrTail=NULL;
20.                     return;
21.             }
22.             while(currNode!=NULL)
23.             {
24.                     nextNode=currNode->next;
25.                     if(nextNode==ptrDel)//node to be deleated
26.                     {
27.                             currNode->next=nextNode->next;
28.                             nextNode->next->prev=currNode;
29.                             if(nextNode==*ptrTail)
30.                                     *ptrTail=nextNode->prev;//last node
31.                             free(nextNode);
32.                     }
33.                     else
34.                     {
35.                     currNode=nextNode;
36.                     }
37.             }
38.     }
```

Analysis: Traverse the list find the node which need to be deleted. Then remove it and adjust next pointer of the node previous to it and prev pointer of the node next to it.

Remove Duplicate

Example 7.36:

```
1.      /*  Remove Duplicate */
2.      void removeDuplicate(Node *head)
3.      {
4.              NodePtr deleteMe;
5.              while(head)
6.              {
7.                      if((head->next) && head->value==head->next->value)
8.                      {
9.                              deleteMe=head->next;
10.                             head->next=deleteMe->next;
11.                             head->next->prev=head;
12.                             if(deleteMe == tail)
13.                             {
14.                                     tail = curr;
15.                             }
16.                             free(deleteMe);
17.                     }
18.                     else
19.                     {
20.                             head=head->next;
21.                     }
22.             }
23.     }
```

Analysis: Remove duplicate is same as single linked list case. Consider the list as sorted remove the repeated value nodes of the list.

Copy List Reversed

Example 7.37:

```
1.      void copyListReversed(NodePtr head, NodePtr* ptrHead2)
2.      {
3.              printf("copy list");
4.              NodePtr tempNode=NULL;
5.              NodePtr tempNode2=NULL;
6.              while(head)
7.              {
8.                      tempNode2=(NodePtr)malloc(sizeof(Node));
9.                      tempNode2->value=head->value;
10.                     tempNode2->next=tempNode;
11.                     tempNode2->prev=NULL;
12.                     tempNode->prev=tempNode2;
13.                     tempNode=tempNode2;
14.                     head=head->next;
15.             }
16.             *ptrHead2=tempNode;
17.     }
```

Analysis: Traverse through the list and copy the value of the nodes into another list. Always add the next node value to the start of the new list there by forming a reversed list.

Copy List

Example 7.38:

```
1.      void copyList(NodePtr head, NodePtr* ptrHead2)
2.      {
3.              printf("copy list");
4.              NodePtr headNode=NULL;
5.              NodePtr tailNode=NULL;
6.              NodePtr tempNode=NULL;
7.              if(head==NULL)
8.                      return;
9.              headNode=(NodePtr)malloc(sizeof(Node));
10.             tailNode=headNode;
11.             headNode->value=head->value;
12.             headNode->next=NULL;
13.             headNode->prev=NULL;
14.             head=head->next;
15.             while(head)
16.             {
17.                     tempNode=(NodePtr)malloc(sizeof(Node));
18.                     tempNode->value=head->value;
19.                     tempNode->next=NULL;
20.                     tailNode->next=tempNode;
21.                     tempNode->prev=tailNode;
22.                     tailNode=tailNode->next;
23.                     head=head->next;
24.             }
25.             *ptrHead2=headNode;
26.     }
```

Analysis: Traverse the list, value of the nodes are added to another list always at the end. Use tail pointer to keep track of the end of the new list.

Circular Linked List

This type is similar to the singly linked list except that the last element points to the first node of the list. The link portion of the last node contains the address of the first node.

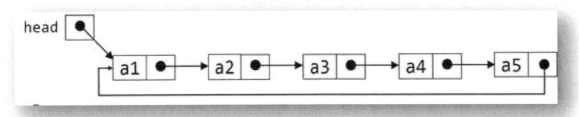

```
typedef struct Node{
        int value;
        struct Node* next;
}Node_t;

typedef Node_t* NodePtr;
```

Insert element in front

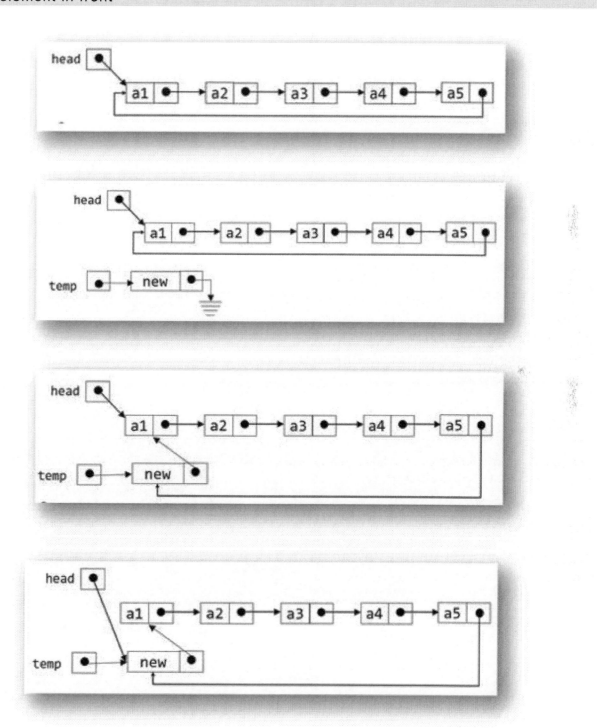

Example 7.39:

```
1.        /* Insert element in front */
2.        int insertNodeAtFront(NodePtr* ptrHead, NodePtr* ptrTail, int value)
3.        {
4.                printf(" \n INSERT NODE AT FRONT\n");
5.                NodePtr temp = (NodePtr)malloc(sizeof(Node_t));
6.                if (!temp)
7.                        return 0;
8.                temp->value = value;
9.                NodePtr head = *ptrHead;
10.               NodePtr tail = *ptrTail;
11.               if (!head)
12.               {
13.                       temp->next = temp;
14.                       *ptrTail = temp;
15.                       *ptrHead = temp;
16.               }
17.               else
18.               {
19.                       temp->next = head;
20.                       tail->next = temp;
21.                       *ptrHead = temp;
22.               }
23.               return 1;
24.       }
```

Analysis:

Line 11-16: When the list is empty the node is created. Head and tail is pointing to this node.

Line 17-22: New node is created its next will point to head and head will point to this new node. Tail nodes next will point to the new node.

Insert element at the end

Example 7.40:

```
1.        /* Insert element at the end */
2.        int insertNodeAtEnd(NodePtr* ptrHead, NodePtr* ptrTail, int value)
3.        {
4.                printf("\n INSERT NODE AT END\n");
5.                NodePtr temp = (NodePtr)malloc(sizeof(Node_t));
6.                if (!temp)
7.                        return 0;
8.                temp->value = value;
9.                NodePtr head = *ptrHead;
10.               NodePtr tail = *ptrTail;
11.               if (!head)
12.               {
13.                       temp->next = temp;
14.                       *ptrTail = temp;
15.                       *ptrHead = temp;
16.               }
```

```
17.            else
18.            {
19.                    temp->next = head;
20.                    tail->next = temp;
21.                    *ptrTail = temp;
22.            }
23.            return 1;
24.    }
```

Analysis: Adding node at the end is same as adding at the beginning. Just need to modify tail pointer in place of the head pointer.

printList

Example 7.41:

```
1.      /* Print A singly linked list */
2.      void printList(NodePtr head)
3.      {
4.              printf("LIST IS:: ");
5.              NodePtr currNode = head;
6.              if (currNode != NULL)
7.              {
8.                      printf(" %d  ", currNode->value);
9.                      currNode = currNode->next;
10.             }
11.             while (currNode != head)
12.             {
13.                     printf(" %d  ", currNode->value);
14.                     currNode = currNode->next;
15.             }
16.     }
```

Analysis: In circular list end of list is not there so we cannot check with NULL. In place of NULL head is used to check end of the list.

Delete List

Example 7.42:

```
1.      /* Delete a circular linked list */
2.      void deleteList(NodePtr* ptrHead)
3.      {
4.              printf("\n DELETE LIST \n");
5.              NodePtr const head = *ptrHead;
6.              NodePtr currNode = *ptrHead;
7.              NodePtr nextNode;
8.              if (currNode != NULL)
9.              {
10.                     nextNode = currNode->next;
11.                     free(currNode);
12.                     currNode = nextNode;
13.             }
```

```
14.          while (currNode != head)
15.          {
16.                  nextNode = currNode->next;
17.                  free(currNode);
18.                  currNode = nextNode;
19.          }
20.          *ptrHead = NULL;
21.     }
```

Analysis: Traverse through the list and delete nodes till you reach the start of the list.

Delete a node given its pointer

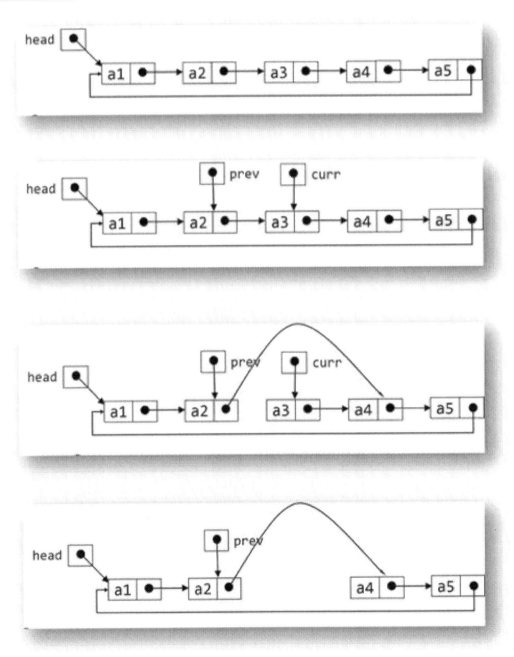

Example 7.43:

```
1.      /* Delete a node given its pointer */
2.      void deleteNodePtr(NodePtr* ptrHead, NodePtr* ptrTail, NodePtr ptrDel)
3.      {
4.              printf("\n DELETE NODE GIVEN ITS POINTER \n");
5.              if (ptrDel == NULL || ptrHead == NULL || ptrTail == NULL)
6.                      return;
7.              NodePtr head = *ptrHead;
8.              NodePtr tail = *ptrTail;
9.              NodePtr currNode = head;
10.             NodePtr prevNode;
11.             if (head == NULL || tail == NULL)
12.                     return;
13.             if (currNode == ptrDel)/* one element and first element case */
14.             {
15.                     if (currNode->next == currNode)
16.                     {
17.                             *ptrHead = NULL;
18.                             *ptrTail = NULL;
19.                             free(currNode);
20.                             return;
21.                     }
22.                     else
23.                     {
24.                             *ptrHead = currNode->next;
25.                             tail->next = currNode->next;
26.                             free(currNode);
27.                             return;
28.                     }
29.             }
30.             prevNode = currNode;
31.             currNode = currNode->next;
32.             while (currNode != head)
33.             {
34.                     if (currNode == ptrDel)
35.                     {
36.                             if (currNode == tail)/* tail change case */
37.                                     *ptrTail = prevNode;
38.                             prevNode->next = currNode->next;
39.                             free(currNode);
40.                             return;
41.                     }
42.                     prevNode = currNode;
43.                     currNode = currNode->next;
44.             }
45.     }
```

Analysis: Find the node that need to free. Only difference is that while traversing the list end of list is tracked by the head pointer in place of NULL.

Delete a node given its value

Example 7.44:

```
1.      /* Delete a node given its value */
2.      void deleteNodeValue(NodePtr* ptrHead, NodePtr* ptrTail, int value)
3.      {
4.              printf("\n DELETE NODE GIVEN ITS VALUE \n");
5.              if (ptrHead == NULL || ptrTail == NULL)
6.                      return;
7.              NodePtr head = *ptrHead;
8.              NodePtr tail = *ptrTail;
9.              NodePtr currNode = head;
10.             NodePtr prevNode;
11.             if (head == NULL || tail == NULL)
12.                     return;
13.             if (currNode->value == value)/* one element and first element case */
14.             {
15.                     if (currNode->next == currNode)
16.                     {
17.                             *ptrHead = NULL;
18.                             *ptrTail = NULL;
19.                             free(currNode);
20.                             return;
21.                     }
22.                     else
23.                     {
24.                             *ptrHead = currNode->next;
25.                             tail->next = currNode->next;
26.                             free(currNode);
27.                             return;
28.                     }
29.             }
30.             prevNode = currNode;
31.             currNode = currNode->next;
32.             while (currNode != head)
33.             {
34.                     if (currNode->value == value)
35.                     {
36.                             if (currNode == tail)/* tail change case */
37.                                     *ptrTail = prevNode;
38.                             prevNode->next = currNode->next;
39.                             free(currNode);
40.                             return;
41.                     }
42.                     prevNode = currNode;
43.                     currNode = currNode->next;
44.             }
45.     }
```

Analysis: Find the node that need to free. Only difference is that while traversing the list end of list is tracked by the head pointer in place of NULL.

Remove Duplicate

Example 7.45:

```
1.      /* Remove Duplicate */
2.      void removeDuplicate(NodePtr* ptrHead, NodePtr* ptrTail)
3.      {
4.              printf("\n Remove Duplicate \n");
5.              NodePtr head = *ptrHead;
6.              NodePtr current = head;
7.              NodePtr deleteMe;
8.              if (!head)
9.                      return;
10.             while (current->next != head)
11.             {
12.                     if (current->value == current->next->value)
13.                     {
14.                             deleteMe = current->next;
15.                             current->next = deleteMe->next;
16.                             if (deleteMe == *ptrTail)
17.                             {
18.                                     *ptrTail = current;
19.                             }
20.                             free(deleteMe);
21.                     }
22.                     else
23.                     {
24.                             current = current->next;
25.                     }
26.             }
27.     }
```

Analysis: Considering the list is sorted repeated value nodes will be removed. Only difference is that while traversing the list end of the traversal is not checked with NULL it is checked by head pointer.

Copy List Reversed

Example 7.46:

```
1.      /* Copy List */
2.      void copyListReversed(NodePtr head, NodePtr* newPtrHead, NodePtr* newPtrTail)
3.      {
4.              printf("\n COPY LIST REVERSED \n");
5.              NodePtr curr = head;
6.              if (curr)
7.              {
8.                      insertNodeAtFront(newPtrHead, newPtrTail, curr->value);
9.                      curr = curr->next;
10.             }
```

```
11.            while (curr != head)
12.            {
13.                    insertNodeAtFront(newPtrHead, newPtrTail, curr->value);
14.                    curr = curr->next;
15.            }
16.    }
```

Analysis: The list is traversed and nodes are added to new list at the beginning. There by making the new list reverse of the given list.

Copy List

Example 7.47:

```
1.      /* Copy List */
2.      void copyList(NodePtr head, NodePtr* newPtrHead, NodePtr* newPtrTail)
3.      {
4.              printf("\n COPY LIST \n");
5.              NodePtr curr = head;
6.              if (curr)
7.              {
8.                      insertNodeAtEnd(newPtrHead, newPtrTail, curr->value);
9.                      curr = curr->next;
10.             }
11.             while (curr != head)
12.             {
13.                     insertNodeAtEnd(newPtrHead, newPtrTail, curr->value);
14.                     curr = curr->next;
15.             }
16.     }
```

Analysis:
List is traversed and nodes are added to the new list at the end. There by making the list whose value are same as the input list.

Doubly Circular list

1. For any linked list there are only three cases zero element, one element, general case
2. Any program which is likely to change the head pointer is to be passed a double pointer
3. To doubly linked list we have a few more things
   a) NULL values
   b) Only element (it generally introduces an if statement with null)
   c) Always an "if" before "while". Which will check from this head.
   d) General case (check with the initial head kept)
   e) Avoid using recursion solutions it makes life harder

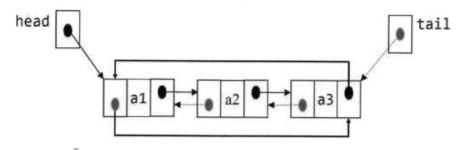

STL implement list using a double circular list.

Insert Node

Example 7.48: Insert value at the front of the list.

```
1.      #include<stdio.h>
2.      #include<stdlib.h>
3.
4.      struct Node{
5.              int value;
6.              struct Node *next;
7.              struct Node *prev;
8.      };
9.      typedef Node* NodePtr;
10.
11.     // Insert value in front
12.     int insertNode(NodePtr* ptrHead, int value)
13.     {
14.             printf("\n INSERT NODE\n");
15.             NodePtr temp=(NodePtr)malloc(sizeof(Node));
16.             if(!temp)
17.                     return 0;
18.             NodePtr head=*ptrHead;
19.             if(!head)
20.             {
21.                     temp->value=value;
22.                     temp->next=temp;
23.                     temp->prev=temp;
24.                     *ptrHead=temp;
25.             }
26.             else
27.             {
28.                     temp->value=value;
29.                     temp->next=head;
30.                     temp->prev=head->prev;
31.                     temp->prev->next = temp
32.                     head->prev=temp;
33.                     *ptrHead=temp;
34.             }
35.             return 1;
36.     }
```

Example 7.49:

```
1.      /*
2.      Delete a node given its pointer
3.      */
4.
5.      void deleteNodePtr(NodePtr* ptrHead, NodePtr ptrDel)
6.      {
7.              printf("\ndeleteNode\n");
8.              NodePtr currNode=*ptrHead;
9.              NodePtr head=*ptrHead;
10.             NodePtr nextNode,prevNode;
11.
12.             if(ptrDel==NULL ||!(*ptrHead))
13.                     return;
14.
15.             if(currNode==ptrDel)//first node
16.             {
17.                     if(currNode->next==currNode)//only node
18.                     {
19.                             *ptrHead=NULL;
20.                             free(currNode);
21.                             return;
22.                     }
23.                     else
24.                     {
25.                             prevNode=currNode->prev;
26.                             *ptrHead=nextNode=currNode->next;
27.                             prevNode->next=nextNode;
28.                             nextNode->prev=prevNode;
29.                             return;
30.                     }
31.             }
32.             currNode = currNode->next;
33.             while(currNode!=head)
34.             {
35.                     if(currNode==ptrDel)
36.                     {
37.                             prevNode=currNode->prev;
38.                             nextNode=currNode->next;
39.                             prevNode->next=nextNode;
40.                             nextNode->prev=prevNode;
41.                             free(currNode);
42.                             return;
43.                     }
44.                     currNode = currNode->next;
45.             }
46.     }
```

Analysis: Delete node in a doubly circular linked list is just same as delete node in a circular linked list. Just few extra prev pointer need to be adjusted.

Remove Duplicate

Example 7.50:

```
1.      /*
2.      *
3.      *REMOVE DUPLICATE
4.      *
5.      */
6.      void removeDuplicate(NodePtr head)
7.      {
8.              NodePtr deleteMe;
9.              NodePtr const tagHead=head;
10.
11.             if(!head)
12.                     return;
13.
14.             head=head->next;
15.
16.             while(head!=tagHead)
17.             {
18.                     if(head==head->next)//this check is to prevent only one node to be
deleted
19.                             break;
20.                     if((head->next) && head->value==head->next->value)
21.                     {
22.                             deleteMe=head->next;
23.                             head->next=deleteMe->next;
24.                             head->next->prev=head;
25.                             free(deleteMe);
26.                     }
27.                     else
28.                     {
29.                             //check for tail
30.                             head=head->next;
31.                     }
32.             }
33.     }
```

Analysis: Remove duplicate is same as remove duplicate in a circular linked list. Just one more prev pointer need to be adjusted.

Copy List Reversed

Example 7.51:

```
1.      void copyListReversed(NodePtr head, NodePtr* ptrHead2)
2.      {
3.              printf("copy list");
4.              NodePtr tempNode=NULL;
5.              NodePtr tempNode2=NULL;
6.              NodePtr const head2=head;
7.
8.              if(head)
9.              {
10.                     tempNode2=(NodePtr)malloc(sizeof(Node));
11.                     tempNode2->value=head->value;
12.                     tempNode2->next=tempNode;
13.                     tempNode2->prev=NULL;
14.                     tempNode=tempNode2;
15.                     head=head->next;
16.             }
17.
18.             while(head!=head2)
19.             {
20.                     tempNode2=(NodePtr)malloc(sizeof(Node));
21.                     tempNode2->value=head->value;
22.                     tempNode2->next=tempNode;
23.                     tempNode2->prev=NULL;
24.                     tempNode=tempNode2;
25.                     head=head->next;
26.             }
27.             *ptrHead2=tempNode;
28.     }
```

Analysis: Copy list is similar to copy list in a circular list. Just prev pointer also need to be adjusted.

Copy List

Example 7.52:

```
1.      void copyList(NodePtr head, NodePtr* ptrHead2)
2.      {
3.              printf("copy list");
4.              NodePtr headNode=NULL
5.              NodePtr tempNode=NULL;
6.              NodePtr const tagHead=head;
7.              NodePtr tailNode;
8.
9.              if(head==NULL)
10.                     return;
11.
```

```
12.          tailNode=headNode=(NodePtr)malloc(sizeof(Node));
13.          headNode->value=head->value;
14.          headNode->next=headNode;
15.          headNode->prev=headNode;
16.          head=head->next;
17.
18.          while(head!=tagHead)
19.          {
20.                  tempNode=(NodePtr)malloc(sizeof(Node));
21.                  tempNode->value=head->value;
22.                  tailNode->next=tempNode;
23.                  tempNode->prev=tailNode;
24.                  tempNode->next=headNode;
25.                  headNode->prev=tempNode;
26.                  head=head->next;
27.          }
28.          *ptrHead2=headNode;
29.   }
```

Analysis: Copy list is similar to copy list in a circular list. Just prev pointer also need to be adjusted.

Exercise

1) Insert an element kth position from the start of linked list. Return 1 if success and if list is not long enough, then return -1.
   Hint: Take a pointer advance it K steps forward, then inserts the node.

2) Insert an element kth position from the end of linked list. Return 1 if success and if list is not long enough, then return -1.
   Hint: Take a pointer advance it K steps forward, then take another pointer and advance both of them simultaneously, so that when the first pointer reach the end of a linked list that is the point where you need to insert the node.

3) Consider there is a loop in a linked list, Write a program to remove loop if there is a loop in this linked list.

4) In the above SearchList program return the count of how many instances of same value found else if value not found then return 0. For example, if the value passed is "4". The elements in the list are 1,2,4,3 & 4. The program should return 2.
   Hint: In place of return 1 in the above program increment a counter and then return counter at the end.

5) If linked list having a loop is given. Count the number of nodes in the linked list

6) We were supposed to write the complete code for the addition of polynomials using Linked Lists. This takes time if you don't have it by heart, so revise it well.

7) Given two linked lists. We have to find that whether the data in one is reverse that of data in another. No extra space should be used and traverse the linked lists only once.

8) Find the middle element in a singly linked list. Tell the complexity of your solution.
   Hint:-
   - *Approach 1:* find the length of linked list. And then find the middle element and return it.
   - *Approach 2:* use two pointer one will move fast and one will move slow make sure you handle border case properly. (Even length and odd length linked list cases.)

9) Print list in reverse order.
   Hint: Use recursion.

CHAPTER 8: STACK

Introduction

A stack is a basic data structure that organized items in last-in-first-out (LIFO) manner. Last element inserted in a stack will be the first to be removed from it.

The real-life analogy of the stack is "chapattis in hotpot", "stack of plates". Imagine a stack of plates in a dining area everybody takes a plate at the top of the stack, thereby uncovering the next plate for the next person.

Stack allow to only access the top element. The elements that are at the bottom of the stack are the one that is going to stay in the stack for the longest time.

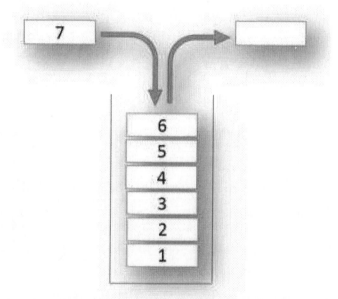

Computer science also has the common example of a stack. Function call stack is a good example of a stack. Function main() calls function foo() and then foo() calls bar(). These function calls are implemented using stack first bar() exists, then go() and then finally main().

As we navigate from web page to web page, the URL of web pages are kept in a stack, with the current page URL at the top. If we click back button, then each URL entry is popped one by one.

The Stack Abstract Data Type

Stack abstract data type is defined as a structure, which follows LIFO or last-in-first-out for the elements, added to it.
The stack should support the following operation:
1. Push(): which add a single element at the top of the stack
2. Pop(): which remove a single element from the top of a stack.
3. Top(): Reads the value of the top element of the stack (does not remove it)
4. isEmpty(): Returns 1 if stack is empty
5. Size(): returns the number of elements in a stack.

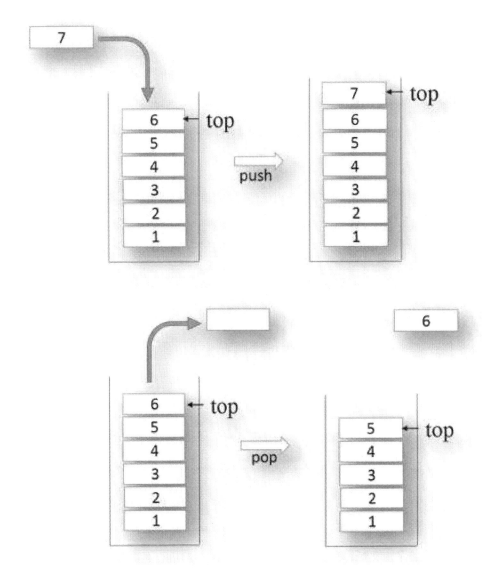

void push(int n);
Add n to the top of a stack.
int pop();
Remove the top element of the stack and return it to the caller function.

The stack can be implemented using an array or a linked list.
In array case, there are two types of implementations
- One in which array size is fixed, so it the capacity of the stack.
- Another approach is variable size array in which memory of the array is allocated using malloc and when the array is filled the size if doubled using realloc (when the stack size decreases below half the capacity is again reduced using realloc).
In case of a linked list, there is no such limit on the number of elements it can contain.

When a stack is implemented, using an array top of the stack is managed using an index variable called top.

When a stack is implemented using a linked list, push() and pop() is implemented using insert at the head of the linked list and remove from the head of the linked list.

Stack using Array (Macro)

Implement a stack using a fixed length array.

Example 8.1:

```
#define MAX_WIDTH 50

typedef struct stack{
        int top;
        int data[MAX_WIDTH];
}Stack;
```

The capacity of the stack is defined by MAX_WIDTH compile time constant.
Stack is defined which will contain the array to store the data and index to indicate the number of elements in the stack.

```
void StackInitialize(Stack* stk)
{
        stk->top = -1;
}
```

Number of elements in the stack is governed by the "top" index and top is initialized to -1 when a stack is initialized. Top index value of -1 indicates that the stack is empty in the beginning.

```
void StackPush(Stack* stk, int value)
{
        if (stk->top < MAX_WIDTH - 1)
        {
                stk->top++;
                stk->data[stk->top] = value;
                //printf("value push : %d \n", value);
        }
        else
        {
                printf("stack overflow\n");
        }
}
```

StackPush() function checks whether the stack has enough space to store one more element, then it increases the "top" by one. Finally sort the data in the stack "data" array. In case, stack is full then "stack overflow" message is printed and that value will not be added to the stack and will be ignored.

```
int StackPop(Stack* stk)
{
        if (stk->top >= 0)
        {
                int value = stk->data[stk->top];
                stk->top--;
                //printf("value pop : %d \n", value);
                return value;
        }
        printf("stack empty\n");
        return 0;
}
```

The StackPop() function is implemented, first it will check that there are some elements in the stack by checking its top index. If some element is there in the stack, then it will store the top most element value in a variable "value". The top index is reduced by one. Finally, that value is returned.

```
int StackTop(Stack* stk)
{
        int value = stk->data[stk->top];
        return value;
}
```

StackTop() function returns the value of stored in the top element of stack (does not remove it)

```
int StackIsEmpty(Stack* stk)
{
        return(stk->top == -1);
}
```

StackIsEmpty() function returns 1 if stack is empty or 0 in all other cases. By comparing the top index value with -1.

```
int StackSize(Stack* stk)
{
        return(stk->top + 1);
}
```

StackSize() function returns the number of elements in the stack. It just returns "top+1". As the top is referring the array index of the stack top variable so we need to add one to it.

Analysis:
- The user of the stack will create a stack local variable.
- Then will init it.
- Use push() and pop() functions to add / remove variables to the stack.
- Read the top element using the top() function call.
- Query regarding size of the stack using size() function call
- Query if stack is empty using isEmpty() function call

Stack using Array (Dynamic memory)

Create a stack using an array, but the memory of the array need to be taken from heap/ or the memory need to be dynamically allocated.

Example 8.2:

```
1.      #include "stdio.h"
2.      #include "stdlib.h"
3.
4.      typedef struct stack{
5.              int top;
6.              int * data;
7.              int max;
8.      }Stack;
9.
10.     void StackInitialize(Stack* stk, int size)
11.     {
12.             stk->data = (int*)malloc(size * sizeof(int));
13.             stk->top = -1;
14.             stk->max = size;
15.     }
16.
17.     int main()
18.     {
19.             Stack s;
20.             StackInitialize(&s, 10);
21.             for (int i = 0; i < 20; i++)
22.                     StackPush (&s, i);
23.             for (int i = 0; i < 20; i++)
24.                     StackPop(&s);
25.             return 0;
26.     }
```

Analysis:

Line 1: 4-8: stack structure is defined which contain its "top" index, A pointer data that will be used to point to memory allocated using malloc in *Line 12*. We keep track of the capacity of an array in a max variable of a stack structure.

Line 10: in init() function, we are passing the stack pointer and the size of memory that need to be allocated to the stack.

Line 12: we are allocating the memory sufficient to store "size" number of *integer* s. Moreover, this memory location is stored in the data field of a stack structure. Max is set to the size of the stack passed.

Line 19-20: Stack variable is created and initialized, a stack is initialized so that it will be able to contain at most 10 elements.

Line 22: push is used to add elements to the stack.

Line 24: pop is used to read and remove the top element of the stack.
Note: All the other function like, StackPush(), StackPop(), StackIsEmpty(), StackSize() and StackTop() will work for dynamically allocated stack array too.

Stack using Array (Growing capacity implementation)

In the above dynamic array implementation of a stack. Make the capacity of stack variable so that when it is nearly filled, then double the capacity of the stack.

Example 8.3:

```
1.      void StackPush(Stack* stk, int value)
2.      {
3.
4.              if (stk->top < stk->max - 1)
5.              {
6.                      stk->top++;
7.                      stk->data[stk->top] = value;
8.                      printf("value push : %d \n", value);
9.              }
10.             else
11.             {
12.                     stk->max = stk->max * 2;
13.                     stk->data = (int*)realloc(stk->data, stk->max * sizeof(int));
14.                     printf("stack size doubled");
15.                     StackPush(stk, value);
16.             }
17.     }
```

Analysis:
Line 12: In this line, we are doubling the max capacity variable of the stack.

Line 13: Size of the memory is reallocated to a bigger value in this line. The realloc function is used to increase or decrease the size of memory allocated. All the data on the stack is copied into the new location.

Line 15: finally the StackPush() function is called recursively to push the value into the increased capacity stack.

Stack using Array (Growing-Reducing capacity implementation)

You can also write a program, which can reduce the size of a dynamic array by two when the number of elements fall below max/2.

You do not want to let the capacity of the stack below the initially allocated size. You can define min length when init is called. And till that size reduce the size of the stack.

Example 8.4:

```
1.      typedef struct stack{
2.              int top;
3.              int * data;
4.              int max;
5.              int min;
6.      }Stack;
7.
```

```
8.      void initStack(Stack* stk, int size)
9.      {
10.             stk->data = (int*)malloc(size * sizeof(int));
11.             stk->top = -1;
12.             stk->max = size;
13.             stk->min = size;
14.     }
15.
16.     int StackPop (Stack* stk)
17.     {
18.             if (stk->top >= 0)
19.             {
20.                     int value = stk->data[stk->top];
21.                     stk->top--;
22.                     if (stk->top < (stk->max / 2) && stk->max > stk->min)
23.                     {
24.                             stk->max = stk->max / 2;
25.                             stk->data = (int*)realloc(stk->data, stk->max * sizeof(int));
26.                             printf("stack size halfed");
27.                     }
28.                     printf("value pop : %d \n", value);
29.                     return value;
30.             }
31.             printf("stack empty\n");
32.     }
33.
34.     int main()
35.     {
36.             Stack s;
37.             initStack(&s, 10);
38.             for (int i = 0; i < 20; i++)
39.                     StackPush(&s, i);
40.             for (int i = 0; i < 20; i++)
41.                     StackPop(&s);
42.             return 0;
43.     }
```

Analysis:

Line 22: the size of the stack is checked if it goes below half of the capacity and is greater than the minimum size.

Line 23-25: the capacity of the stack is divided by 2 and memory is reallocated to point to half size memory.

Example 8.5:

```
1.      #include<stdlib.h>
2.      #include<stdio.h>
3.
4.      struct stackNode_t{
5.              int value;
6.              stackNode_t *next;
7.      };
8.      typedef stackNode_t* stackPtr;
9.      #define ERROR_VALUE -99999
```

```
1.      void StackPush(stackPtr* dPtrHead, int value)
2.      {
3.              stackPtr tempNode=(stackPtr)malloc(sizeof(stackNode_t));
4.              if(!tempNode)
5.              {
6.                      Printf("memory shortage unable to push");
7.                      return;
8.              }
9.              tempNode->value=value;
10.             tempNode->next=*dPtrHead;
11.             *dPtrHead=tempNode;
12.     }
```

Analysis: Stack implemented using a linked list is simply insertion and deletion at the head of the linked list. In StackPush() function, memory is created for one node. Then the value is stored into that node. Finally, the node is inserted at the beginning of the list.

popNode

Implement popNode function that will return a first node pointer of the stack

Example 8.6:

```
1.      stackPtr popNode(stackPtr* dPtrHead)//free the returned node yourself
2.      {
3.              stackPtr deleteMe;
4.              if(*dPtrHead)
5.              {
6.                      deleteMe=*dPtrHead;
7.                      *dPtrHead=deleteMe->next;
8.                      return deleteMe;
9.              }
10.             else
11.             {
12.                     printf("stack empty \n");
13.                     return NULL;
14.             }
15.     }
```

Analysis:

Line 1-15: popNode() function will take the first element of the list and will return its pointer to the caller. The caller of this function will be responsible for the deletion of the memory.

Line 13: In case the stack is empty NULL will be returned.

Pop

Example 8.7: Implement the pop function that will return the value at the top of the stack.

```
1.      int pop(stackPtr* dPtrHead)//free the returned node yourself
2.      {
3.              stackPtr deleteMe;
4.              int value;
5.              if(*dPtrHead)
6.              {
7.                      deleteMe=*dPtrHead;
8.                      *dPtrHead=deleteMe->next;
9.                      value = deleteMe->data;
10.                     free(deleteMe);
11.                     return value;
12.             }
13.             else
14.             {
15.                     printf("stack empty \n");
16.                     return ERROR_VALUE;
17.             }
18.     }
```

Analysis:

Line 1-18: in pop() function first element of the list is pointed by a temporary pointer variable "deleteMe". The value of the first node is stored into a local variable "value". Head of the list will point to the next element. Then the memory pointed by deleteMe will be freed using free() and finally value is returned.

Line 16: in case stack is empty ERROR_VALUE will be returned.

Problems in Stack

Balanced Parenthesis

Example 8.8: Stacks can be used to check a program for balanced symbols (such as {}, (), []). The closing symbol should be matched with the most recently seen opening symbol.
Example: {()} is legal, {()({})} is legal, but {((} and {(}) are not legal

```c
int isBalancedParenthesis (char* expn)
{
        Stack stk;
        StackInitialize(&stk);
        int i = 0;
        char ch;
        while ((ch = expn[i++]) != '\0')
        {
                switch (ch)
                {
                case '{':
                case '[':
                case '(':
                        StackPush(&stk,ch);
                        break;

                case '}':
                        if (StackPop(&stk) != '{')
                                return 0;
                        break;

                case ']':
                        if (StackPop(&stk) != '[')
                                return 0;
                        break;

                case ')':
                        if (StackPop(&stk) != '(')
                                return 0;
                        break;
                }
        }

        return StackIsEmpty(&stk);
}
```

Analysis:
Traverse the input string when we get a opening parenthesis we push it into stack. And when we get a closing parenthesis then we pop a parenthesis from the stack and compare if it is the corresponding to the one on the closing parenthesis.
We return 0 / error if there is a mismatch of parenthesis.
If at the end of the whole staring traversal we reached to the end of the string and the stack is empty then we have balanced parenthesis.

```
int main()
{
        char expn[50] = "{()}";
        int value = isBalancedParenthesis (expn);
        printf("\n Given Expn: %s\n", expn);
        printf("\n Result after isParenthesisMatched: %d\n", value);
        return 0;
}
```

Infix, Prefix and Postfix Expressions

When we have an algebraic expression like A + B then we know that the variable is being added to variable B. This type of expression is called **infix** expression because the operator "+" is between operands A and operand B.

Now consider another infix expression A + B * C. In this expression there is a problem that in which order + and * works. Does A and B are added first and then the result is multiplied. Or B and C are multiplied first and then the result is added to A. This makes the expression ambiguous. To deal with this ambiguity we define the precedence rule or use parentheses to remove ambiguity.

So if we want to multiply B and C first and then add the result to A. Then the same expression can be written unambiguously using parentheses as A + (B * C). On the other hand, if we want to add A and B first and then the sum will be multiplied by C we will write it as (A + B) * C. So in the infix expression to make the expression unambiguous, we need parenthesis.

Infix expression: in this notation we place operator in the middle of the operands.
< operand > < operator > < operand >

Prefix expressions: In this notation we place operator at the beginning of the operands.
< operator > < operand > < operand >

Postfix expression: in this notation we place operator at the end of the operands.
< operand > < operand > < operator >

Infix Expression	Prefix Expression	Postfix Expression
A + B	+ A B	A B +
A + (B * C)	+ A * B C	A B C * +
(A + B) * C	* + ABC	A B + C *

Now comes the most obvious question why we need so unnatural Prefix or Postfix expressions when we already have infix expressions which words just fine for us.

The answer to this is that infix expressions are ambiguous and they need parenthesis to make them unambiguous. While postfix and prefix notations don't need any parenthesis.

Example 8.9:

```
void infixToPostfix(char* expn,char* output)
{
        Stack stk;
        StackInitialize(&stk);
        char ch, op;
        int i = 0;
        int index =0;
        int digit = 0;
        while ((ch = expn[i++]) != '\0')
        {
                if (isdigit(ch))
                {
                        output[index++] = ch;
                        digit=1;
                }
                else
                {
                        if(digit)
                        {
                                output[index++] = ' ';
                                digit = 0;
                        }
                        switch (ch)
                        {
                        case '+':
                        case '-':
                        case '*':
                        case '/':
                        case '%':
                        case '^':
                                while (!StackIsEmpty(&stk) && precedence(ch) <=
                                                        precedence(StackTop(&stk)))
                                {
                                        op = StackPop(&stk);
                                        output[index++] = op;
                                        output[index++] = ' ';
                                }
                                StackPush(&stk, ch);
                                break;
                        case '(':
                                StackPush(&stk, ch);
                                break;
                        case ')':
                                while (!StackIsEmpty(&stk) && (op = StackPop(&stk)) != '(')
                                {
                                        output[index++] = op;
                                        output[index++] = ' ';
                                }
```

```
                              break;
                         }
                    }
               }
          while (!StackIsEmpty(&stk))
          {
               op = StackPop(&stk);
               output[index++] = op;
               output[index++] = ' ';
          }
          output[index++] = '\0';
     }
int precedence(char x)
{
     if (x == '(')
          return(0);
     if (x == '+' || x == '-')
          return(1);
     if (x == '*' || x == '/' || x == '%')
          return(2);
     if (x == '^')
          return(3);
     return(4);
}
```

Analysis:

1. Print operands in the same order as they arrive.

2. If the stack is empty or contains a left parenthesis "(" on top, we should push the incoming operator in the stack.

3. If the incoming symbol is a left parenthesis "(", push left parenthesis in the stack.

4. If the incoming symbol is a right parenthesis ")", pop from the stack and print the operators till you see a left parenthesis ")". Discard the pair of parentheses.

5. If the precedence of incoming symbol is higher than the operator at the top of the stack, then push it to the stack.

6. If the incoming symbol has an equal precedence compared to the top of the stack, use association. If the association is left to right then pop and print the symbol at the top of the stack and then push the incoming operator. If the association is right to left, then push the incoming operator.

7. If the precedence of incoming symbol is lower than the operator on the top of the stack, then pop and print the top operator. Then compare the incoming operator against the new operator at the top of the stack.

8. At the end of the expression, pop and print all operators on the stack.

Infix-to-Prefix Conversion

Example 8.10:

```
void infixToPrefix(char* expn,char* output)
{
     reverseString(expn);
     replaceParanthesis(expn);
     infixToPostfix(expn, output);
     reverseString(output);
}
```

```
void reverseString(char *a)
{
        int lower=0;
        int upper=strlen(a)-1;
        char tempChar;
        while(lower<upper)
        {
                tempChar=a[lower];
                a[lower]=a[upper];
                a[upper]=tempChar;

                lower++;
                upper--;
        }
}
```

```
void replaceParanthesis(char *a)
{
        int lower=0;
        int upper=strlen(a)-1;
        char tempChar;
        while(lower<=upper)
        {
                if(a[lower]  == '(')
                        a[lower]  = ')';
                else if(a[lower]  == ')')
                        a[lower]  = '(';
                lower++;
        }
}
```

```
int main()
{
        char expn[50] = "10 + ((3)) * 5 / (16 - 4)";
        printf("\n Given Expn: %s\n", expn);
        infixToPostFix(expn);

        char expn2[50] = "(5 * 3) ^ (4 - 2)";
        printf("\n Given Expn: %s\n", expn2);
        infixToPostFix(expn2);

        return 0;
}
```

Analysis:

1. Reverse the given infix expression.
2. Replace '(' with ')' and ')' with '(' in the reversed expression.
3. Now apply infix to postfix subroutine already discussed.
4. Reverse the generated postfix expression and this will give required prefix expression.

Postfix Evaluate

Write a postfixEvaluate() function to evaluate a postfix expression.
Such as: 1 2 + 3 4 + *

Example 8.11:

```
int postfixEvaluate(char* postfx)
{
        Stack s;
        StackInitialize(&s);
        int i = 0, op1, op2;
        char ch;
        int digit = 0;
        int value = 0;
        while ((ch = postfx[i++]) != '\0')
        {
                if (isdigit(ch))
                {
                        digit = 1;
                        value = value * 10 + (ch - '0');
                }
                else if (ch == ' ')
                {
                        if (digit == 1)
                        {
                                StackPush(&s, value); /* Push the operand */
                                digit = 0;
                                value = 0;
                        }
                }
                else
                {
                        op2 = StackPop(&s);
                        op1 = StackPop(&s);
                        switch (ch)
                        {
                        case '+': StackPush(&s, op1 + op2); break;
                        case '-': StackPush(&s, op1 - op2); break;
                        case '*': StackPush(&s, op1 * op2); break;
                        case '/': StackPush(&s, op1 / op2); break;
                        }
                }
        }
        return StackTop(&s);
}
```

```
int main()
{
        char postfx[50] = "6 5 2 3 + 8 * + 3 + *";
        int value = postfixEvaluate (postfx);
        printf("\n Given Postfix Expn: %s\n", postfx);
        printf("\n Result after Evaluation: %d\n", value);
        return 0;
}
```

Analysis:

1) Create a stack to store values or operands.
2) Scan through the given expression and do following for each element:
   a)   If the element is a number, then push it into the stack.
   b)   If the element is a operator, then pop values from the stack. Evaluate the operator over the values and push the result into the stack.
3) When the expression is scanned completely, the number in the stack is the final result.

Min stack

Design a stack in which get minimum value in stack should also work in *O(1) Time Complexity*.

Hint: Keep two stack one will be general stack which will just keep the elements. The second will keep the min value.
   1.   Push: Push an element to the top of stack1. Compare the new value with the value at the top of the stack2. If the new value is smaller, then push the new value into stack2. Or push the value at the top of the stack2 to itself once more.
   2.   Pop: Pop an element from top of stack1 and return. Pop an element from top of stack2 too.
   3.   Min: Read from the top of the stack2 this value will be the min.

Palindrome string

Find if given string is a palindrome or not using a stack.
Definition of palindrome: A palindrome is a sequence of characters which is same backward or forward.
Eg. "AAABBBCCCBBBAAA", "ABA" & "ABBA"

Hint: Push characters to the stack till the half length of the string. Then pop these characters and then compare. Make sure you take care of the odd length and even length.

Reverse Stack

Given a stack how to reverse the elements of the stack without using any other data-structure. You cannot use another stack too.
Time Complexity and *Space Complexity* is wrong, it is *O(n)* for both cases.

Hint: Use recursion (system stack.) When you go inside the stack pop elements from stack in each subsequent call till stack is empty. Then push these elements one by one when coming out of the recursion. The elements will be reversed.

Example 8.12:

```
void reverseStack(Stack* stk)
{
        int data;
        if (StackIsEmpty(stk))
                return;
        data = StackPop(stk);
        reverseStack(stk);
        insertAtBottom(stk, data);
}
```

Insert At Bottom

Example 8.13:

```
void insertAtBottom(Stack* stk, int value)
{
        if (StackIsEmpty(stk))
                StackPush(stk, value);
        else
        {

                int temp = StackPop(stk);
                insertAtBottom(stk, value);
                StackPush(stk, temp);

        }
}
```

Depth-First Search with a Stack

In a depth-first search we traverse down a path until we get a dead end; then we *backtrack* by popping a stack to get an alternative path.
- Create a stack
- Create a start point
- Push the start point onto the stack
- While (value searching not found and the stack is not empty)
  - Pop the stack
  - Find all possible points after the one which we just tried
  - Push these points onto the stack

Stack using a queue

How to implement a stack using a queue. Analyze the running time of the stack operations.

See queue chapter for this.

Example 8.14: How to implement two stacks using one single array.

```
#define MAX_SIZE 50

typedef struct stack{
        int top1;
        int top2;
        int data[MAX_SIZE];
}Stack;
```

```
void StackInitialize(Stack* stk)
{
        stk->top1 = -1;
        stk->top2 = MAX_SIZE;
}
```

```
void StackPush1 (Stack* stk, int data)
{
  if (stk->top1 < stk->top2 - 1)
  {
    stk->data[++stk->top1] = data;
  }
  else
  {
    printf ("Stack is Full!\n");
  }
}
```

```
int StackPop1 (Stack* stk)
{
  if (stk->top1 >= 0)
  {
    int value = stk->data[stk->top1--];
    printf ("%d is being popped from Stack 1\n", value);
        return value;
  }
  else
  {
    printf ("Stack Empty! Cannot Pop\n");
  }
  return INT_MIN;
}
```

```
void StackPush2 (Stack* stk, int data)
{
  if (stk->top1 < stk->top2 - 1)
  {
    stk->data[--stk->top2] = data;
  }
  else
  {
    printf ("Stack is Full!\n");
  }
}
```

```
int StackPop2 (Stack* stk)
{
  if (stk->top2 < MAX_SIZE)
  {
    int value = stk->data[stk->top2++];
    printf ("%d is being popped from Stack 2\n", value);
        return value;
  }
  else
  {
    printf ("Stack Empty! Cannot Pop\n");
  }
  return INT_MIN;
}
```

Analysis: Same array is used to implement two stack. First stack is filled from the beginning of the array and second stack is filled from the end of the array. Overflow and underflow conditions need to be taken care of carefully.

Stock Span Problem

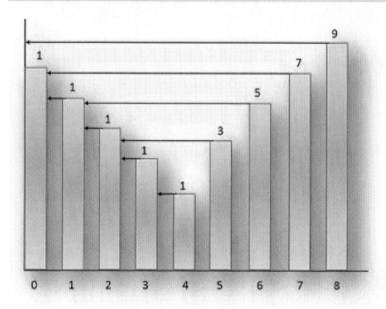

187

Approach 1:

```
int*  StockSpanRange(int arr[], int size)
{
        int *SR = (int*)malloc(size * sizeof(int));
        SR[0] = 1;

        for (int i = 1; i < size; i++)
        {
                SR[i] = 1;
                for (int j = i - 1; (j >= 0) && (arr[i] >= arr[j]); j--)
                        SR[i]++;
        }
        return SR;
}
```

Approach 2:

```
int* StockSpanRange (int arr[], int size)
{
        Stack stk;
        int *SR = (int*)malloc(size * sizeof(int));
        StackInitialize(&stk);
        StackPush(&stk, 0);
        SR[0] = 1;

        for (int i = 1; i < size; i++)
        {
                while (!StackIsEmpty(&stk) && arr[StackTop(&stk)] <= arr[i])
                {
                        StackPop(&stk);
                }

                SR[i] = (StackIsEmpty(&stk)) ? (i + 1) : (i - StackTop(&stk));
                StackPush(&stk, i);
        }
        return SR;
}
```

Get Max Rectangular Area in a Histogram

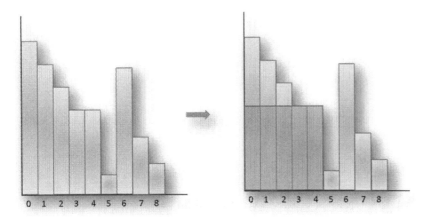

Approach 1

```
int GetMaxArea(int arr[], int size)
{
        int maxArea = -1;
        int currArea;
        int minHeight = 0;
        for (int i = 1; i < size; i++)
        {
                minHeight = arr[i];
                for (int j = i - 1; j >= 0; j--)
                {
                        if (minHeight > arr[j])
                                minHeight = arr[j];

                        currArea = minHeight * (i - j + 1);

                        if (maxArea < currArea)
                                maxArea = currArea;
                }
        }
        return maxArea;
}
```

Approach 2: Divide and conquer

Approach 3

```
int GetMaxArea(int arr[], int size)
{
        Stack stk;
        StackInitialize(&stk);
        int maxArea = 0;
        int top;
        int topArea;
        int i = 0;
        while (i < size)
        {
                while ( (i < size) && (StackIsEmpty(&stk) || arr[StackTop(&stk)] <= arr[i]) )
                {
                        StackPush(&stk, i);
                        i++;
                }
                while ( !StackIsEmpty(&stk) && ( i == size || arr[StackTop(&stk)] > arr[i]) )
                {
                        top = StackTop(&stk);
                        StackPop(&stk);
                        topArea = arr[top] * (StackIsEmpty(&stk) ? i : i - StackTop(&stk) - 1);
                        if (maxArea < topArea)
                                maxArea = topArea;
```

```
        }
        return maxArea;
}
```

Pros and cons of array and linked list implementation of stack.

Linked lists: List implementation uses 1 pointer extra memory per item. There is no size restriction.

Arrays: Allocated a constant amount of space, when the stack is nearly empty, then lost of space is waste as it's not used. Maximum size is determined when the stack is created.

Uses of Stack

- Recursion can also be done using stack. (In place of the system stack)
- The function call is implemented using stack.
- Some problems when we want to reverse a sequence, we just push everything in stack and pop from it.
- Grammar checking, balance parenthesis, infix to postfix conversion, postfix evaluation of expression etc.

Exercise

Ex 1: Converting Decimal Numbers to Binary Numbers using stack data structure.

Hint: store reminders into the stack and then print the stack.

Ex 2: Convert an infix expression to prefix expression.

Hint: Reverse given expression, Apply infix to postfix, and then reverse the expression again.
Step 1. Reverse the infix expression.
        5^E+D*)C^B+A(
Step 2. Make Every '(' as ')' and every ')' as '('
        5^E+D*(C^B+A)
Step 3. Convert an expression to postfix form.

Step 4. Reverse the expression.
        +*+A^BCD^E5

Ex 3: Write an HTML opening tag and closing tag matching program.
Hint: parenthesis matching.

Ex 4: Write a function that will do Postfix to Infix Conversion

Ex 5: : Write a function that will do Prefix to Infix Conversion

Ex 6 : Write a palindrome matching function which ignore characters other than English alphabet and digits.
String "Madam, I'm Adam." should return true.

CHAPTER 9: QUEUE

Introduction

A queue is a basic data structure that organized items in first-in-first-out (FIFO) manner. First element inserted into a queue will be the first to be removed. It is also known as "first-come-first-served".

The real life analogy of queue is typical lines in which we all participate time to time.
- We wait in a line of railway reservation counter.
- We wait in the cafeteria line (to pop a plate from "stack of plates").
- We wait in a queue when we call to some customer case.

The elements which are at the front of the queue are the one which stayed in the queue for the longest time.

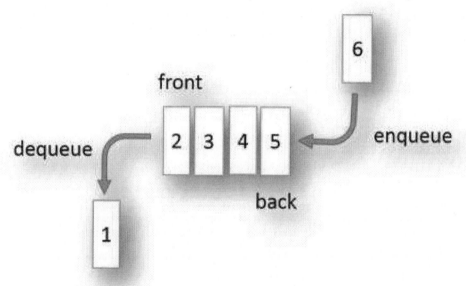

Computer science also has common examples of queues. We issue a print command from our office to a single printer per floor, print task gets lined up in a printer queue. The print command that was issued first will be printed before the next commands in line.

In addition to printing queues operating system is also using different queues to control process scheduling. Processes are added to processing queue which is used by an operating system for various scheduling algorithms.

Soon we will be reading about graphs and will come to know about breadth-first traversal which uses a queue.

The Queue Abstract Data Type

Queue abstract data type is defined as a structure which follows FIFO or first-in-first-out for the elements added to it.
Queue should support the following operation:
1. enqueue(): Which add a single element at the back of a queue
2. dequeue(): Which remove a single element from the front of a queue.
3. isEmpty(): Returns 1 if the queue is empty
4. size(): Returns the number of elements in a queue.

0	1	2	3	4	5	6	7	8	9
1	2	3	4	5	6	7			

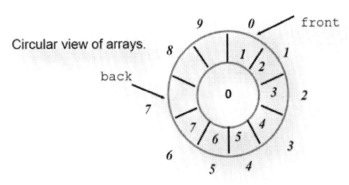

Circular view of arrays.

Example 9.1:

```
#define SIZE 100
#define ERROR_VALUE -999

typedef struct Queue_t{
        int front;
        int back;
        int size;
        int data[SIZE];
}Queue;
```

```
void QueueInitialize(Queue* que)
{
        que->back = 0;
        que->front = 0;
        que->size = 0;
}
```

```
int QueueIsEmpty(Queue* que)
{
        return que->size == 0;
}
```

```
int QueueSize(Queue* que)
{
        return que->size;
}
```

```c
void Enqueue(Queue* que, int value)
{
        if (que->size >= SIZE )
        {
                printf("\n Queue is full.");
                return;
        }
        else
        {
                que->size++;
                que->data[que->back] = value;
                que->back = (++(que->back)) % (SIZE - 1);
                //printf("\n enqueue: %d ", value);
        }
}
```

```c
int Dequeue(Queue* que)
{
        int value;
        if (que->size <= 0)
        {
                printf("\n Queue is empty.");
                return ERROR_VALUE;
        }
        else
        {
                que->size--;
                value = que->data[que->front];
                que->front = (++(que->front)) % (SIZE - 1);
        }
        return value;
}
```

```c
int main()
{
        Queue que;
        QueueInitialize(&que);
        for (int i = 0; i < 20; i++)
        {
                Enqueue(&que,i);
        }
        for (int i = 0; i < 20; i++)
        {
                Dequeue(&que);
        }
        return 0;
}
```

193

Analysis:

1. Hear queue is created from an array of size 100.
2. QueueInitialize function initialize the number of element in queue to zero. By assigning front, back and size of queue to zero.
3. Enqueue insert one element at the back of the queue.
4. Dequeue delete one element from the front of the queue.

Queue Using linked list

```
struct queueNode_t{
        int value;
        queueNode_t *next;
};
typedef queueNode_t* queuePtr;
#define ERROR_VALUE -99999
```

A node of a queue using linked list looks same as linked list.

Enqueue

Enqueue into a queue using linked list. Nodes are added to the end of the linked list. Below diagram indicates how a new node is added to the list. The tail is modified every time when a new value is added to the queue. But the head is also updated in the case when there is no element in the queue and when that first element is added to the queue both head and tail will be pointing to it.

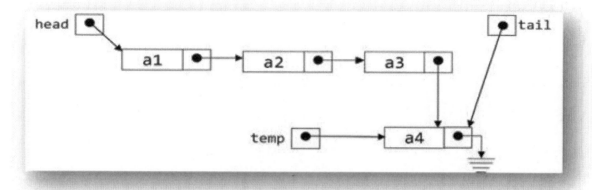

Example 9.2:

```
1.      void enqueue(queuePtr* dPtrHead,queuePtr* dPtrTail,int value)
2.      {
3.              queuePtr tempNode=(queuePtr)malloc(sizeof(queueNode_t));
4.              if(!tempNode)
5.              {
6.                      Printf("memory shortage unable to enqueue");
7.                      return;
8.              }
9.              tempNode->value=value;
10.             tempNode->next=NULL;
11.             if(*dPtrHead==NULL)
12.             {
13.                     *dPtrTail=tempNode;
14.                     *dPtrHead=tempNode;
15.             }
16.             else
17.             {
18.                     (*dPtrTail)->next=tempNode;
19.                     *dPtrTail=tempNode;
20.             }
21.     }
```

Analysis: Enqueue operation add one element at the end of the Queue (linked list).

Dequeue

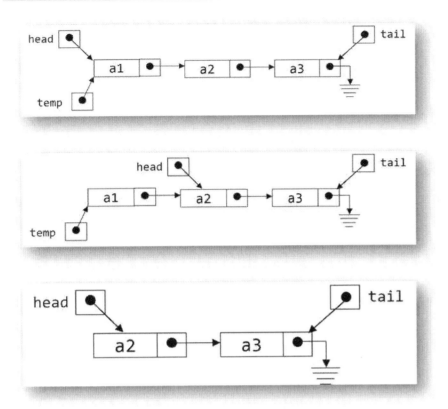

In this we need the tail pointer as it may be the case there was only one element in the list and the tail pointer will also be modified in case of the dequeue.

Example 9.3:

```
1.      int dequeue(queuePtr* dPtrHead,queuePtr* dPtrTail)
2.      {
3.              int value;
4.              queuePtr deleteMe;
5.              if(*dPtrHead)
6.              {
7.                      deleteMe=*dPtrHead;
8.                      *dPtrHead=deleteMe->next;
9.                      value=deleteMe->value;
10.                     free(deleteMe);
11.                     if(*dPtrHead==NULL)
12.                             *dPtrTail=NULL;
13.                     return value;
14.             }
15.             else
16.             {
17.                     Printf("queue empty \n");
18.                     return ERROR_VALUE;
19.             }
20.     }
```

Analysis:
Dequeue operation removes first node from the start of the queue(linked list).

Queue using a stack

How to implement a queue using a stack. You can use more than one stack.

Solution: We can use two stack to implement queue. We need to simulate first in first our using stack.
   a) Enqueue Operation: new elements are added to the top of first stack.
   b) Dequeue Operation: elements are popped from the second stack and when second stack is empty then all the elements of first stack are popped one by one and pushed to second stack.

Example 9.4:

```
#include "Stack.h"

typedef struct SQueue_t
{
        Stack stk1;
        Stack stk2;
}SQueue;
```

```
void QueueInitialize(SQueue* que)
{
        StackInitialize(&que->stk1);
        StackInitialize(&que->stk2);
}
```

```
void Enqueue(SQueue* que, int value)
{
        StackPush(&que->stk1, value);
}
```

```
int Dequeue(SQueue* que)
{
        int value;
        if (!StackIsEmpty(&que->stk2))
                return StackPop(&que->stk2);

        while (!StackIsEmpty(&que->stk1))
        {
                value = StackPop(&que->stk1);
                StackPush(&que->stk2, value);
        }
        return StackPop(&que->stk2);
}
```

```
int main()
{
        SQueue que;
        QueueInitialize(&que);
        Enqueue(&que,1);
        Enqueue(&que, 11);
        Enqueue(&que, 111);
        printf("%d ", Dequeue(&que));
        printf("%d ", Dequeue(&que));
        printf("%d ", Dequeue(&que));
}
```

Stack using a Queue

Implement stack using a queue.

Solution 1: use two queue
Push: enqueue new elements to queue1.
Pop: while size of queue1 is bigger than 1. Push all items from queue 1 to queue 2 except the last item. Switch the name of queue 1 and queue 2. And return the last item.
Push operation is *O(1)* and Pop operation is *O(n)*

Solution 2: This same can be done using just one queue.
Push: enqueue the element to queue.
Pop: find the size of queue. If size is zero then return error. Else if size is positive then dequeue size- 1 elements from the queue and again enqueue to the same queue. At last dequeue the next element and return it.
Push operation is *O(1)* and Pop operation is *O(n)*

Solution 3: In the above solutions the push is efficient and pop is un efficient can we make pop efficient *O(1)* and push inefficient *O(n)*
Push : enqueue new elements to queue2. Then enqueue all the elements of queue 1 to queue 2. Then switch names of queue1 and queue 2.
Pop: dequeue from queue1
Push operation is *O(n)* and Pop operation is *O(1)*

Reverse a stack

Reverse a stack using queue
Solution:
   a) Pop all the elements of stack and enqueue them into a queue.
   b) Then dequeue all the elements of the queue into stack
   c) We have the elements of the stack reversed.

Reverse a queue

Reverse a queue using stack
Solution:
   a) Dequeue all the elements of the queue into stack
   b) Then pop all the elements of stack and enqueue them into a queue.
   c) We have the elements of the queue reversed.

Breadth-First Search with a Queue

In breadth-first search, we explore all the nearest nodes first by finding all possible successors and enqueue them to a queue.

a) Create a queue
b) Create a start point
c) Enqueue the start point onto the queue
d) while (value searching not found and the queue is not empty)
   o Dequeue from the queue
   o Find all possible points after the last one tried
   o Enqueue these points onto the queue

Josephus problem

There are n people standing in a queue waiting to be executed. The counting begins at the front of the queue. In each step, k number of people are dequeued and again enqueued one by one from the queue. Then the next person is executed. The execution proceeds around the circle until only the last person remains, who is given freedom.

Find that position where you want to stand and gain your freedom.

Solution:

1) Just insert *integer* for 1 to k in a queue. (corresponds to k people)
2) Define a Kpop() function such that it will dequeue and enqueue the queue k-1 times and then dequeue one more time. (This man is dead.)
3) Repeat second step till size of queue is 1.
4) Print the value in the last element. This is the solution.

Exercise

1) Implement queue using dynamic memory allocation. Such that the implementation should follow the following constraints.

   a) The user should use memory allocation from the heap using malloc() function. In the above code make this change in the init() function. In this, you need to take care of the max value in the queue structure. (You don't need # define).

   b) Once you are done with the above exercise and you are able to test your queue. Then you can add some more complexity to your code. In enqueue() function when the queue is full in place of printing "Queue is full" you should allocate more space using realloc() function call.

   c) Once you are done with the above exercise. Now in dequeue function once you are below half of the capacity of the queue, you need to decrease the size of the queue by half. You should add one more variable "min" to queue structure so that you can track what is the original value capacity passed at init() function. And the capacity of the queue will not go below the value passed in the init() function.

(If you are not able to solve the above exercise, then have a look into stack chapter where we have done similar for stack)

2) Implement the below function for the queue:

   a. IsEmpty: This is left as an exercise for the user. Take a variable which will take care of the size of a queue if the value of that variable is zero, isEmpty should return 1 (true). If the queue is not empty, then it should return 0 (false).

    b.   Size: Use the size variable to be used under size function call. Size() function should return the number of elements in the queue.

3) Implement stack using a queue. Write a program for this problem. You can use just one queue.

4) Write a program to Reverse a stack using queue

5) Write a program to Reverse a queue using stack

6) Write a program to solve Josephus problem (algo already discussed.). There are n people standing in a queue waiting to be executed. The counting begins at the front of the queue. In each step, k number of people are dequeued and again enqueued one by one from the queue. Then the next person is executed. The elimination proceeds around the circle until only the last person remains, who is given freedom. Find that position where you want to stand and gain your freedom.

7) Write a CompStack() function which takes a pointer to two stack structure as an argument and return true or false depending upon whether all the elements of the stack are equal or not. You are given isEqual(int, int) which will compare and return 1 if both values are equal and 0 if they are different.

CHAPTER 10: TREE

Introduction

We have already read about various linear data structures like an array, linked list, stack, queue etc. Both array and linked list have a drawback of linear time required for searching an element.

A tree is a nonlinear data structure which is used to represent hierarchical relationships (parent-child relationship). Each node is connected by another node by directed edges.

Example 1: Tree in organization

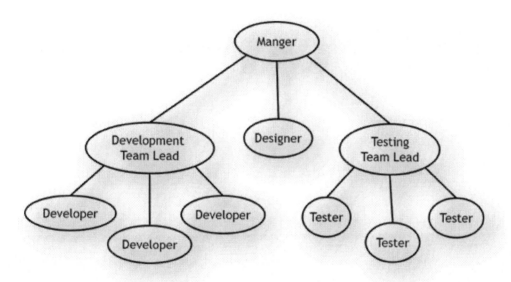

Example 2: Tree in a file system

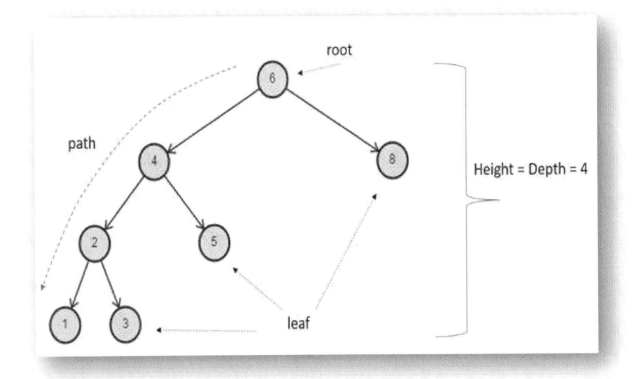

Root: The root of the tree is the only node in the tree that has no incoming edges. It is the top node of a tree.

Node: It is a fundamental element of a tree. Each node has data and two pointers which may point to null or its child's.

Edge: It is also a fundamental part of a tree which is used to connect two nodes.

Path: A path is an ordered list of nodes that are connected by edges.

Leaf: A leaf node is a node that has no children.

Height of the tree: The height of a tree is the number of edges on the longest path between the root and a leaf.

The level of node: The level of a node is the number of edges on the path from the root node to that node.

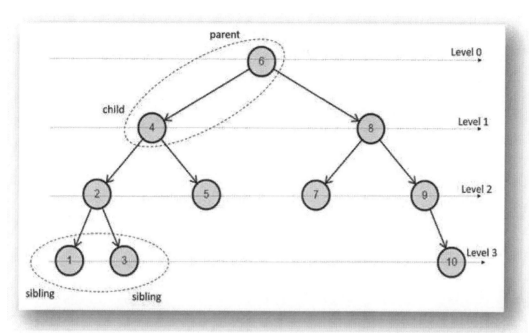

Children: Nodes that have incoming edges from the same node to be said to be the children of that node.

Parent: Node is a parent of all the child nodes which are linked by outgoing edges.

Sibling: Nodes in the tree that are children of the same parent are said to be siblings'

Ancestor: A node reachable by repeated moving from child to parent.

Binary Tree

A binary tree is a type tree in which each node has at most two children (0, 1 or 2), which are referred to as the left child and the right child.

Below is a node of the binary tree with "a" stored as data and whose left child (lChild) and whose right child (rchild) both pointing towards NULL.

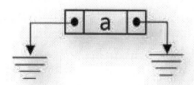

Below is a structure used to define node, we have typedef node pointer to treeptr

```
struct treeNode_t{
        int value;
        treeNode_t * lChild;
        treeNode_t * rChild;
};

typedef treeNode_t* treePtr;
```

203

Below is a binary tree whose nodes contains data from 1 to 10

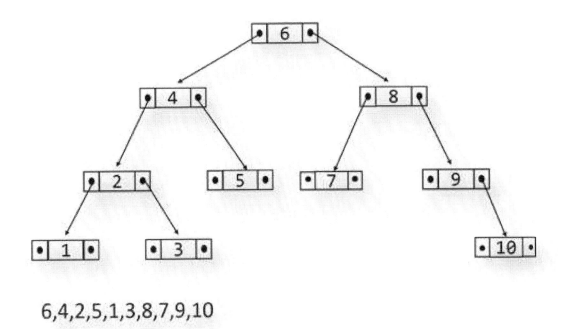

6,4,2,5,1,3,8,7,9,10

In the rest of the book binary tree will be represented as below:

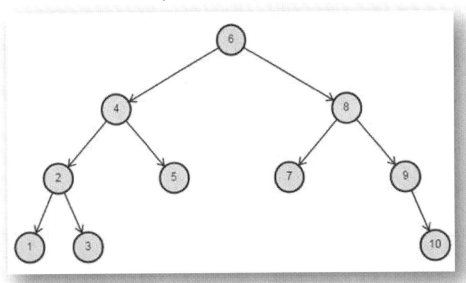

Properties of Binary tree are:
1. The maximum number of nodes on level i of a binary tree is 2^i , where i >= 1
2. The maximum number of nodes in a binary tree of depth k is 2^{k+1}, where k >= 1
3. There is exactly one path from the root to any nodes in a tree.
4. A tree with N nodes have exactly N-1 edges connecting these nodes.
5. The height of a complete binary tree of N nodes is $\log_2 N$.

Types of Binary trees

Complete binary tree

In a complete binary tree, every level except the last one is completely filled. All nodes in the left are filled first, then the right one.
A binary heap is an example of a complete binary tree.

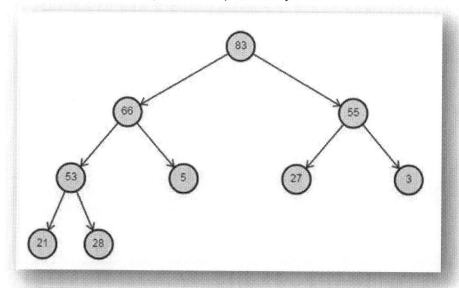

Full/ Strictly binary tree

The full binary tree is a binary tree in which each node has exactly zero or two children.

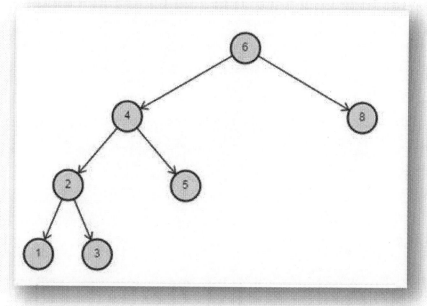

Perfect binary tree

The perfect binary tree is a type of full binary tree in which each non leaf node has exactly two child nodes.
All leaf nodes have identical path length and all possible node slots are occupied

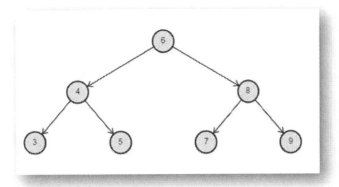

Right skewed binary tree

A binary tree in which each node is having either only a right child or no child (leaf) is called as right skewed binary tree

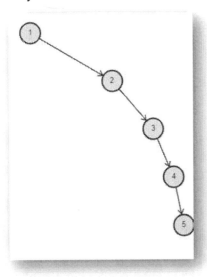

Left skewed binary tree

A binary tree in which each node is having either only a left child or no child (leaf) is called as Left skewed binary tree

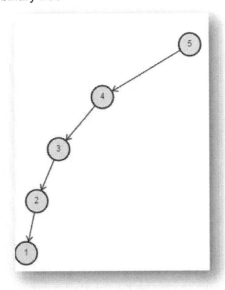

Height-balanced Binary Tree

A height-balanced binary tree is a binary tree such that the left & right subtrees for any given node differ in height by max one.

Note: Each complete binary tree is a height-balanced binary tree

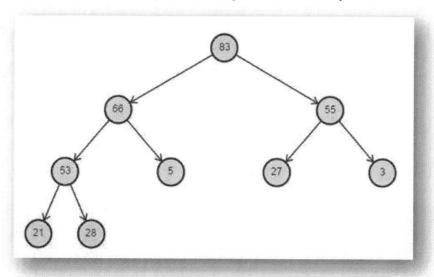

AVL tree and RB tree are an example of height balanced tree we will discuss these trees in advance tree topic.

Problems in Binary Tree

Create a Complete binary tree

Create a binary tree given a list of values in an array.

Solution: Since there is no order defined in a binary tree, so nodes can be inserted in any order so it can be a skewed binary tree. But it is inefficient to do anything in a skewed binary tree so we will create a Complete binary tree. At each node the middle value stored in the array is assigned to node and left of array is passed to the left child of the node to create left sub-tree. And right portion of array is passed to right child of the node to crate right sub-tree.

Example 10.1:

```
treePtr CompleteBinaryTree(int* arr, int start, int size)
{
        treePtr root = NULL;

        root = createNode(arr[start]);

        int left = 2 * start + 1;
        int right = 2 * start + 2;

        if (left < size)
                root->lChild = CompleteBinaryTree(arr, left, size);
        if (right < size)
                root->rChild = CompleteBinaryTree(arr, right, size);

        return root;
}
```

```
treePtr createNode(int val)
{
        treePtr root = (treePtr)malloc(sizeof(treeNode_t));
        root->value = val;
        root->lChild = root->rChild = NULL;
        return root;
}
```

```
int main()
{
        treePtr root = NULL;
        int A[] = { 1, 2, 3, 4, 5, 6, 7, 8, 9, 10 };
        root = CompleteBinaryTree(A, 0, 10);
        return 0;
}
```

Complexity Analysis:
This is an efficient algorithm for creating a complete binary tree.
Time Complexity: $O(n)$ Space Complexity: $O(n)$

Pre-Order Traversal

Traversal is a process of visiting each node of a tree. In Pre-Order Traversal parent is visited/traversed first, then left child and right child. Pre-Order traversal is a type of depth-first traversal.

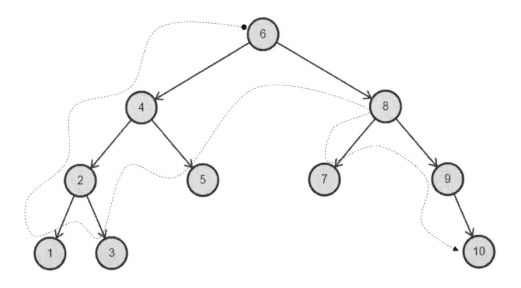

Solution:
Preorder traversal is done using recursion. At each node first the value stored in it is printed and then followed by the value of left child and right child. At each node its value is printed followed by calling printTree() function to its left and right child to print left and right sub-tree.

Example 10.2:

```
1.      void printPreorder (treePtr root) /* pre order */
2.      {
3.              if(root)
4.              {
5.                      printf("%d ", root->value);
6.                      printPreorder (root->lChild);
7.                      printPreorder (root->rChild);
8.              }
9.      }
```

Output:

```
6 4 2 1 3 5 8 7 9 10
```

Complexity Analysis: Time Complexity: $O(n)$ Space Complexity: $O(n)$

Note: When there is an algorithm in which all nodes are traversed, then complexity can't be less then $O(n)$. When there is a large portion of the tree which is not traversed then complexity reduces.

Post-Order Traversal

In Post-Order Traversal left child is visited/traversed first, then right child and last parent
Post-Order traversal is a type of depth-first traversal.

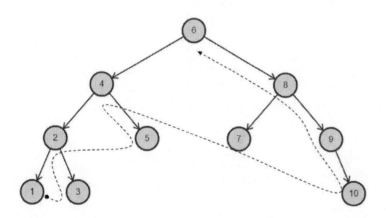

Solution: In post order traversal first the left child is traversed then right child and in the end current node value is printed to the screen.

Example 10.3:

```
1.      void printPostorder(treePtr root) /* post order */
2.      {
3.              if(root)
4.              {
5.                      printPostorder (root->lChild);
6.                      printPostorder (root->rChild);
7.                      printf("%d ", root->value);
8.              }
9.      }
```

Output:

1 3 2 5 4 7 10 9 8 6

Complexity Analysis: Time Complexity: $O(n)$ Space Complexity: $O(n)$

In-Order Traversal

In In-Order Traversal left child is visited/traversed first, then the parent and last right child
In-Order traversal is a type of depth-first traversal. The output of In-Order traversal of BST is a sorted list.

Solution:

In In-Order traversal first the value of left child is traversed, then the value of node is printed to the screen and then the value of right child is traversed.

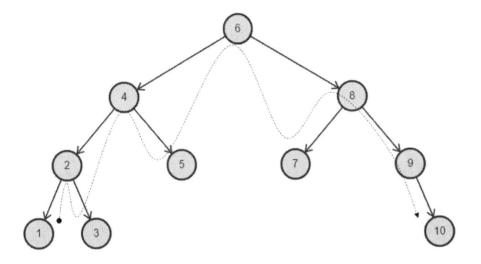

Example 10.4:

```
1.      void printInorder (treePtr root) /* in order */
2.      {
3.              if(root)
4.              {
5.                      printInorder (root->lChild);
6.                      printf("%d ", root->value);
7.                      printInorder (root->rChild);
8.              }
9.      }
```

Output:

1 2 3 4 5 6 7 8 9 10

Complexity Analysis: Time Complexity: $O(n)$ Space Complexity: $O(n)$

Note: Pre-Order, Post-Order, and In-Order traversal are for all binary trees. They can be used to traverse any kind of a binary tree.

Level order traversal / Breadth First traversal

Write C code to implement level order traversal of a tree. Such that nodes at depth k is printed before nodes at depth k+1.

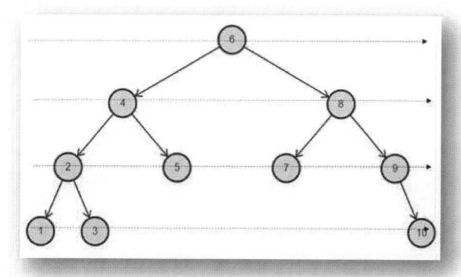

Solution:

Level order traversal or Breadth First traversal of a tree is done using a queue. At the start the root node pointer is added to queue. The traversal of tree happens till its queue is empty. When we traverse the tree we first dequeue an element from the queue, print the value stored in that node and then its left child and right child will be added to the queue.

Example 10.5:

```
1.      void printBredthFirst(treePtr root)
2.      {
3.              std::queue<treePtr> que;
4.              treePtr temp;
5.              que.push(root);
6.              while(!que.empty())
7.              {
8.                      temp= que.front();
9.                      que.pop();
10.                     printf(" %d ", temp->value);
11.                     if(temp->lChild)
12.                             que.push(temp->lChild);
13.                     if(temp->rChild)
14.                             que.push(temp->rChild);
15.             }
16.     }
```

Complexity Analysis:

Time Complexity: $O(n)$ Space Complexity: $O(n)$

Print Depth First without using the recursion / system stack.

Solution: Depth first traversal of the tree is done using recursion by using system stack. The same can be done using stack. In the start root node pointer is added to the stack. The whole tree is traversed till the stack is empty. In each iteration an element is popped from the stack its value is printed to screen. Then right child and then left child of the node is added to stack.

Example 10.6:

```
1.      void printDepthFirst(treePtr root)
2.      {
3.              std::stack<treePtr> st;
4.              treePtr temp;
5.              st.push(root);
6.              while(!st.empty() )
7.              {
8.                      temp=st.top();
9.                      st.pop();
10.                     printf( " %d ", temp->value);
11.                     if(temp->rChild)
12.                             st.push(temp->rChild);
13.                     if(temp->lChild)
14.                             st.push(temp->lChild);
15.             }
16.     }
```

Complexity Analysis: Time Complexity: $O(n)$ Space Complexity: $O(n)$

Tree Depth

Solution: Depth is tree is calculated recursively by traversing left and right child of the root. At each level of traversal depth of left child is calculated and depth of right child is calculated. The greater depth among the left and right child is added by one (which is the depth of the current node) and this value is returned.

Example 10.7:

```
1.      int treeDepth(treePtr root)
2.      {
3.              if(!root)
4.                      return 0;
5.              else
6.              {
7.                      int lDepth=treeDepth(root->lChild);
8.                      int rDepth=treeDepth(root->rChild);
9.                      if(lDepth > rDepth)
10.                             return lDepth+1;
11.                     else
12.                             return rDepth+1;
13.             }
14.     }
```

Complexity Analysis: Time Complexity: $O(n)$ Space Complexity: $O(n)$

Nth Pre-Order

Solution: We want to print the node which will be at the nth index when we print the tree in PreOrder traversal. So we keep a counter to keep track of the index. When the counter is equal to index, then we print the value and return the Nth preorder index node.

Example 10.8:

```
1.      treePtr NthPreOrder(treePtr root, int index)/* pre order */
2.      {
3.              static int counter=0;
4.              treePtr temp=NULL;
5.              if(root)
6.              {
7.                      counter ++;
8.                      if(counter == index)
9.                      {
10.                             printf(" %d ", root->value);
11.                             return root;
12.                     }
13.                     temp=NthPreOrder(root->lChild,index);
14.                     if(temp)
15.                             return temp;
16.                     temp=NthPreOrder(root->rChild,index);
17.                     if(temp)
18.                             return temp;
19.             }
20.             return NULL;
21.     }
```

Complexity Analysis: Time Complexity: $O(n)$ Space Complexity: $O(n)$

Nth Post Order

Solution: We want to print the node which will be at the nth index when we print the tree in post order traversal. So we keep a counter to keep track of the index, but at this time we will increment the counter after left child and right child traversal. When the counter is equal to index, then we print the value and return the nth post order index node.

Example 10.9

```
1.      treePtr NthPostOrder(treePtr root, int index)/* post order */
2.      {
3.              static int count=0;
4.              treePtr temp=NULL;
5.              if(root)
6.              {
7.                      temp=NthPostOrder(root->lChild,index);
8.                      if(temp)
9.                              return temp;
10.                     temp=NthPostOrder(root->rChild,index);
```

```
11.                    if(temp)
12.                            return temp;
13.                    count++;
14.                    if(count == index)
15.                    {
16.                            printf(" %d ", root->value);
17.                            return root;
18.                    }
19.            }
20.            return NULL;
21.    }
```

Complexity Analysis:

Time Complexity: $O(n)$ Space Complexity: $O(n)$

Nth In Order

Solution:

We want to print the node which will be at the nth index when we print the tree in in-order traversal. So we keep a counter to keep track of the index, but at this time we will increment the counter after left child traversal but before the right child traversal. When the counter is equal to index, then we print the value and return the nth in-order index node.

Program 10.10:

```
1.      treePtr NthInOrder(treePtr root, int index)/* in order */
2.      {
3.              static int count=0;
4.              treePtr temp=NULL;
5.              if(root)
6.              {
7.                      temp=NthInOrder(root->lChild,index);
8.                      if(temp)
9.                              return temp;
10.                     count++;
11.                     if(count == index)
12.                     {
13.                             printf("%d ", root->value);
14.                             return root;
15.                     }
16.
17.                     temp=NthInOrder(root->rChild,index);
18.                     if(temp)
19.                             return temp;
20.             }
21.             return NULL;
22.     }
```

Complexity Analysis:

Time Complexity: $O(n)$ Space Complexity: $O(1)$

Copy Tree

Solution: Copy tree is done by copy nodes of the input tree at each level of the traversal of the tree. At each level of the traversal of nodes of tree a new node is created and the value of the input tree node is copied to it. The left child tree is copied recursively and then pointer to new subtree is returned will be assigned to the left child of the current new node. Similarly for the right child too. Finally the tree is copied.

Example 10.11:

```
1.      treePtr copyTree(treePtr root)
2.      {
3.              treePtr  temp;
4.              if(root != NULL)
5.              {
6.                      temp=(treePtr)malloc(sizeof(treeNode_t));
7.                      if(!temp)
8.                              return NULL;
9.                      temp->value=root->value;
10.                     temp->lChild=copyTree(root->lChild);
11.                     temp->rChild=copyTree(root->rChild);
12.                     return temp;
13.             }
14.             else
15.                     return NULL;
16.     }
```

Complexity Analysis: Time Complexity: $O(n)$ Space Complexity: $O(n)$

Copy Mirror Tree

Solution: Copy, mirror image of the tree is done same as copy tree, but in place of left child pointing to the tree formed by left child traversal of input tree, this time left child points to the tree formed by right child traversal. Similarly right child point to the traversal of the left child of the input tree.

Example 10.12:

```
1.      treePtr copyMirrorTree(treePtr root)
2.      {
3.              treePtr  temp;
4.              if(root != NULL)
5.              {
6.                      temp=(treePtr)malloc(sizeof(treeNode_t));
7.                      if(!temp)
8.                              return NULL;
9.                      temp->value=root->value;
10.                     temp->lChild=copyMirrorTree(root->rChild);
11.                     temp->rChild=copyMirrorTree(root->lChild);
12.                     return temp;
13.             }
14.             else
15.                     return NULL;
16.     }
```

Complexity Analysis: Time Complexity: $O(n)$ Space Complexity: $O(n)$

Number of Element

Solution: Number of nodes at the right child and the number of nodes at the left child is added by one and we get the total number of nodes in any tree/sub-tree.

Example 10.13:

```
1.      int numElement(treePtr root)
2.      {
3.              if(!root)
4.                      return 0;
5.              else
6.                      return (1 + numElement(root->rChild) + numElement(root->lChild) );
7.      }
```

Complexity Analysis: Time Complexity: $O(n)$ Space Complexity: $O(n)$

Number of Leaf nodes

Solution: If we add the number of leaf node in the right child with the number of leaf nodes in the left child, we will get the total number of leaf node in any tree or subtree.

Example 10.14:

```
1.      int numLeafs(treePtr root)
2.      {
3.              if(!root)
4.                      return 0;
5.              if( !root->lChild && !root -> rChild )
6.                      return 1;
7.              else
8.                      return (numLeafs(root->rChild) + numLeafs(root->lChild) );
9.      }
```

Complexity Analysis: Time Complexity: $O(n)$ Space Complexity: $O(n)$

Print Mirror

Solution: Print mirror tree is very simple in place of printing the left child first print the right child first so that the tree is printed is preorder traversal of mirror of the input tree.

Example 10.15:

```
1.      void printMirror(treePtr root) /* pre order */
2.      {
3.              if(root != NULL)
4.              {
5.                      printf(" %d ", root->value);
6.                      printMirror(root->rChild);
7.                      printMirror(root->lChild);
8.                      return;
9.              }
10.             else
11.                     return;
12.     }
```

Complexity Analysis: Time Complexity: $O(n)$ Space Complexity: $O(n)$

216

Identical

Solution: Two trees have identical values if at each level the value is equal.

Example 10.16:

```
1.      int identical(treePtr root1, treePtr root2)
2.      {
3.              if(!root1 && !root2)
4.                      return 1;
5.              else if(!root1 || !root2)
6.                      return 0;
7.              else
8.                      return ( identical(root1->lChild, root2->lChild) && identical(root1-
>rChild, root2->rChild) && (root1->value == root2->value));
9.      }
```

Complexity Analysis: Time Complexity: $O(n)$ Space Complexity: $O(n)$

Free Tree

Solution: The tree is traversed and nodes of tree are freed in such a manner such that all child nodes are freed before it.

Example 10.17:

```
1.      treePtr freeTree(treePtr root)
2.      {
3.              if(root)
4.              {
5.                      root->lChild=freeTree(root->lChild);
6.                      root->rChild=freeTree(root->rChild);
7.                      if(root->lChild == NULL&&root->rChild == NULL)
8.                      {
9.                              free(root);
10.                             return NULL;
11.                     }
12.             }
13.             return NULL;
14.     }
```

```
1.      void freeTree(treePtr* rootPtr)
2.      {
3.              *rootPtr=freeTree(*rootPtr);
4.      }
```

Complexity Analysis:
Time Complexity: $O(n)$ Space Complexity: $O(n)$

Solution: Tree to the list is done recursively. At each node we will suppose that the tree to list function will do its job for the left child and right child. Then we will combine the result of the left child and right child traversal. We need a head and tail pointer of the left list and right list to combine them with the current node. In the process of integration the current node will be added to the tail of the left list and current node will be added to the head to the right list. Head of the left list will become the head of the newly formed list and tail of the right list will become the tail of the newly created list.

Example 10.18:

```
treePtr treeToListRec(treePtr curr)
{
        treePtr Head, Tail, tempHead;
        if(!curr)
                return NULL;

        if(curr->lChild == NULL && curr->rChild == NULL)
        {
                curr->lChild = curr;
                curr->rChild = curr;
                return root;
        }
        if(curr->lChild)
        {
                Head = treeToListRec(curr->lChild);
                Tail = Head->lChild;
                curr->lChild = Tail;
                Tail->rChild = curr;
        }
        else
                Head=curr;

        if(curr->rChild)
        {
                tempHead = treeToListRec(curr->rChild);
                Tail = tempHead->lChild;
                curr->rChild = tempHead;
                tempHead->lChild = curr;
        }
        else
                Tail = curr;

        Head->lChild = Tail;
        Tail->rChild = Head;
        return Head;
}
```

Complexity Analysis:

Time Complexity: $O(n)$ Space Complexity: $O(n)$

Print all the paths

Print all the paths from the roots to the leaf

Solution: Whenever we traverse a node we add that node to the list. When we reach a leaf we print the whole list. When we return from a function, then we remove the element that was added to the list when we entered this function.

Example 10.19:

```
1.    #include<iostream>
2.    #include<list>
```

```
1.    void printList(list<int> L1)
2.    {
3.            list<int>::iterator iterB= L1.begin();
4.            list<int>::iterator iterE = L1.end();
5.            while(iterB != iterE)
6.            {
7.                    cout<<(*iterB)<<"  ";
8.                    iterB++;
9.            }
10.           cout<<endl;
11.   }
```

```
1.    void printPath(treePtr head, list<int>& L1)
2.    {
3.            if(!head)
4.                    return;
5.            If(head->rChild == null || head->lChild == null)
6.            {
7.                    printList(L1);
8.                    L1.pop_back();
9.                    return;
10.           }
11.           L1.push_back(head->value);
12.           printPath(head->rChild,L1);
13.           printPath(head->lChild,L1);
14.           L1.pop_back();
15.   }
```

```
1.    void printPathWrapper(treePtr head)
2.    {
3.            list<int> L1;
4.            printPath(head,L1);
5.    }
```

Complexity Analysis:
Time Complexity: $O(n)$, Space Complexity: $O(n)$

Least Common Ancestor

Solution: We recursively traverse the nodes of a binary tree. And we find any one of the node we are searching for then we return that node. And when we get both the left and right as some valid pointer location other than NULL we will return that node as the common ancestor.

Example 10.20:

```
1.      treePtr LCA(treePtr root, treePtr firstPtr, treePtr secondPtr)
2.      {
3.              treePtr left, right;
4.
5.              if (root == NULL)
6.                      return NULL;
7.
8.              if (root == firstPtr || root == secondPtr)
9.                      return root;
10.
11.             left = LCA(root->lChild, firstPtr, secondPtr);
12.             right = LCA(root->rChild, firstPtr, secondPtr);
13.
14.             if (left && right)
15.                     return root;
16.             else if (left)
17.                     return left;
18.             else
19.                     return right;
20.     }
```

Complexity Analysis: Time Complexity: $O(n)$ Space Complexity: $O(n)$

Find Max in Binary Tree

Solution: We recursively traverse the nodes of a binary tree. We will find the maximum value in the left and right subtree of any node then will compare the value with the value of the current node and finally return the largest of the three values.

Example 10.21:

```
1.      int findMaxBT(treePtr root)
2.      {
3.              int max;
4.              int left, right;
5.
6.              if (root == NULL)
7.                      return INT_MIN;
8.
9.              max = root->value;
10.
11.             left = findMaxBT(root->lChild);
12.             right = findMaxBT(root->rChild);
13.
```

```
14.             if (left > max)
15.                 max = left;
16.             if (right > max)
17.                 max = right;
18.
19.             return max;
20.     }
```

Search value in a Binary Tree

Solution: To find if some value is there in a binary tree or not is done using exhaustive search of the binary tree. First the value of current node is compared with the value which we are looking for. Then it is compared recursively inside the left child and right child.

Example 10.22:

```
1.      int searchBT(treePtr root, int value)
2.      {
3.              int max;
4.              int left, right;
5.
6.              if (root == NULL)
7.                      return 0;
8.
9.              if(root->value== value)
10.                     return 1;
11.
12.             left = searchBT(root->lChild, value);
13.             if (left)
14.                     return 1;
15.
16.             right = searchBT(root->rChild, value);
17.             if (right)
18.                     return 1;
19.
20.             return 0;
21.     }
```

Maximum Depth in a Binary Tree

Solution: To find the maximum depth of a binary tree we need to find the depth of the left tree and depth of right tree then we need to store the value and increment it by one so that we get depth of the given node.

Example 10.23:

```
1.      int maxDepthBT(treePtr root)
2.      {
3.              int max;
4.              int left, right;
5.
6.              if (root == NULL)
7.                      return 0;
8.
9.              left = findMaxBT(root->lChild);
10.             right = findMaxBT(root->rChild);
11.
12.             if (left > max)
13.                     max = left;
14.             if (right > max)
15.                     max = right;
16.
17.             return max+1;
18.     }
```

Number of Full Nodes in a BT

Solution: A full node is a node which have both left and right child. We will recursively travers the whole tree and will increase the count of full node as we find them.

Example 10.24:

```
1.      int numFullNodesBT(treePtr root)
2.      {
3.              int count=0;
4.              int left, right;
5.
6.              if (root == NULL)
7.                      return 0;
8.
9.              left = findMaxBT(root->lChild);
10.             right = findMaxBT(root->rChild);
11.
12.             count = left + right;
13.
14.             if(root->lChild && root->rChild)//this line can be changed to solve many
problems.
15.                     count++;
16.
17.             return count;
18.     }
```

Maximum Length Path in a BT/ Diameter of BT

Solution: To find the diameter of BT we need to find the depth of left child and right child then will add these two values and increment it by one so that we will get the maximum lenght path (diameter candidate) which contains the current node. Then we will find max length path in the left child sub-tree. And will also find the max length path in the right child sub-tree. Finally, we will compare the three values and return the maximum value out of these this will be the diameter of the Binary tree.

Example 10.25:

```
1.      int maxLengthPathBT(treePtr root)//diameter
2.      {
3.              int max;
4.              int leftPath, rightPath;
5.              int leftMax, rightMax;
6.
7.              if (root == NULL)
8.                      return 0;
9.
10.             leftPath = maxDepthBT(root->lChild);
11.             rightPath = maxDepthBT(root->rChild);
12.
13.             max = leftPath + rightPath + 1;
14.
15.             leftMax = maxLengthPathBT(root->lChild);
16.             rightMax = maxLengthPathBT(root->rChild);
17.
18.             if (leftMax > max)
19.                     max = leftMax;
20.
21.             if (rightMax > max)
22.                     max = rightMax;
23.
24.             return max;
25.     }
```

Sum of All nodes in a BT

Solution: We will find the sum of all the nodes recursively. sumAllBT() will return the sum of all the node of left and right subtree then will add the value of current node and will return the final sum.

Example 10.26:

```
1.      int sumAllBT(treePtr root)
2.      {
3.              int sum;
4.              int left, right;
5.
6.              if (root == NULL)
7.                      return 0;
8.
9.              left = sumAllBT(root->lChild);
10.             right = sumAllBT(root->rChild);
11.
12.             sum = left + right + root->value;
13.
14.             return sum;
15.     }
```

Iterative Pre-order

Solution: In place of using system stack in recursion, we can traverse the tree using stack data structure.

Example 10.27:

```
/* Iterative preorder, postorder, inorder us your own stack don't use system provided */
1.      #define maxStackSize 100
2.      void iterativePreorder(treePtr root)
3.      {
4.              struct structStack{
5.                      treePtr ptr;
6.                      int visited;
7.              };
8.              treePtr tempRoot=NULL;
9.              int tempVisit=0;
10.             structStack stack[maxStackSize];
11.             int top=1;
12.             stack[top].ptr=root;
13.             stack[top].visited=0;
14.             while(top)
15.             {
16.                     tempRoot=stack[top].ptr;
17.                     tempVisit=stack[top].visited;
18.                     top--;
19.                     if(tempVisit)
20.                     {
21.                             printf("[ %d ]", tempRoot->value);
22.                     }
```

```
23.                    else
24.                    {
25.                        if(tempRoot->rChild != NULL) /* right child always goes first
then left child */
26.                        {
27.                            top++;
28.                            stack[top].ptr=tempRoot->rChild;
29.                            stack[top].visited=0;
30.                        }
31.                        if(tempRoot->lChild != NULL)
32.                        {
33.                            top++;
34.                            stack[top].ptr=tempRoot->lChild;
35.                            stack[top].visited=0;
36.                        }
37.                        top++;
38.                        stack[top].ptr=tempRoot;
39.                        stack[top].visited=1;
40.                    }
41.            }
42.    }
```

Complexity Analysis:

Time Complexity: $O(n)$ Space Complexity: $O(n)$

Iterative Post-order

Solution: In place of using system stack in recursion, we can traverse the tree using stack data structure.

Example 10.28:

```
1.      void iterativePostorder(treePtr root)
2.      {
3.              struct structStack{
4.              treePtr ptr;
5.              int visited;
6.              };
7.              treePtr tempRoot=NULL;
8.              int tempVisit=0;
9.              structStack stack[maxStackSize];
10.             int top=1;
11.             stack[top].ptr=root;
12.             stack[top].visited=0;
13.             while(top)
14.             {
15.                     tempRoot=stack[top].ptr;
16.                     tempVisit=stack[top].visited;
17.                     top--;
18.                     if(tempVisit)
```

```
19.                  {
20.                          printf("[ %d ]", tempRoot->value);
21.                  }
22.                  else
23.                  {
24.                          top++;
25.                          stack[top].ptr=tempRoot;
26.                          stack[top].visited=1;
27.                          if(tempRoot->rChild != NULL) /* right chld always goes first
then right child */
28.                          {
29.                                  top++;
30.                                  stack[top].ptr=tempRoot->rChild;
31.                                  stack[top].visited=0;
32.                          }
33.                          if(tempRoot->lChild != NULL)
34.                          {
35.                                  top++;
36.                                  stack[top].ptr=tempRoot->lChild;
37.                                  stack[top].visited=0;
38.                          }
39.                  }
40.          }
41.  }
```

Complexity Analysis: Time Complexity: $O(n)$ Space Complexity: $O(n)$

Iterative In-order

Solution: In place of using system stack in recursion, we can traverse the tree using stack data structure.

Example 10.29:

```
1.      void iterativeInorder(treePtr root)
2.      {
3.              struct structStack{
4.                      treePtr ptr;
5.                      int visited;
6.              };
7.              treePtr tempRoot=NULL;
8.              int tempVisit=0;
9.              structStack stack[maxStackSize];
10.             int top=1;
11.             stack[top].ptr=root;
12.             stack[top].visited=0;
13.             while(top)
14.             {
15.                     tempRoot=stack[top].ptr;
16.                     tempVisit=stack[top].visited;
```

```
17.                     top--;
18.                     if(tempVisit)
19.                     {
20.                             printf("[ %d ]", tempRoot->value);
21.                     }
22.                     else
23.                     {
24.                             if(tempRoot->rChild != NULL) /* right chld always goes first
then right child */
25.                             {
26.                                     top++;
27.                                     stack[top].ptr=tempRoot->rChild;
28.                                     stack[top].visited=0;
29.                             }
30.                             top++;
31.                             stack[top].ptr=tempRoot;
32.                             stack[top].visited=1;
33.                             if(tempRoot->lChild != NULL)
34.                             {
35.                                     top++;
36.                                     stack[top].ptr=tempRoot->lChild;
37.                                     stack[top].visited=0;
38.                             }
39.                     }
40.             }
41.     }
```

Complexity Analysis:

Time Complexity: $O(n)$ Space Complexity: $O(n)$

Binary Search Tree (BST)

A binary search tree (BST) is a binary tree on which nodes are ordered in the following way:
- The key in the left subtree is less than the key in its parent node.
- The key in the right subtree is greater the key in its parent node.
- No duplicate key allowed.

Note: there can be two separate key and value fields in the tree node. But for simplicity, we are considering value as the key. All problems in the binary search tree are solved using this supposition that the value in the node is key for the tree.

Note: Since binary search tree is a binary tree to all the above algorithm of a binary tree are applicable to a binary search tree.

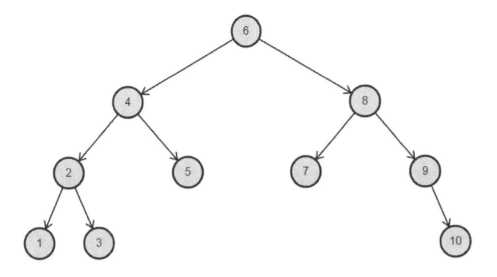

Problems in Binary Search Tree (BST)

All binary tree algorithms are valid for binary search tree too.

Create a binary search tree

Create a binary tree given list of values in an array in sorted order

Solution: Since the elements in the array are in sorted order and we want to create a binary search tree in which left subtree nodes are having values less than the current node and right subtree nodes have value greater than the value of the current node.

We have to find the middle node to create a current node and send the rest of the array to construct left and right subtree.

Example 10.30:

```
treePtr CreateBinaryTree (int* arr, int start, int end)
{
        treePtr root= NULL;
        if (start > end)
                return NULL;

        int mid = ( start + end ) / 2;
        root = createNode(arr[mid]);
        root ->left = CreateBinaryTree (arr, start, mid-1);
        root ->right = CreateBinaryTree (arr, mid+1, end);
        return root;

}
```

```
treePtr createNode(int val)
{
        treePtr root = (treePtr)malloc(sizeof(treeNode_t));
        root->value = val;
        root->lChild = root->rChild = NULL;
        return root;
}
```

```
int main()
{
        treePtr root = NULL;
        int A[] = { 1, 2, 3, 4, 5, 6, 7, 8, 9, 10 };
        root = CreateBinarySearchTree ( A, 0, 10);
        return 0;
}
```

Insertion

Nodes with key 6,4,2,5,1,3,8,7,9,10 are inserted in a tree. Below is step by step tree after inserting nodes in the order.

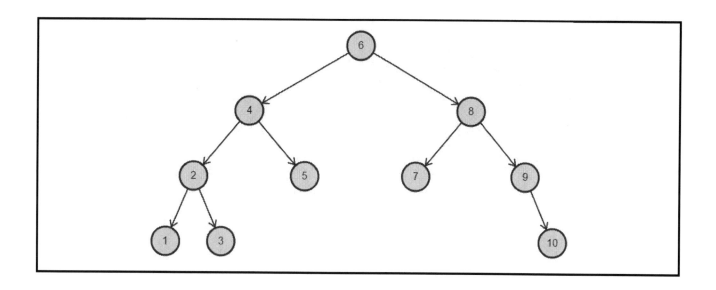

Solution: Smaller values will be added to the left child sub-tree of a node and grater value will be added to the right child sub-tree of the current node.

Example 10.31:

```
1.      treePtr insertNode(int value, treePtr root)
2.      {
3.              if(root == NULL)
4.              {
5.                      root=(treePtr)malloc(sizeof(treeNode_t));
6.                      if(root == NULL)
7.                      {
8.                              printf("filled memory shortage ");
9.                              return root;
10.                     }
11.                     root->value=value;
12.                     root->lChild=root->rChild=NULL;
13.             }
14.             else
15.             {
16.                     if(root->value > value)
17.                     {
18.                             root->lChild=insertNode(value, root->lChild);
19.                     }
20.                     else
21.                     {
22.                             root->rChild=insertNode(value, root->rChild);
23.                     }
24.             }
25.             return root;
26.     }
```

```
1.      void insertNode(int value, treePtr * ptrRoot)
2.      {
3.              *ptrRoot = insertNode(value,*ptrRoot);
4.      }
```

Complexity Analysis:

Time Complexity: $O(n)$ Space Complexity: $O(n)$

Find Node

Find the node with the value given.

Solution: The value grater then the current node value will be in the right child sub-tree and the value smaller then the current node is in the left child sub-tree.

Example 10.32:

```
1.      treePtr findNode(treePtr root, int value)
2.      {
3.              if(!root)
4.                      return NULL;
5.              if(root->value == value)
6.                      return root;
7.              else
8.              {
9.                      if(root->value > value)
10.                             return findNode(root->lChild, value);
11.                     else
12.                             return findNode(root->rChild, value);
13.             }
14.     }
```

Complexity Analysis:

Time Complexity: $O(n)$ Space Complexity: $O(1)$

Find Node Iterative

Solution: The value grater then the current node value will be in the right child sub-tree and the value smaller then the current node is in the left child sub-tree. We can find a value by traversing the left or ritht subtree iteratively.

Example 10.33:

```
1.      treePtr findNodeIterative(treePtr root, int value) /* iterative */
2.      {
3.              while(root)
4.              {
5.                      if(root->value == value)
6.                              return root;
7.                      else if(root->value > value)
8.                              root=root->lChild;
9.                      else
10.                             root=root->rChild;
```

```
11.          }
12.              return NULL;
13.      }
```

Complexity Analysis: Time Complexity: $O(n)$ Space Complexity: $O(1)$

Example 10.34: Operators are generally read from left to right

```
1.      treePtr findNodeIterative_optimized(treePtr root, int value)
2.      {
3.              while(root && root->value != value)
4.                      (root->value > value)? root = root->lChild : root=root->rChild;
5.              return root;
6.      }
```

Complexity Analysis: Time Complexity: $O(n)$ Space Complexity: $O(n)$

Find Min

Find the node with the minimum value.

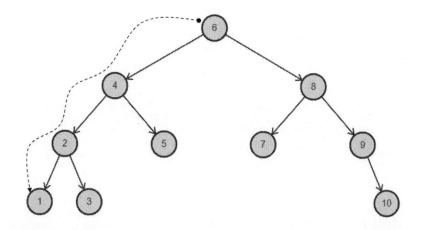

Solution: left most child of the tree will be the node with the minimum value.

Example 10.35:

```
1.      treePtr findMin(treePtr root)
2.      {
3.              if(root)
4.              {
5.                      while(root->lChild)
6.                      {
7.                              root=root->lChild;
8.                      }
9.              }
10.             return root;
11.     }
```

Complexity Analysis: Time Complexity: $O(n)$ Space Complexity: $O(1)$

Find Min Recursive

Find the node with a minimum value, provide a recursive solution.
Example 10.36:

```
1.      treePtr findMinRec(treePtr root)
2.      {
3.              if(!root)
4.                      return NULL;
5.              if(root->lChild == NULL)
6.                      return root;
7.              else
8.                      return findMinRec(root->lChild);
9.      }
```

Complexity Analysis: Time Complexity: $O(n)$ Space Complexity: $O(n)$

Find Max

Find the node in the tree with the maximum value.

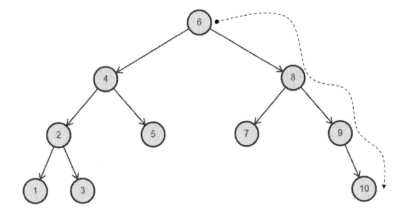

Solution: Right most node of the tree will be the node with the maximum value.
Example 10.37:

```
1.      treePtr findMax(treePtr root)
2.      {
3.              if(root)
4.              {
5.                      while(root->rChild)
6.                      {
7.                              root=root->rChild;
8.                      }
9.              }
10.             return root;
11.     }
```

Complexity Analysis: Time Complexity: $O(n)$ Space Complexity: $O(1)$

Find Max Recursive

Find the node in the tree with the maximum value, provide a recursive solution.

Example 10.38:

```
1.      treePtr findMaxRec(treePtr root)
2.      {
3.      if(!root)
4.              return NULL;
5.      if(root->rChild == NULL)
6.              return root;
7.      else
8.              return findMaxRec(root->rChild);
9.      }
```

Complexity Analysis: Time Complexity: $O(n)$ Space Complexity: $O(n)$

Max Value

Example 10.39:

```
1.      int maxValue(treePtr root)
2.      {
3.              if(root)
4.              {
5.                      while(root->rChild)
6.                      {
7.                              root=root->rChild;
8.                      }
9.                      return root->value;
10.             }
11.             return -999;
12.     }
```

Complexity Analysis: Time Complexity: $O(n)$ Space Complexity: $O(1)$

Min Value

Example 10.40:

```
1.      int minValue(treePtr root)
2.      {
3.              if(root)
4.              {
5.                      while(root->lChild)
6.                      {
7.                              root=root->lChild;
8.                      }
9.                      return root->value;
10.             }
11.             return -999;
12.     }
```

Complexity Analysis: Time Complexity: $O(n)$ Space Complexity: $O(1)$

Solution: At each node we check, max value of left subtree is smaller then the value of current node and min value of right subtree is grater then the current node.

Example 10.41:

```
1.      int isBST(treePtr root)
2.      {
3.              if(!root)
4.                      return 1;
5.              if(root->lChild && maxValue(root->lChild) > root->value )
6.                      return 0;
7.              if(root->rChild && minValue(root->rChild) <= root->value )
8.                      return 0;
9.              return (isBST(root->lChild) && isBST(root->rChild));
10.     }
```

Complexity Analysis:

Time Complexity: $O(n^2)$ Space Complexity: $O(n)$

The above solution is correct but it is not efficient as same tree nodes are traversed many times.

Solution: An another better solution will be the one in which we will look into each node only once. This is done by narrowing the range. We will be using a isBSTUtil() funciton which will take the max and min range fo the vlaues of the nodes. The initial value of min and max will be INT_MIN and INT_MAX.

Example 10.42:

```
1.      int isBSTUtil(treePtr root, int min, int max)
2.      {
3.              if(!root)
4.                      return 1;
5.
6.              if(root->value < min || root->value > max)
7.                      return 0;
8.
9.              return isBSTUtil(root->lChild, min, root->value) &&
        isBSTUtil(root->rChild,root->value+1,max);
10.     }
11.
12.     int isBST(treePtr root)
13.     {
14.             return isBSTUtil(root, INT_MIN, INT_MAX);
15.     }
```

Complexity Analysis:

Time Complexity: $O(n)$ Space Complexity: $O(n)$ for stack

Solution: Above method is correct and efficient but there is an another easy method to do the same. We can do in-order traversal of nodes and see if we are getting a strictly increasing sequence

Example 10.43:

```
1.      int isBST(treePtr root, int* value )/*  in order  traversal */
2.      {
3.              int ret;
4.              if(root)
5.              {
6.                      ret = isBST(root->lChild,value);
7.                      if(!ret)
8.                              return 0;
9.
10.                     if(*value > root->value)
11.                             return 0;
12.
13.                     *value = root->value;
14.
15.                     ret = isBST(root->rChild,value);
16.                     if(!ret)
17.                             return 0;
18.             }
19.             return 1;
20.     }
```

Complexity Analysis: Time Complexity: $O(n)$ Space Complexity: $O(n)$ for stack

Delete Node

Description: Remove the node x from the binary search tree, making the necessary, reorganize nodes of binary search tree to maintain its properties.

There are three cases in delete node, lets call the node that need to be deleted as x.
Case 1: node x has no children. Just delete it (i.e. Change parent node so that it doesn't point to x)
Case 2: node x has one child. Splice out x by linking x's parent to x's child
Case 3: node x has two children. Splice out the x's successor and replace x with x's successor

When the node to be deleted have no children
This is a trival case in this case we directly delete the node and return null.

When the node to be deleted have only one child.
In this case we save the child in a temp variable and then delete current node and finally return the child.

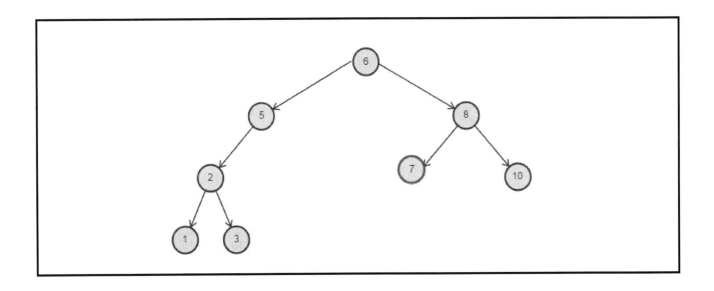

When the node to be deleted has two children.

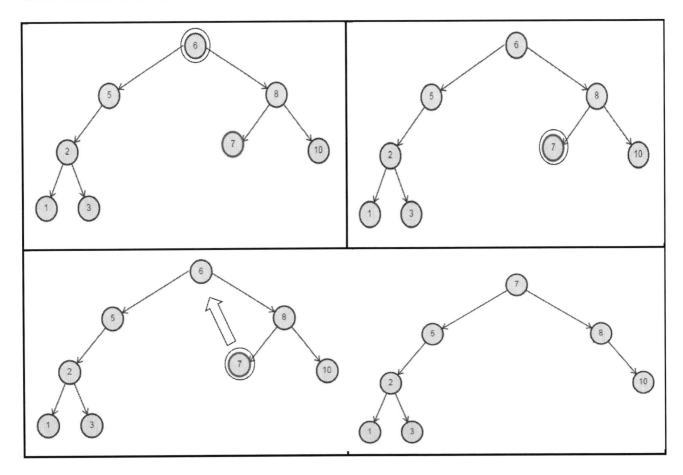

Example 10.44:

```
1.      void deleteNode(treePtr* rootPtr, int value)
2.      {
3.              *rootPtr=deleteNode(*rootPtr, value);
4.      }
```

```
1.treePtr deleteNode(treePtr root, int value)
2.{
3.        treePtr temp=NULL;
4.        if(root)
5.        {
6.                if(root->value == value)
7.                {
8.                        if(root->lChild == NULL && root->rChild == NULL)
9.                        {
10.                                free(root);
11.                                return NULL;
12.                        }
13.                        else
14.                        {
15.                                if(root->lChild == NULL)
16.                                {
17.                                        temp=root->rChild;
18.                                        free(root);
19.                                        return temp;
20.                                }
21.                                if(root->rChild == NULL)
22.                                {
23.                                        temp=root->lChild;
24.                                        free(root);
25.                                        return temp;
26.                                }
27.                                temp=findMin(root->rChild);
28.                                root->value=temp->value;
29.                                root->rChild=deleteNode(root->rChild,temp->value);
30.                        }
31.                }
32.                else
33.                {
34.                        if(root->value > value)
35.                        {
36.                                root->lChild=deleteNode(root->lChild,value);
37.                        }
38.                        else
39.                        {
40.                                root->rChild=deleteNode(root->rChild,value);
41.                        }
42.                }
43.        }
44.        return root;
45.}
```

Analysis:

Time Complexity: $O(n)$ Space Complexity: $O(n)$

Least Common Ancestor

In a tree T. The least common ancestor between two nodes n1 and n2 is defined as the lowest node in T that has both n1 and n2 as descendants.

Example 10.45:

```
1.      treePtr LcaBST(treePtr root, treePtr firstPtr, treePtr secondPtr)
2.      {
3.              if(!firstPtr || !secondPtr || !root)
4.              {
5.                      return root;
6.              }
7.
8.              if(root->value > firstPtr->value &&
9.                      root->value > secondPtr->value)
10.             {
11.                     return LcaBST(root->lChild, firstPtr, secondPtr);
12.             }
13.             if(root->value < firstPtr->value &&
14.                     root->value < secondPtr->value)
15.             {
16.                     return LcaBST(root->rChild, firstPtr, secondPtr);
17.             }
18.             return root;
19.     }
```

Path Length

Given two nodes find the path length between them.

Solution: This problem solution is simply finding the least common ansistor of the two node and then find the length of each of node from there parent.

Example 10.46:

```
1.      int pathLength(treePtr root, treePtr firstPtr, treePtr secondPtr)
2.      {
3.              treePtr parent = LcaBST(root, firstPtr, secondPtr);
4.              int first = findNodeDepth(parent, firstPtr);
5.              int second = findNodeDepth(parent, secondPtr);
6.              return first + second;
7.      }
```

```
1.      int findNodeDepth(treePtr root, treePtr dstPtr)
2.      {
3.              int value;
4.              if (!root || !dstPtr)
5.                      return -1;
6.
7.              if (root->value == dstPtr->value)
8.                      return 0;
9.              else
10.             {
11.                     if (root->value > dstPtr->value)
12.                             value = findNodeDepth(root->lChild, dstPtr);
13.                     else
14.                             value = findNodeDepth(root->rChild, dstPtr);
15.
16.                     if (value != -1)
17.                             return (value + 1);
18.             }
19.     }
```

Trim the Tree nodes which are Outside Range

Given a range as min, max. we need to delete all the nodes of the tree which are out of this range.

Solution: Traverse the tree and each node which is having value outside the range will delete itself. All the deletion will happen from inside out so we don't have to care about the children of a node as if they are out of range then they already had deleted themselves.

Example 10.47:

```
1.      treePtr trimOutsideRange(treePtr root, int min, int max)
2.      {
3.              treePtr tempNode;
4.              if (root == NULL)
5.                      return NULL;
6.
7.              root->lChild=trimOutsideRange(root->lChild, min, max);
8.              root->rChild=trimOutsideRange(root->rChild, min, max);
9.
10.             if (root->value < min)
11.             {
12.                     tempNode = root->rChild;
13.                     delete root;
14.                     return tempNode;
15.             }
16.
```

```
17.             if (root->value > max)
18.             {
19.                     tempNode = root->lChild;
20.                     delete root;
21.                     return tempNode;
22.             }
23.
24.             return root;
25. }
```

Print Tree nodes which are in Range

Print only those nodes of the tree whose value is in the range given.

Solution: Just normal inorder traversal and at the time of printing we will check if the value is inside the range provided.

Example 10.48:

```
1. void printInRange(treePtr root, int min, int max)
2. {
3.       if(!root)
4.               return;
5.
6.       printInRange(root->lChild, min, max);
7.
8.       if(root->value >= min && root->value <= max)
9.               printf(" %d ", root->value);
10.
11.      printInRange(root->rChild, min, max);
12. }
```

Find Ceil and Floor value inside BST given key

Given a tree and a value we need to find the ceil value of node in tree which is smaller then the given value and also need to find the floor value of node in tree which is bigger. Our aim is to find ceil and floor value as close as possible then the given value.

Example 10.49:

```
1.       void CeilFloorBST(treePtr root, int value, int* ceil, int* floor )
2.       {
3.               while (root)
4.               {
5.                       if (root->value == value)
6.                       {
7.                               *ceil = root->value;
8.                               *floor = root->value;
9.                               break;
10.                      }
```

```
11.                    else if (root->value > value)
12.                    {
13.                            *ceil = root->value;
14.                            root = root->lChild;
15.                    }
16.                    else
17.                    {
18.                            *floor = root->value;
19.                            root = root->rChild;
20.                    }
21.            }
22.    }
```

Tree to Doubly Linked list

We need to convert a binary tree to double linked list. Such that the inorder traversal of the tree is saved as a sequence of node in double linked list.

Solution: We will use TreeToList() funciton. At each node we will call TreeToList() funciton for both left child and right child. These two funciton call will crate double linked list of left child and right child respectively. Then we just have to worry about the current node. We will append the two linked list formed by the recursive call and the join them and the final list is prepared.

Example 10.50:

```
1.      void connect(treePtr a, treePtr b)
2.      {
3.              a->rChild=b;
4.              b->lChild=a;
5.      }
```

```
1.      treePtr  append(treePtr a, treePtr b)
2.      {
3.              treePtr aLast, bLast;
4.              if (a == NULL)
5.                      return(b);
6.              if (b == NULL)
7.                      return(a);
8.              aLast = a->lChild;
9.              bLast = b->lChild;
10.             connect(aLast, b);
11.             connect(bLast, a);
12.             return (a);
13.     }
```

```
1.      treePtr treeToList(treePtr root)
2.      {
3.             treePtr aList, bList;
4.             if (root == NULL)
5.                    return (NULL);
6.             aList = treeToList(root->lChild);
7.             bList = treeToList(root->rChild);
8.             root->lChild = root;
9.             root->rChild = root;
10.            aList = append(aList, root);
11.            aList = append(aList, bList);
12.            return (aList);
13.     }
```

Analysis:

Time Complexity: $O(n)$ Space Complexity: $O(1)$

Exercise

1. Construct a tree given its in-order and pre-order traversal strings.
   - inorder : 1 2 3 4 5 6 7 8 9 10
   - pre-order: 6 4 2 1 3 5 8 7 9 10

2. Construct a tree given its in-order and post-order traversal strings.
   - inorder: 1 2 3 4 5 6 7 8 9 10
   - post-order: 1 3 2 5 4 7 10 9 8 6

3. Write a delete node function in Binary tree.

4. Write a function print depth first in a binary tree without using system stack (use STL queue or stack etc.)

Hint: you may want to keep another element to tree node like visited flag.

5. Check whether a given Binary Tree is Complete or not
   - In a complete binary tree, every level except the last one is completely filled. All nodes in the left are filled first, then the right one.

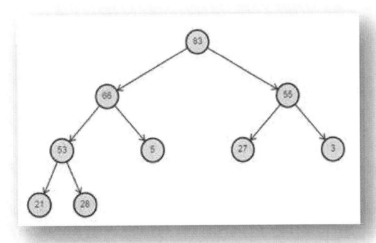

6. Check whether a given Binary Tree is Full/ Strictly binary tree or not
   o The full binary tree is a binary tree in which each node has zero or two children.

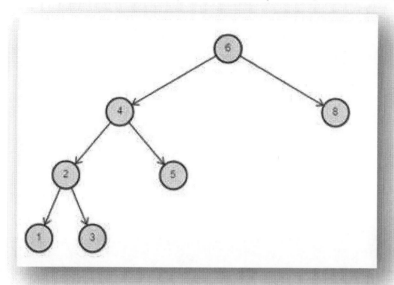

7. Check whether a given Binary Tree is a Perfect binary tree or not
   o The perfect binary tree- is a type of full binary trees in which each non leaf node has exactly two child nodes.

8. Check whether a given Binary Tree is Height-balanced Binary Tree or not
   o A height-balanced binary tree is a binary tree such that the left & right subtrees for any given node differ in height by no more than one

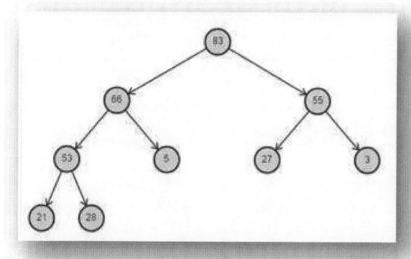

9. Isomorphic: two trees are isomorphic if they have the same shape, it does not matter what the value is. Write a program to find if two given tree are isomorphic or not.

10. The worst-case run *Time Complexity* of building a BST with n nodes
    o O(n²)
    o O(n * log n)
    o O(n)
    o O(logn)

11. The worst-case run*Time Complexity* of insertion into a BST with n nodes is
    - O(n2)
    - O(n * log n)
    - O(n)
    - O(logn)

12. The worst-case run*Time Complexity* of a search of a value in a BST with n nodes.
    - O(n²)
    - O(n * log n)
    - O(n)
    - O(logn)

13. Which of the following traversals always gives the sorted sequence of the elements in a BST?
    - Preorder
    - Ignored
    - Postorder
    - Undefined

14. The height of a Binary Search Tree with n nodes in the worst case?
    - O(n * log n)
    - O(n)
    - O(logn)
    - O(1)

15. Try to optimize the above solution to give a DFS traversal without using recursion use some stack or queue.

16. This is an open exercise for the readers. Every algorithm that is solved using recursion (system stack) can also be solved using user defined or library defined (STL) stack. So try to figure out what all algorithms which are using recursion and try to figure out how you will do this same issue using user layer stack.

17. In a binary tree print the nodes in zigzag order. In the first level nodes are printed in the left to right order. In the second level nodes are printed in right to left and in the third level again in the order left to right.
    - *Hint:* Use two stacks. Pop from first stack and push into another stack. Swap the stacks alternatively.

18. Find nth smallest element in a binary search tree.
    - *Hint:* Nth inorder in a binary tree.

19. Find the floor value of key which is inside a BST.

20. Find the Ceil value of key which is inside a BST.

21. What is *Time Complexity* of the below code:

```c
void DFS(treePtr head)
{
        treePtr curr = head, *prev;
        int count = 0;
        while (curr && ! curr->visited)
        {
                count++;
                if (curr->lChild && ! curr->lChild->visited)
                {
                        curr= curr->lChild;
                }
                else if (curr->rChild && ! curr->rChild->visited)
                {
                        curr= curr->rChild;
                }
                else
                {
                        printf("%d  ", curr->value);
                        curr->visited = 1;
                        curr = head;
                }
        }
        printf("\n count is : %d ",count);
}
```

CHAPTER 11: PRIORITY QUEUE

Introduction

A Priority-Queue also knows as Binary-Heap, is a variant of queue. Items are removed from the start of the queue. But in a Priority-Queue the logical ordering of objects is determined by their priority. The highest priority item are at the front of the Priority-Queue. When you enqueue an item to Priority-Queue the new item can more to the front of the queue. A Priority-Queue is a very important data structure. Priority-Queue is used in various Graph algorithms like Prim's Algorithm and Dijkstra's algorithm. Priority-Queue is also used in the timer implementation etc.

A Priority-Queue is implemented using a Heap (Binary Heap). A Heap data structure is an array of elements that can be observed as a complete binary tree. The tree is completely filled on all levels except possibly the lowest. And heap satisfies the heap ordering property. A heap is a complete binary tree so the height of tree with N nodes is always *O(logn)*.

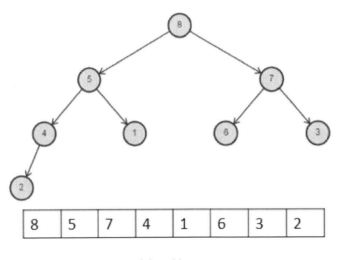

Max Heap

A heap is not a sorted structure and can be regarded as partially ordered. As you see from the picture, there is no relationship among nodes at any given level, even among the siblings.

Heap is implemented using an array. And because heap is a complete binary tree, the left child of a parent (at position x) is the node that is found in position 2x in the array. Similarly, the right child of the parent is at position 2x+1 in the array. To find the parent of any node in the heap, we can simply division. Given the index y of a node, the parent index will by y/2.

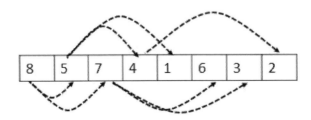

Types of Heap

There are two types of heap and the type depends on the ordering of the elements. The ordering can be done in two ways: Min-Heap and Max-Heap

Max Heap

Max-Heap: the value of each node is less than or equal to the value of its parent, with the lagest-value element at the root.

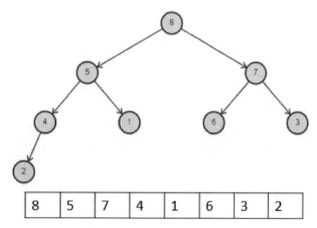

| 8 | 5 | 7 | 4 | 1 | 6 | 3 | 2 |

Max Heap

Max Heap Operations

Insert	O(logn)
DeleteMax	O(logn)
Remove	O(logn)
FindMax	O(1)

Min Heap

Min-Heap: the value of each node is greater than or equal to the value of its parent, with the minimum-value element at the root.

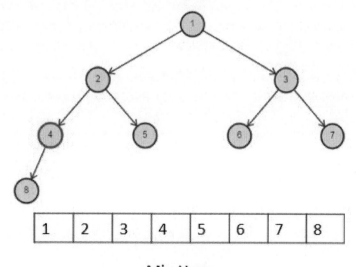

| 1 | 2 | 3 | 4 | 5 | 6 | 7 | 8 |

Min Heap

Use it whenever you need quick access to the smallest item, because that item will always be at the root of the tree or the first element in the array. However, the remainder of the array is kept partially sorted. Thus, instant access is only possible for the smallest item.

Min Heap Operations

Insert	O(logn)
DeleteMin	O(logn)
Remove	O(logn)
FindMin	O(1)

Throughout this chapter the word "heap" will always refer to a max-heap. The implementation of min-heap is left for the user to do it as an exercise.

Heap ADT Operations

The basic operations of binary heap are as follows:

Binary Heap	Create a new empty binary heap	O(1)
Insert	Adding a new element to the heap	O(logn)
DeleteMax	Delete the maximum element form the heap.	O(logn)
FindMax	Find the maximum element in the heap.	O(1)
isEmpty	return true if the heap is empty else return false	O(1)
Size	Return the number of elements in the heap.	O(1)
BuildHeap	Build a new heap from the array of elements	O(logn)

Operation on Heap

Create Heap from an array

1. Starts by putting the elements to an array.
2. Starting from the middle of the array move downward towards the start of the array. At each step compare parent value with its left child and right child. And restore the heap property by shifting the parent value with its greatest-value child. Such that the parent value will always be greater than or equal to left child and right child.
3. For all elements from middle of the array to the start of the array. We are doing comparisons and shift till we reach the leaf nodes of the heap. The *Time Complexity* of build heap is *O(N)*.

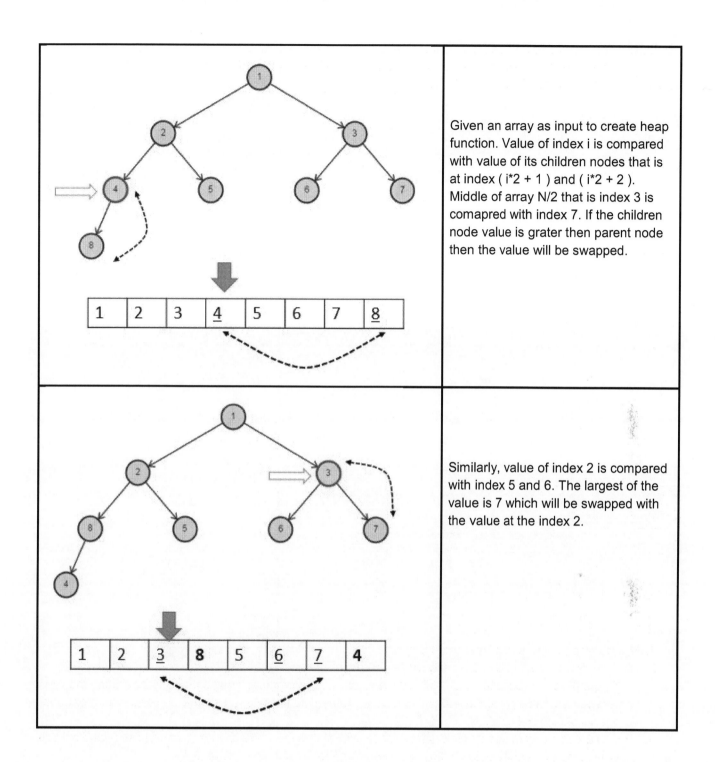

Given an array as input to create heap function. Value of index i is compared with value of its children nodes that is at index (i*2 + 1) and (i*2 + 2). Middle of array N/2 that is index 3 is comapred with index 7. If the children node value is grater then parent node then the value will be swapped.

Similarly, value of index 2 is compared with index 5 and 6. The largest of the value is 7 which will be swapped with the value at the index 2.

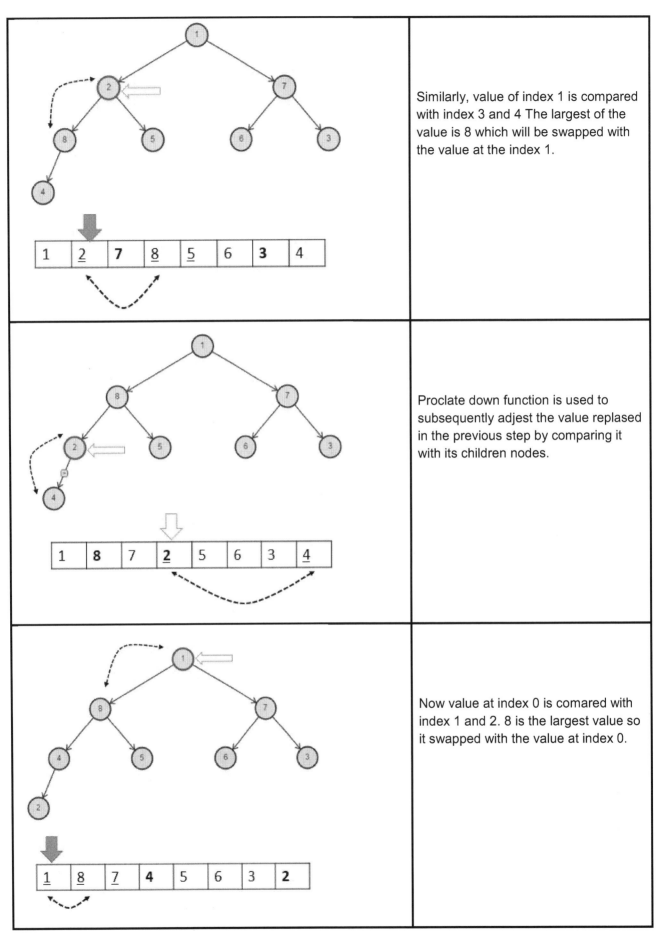

Similarly, value of index 1 is compared with index 3 and 4 The largest of the value is 8 which will be swapped with the value at the index 1.

Proclate down function is used to subsequently adjest the value replased in the previous step by comparing it with its children nodes.

Now value at index 0 is comared with index 1 and 2. 8 is the largest value so it swapped with the value at index 0.

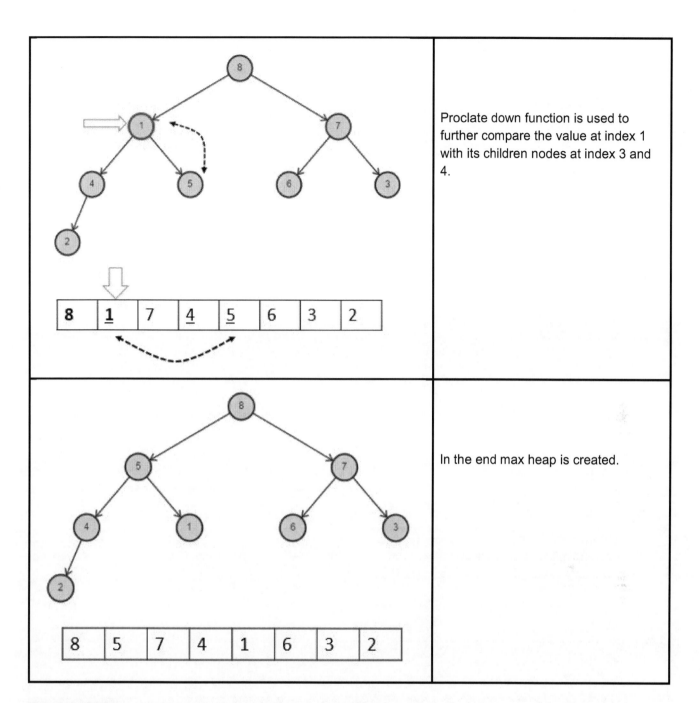

Proclate down function is used to further compare the value at index 1 with its children nodes at index 3 and 4.

In the end max heap is created.

Example 11.1:

```
PtrHeap BuildHeap(int *arr,int size,int capacity)
{
        PtrHeap pHeap=(PtrHeap)malloc(sizeof(Heap));
        pHeap->Size = size;
        pHeap->Capacity = capacity;
        pHeap->Array = arr;

        for(int i=(pHeap->Size)/2;i>0;i--)
                ProclateDown(pHeap->Array,i,pHeap->Size);

        return pHeap;
}
```

```
void ProclateDown(int *arr,int position,int size)
{
        int lChild=2*position+1;
        int rChild=lChild+1;
        int small=-1;

        if(lChild < size)
                small = lChild;

        if( rChild < size && arr[rChild] < arr[lChild] )
                small = rChild;

        if(small!=-1 && arr[small]< arr[position])
        {
                int temp = arr[position];
                arr[position] = arr[small];
                arr[small] = temp;
                ProclateDown(arr,small,size);
        }
}
```

Initializing an empty Heap

Example 11.2:

```
void HeapInitialize(PtrHeap pHeap,int capacity)
{
        pHeap->Size=0;
        pHeap->Capacity= capacity;
        pHeap->Array=(int*)malloc((capacity)*sizeof(int));
}
```

Enqueue / Insert

1. Add the new element at the end of the array. This keeps the structure as a complete binary tree, but it might no longer be a heap since the new element might have a value greater than its parent.
2. Swap the new element with its parent till it has value greater than its parents.
3. Step 2 will terminate when the new element reaches the root or when the new element's parent have a value greater than or equal to the new element's value.

Lets take and example of the Max heap created in the above example.

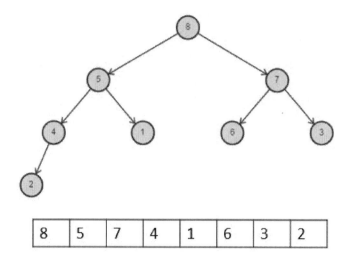

8	5	7	4	1	6	3	2

Lets take an example by inserting element with value 9 to the heap. The element is added to the end of the heap array. Now the value will be proclate up by comparing it with the parent. The value is added to index 8 and its parent will be (N-1)/2 = index 3.

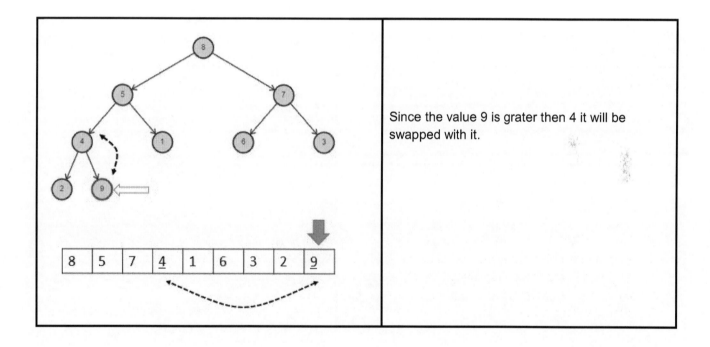

Since the value 9 is grater then 4 it will be swapped with it.

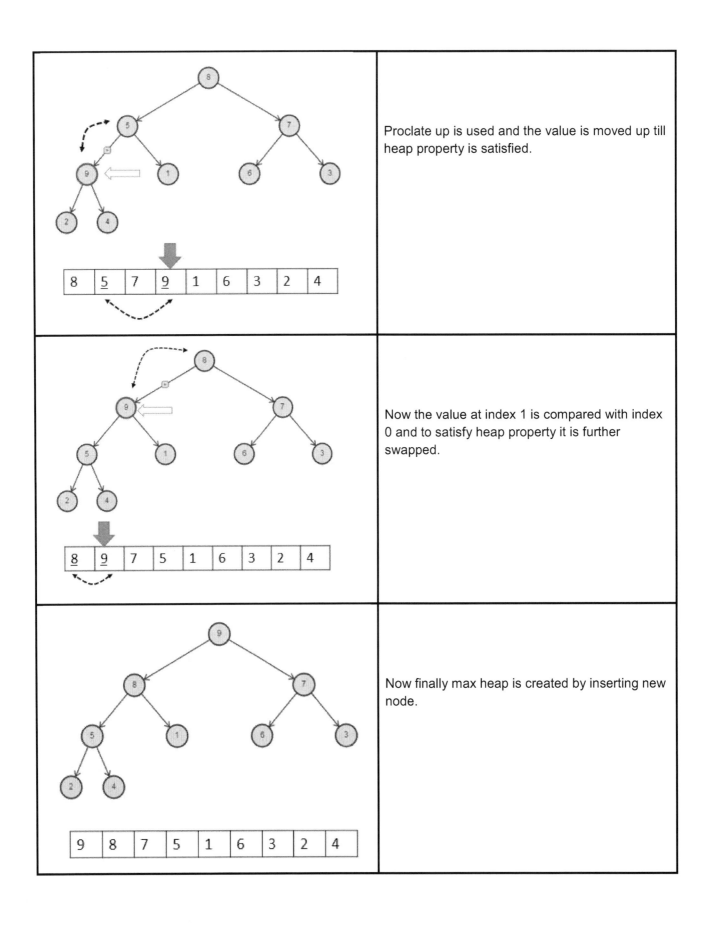

Proclate up is used and the value is moved up till heap property is satisfied.

Now the value at index 1 is compared with index 0 and to satisfy heap property it is further swapped.

Now finally max heap is created by inserting new node.

Example 11.3:

```
void HeapInsert(PtrHeap pHeap,int value)
{
        pHeap->Array[pHeap->Size]=value;
        ProclateUp(pHeap->Array,pHeap->Size);
        pHeap->Size++;
}
```

```
void ProclateUp(int *arr,int position)
{
        int parent=(position – 1)/2;

        if(position != 0)
        {
                if(arr[parent] >arr[position])
                {
                        int temp = arr[position];
                        arr[position] = arr[parent];
                        arr[parent] = temp;

                        ProclateUp(arr,parent);
                }
        }
}
```

Dequeue / Delete

1. Copy the value at the root of the heap to the variable used to return a value.
2. Copy the last element of the heap to the root, and then reduce the size of heap by 1. This element is called the "out-of-place" element.
3. Restore heap property by swapping the out-of-place element with its greatest-value child. Repeat this process until the out-of-place element reaches a leaf or it has a value that is greater or equal to all its children.
4. Return the answer that was saved in Step 1.

To dequeue an element from heap its top value is swapped to the end of the heap array and size fo heap is reduced by 1.

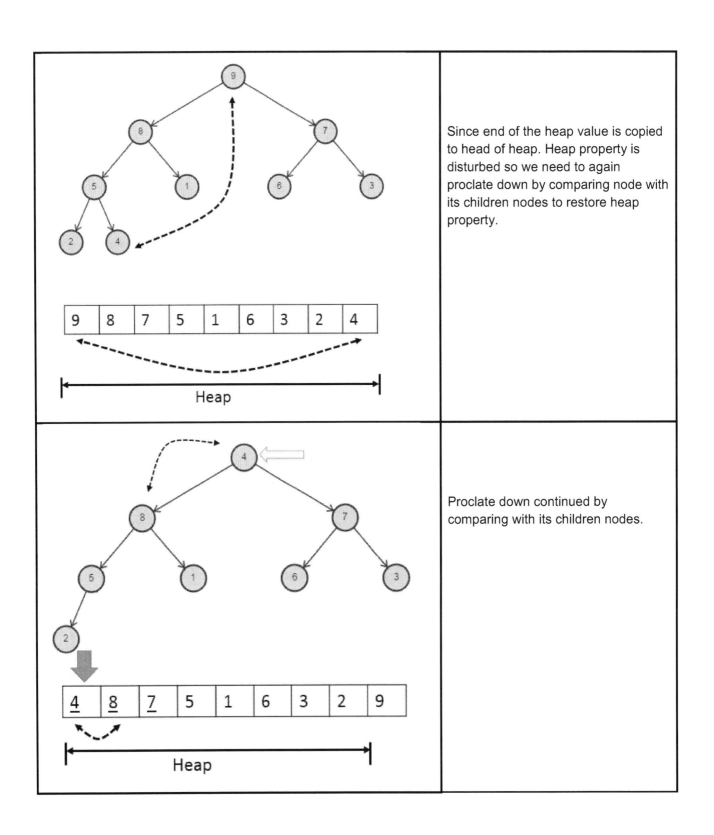

Since end of the heap value is copied to head of heap. Heap property is disturbed so we need to again proclate down by comparing node with its children nodes to restore heap property.

Proclate down continued by comparing with its children nodes.

258

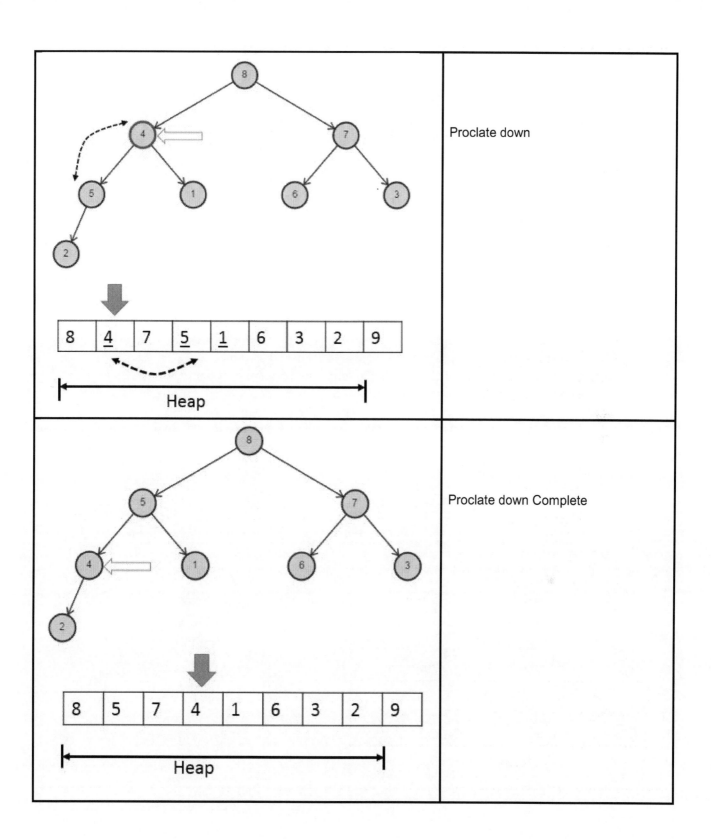

Proclate down

Proclate down Complete

Example 11.4:

```
int HeapDelete(PtrHeap pHeap)
{
        int value=(pHeap->Array[0]);
        pHeap->Array[0]=pHeap->Array[pHeap->Size -1];
        pHeap->Size--;
        ProclateDown(pHeap->Array,0,pHeap->Size);
        return value;
}
```

Heap-Sort

1. Use create heap function to build a max heap from the given array of elements. This operation will take **O(N)** time.
2. Dequeue the max value from the heap and store this value to the end of the array at location arr[size-1]
   a) Copy the value at the root of the heap to end of the array.
   b) Copy the last element of the heap to the root, and then reduce the size of heap by 1. This element is called the "out-of-place" element.
   c) Restore heap property by swapping the out-of-place element with its greatest-value child. Repeat this process until the out-of-place element reaches a leaf or it has a value that is greater or equal to all its children
3. Repeat this operation till there is just one element in the heap.

Let's take example of the heap which we had created at the start of the chapter. Heap sort is algorithm starts by creating a heap of the given array which is done in leniar time. Then at each step head of the heap is swapped with the end of the heap and the heap size is reduced by 1. Then proclate down is used to restore the heap property. And this same is done multiple times till the heap contain just one element.

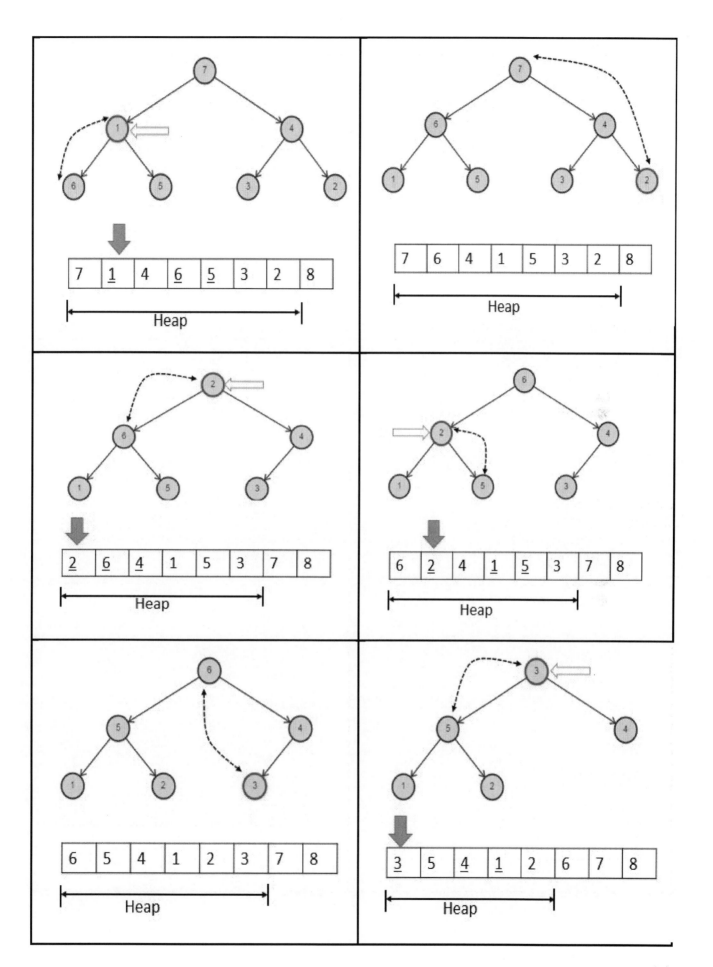

7	1	4	6	5	3	2	8

Heap

7	6	4	1	5	3	2	8

Heap

2	6	4	1	5	3	7	8

Heap

6	2	4	1	5	3	7	8

Heap

6	5	4	1	2	3	7	8

Heap

3	5	4	1	2	6	7	8

Heap

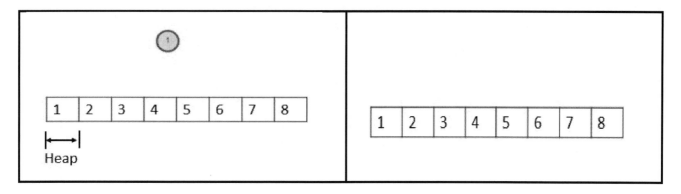

Example 11.5:

```
void HeapSort(int *arr, int size)
{
        int temp;
        for (int i = size/2; i>0; i--)
                ProclateDown(arr, i, size);

        while (size)
        {
                temp = arr[0];
                arr[0] = arr[size - 1];
                arr[size - 1] = temp;
                size--;
                ProclateDown(arr, 0, size);
        }
}
```

```
void ProclateDown(int *arr,int position,int size)
{
        int lChild=2*position + 1;
        int rChild=lChild+1;
        int small=-1;

        if(lChild < size)
                small = lChild;

        if( rChild < size && compare( arr[rChild], arr[lChild] ))//compare function decide min
        {                                                        // or max heap
                small = rChild;
        }

        if(small!=-1 && compare( arr[small], arr[position] ))
        {
                int temp = arr[position];
                arr[position] = arr[small];
                arr[small] = temp;
                ProclateDown(arr,small,size);
        }
}
```

```
//Swap, when the parent is less then child, will give max heap.
//Swap when a parent is grater then a child. it will give min heap.
int compare(int parentVal, int childVal)
{
        return (parentVal < childVal);
}
```

```
int main()
{
        int a[10] = { 4, 5, 3, 2, 6, 7, 11, 8, 9, 10 };
        heapSort(a, sizeof(a) / sizeof(int));
}
```

Data structure	Array
Worst Case Time Complexity	O(nlogn)
Best Case Time Complexity	O(nlogn)
Average Time Complexity	O(nlogn)
Space Complexity	O(1)

Note: Heap-Sort is not a Stable sort and do not require any extra space for sorting a list.

Uses of Heap

1. **Heapsort**: One of the best sorting methods being in-place and log(N) time complexity in all scenarios.

2. **Selection algorithms**: Finding the min, max, both the min and max, median, or even the kth largest element can be done in linear time (often constant time) using heaps.

3. **Priority Queues**: Heap Implemented priority queues are used in Graph algorithms like Prim's Algorithm and Dijkstra's algorithm. A heap is a useful data structure when you need to remove the object with the highest (or lowest) priority. Schedulers, timers

4. **Graph algorithms**: By using heaps as internal traversal data structures, run time will be reduced by polynomial order. Examples of such problems are Prim's minimal

5. Because of the lack of pointers, the operations are faster than a binary tree. Also, some more complicated heaps (such as binomial) can be merged efficiently, which isn't easy to do for a binary tree.

Problems in Heap

Kth Smallest in a Min Heap

Just call DeleteMin() operation K-1 times and then again call DeleteMin() this last operation will give Kth smallest value. *Time Complexity O(KlogN)*

Kth Largest in a Max Heap

Just call DeleteMax() operation K-1 times and then again call DeleteMax () this last operation will give Kth smallest value. *Time Complexity* O(KlogN)

100 Largest in a Stream

There are billions of *integer* s coming out of a stream some getInt() function is providing *integer* s one by one. How would you determine the largest 100 numbers?

> *Solution:* Large hundred (or smallest hundred etc.) such problems are solved very easily using a Heap. In our case, we will create a min heap.

1. First from 100 first *integer* s builds a min heap.
2. Then for each coming *integer* compare if it is greater than the top of the min heap.
3. If not, then look for next *integer* . If yes, then remove the top min value from the min heap and insert the new value at the top of the heap and use procolateDown and move it to its proper position down the heap.
4. Every time you have largest 100 values stored in your head

Merge two Heap

How can we merge two heaps?

Solution: There is no single solution for this. Let us suppose the size of the bigger heap is N and the size of the smaller heap is M.

1. If both heaps are comparable size, then put both heap arrays in same bigger arrays. Or in one of the arrays if they are big enough. Then apply CreateHeap() function which will take theta(N+M) time.
2. If M is much smaller then N then enqueue() each element of M array one by one to N heap. This will take O(MlogN) the worst case or O(M) best case.

Min / Max Heap using function pointer

Example 11.6: Same heap data structure can be used to create boty min heap and max heap only the compare function will change.

```
typedef struct Heap_t{
        int Capacity;
        int Size;
        int *Array;
        bool(*compare)(int, int);
}Heap;
```

```
void HeapInitialize(PtrHeap pHeap, int capacity, bool(*comp)(int, int))
{
        pHeap->Size = 0;
        pHeap->Capacity = capacity;
        pHeap->Array = (int*)malloc((capacity)*sizeof(int));
        pHeap->compare = comp;
}
```

```
void HeapInsert(PtrHeap pHeap, int value)
{
        pHeap->Array[pHeap->Size] = value;
        ProclateUp(pHeap->Array, pHeap->Size,pHeap->compare);
        pHeap->Size++;
}
```

```
void ProclateUp(int *arr, int position, bool(*comp)(int, int))
{
        int parent = (position - 1) / 2;

        if (position != 0)
        {
                if (comp(arr[parent], arr[position]))
                {
                        int temp = arr[position];
                        arr[position] = arr[parent];
                        arr[parent] = temp;
                        ProclateUp(arr, parent);
                }
        }
}
```

```
void ProclateDown(int *arr, int position, int size, bool(*comp)(int, int))
{
        int lChild = 2 * position + 1;
        int rChild = lChild + 1;
        int small = -1;

        if (lChild < size)
                small = lChild;

        if (rChild < size && comp(arr[rChild], arr[lChild]))
                small = rChild;

        if (small != -1 && comp(arr[small], arr[position]))
        {
                int temp = arr[position];
                arr[position] = arr[small];
                arr[small] = temp;
                ProclateDown(arr, small, size);
        }
}
```

```
int HeapDelete(PtrHeap pHeap)
{
        int value = (pHeap->Array[0]);
        pHeap->Array[0] = pHeap->Array[pHeap->Size - 1];
        pHeap->Size--;
        ProclateDown(pHeap->Array, 0, pHeap->Size,pHeap->compare);
        return value;
}
```

```
// Greater used as comparator, swap when parent is grater then child, min heap
bool  Greater(int  a, int  b)
{
   return  a > b;
}
```

```
// Smaller used as comparator, swap when parent is smaller then child, max heap
bool  Smaller(int  a, int  b)
{
   return  a < b;
}
```

```
int HeapSize(PtrHeap pHeap)
{
        return pHeap->Size;
}
```

Get Median function

Example 11.7: Give a data structure which will provide median of given values in constant time.

Solution: We will be using two heap one min heap and other max heap. First, there will be a max heap which will contain the first half of data and there will be an another min heap which will contain the second half of the data. Max heap will contain the smaller half of the data and its max value which is at the top of the heap will be the median contender. Similarly the Min heap will contain the larger values of the data and its min value which is at its top will contain the median contender. We will keep track of the size of heaps. Whenever we insert a value to heap we will make sure that the size of two heaps differs by max one element, otherwise we will pop one element from one and insert into another to keep them balanced.

```
void MedianHeapInit(MedianHeap* heap)
{
        HeapInitialize(&heap->minHeap, 100, Greater);
        HeapInitialize(&heap->maxHeap, 100, Smaller);
}
```

```
void MedianHeapInsert(MedianHeap* heap, int value)
{
        if (HeapSize(&heap->maxHeap) == 0 || HeapTop(&heap->maxHeap) >= value )
        {
                HeapInsert(&heap->maxHeap, value);
        }
        else
        {
                HeapInsert(&heap->minHeap, value);
        }
        //size balancing
        if (HeapSize(&heap->maxHeap) > HeapSize(&heap->minHeap) + 1)
        {
                value = HeapDelete(&heap->maxHeap);
                HeapInsert(&heap->minHeap, value);
        }
        if (HeapSize(&heap->minHeap) > HeapSize(&heap->maxHeap) + 1)
        {
                value = HeapDelete(&heap->minHeap);
                HeapInsert(&heap->maxHeap, value);
        }
}
```

```
int getMedian(MedianHeap* heap)
{
        if (HeapSize(&heap->maxHeap) == 0 && HeapSize(&heap->minHeap) == 0)
                return INT_MIN;

        if (HeapSize(&heap->maxHeap) == HeapSize(&heap->minHeap))
                return (HeapTop(&heap->maxHeap) + HeapTop(&heap->minHeap)) / 2;
        else if (HeapSize(&heap->maxHeap) > HeapSize(&heap->minHeap))
                return HeapTop(&heap->maxHeap);
        else
                return HeapTop(&heap->minHeap);
}
```

```
int main()
{
        int arr[] = { 1, 9, 2, 8, 3, 7, 4, 6, 5, 1, 9, 2, 8, 3, 7, 4, 6, 5, 10, 10 };

        MedianHeap heap;
        MedianHeapInit(&heap);
        for (int i = 0; i < 20; i++)
        {
                MedianHeapInsert(&heap, arr[i]);
                printf("Median after insertion of %d is %d \n", arr[i], getMedian(&heap));
        }
        return 0;
}
```

Is Min Heap

Given an array find if it is a binary Heap is Min Heap

Example 11.8:

```
int IsMinHeap(int arr[], int size)
{
        for (int i = 0; i <= (size - 2) / 2; i++)
        {
                if (2 * i + 1 < size)
                {
                        if (arr[i] > arr[2 * i + 1])
                                return 0;
                }
                if (2 * i + 2<size)
                {
                        if (arr[i] > arr[2 * i + 2])
                                return 0;
                }
        }
        return 1;
}
```

Is Max Heap

Given an array find if it is a binary Heap Max heap

Example 11.9:

```
int IsMaxHeap(int arr[], int size)
{
        for (int i = 0; i <= (size - 2) / 2; i++)
        {
                if (2 * i + 1 < size)
                {
                        if (arr[i] < arr[2 * i + 1])
                                return 0;
                }
                if (2 * i + 2 < size)
                {
                        if (arr[i] < arr[2 * i + 2])
                                return 0;
                }
        }
        return 1;
}
```

Traversal in Heap

Heaps are not designed to traverse to find some element they are made to get min or max element fast. But still if you want to traverse a heap just traverse the array sequentially. This traversal will be level order traversal. This traversal will have linear *Time Complexity*.

Deleting Aribtery element from Min Heap

Again heap is not designed to delete an arbitrary element, but still if you want to do so. Find the element by linear search in the heap array. Replace it with the value stored at the end of the Heap value. Reduce the size of the heap by one. Compare the new inserted value with its parent. If its value is smaller than the parent value, then percolate up. Else if its value is greater than its left and right child then percolate down. *Time Complexity* is **O(logn)**

Deleting Kth element from Min Heap

Again heap is not designed to delete an arbitrary element, but still if you want to do so. Replace the kth value with the value stored at the end of the Heap value. Reduce the size of the heap by one. Compare the new inserted value with its parent. If its value is smaller than the parent value, then percolate up. Else if its value is greater than its left and right child then percolate down. *Time Complexity* is **O(logn)**

Print value in Range in Min Heap

Linearly traverse through the heap and print the value which are in the given range.

Exercise

1. What is the worst-case runTime Complexity of finding the smallest item in a min-heap?

2. Find max in a min heap.
   Hint: normal search in the complete array. There is one more optimization you can search from the mid of the array at index N/2

3. What is the worst-case time Complexity of finding the largest item in a min-heap?

4. What is the worst-case time Complexity of deleteMin in a min-heap?

5. What is the worst-case time Complexity of building a heap by insertion?

6. Is a heap full or complete binary tree?

7. What is the worst time runTime Complexity of sorting an array of N elements using heapsort?

8. Given a sequence of numbers: 1, 2, 3, 4, 5, 6, 7, 8, 9
   a. Draw a binary Min-heap by inserting the above numbers one by one
   b. Also draw the tree that will be formed after calling Dequeue() on this heap

9. Given a sequence of numbers: 1, 2, 3, 4, 5, 6, 7, 8, 9
   a. Draw a binary Max-heap by inserting the above numbers one by one
   b. Also draw the tree that will be formed after calling Dequeue() on this heap

10. Given a sequence of numbers: 3, 9, 5, 4, 8, 1, 5, 2, 7, 6. Construct a Min-heap by calling CreateHeap function.

11. Show an array that would be the result after the call to deleteMin() on this heap

12. Given an array: [3, 9, 5, 4, 8, 1, 5, 2, 7, 6]. Apply heapify over this to make a min heap and sort the elements in decreasing order?

13. In Heap-Sort once a root element has been put in its final position, how much time does it take to re-heapify the structure so that the next removal can take place? In other words, what is the *Time Complexity* of a single element removal from the heap of size N?

14. What do you think the overall *Time Complexity* for heapsort is? Why do you feel this way?

CHAPTER 12: HASH-TABLE

Introduction

In the previous chapter, we have looked into various searching techniques. Consider a problem of searching a value in an array. If the array is not sorted then we have no other option but to look into each and every element one by one so the searching *Time Complexity* will be **O(n)**. If the array is sorted then we can search the value we are looking for in **O(logn)** logarithmic time using binary search.

What if we have a function which can tell us the location/index of the value we are looking for in the array? We can directly go into that location and tell whether our object we are searching for is present or not in just **O(1)** constant time. Such a function is called a Hash function.

In real life when a letter is handed over to a postman, by looking at the address on the letter, postman precisely knows to which house this letter needs to be delivered. He is not going to ask for a person door to door.

Hash Function

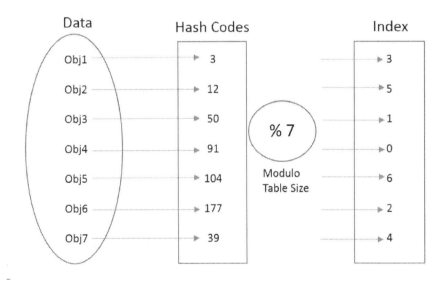

The process of storing objects using a hash function is as follows:
1.   Create an array of size M to store objects, this array is called Hash-Table.
2.   Find a hash code of an object by passing it through the hash function.
3.   Take module of hash code by the size of Hashtable to get the index of the table where objects will be stored.
4.   Finally store these objects in the designated index.

The process of searching objects in Hash-Table using a hash function is as follows:
1.   Find a hash code of the object we are searching for by passing it through the hash function.
2.   Take module of hash code by the size of Hashtable to get the index of the table where objects are stored.
3.   Finally, retrieve the object from the designated index.

Hash-Table

A Hash-Table is a data structure which maps keys to values. Each position of the Hash-Table is called a slot. The Hash-Table uses a hash function to calculate an index of an array of slots. We use the Hash-Table when the number of keys actually stored is small relatively to the number of possible keys.

Hash-Table Abstract Data Type (ADT)

ADT of Hash-Table contains the following functions:
1. Insert(x), add object x to the data set.
2. Delete(x), delete object x from the data set.
3. Search(x), search object x in data set.

Hash Function

A hash function is a function which generates an index in a table for a given object.

An ideal hash function should generate a unique index for each and every object is called the perfect hash function.

Example 12.1: Most simple hash function

```
unsigned int Hash(int key, int tableSize)//division method
{
        unsigned int hashValue = 0;
        hashValue = key;
        return hashValue % tableSize;
}
```

There are many hash functions, but this is the minimum that a hash function should do. Various hash generation logics will be added to this function to generate a better hash.

Properties of good hash function:

1. It should provide a uniform distribution of hash values. A non-uniform distribution increased the number of collisions and the cost of resolving them.
2. Choose a hash function which can be computed quickly and returns values within the range of the Hash-Table.
3. Chose a hash function with a good collision resolution algorithm which can be used to compute alternative index if the collision occurs.
4. Choose a hash function which uses the necessary information provided in the key.
5. It should have high load factor for a given set of keys.

Load Factor

Load factor = Number of elements in Hash-Table / Hash-Table size

Based on the above definition, Load factor tells whether the hash function is distributing the keys uniformly or not. So it helps in determining the efficiency of the hashing function. It also works as decision parameter when we want to expand or rehash the existing Hash-Table entries.

Collisions

When a hash function generates the same index for the two or more different objects, the problem known as the collision. Ideally hash function should return a unique address for each key, but practically it is not possible.

Collision Resolution Techniques

Hash collisions are practically unavoidable when hashing large number of objects. Techniques which are used to find the alternate location in the Hash-Table is called collision resolution. There are a number of collision resolution techniques to handle the collision in hashing.

Most common and widely used techniques are:
- Open addressing
- Separate chaining

Hashing with Open Addressing

When using linear open addressing, the Hash-Table is represented by a one-dimensional array with indices that range from 0 to the desired table size-1.

One method of resolving collision is the look into a Hash-Table and find another free slot the hold the object which have caused the collision. A simple way is to move from one slot to another in some sequential order until we find a free space. This collision resolution process is called Open Addressing.

Linear Probing

In Linear Probing, we try to resolve the collision of an index of a Hash-Table by sequentially searching the Hash-Table for free location. Let us suppose, if k is the index retrieved from the hash function. If the kth index is already filled then we will look for (k+1) %M, then (k+2) %M and so on. When we get a free slot we will insert the object into that free slot.

Example 12.2: The resolver function of linear probing

```
int resolverFun(int i)
{
        return i;
}
```

Quadratic Probing

In Quadratic Probing, we try to resolve the collision of the index of a Hash-Table by quadratic ally increasing the search index for free location. Let us suppose, if k is the index retrieved from the hash function. If the kth index is already filled then we will look for (k+1^2) %M, then (k+2^2) %M and so on. When we get a free slot we will insert the object into that free slot.

Example 12.3: The resolver function of quadratic probing

```
int resolverFun(int i)
{
        return i * i;
}
```

Table size should be a prime number to prevent early looping shouldn't be too close to 2powN

Linear Probing implementation

Example 12.4: Below is a linear probing collision resolution Hash-Table implementation.

```
#include <stdio.h>
#include <stdlib.h>

#define TABLE_SIZE 50
#define EMPTY_NODE -1
#define LAZY_DELETED -2
```

Table array size will be 50 and we have defined two constant values EMPTY_NODE and LAZY_DELETED.

```
unsigned int ComputeHash(int key, int tableSize)//division method
{
        unsigned int hashValue = 0;
        hashValue = key;
        return hashValue % tableSize;
}
```

This is the most simple hash generation function which does nothing but just take the modulus of the key.

```
int ResolverFun(int i)
{
        return i;
}
```

When the hash index is already occupied by some element the value will be placed in some other location to find that new location resolver function is used.

```
struct hashhash_t{
        int tableSize;
        int* intArray;
};
typedef hashhash_t* hashPtr;
```

Hash-Table has two component one is table size and other is pointer to array.

```
hashPtr HashInitialize()
{
        hashPtr hash;
        hash = (hashPtr)malloc(sizeof(hashhash_t));

        hash->tableSize = TABLE_SIZE;
        hash->intArray = (int*)malloc(hash->tableSize*sizeof(int));

        for (int i = 0; i<hash->tableSize; i++)
                hash->intArray[i] = EMPTY_NODE;

        return hash;
}
```

initializeTable is the first function which will initialize the Hash-Table. This is the first function called after a Hash-Table before any insert, search or delete operation.

Example **12.5:**

```
int HashInsert(hashPtr hash, int value)
{
        int hashValue = ComputeHash(value, hash->tableSize);
        int i = 0;
        for (i = 0; i < hash->tableSize; i++)
        {

                if (hash->intArray[hashValue] == EMPTY_NODE ||
                        hash->intArray[hashValue] == LAZY_DELETED)
                {

                        hash->intArray[hashValue] = value;
                        return 1;

                }
                hashValue = hashValue + ResolverFun(i);
                hashValue = hashValue % hash->tableSize;

        }
        return -1;

}
```

An insert node function is used to add values to the array. First hash is calculated. And then we try to place that value in the Hash-Table. We look for empty node or lazy deleted node to insert value. In case insert did not success we try new location using a resolver function.

Example 12.6:

```
int HashFind(hashPtr hash, int value)
{
        int hashValue = ComputeHash(value, hash->tableSize);
        for (int i = 0; i < hash->tableSize; i++)
        {

                if (hash->intArray[hashValue] == value ||
                        hash->intArray[hashValue] == EMPTY_NODE)
                {

                        break;

                }
                hashValue = hashValue + ResolverFun(i);
                hashValue = hashValue % hash->tableSize;

        }

        if (hash->intArray[hashValue] == value)
                return hashValue;
        else
                return -1;//value not found

}
```

Find node function is used to search values in the array. First hash is calculated. And then we try to find that value in the Hash-Table. We look for over desired value or empty node. In case we find the value we are looking for then we return that value or in case we don't we return -1. We use a resolver function to find the next probable index to search.

276

Example 12.7:

```
int HashDelete(hashPtr hash, int value)
{
        int hashValue = ComputeHash(value, hash->tableSize);

        for (int i = 0; i < hash->tableSize; i++)
        {
                if (hash->intArray[hashValue] == EMPTY_NODE)
                        return -1;

                if (hash->intArray[hashValue] == value)
                {
                        hash->intArray[hashValue] = LAZY_DELETED;
                        return 1;//deleted properly
                }

                hashValue = hashValue + ResolverFun(i);
                hashValue = hashValue%hash->tableSize;
        }
        return -1;//value not found
}
```

Delete node function is used to delete values from a Hashtable. We don't actually delete the value we just mark that value as LAZY_DELETED. Same as the insert and search we use resolverFun to find the next probable location of the key.

Example 12.8:

```
void PrintHash(hashPtr hash, int tableSize)//print key wise values
{
        for (int i = 0; i< hash->tableSize; i++)
                printf("index %d value :: %d \n", i, hash->intArray[i]);
}
int main()
{
        hashPtr myHash = HashInitialize();
        for (int i = 100; i < 110; i++)
                HashInsert(myHash, i);
        printf("search 100 :: %d \n", HashFind(myHash, 100));
        printf("remove 100 :: %d \n", HashDelete(myHash, 100));
        printf("search 100 :: %d \n", HashFind(myHash, 100));
        printf("remove 100 :: %d \n", HashDelete(myHash, 100));
        PrintHash(myHash, TABLE_SIZE);
}
```

Quadratic Probing implementation.

Everything will be same as linear probing implementation only resolver function will be changed.

```
int resolverFun(int i)
{       return i * i;
}
```

Hashing with Separate chaining

Another method for collision resolution is based on an idea of putting the keys that collide in a linked list. This method is called separate chaining. To speed up search we use Insertion-Sort or keeping the linked list sorted.

Table

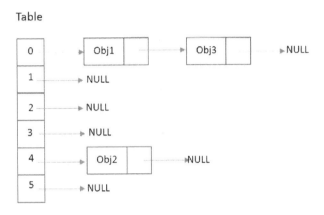

Separate Chaining implementation

'

Example 12.9: Below is separate chaining implementation of hash tables.

```
#include <stdio.h>
#include <stdlib.h>

#define TABLE_SIZE 517
#define TABLE_BITS 9

struct listNode_t{
        int value;
        listNode_t* next;
};

typedef listNode_t* ptrList;
```

```
struct hashTable_t{
        int tableSize;
        ptrList* listArray;//double pointer
};
typedef hashTable_t* hashPtr;
```

```c
unsigned int ComputeHash(int key, int tableSize)//division method
{
        unsigned int hashValue = 0;
        hashValue = key;
        return hashValue % tableSize;
}
```

```c
hashPtr HashInitialize(int size)
{
        hashPtr hTable = (hashPtr)malloc(sizeof(hashTable_t));
        hTable->tableSize = size;
        hTable->listArray = (ptrList*)malloc(hTable->tableSize * sizeof(ptrList));

        for (int i = 0; i<hTable->tableSize; i++)
                hTable->listArray[i] = NULL;
        return hTable;
}
```

```c
void PrintHash(hashPtr hTable, int tableSize)//print key wise values
{
        for (int i = 0; i<hTable->tableSize; i++)
        {
                printf("\n Printing for index value ::( %d ) List of value printing :: ", i);
                ptrList   head = hTable->listArray[i];
                while (head)
                {
                        printf(" %d ", head->value);
                        head = head->next;
                }
        }
}
```

```c
int HashFind(hashPtr hTable, int value)
{
        ptrList possition;
        int index = ComputeHash(value, hTable->tableSize);
        possition = hTable->listArray[index];
        while (possition && possition->value != value)
        {
                possition = possition->next;
        }
        return !(possition == NULL);
}
```

```
void HashInsert(hashPtr hTable, int value)
{
        int index = ComputeHash(value, hTable->tableSize);
        ptrList tempPtr = (ptrList)malloc(sizeof(listNode_t));
        tempPtr->value = value;
        tempPtr->next = hTable->listArray[index];
        hTable->listArray[index] = tempPtr;
}
```

```
int HashDelete(hashPtr hTable, int value)
{
        ptrList currNode, nextNode;
        int index = ComputeHash(value, hTable->tableSize);
        currNode = hTable->listArray[index];

        if (currNode && currNode->value == value)
        {
                hTable->listArray[index] = currNode->next;
                free(currNode);
                return 1;
        }
        while (currNode)
        {
                nextNode = currNode->next;
                if (nextNode && nextNode->value == value)
                {
                        currNode->next = nextNode->next;
                        free(nextNode);
                        return 1;
                }
                else
                {
                        currNode = nextNode;
                }
        }
        return 0;
}
```

```
int main()
{
        hashPtr myTable = HashInitialize(TABLE_SIZE);
        for (int i = 100; i < 110; i++)
                HashInsert(myTable, i);
        printf("search 100 :: %d \n", HashFind(myTable, 100));
        printf("remove 100 :: %d \n", HashDelete(myTable, 100));
        printf("search 100 :: %d \n", HashFind(myTable, 100));
        printf("remove 100 :: %d \n", HashDelete(myTable, 100));
        PrintHash(myTable, TABLE_SIZE);
}
```

Note: It is important to note that the size of the "skip" must be such that all the slots in the table will eventually be occupied. Otherwise, part of the table will be unused. To ensure this, it is often suggested that the table size being a prime number. This is the reason we have been using 11 in our examples.

Problems in Hashing

Anagram solver

An anagram is a word or phrase formed by reordering the letters of another word or phrase.

Example 12.10: Two words are anagram if they are of same size and there chracters are same.

```
int isAnagram(char str1[], char str2[])
{
        int curr = 0;
        int size1 = strlen(str1);
        int size2 = strlen(str2);
        if (size1 != size2)
                return 0;
        hashPtr pHash = HashInitialize();

        while (str1[curr])
        {
                HashInsert(pHash, str1[curr]);
                curr++;
        }
        curr = 0;
        while (str2[curr])
        {
                if (!HashDelete(pHash, str2[curr]))
                        return 0;
                curr++;
        }
        return 1;
}
```

Remove Duplicate

Remove duplicates in an array of numbers.

Solution: We can use a second array or the same array, as the output array. In the below example Hash-Table is used to solve this problem.

Example 12.11:

```
void removeDuplicate(char str[])
{
        int curr = 0, end = 0;
        int size = strlen(str);
        hashPtr pHash = HashInitialize();

        while (str[curr])
        {
                if (!HashFind(pHash, str[curr]))
                {
                        str[end++] = str[curr];
                        HashInsert(pHash, str[curr]);
                }
                curr++;
        }
        str[end] = '\0';
}
```

Find Missing

Example 12.12: There is a list of integers we need to find the missing number in the list.

```
int findMissing(int arr[], int size)
{
        int curr = 0;
        int n = size + 1;
        hashPtr pHash = HashInitialize();

        while (arr[curr])
        {
                HashInsert(pHash, arr[curr]);
                curr++;
        }

        for(curr = 1; curr <= n; curr++)
        {
                if (!HashFind(pHash, curr))
                        return curr;
        }
        return 1;
}
```

Print Repeating

Example 12.13: Print the repeting integer in a list of integers.

```
void printRepeating(int arr[], int size)
{
        int i;
        hashPtr pHash = HashInitialize();

        printf("Repeating elements are ");
        for (i = 0; i < size; i++)
        {
                if (HashFind(pHash, arr[i]))
                        printf(" %d ", arr[i]);
                else
                        HashInsert(pHash, arr[i]);
        }
}
```

Print First Repeating

Example 12.14: Same as the above problem in this we need to print the first repeting number. Cution should be taken to find the first repeting number. It should be the one number which is repeting. For example 1,2,3,2,1. The answer should be 1 as it is the first number which is repeting.

```
void printFirstRepeating(int arr[], int size)
{
        int i;
        hashPtr pHash = HashInitialize();

        for (i = 0; i < size; i++)
        {
                HashInsert(pHash, arr[i]);
        }
        for (i = 0; i < size; i++)
        {
                HashDelete(pHash, arr[i]);
                if (HashFind(pHash, arr[i]))
                {
                        printf("First Repeating number is : %d ", arr[i]);
                        return;
                }
        }
}
```

1. Design a number (ID) generator system which generate numbers between 0-99999999 (8-digits).
   The system should support two functions:
   a. int getNumber();
   b. int requestNumber();

   getNumber() function should find out a number that is not assigned, than marks it as assigned and return that number.
   requestNumber() function checks the number is assigned or not. If it is assigned returns 0, else marks it as assigned and return 1.

   Hint: You can keep a counter for assigning numbers. Whenever there is a getNumber() call you will check if that number is already assigned in a Hash-Table. If it is already assigned, then increase the counter and check again. If you find a number not in the Hash-Table then add it to Hashtable and increase the counter.
   requestNumber() will look in the Hash-Table if the number is already taken, then it will return 0 else it will return 1 and mark that number as taken inside the Hash-Table.

2. Given a large string, find the most occurring words in the string. What is the *Time Complexity* of the above solution?
   Hint:-
   a. Create a Hashtable which will keep track of <word, frequency>
   b. Iterate through the string and keep track of word frequency by inserting into Hash-Table.
   c. When we have a new word we will insert it into the Hashtable with frequency 1. For all repetition of the word we will increase the frequency.
   d. We can keep track of the most occurring words whenever we are increasing the frequency we can see if this is the most occurring word or not.
   e. The *Time Complexity* is *O(n)* where n is the number of words in the string and *Space Complexity* is the O(m) where m is the unique words in the string.

3. In the above question, What if you are given whole work of OSCAR WILDE, most popular playwrights in the early 1890s.
   Hint:-
   a. Who knows how many books are there, let's assume there is a lot and we can't put everything in memory. First, we need a Streaming Library so that we can read section by section in each document. Then we need a tokenizer which will give words to our program. And we need some sort of dictionary let's say we will use HashTable.
   b. What you need is - 1. A streaming library tokenizer, 2. A tokenizer 3. A hashmap

   Method:
   1. Use streamers to find a stream of the given words
   2. Tokenize the input text
   3. If the stemmed word is in hash map, increment its frequency count else adds a word to hash map with frequency 1
   c. We can improve the performance by looking into parallel computing. We can use the map-reduce to solve this problem. Multiple nodes will read and process multiple documents. Once they are done with their processing, then we can use reduce to merge them.

4. In the above question, What if we wanted to find the most common PHRASE in his writings.
   Hint:- We can keep <phrase, frequency> Hash-Table and do the same process of the 2nd and 3rd problems.

5. Write a hashing algorithm for strings.
Hint: Use Horner's method

```
int hornerHash (char* key, int tableSize )
{
        int size = strlen(key);
        int h = 0;
        int i;
        for (i=0; i < size  ; i++)
        {
                h = (32 * h + key[i]) % tableSize;
        }
        return h;
}
```

6. Pick two data structures to use in implementing a Map. Describe lookup, insert, & delete operations. Give time & *Space Complexity* for each. Give pros & cons for each.

Hint:-

     a) Linked List
        I.   Insert is *O(1)*
        II.   Delete is *O(1)*
        III. Lookup is *O(1)* auxiliary and *O(N)* worst case.
        IV. Pros: Fast inserts and deletes, can use for any data type.
        V.   Cons: Slow lookups.

     b) Balanced Search Tree (RB Tree)
        I.   Insert is *O(logn)*
        II.   Delete is *O(logn)*
        III. Lookup is *O(logn)*
        IV. Pros: Reasonably fast inserts/deletes and lookups.
        V.   Cons: Data needs to have order defined on it.

CHAPTER 13: GRAPHS

Introduction

In this chapter, we will study about Graphs. Graphs can be used to represent many interesting things in the real world. Flights from cities to cities, rods connecting various town and cities. Even the sequence of steps that we take to become ready for jobs daily, or even a sequence of classes that we take to become a graduate in computer science. Once we have a good representation of the map, then we use a standard graph algorithms to solve many interesting problems of real life.

The flight connection between major cities of India can also be represented by the below graph. Each node is a city and each edge is a straight flight path from one city to another. You may want to go from Delhi to Chennai, if given this data in good representation to a computer, through graph algorithms the computer may propose shortest, quickest or cheapest path from soured to destination.

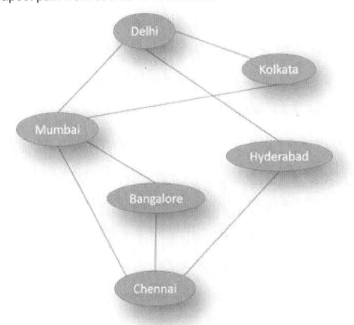

Google map which we use is also a big graph of lots of nodes and edges. And suggest shortest and quickest path to the user.

Graph Definitions

A Graph is represented by G where G = (V, E), where V is a finite set of points called **Vertices** and E is a finite set of **Edges**.

Each **edge** is a tuple (u, v) where u, v ∈ V. There can be a third component weight to the tuple. **Weight** is cost to go from one vertex to another.

Edge in a graph can be directed or undirected. If the edges of graph are one way it is called **Directed graph** or **Digraph**. The graph whose edges are two ways are called **Undirected graph** or just graph.

A **Path** is a sequence of edges between two vertices. The length of a path is defined as the sum of the weight of all the edges in the path.

Two vertices u and v are **adjacent** if there is an edge whose endpoints are u and v.

In the below graph:

V = { V1, V2, V3, V4, V5, V6, V7, V8, V9 } ,

$$E = \left\{ \begin{array}{l} (V1, V0,1), (V2, V1,2), (V3, V2,3), (V3, V4,4), (V5, V4,5), \\ (V1, V5, 6), (V2, V5,7), (V3, V5,8), (V4, V5,9) \end{array} \right\}$$

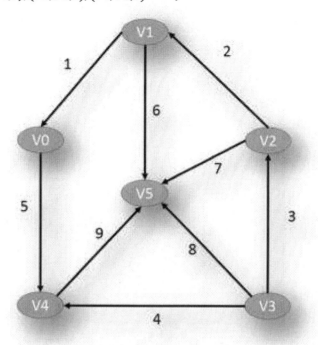

The **in-degree** of a vertex v, denoted by indeg(v) is the number of incoming edges to the vertex v. The **out-degree** of a vertex v, denoted by outdeg(v) is the number of outgoing edges of a vertex v. The **degree** of a vertex v, denoted by deg(v) is the total number of edges whose one endpoint is v.

deg(v) = Indeg (v) + outdeg (v)

In the above graph
deg(V4)=3, indeg(V4)=2 and outdeg(V4)=1

A **Cycle** is a path that starts and ends at the same vertex and include at least one vertex.

An edge is a **Self-Loop** if two if its two endpoints coincide. This is a form of a cycle.

A vertex v is **Reachable** from vertex u or "u reaches v" if there is a path from u to v. In an undirected graph if v is reachable from u then u is reachable from v. But in a directed graph it is possible that u reaches v but there is no path from v to u.

A graph is **Connected** if for any two vertices there is a path between them.

A **Forest** is a graph without cycles.

A **Sub-Graph** of a graph G is a graph whose vertices and edges are a subset of the vertices and edges of G.

A **Spanning Sub-Graph** of G is a graph that connects all the vertices of G.

A **tree** is a acyclic connected graph.

A **Spanning tree** of a graph is a spanning sub-graph which is also a tree which means, a connected graph which connects all the vertices of graph and that does not have a cycle.

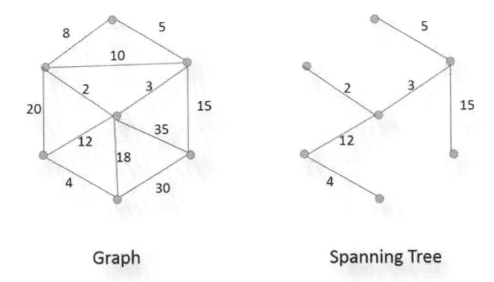

Graph   Spanning Tree

Graph Representation

In this section we introduce the data structure for representing a graph. In the below representations we maintain a collection to store edges and vertices of the graph.

Adjacency Matrix

One of the ways to represent a graph is to use two dimensional matrix. Each combination of row and column represent a vertex in the graph. The value stored at the location row v and column w is the edge from vertex v to vertex w. The nodes that are connected by an edge are called adjacent nodes. This matrix is used to store adjacent relation so it is called the Adjacency Matrix. In the below diagram, we have a graph and its Adjacency matrix.

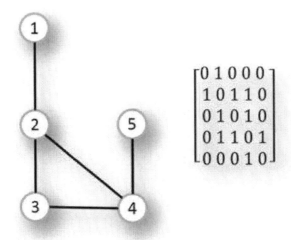

$$\begin{bmatrix} 0 & 1 & 0 & 0 & 0 \\ 1 & 0 & 1 & 1 & 0 \\ 0 & 1 & 0 & 1 & 0 \\ 0 & 1 & 1 & 0 & 1 \\ 0 & 0 & 0 & 1 & 0 \end{bmatrix}$$

In the above graph each node has weight 1 so the adjacency matrix has just 1s or 0s. If the edges are of different weights that that weight will be filled in the matrix.

Pros: Adjacency matrix implementation is simple. Adding/Removing an edge between two vertices is just *O(1)*. Query if there is an edge between two vertices is also *O(1)*

Cons: It always consumes O(V^2) space, which is an inefficient way to store when a graph is a sparse. Sparse Matrix: In a huge graph each node is connected with fewer nodes. So most of the places in adjacency matrix are empty. Such matrix is called sparse matrix. In most of the real world problems adjacency matrix is not a good choice for sore graph data.

Adjacency List

A more space efficient way of storing graph is adjacency list. In adjacency list of pointers to a linked list node. Each pointer corresponds to vertices in a graph. Each pointer will then point to the vertices which are connected to it and store this as a list.

In the below diagram node 2 is connected to 1, 3 and 4. So the pointer at location 2 is pointing to a list which contain 1, 3 and 4.

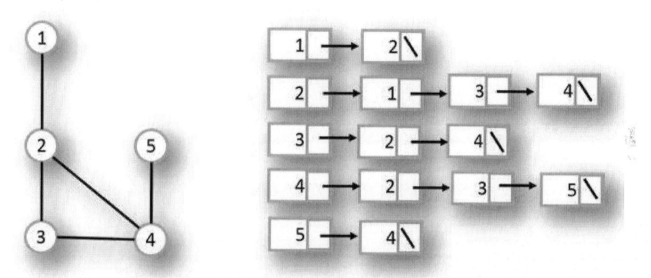

The adjacency list helps us to compactly represent a sparse graph. An adjacency list representation also allows us to find all the vertices which are directly connected to any vertices by just one link list scan. In all our programs we are going to use the adjacency list to store the graph.

Below is C code for adjacency list representation of an undirected graph:

Example 13.1:

```
struct ListNode{
        int weight;
        int index;
        ListNode* next;
};

typedef ListNode* ListPtr;

typedef struct Graph_t{
        ListPtr* dpHead;
        int count;
} Graph;

typedef Graph* GraphPtr;
```

```c
void GraphInit(GraphPtr pGraph, int nodeCount)//one extra sentinel for ease
{
        ListPtr* dpHead =  (ListPtr*)malloc((nodeCount) * sizeof(ListPtr));
        for(int i=0; i<=nodeCount; i++)
                dpHead[i] = NULL;
        pGraph->dpHead = dpHead;
        pGraph->count = nodeCount;
}
```

```c
int GraphInsert(GraphPtr G, int src, int dst, int weight)
{
        ListPtr temp = (ListPtr)malloc(sizeof(ListNode));
        temp->weight = weight;
        temp->index=dst;
        temp->next = G->dpHead[src];
        G->dpHead[src]=temp;
        return 1;
}
```

```c
void UndirectedGraphInsert(GraphPtr G, int src, int dst, int weight)
{
        GraphInsert( G,  src,  dst,  weight);
        GraphInsert( G,  dst,  src,  weight);
}
```

```c
void GraphPrint(GraphPtr G)
{
        int count = G->count, index;
        for (index = 0; index < count; index++)
        {
                ListPtr head = G->dpHead[index];
                printf("\n Adjacency list of index %d are [ ", index);
                while(head)
                {
                        printf(" %d ", head->index);
                        head = head->next;
                }
                printf(" ]\n");
        }
}
```

```
int main()
{
        int nodeCount=8;
        Graph gph;
        GraphInit(&gph,nodeCount);
        UndirectedGraphInsert(&gph, 0,1,1);
        UndirectedGraphInsert(&gph, 0,2,1);
        UndirectedGraphInsert(&gph, 0,3,1);
        UndirectedGraphInsert(&gph, 1,4,1);
        UndirectedGraphInsert(&gph, 2,5,1);
        UndirectedGraphInsert(&gph, 3,6,1);
        UndirectedGraphInsert(&gph, 4,7,1);
        UndirectedGraphInsert(&gph, 5,7,1);
        UndirectedGraphInsert(&gph, 6,7,1);
        GraphPrint(&gph);
        return 0;
}
```

Graph traversals

The **Depth first search (DFS)** and **Breadth first search (BFS)** are the two algorithms used to traverse a graph. These same algorithms can also be used to find some node in the graph, find if a node is reachable etc.

Traversal is the process of exploring a graph by examining all its edges and vertices.

A list of some of the problems that are solved using graph traversal are:
1. Determining a path from vertex u to vertex v, or report an error if there is no such path.
2. Given a starting vertex s, finding the minimum number of edges from vertex s to all the other vertices of the graph.
3. Testing of a graph G is connected.
4. Finding a spanning tree of a Graph.
5. Finding if there is some cycle in the graph.

Depth First Traversal

The DFS algorithm we start from starting point and go into depth of graph till we reach a dead end and then move up to parent node (Backtrack). In DFS we use stack to get the next vertex to start a search. Or we can use recursion (system stack) to do the same.

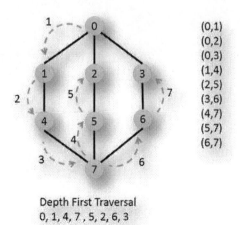

(0,1)
(0,2)
(0,3)
(1,4)
(2,5)
(3,6)
(4,7)
(5,7)
(6,7)

Depth First Traversal
0, 1, 4, 7 , 5, 2, 6, 3

Algorithm steps for DFS
1. Push the starting node in the stack.
2. Loop until the stack is empty.
3. Pop the node from the stack inside loop call this node current.
4. Process the current node. //Print, etc.
5. Traverse all the child nodes of the current node and push them into stack.
6. Repeat steps 3 to 5 until the stack is empty.

Stack based implementation of DFS

Example 13.2:

```
void DFSStack(GraphPtr G)
{
        int count = G->count;
        int* visited = (int*)malloc((count)*sizeof(int));
        int curr;
        Stack stk;
        for (int i = 0; i < count; i++)
                visited[i] = 0;
        StackInitialize(&stk);
        visited[0] = 1;
        StackPush(&stk,0);


        while (!StackIsEmpty(&stk))
        {
                curr = StackPop(&stk);
                printf(" %d ",curr);


                ListPtr head = G->dpHead[curr];
                while(head)
                {
                        if(!visited[head->index])
                        {
                                visited[head->index] = 1;
                                StackPush(&stk, head->index);
                        }
                        head = head->next;
                }
        }
}
```

Recursion based implementation of DFS

Example 13.3:

```
void DFSRec(GraphPtr G, int index, int* visited)
{
        printf(" %d ", index);
        ListPtr head = G->dpHead[index];
        while(head)
        {
                if(!visited[head->index])
                {
                        visited[head->index] = 1;
                        DFSRec( G, head->index, visited);
                }
                head = head->next;
        }
}
```

```
void DFS(GraphPtr G)
{
        int count = G->count;
        int* visited = (int*)malloc((count)*sizeof(int));
        for (int i = 0; i < count; i++)
                visited[i] = 0;

        for (int i = 0; i < count; i++)
                if (visited[i] == 0)
                {
                        visited[i] = 1;
                        DFSRec(G, i, visited);
                }
}
```

Breadth First Traversal

In BFS algorithm a graph is traversed in layer by layer fashion. The graph is traversed closer to the starting point. The queue is used to implement BFS.

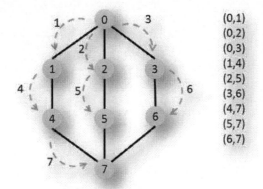

Breadth First Traversal
0, 1, 2, 3, 4, 5, 6, 7

293

Algorithm steps for BFS
1. Push the starting node into the Queue.
2. Loop until the Queue is empty.
3. Remove a node from the Queue inside loop, call this node current.
4. Process the current node.//print etc.
5. Traverse all the child nodes of the current node and push them into Queue.
6. Repeat steps 3 to 5 until Queue is empty.

Example 13.4:

```
void BFSQueue(GraphPtr G, int index, int* visited)
{
        int curr;
        Queue que;
        QueueInitialize(&que);

        visited[index] = 1;
        Enqueue(&que,index);

        while(!QueueIsEmpty(&que))
        {
                curr=Dequeue(&que);
                printf(" %d ", curr);
                ListPtr head = G->dpHead[curr];
                while(head)
                {
                        if(!visited[head->index])
                        {
                                visited[head->index] = 1;
                                Enqueue( &que,head->index);
                        }
                        head = head->next;
                }
        }
}
```

```
void BFS(GraphPtr G)
{
        int count = G->count;
        int* visited = (int*)malloc((count)*sizeof(int));
        for (int i = 0; i < count; i++)
                visited[i] = 0;

        for (int i = 0; i < count; i++)
                if (visited[i] == 0)
                        BFSQueue(G, i, visited);
}
```

A runtime analysis of DFS and BFS traversal is $O(n+m)$ time, where n is the number of edges reachable from source node and m is the number of edges incident on s.

The following problems have O(m+n) time performance:
1. Determining a path from vertex u to vertex v, or report an error if there is no such path.
2. Given a starting vertex s, finding the minimum number of edges from vertex s to all the other vertices of the graph.
3. Testing of a graph G is connected.
4. Finding a spanning tree of a Graph.
5. Finding if there is some cycle in the graph.

Problems in Graph

Determining a path from vertex u to vertex v

IF there is a path from u to v and we are doing DFS from u then v must be visited. And if there is no path them report an error.

Example 13.5:

```
int PathExist(GraphPtr G, int src, int dst)
{
        int count = G->count;
        int* visited = (int*)malloc((count)*sizeof(int));
        for (int i = 0; i < count; i++)
                visited[i] = 0;

        visited[src] = 1;
DFSRec (G, src, visited);
return visited[dst];
}
```

Given a starting vertex s, finding the minimum number of edges from vertex s to all the other vertices of the graph

Look for single source shortest path algorithm for each edge cost as 1 unit.

Testing of a graph G is connected.

We simply start from any arbitrary vertex and do DFS search and should see if there is some vertex which is not visited. If all the vertices are visited then it is a connected graph.

Example 13.6:

```
int isConnected(GraphPtr G)
{
        int count = G->count;
        int* visited = (int*)malloc((count)*sizeof(int));
        for (int i = 0; i < count; i++)
                visited[i] = 0;
        visited[0] = 1;
        DFSRec(G,0, visited);
        for (int i = 0; i < count; i++)
                if(visited[i] == 0)
                        return 0;
        return 1;
}
```

Finding if there is some cycle in the graph.

Modify DFS problem and get this done.

Directed Acyclic Graph

A Directed Acyclic Graph (DAG) is a directed graph with no cycle. A DAG represent relationship which is more general than a tree. Below is an example of DAG, this is how someone becomes ready for work. There are N other real life examples of DAG such as coerces selection to being graduated from college

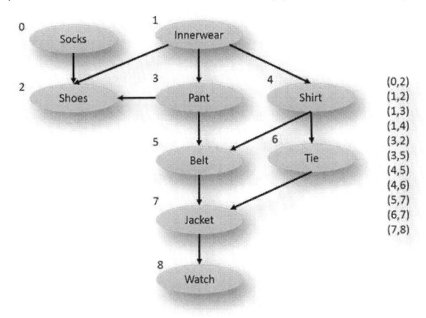

```
(0,2)
(1,2)
(1,3)
(1,4)
(3,2)
(3,5)
(4,5)
(4,6)
(5,7)
(6,7)
(7,8)
```

Topological Sort

A topological sort is a method of ordering the nodes of a directed graph in which nodes represent activities and the edges represent dependency among those tasks. For topological sorting to work it is required that the graph should be a DAG which means it should not have any cycle. Just use DFS to get topological sorting.

Example 13.7:

```
void TopologicalSort(GraphPtr G)
{
        Stack stk;
        StackInitialize(&stk);
        int count = G->count;
        int* visited = (int*)malloc((count)*sizeof(int));
        for (int i = 0; i < count; i++)
                visited[i] = 0;
        for (int i = 0; i < count; i++)
                if (visited[i] == 0)
                {
                        visited[i] = 1;
                        TopologicalSortDFS(G, i, visited, &stk);
                }
        while (!StackIsEmpty(&stk))
                printf(" %d ",StackPop(&stk));
}
```

```
void TopologicalSortDFS(GraphPtr G, int index, int* visited, Stack* stk)
{
        ListPtr head = G->dpHead[index];
        while(head)
        {
                if(!visited[head->index])
                {
                        visited[head->index] = 1;
                        TopologicalSortDFS( G, head->index, visited, stk);
                }
                head = head->next;
        }
        StackPush(stk,index);
}
```

Minimum Spanning Trees (MST)

A Spanning Tree of a graph G is a tree which contains all the edges of the Graph G.
A Minimum Spanning Tree is a tree whose sum of length/weight of edges is minimum as possible.

For example, if you want to setup communication between a set of cities, then you may want to use the least amount of wire as possible. MST can be used to find the network path and wire cost estimate.

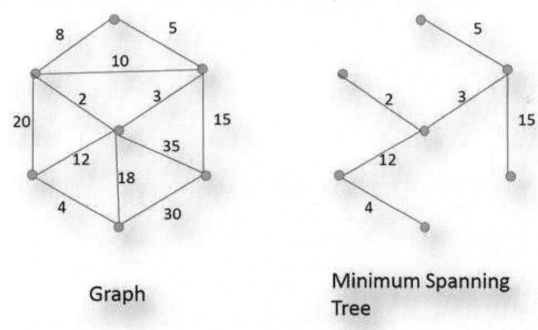

Graph

Minimum Spanning Tree

Prim's Algorithm for MST

Prim's algorithm grows a single tree T, one edge at a time, until it becomes a spanning tree.
We initialize T with zero edges. And U with single node. Where T is spanning tree edges set and U is spanning tree vertex set.

At each step, Prim's algorithm adds the smallest value edge with one endpoint in U and other not in us.
Since each edge adds one new vertex to U, after n − 1 additions, U contain all the vertices of the spanning tree and T becomes a spanning tree.

Example 13.8:

```
// Returns the MST by Prim's Algorithm
// Input: A weighted connected graph G = (V, E)
// Output: Set of edges comprising a MST

Algorithm Prim(G)
        T = {}
        Let r be any vertex in G
        U = {r}
        for i = 1 to |V| - 1 do
                e = minimum-weight edge (u, v)
                        With u in U and v in V-U
                U = U + {v}
                T = T + {e}
        return T
```

Prim's Algorithm using a priority queue (min heap) to get the closest fringe vertex
Time Complexity will be O(m log n) where n vertices and m edges of the MST.

Example 13.9:

```
void PrimMST(GraphPtr G)
{
        int i,src=1;
        int count = G->count;// Get the number of vertices in graph
        int* distance= (int*)malloc((count)*sizeof(int));
        int* path= (int*)malloc((count)*sizeof(int));

        Heap que;
        HeapInitialize(&que, 100);

        for ( i = 0; i < count; i++)
                distance[i] = -1;

        ListPtr head;
        Edge e;
        e.src = src;
        e.dst = src;
        e.weight = 0;
        HeapInsert(&que,e);
        distance[src]=0;
        path[src]=-1;
        Edge curr;
        while(que.Size)
        {
                curr=HeapDeleteMin(&que);
                head = G->dpHead[curr.dst];
```

298

```
                    while(head)
                    {
                            int disUpdate = head->weight;
                            if(distance[head->index] == -1 ||
                            distance[head->index] > disUpdate )
                            {
                                    distance[head->index] = disUpdate;
                                    path[head->index]=curr.dst;
                                    e.src = curr.dst;
                                    e.dst = head->index;
                                    e.weight = distance[head->index];
                                    HeapInsert( &que,e);
                            }
                            head = head->next;
                    }
            }
        for(int i=0;i<count;i++)
                printf("%d  to  %d weight %d \n", path[i], i , distance[i]);
}
```

Kruskal's Algorithm

Kruskal's Algorithm repeatedly chooses the smallest-weight edge that does not form a cycle.
Sort the edges in non-decreasing order of cost: $c(e1) \leq c(e2) \leq \cdots \leq c(em)$.
Set T to be the empty tree. Add edges to tree one by one if it does not create a cycle.

Example 13.10:

```
// Returns the MST by Kruskal's Algorithm
// Input: A weighted connected graph G = (V, E)
// Output: Set of edges comprising a MST

Algorithm Kruskal(G)
        Sort the edges E by their weights
        T = {}
        while |T| + 1 < |V| do
                e = next edge in E
                if T + {e} does not have a cycle then
                        T = T + {e}
        return T
```

Kruskal's Algorithm is O(E log V) using efficient cycle detection.

Shortest Path Algorithms in Graph

Single Source Shortest Path

For a graph G= (V, E), the single source shortest path problem is to find the shortest path from a given source vertex s to all the vertices of V.

Single Source Shortest Path for unweighted Graph.

Find single source shortest path for unweighter graph or a graph whose all the vertices have same weight.

Example 13.11:

```
void ShortestPath(GraphPtr G, int src)
{
        int curr;
        int count = G->count;
        int* distance= (int*)malloc((count)*sizeof(int));
        int* path= (int*)malloc((count)*sizeof(int));

        Queue que;
        QueueInitialize(&que);

        for (int i = 0; i < count; i++)
                distance[i] = -1;

        Enqueue(&que,src);
        distance[src]=0;

        while(!QueueIsEmpty(&que))
        {
                curr=Dequeue(&que);
                ListPtr head = G->dpHead[curr];
                while(head)
                {
                        if(distance[head->index] == -1)
                        {
                                distance[head->index] = distance[curr] + 1;
                                path[head->index]=curr;
                                Enqueue( &que,head->index);
                        }
                        head = head->next;
                }
        }
        for(int i=0;i<count;i++)
                printf("%d to %d weight %d \n", path[i], i , distance[i]);
}
```

Dijkstra's algorithm

Dijkstra's algorithm for single-source shortest path problem for weighted edges with no negative weight.

Given a weighted connected graph G, find shortest paths from the source vertex s to each of the other vertices. Dijkstra's algorithm is similar to prims algorithm. It maintains a set of nodes for which shortest path is known.

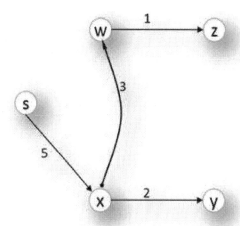

Single-Source shortest path

The algorithm starts by keeping track of the distance of each node and its parents. All the distance is set to infinite in the beginning as we don't know the actual path to the nodes and parents of all the vertices are set to null. All the vertices are added to a priority queue (min heap implementation)

At each step algorithm takes one vertex from the priority queue (which will be the source vertex in the beginning). Then update the distance array corresponding to all the adjacent vertices. When the queue is empty, then we will have the distance and parent array fully populated.

Example 13.12:

```
// Solves SSSP by Dijkstra's Algorithm
// Input: A weighted connected graph G = (V, E)
// with no negative weights, and source vertex v
// Output: The length and path from s to every v

Algorithm Dijkstra(G, s)
        for each v in V do
                D[v] = infinite    // Unknown distance
                P[v] = null        //unknown previous node
                add v to PQ        //adding all nodes to priority queue

        D[source] = 0 // Distance from source to source

        while (PQ is not empty)
                u = vertex from PQ with smallest D[u]
                remove u from PQ
                for each v adjacent from u do
                        alt = D[u] + length ( u , v)
                        if  alt < D[v] then
                                D[v] = alt
                                P[v] = u
        Return D[] , P[]
```

Time Complexity will be O(|E|log|V|)

Note: Dijkstra's algorithm does not work for graphs with negative edges weight.
Note: Dijkstra's algorithm is applicable to both undirected and directed graphs.

Example 13.13:

```
void DijkstraShortestPath(GraphPtr G, int src)
{
        Edge curr;
        int i;
        int count = G->count;

        int* distance= (int*)malloc((count)*sizeof(int));
        int* path= (int*)malloc((count)*sizeof(int));

        Heap que;
        HeapInitialize(&que, 100);

        for ( i = 0; i < count; i++)
                distance[i] = -1;

        ListPtr head;
        Edge e;
        e.src = src;
        e.dst = src;
        e.weight = 0;

        HeapInsert(&que,e);
        distance[src]=0;
        path[src]=-1;

        while(que.Size)
        {
                curr=HeapDeleteMin(&que);
                head = G->dpHead[curr.dst];
                while(head)
                {
                        int disUpdate = distance[curr.dst] + head->weight;
                        if(distance[head->index] == -1 ||
distance[head->index] > disUpdate )
                        {
                                distance[head->index] = disUpdate;
                                path[head->index]=curr.dst;
                                e.src = curr.dst;
                                e.dst = head->index;
                                e.weight = distance[head->index];
                                HeapInsert( &que,e);
                        }
                        head = head->next;
                }
        }
        for(int i=0;i<count;i++)
                printf("%d to %d weight %d \n", path[i], i , distance[i]);
}
```

Bellman Ford Shortest Path

The bellman ford algorithm works even when there are negative weight edges in the graph. It does not work if there is some cycle in the graph whose total weight is negative.

Example 13.14:

```c
#define INF 123456789
void BellmanFordShortestPath(GraphPtr G, int src)
{
        int curr;
        int count = G->count;

        int* distance= (int*)malloc((count)*sizeof(int));
        int* path= (int*)malloc((count)*sizeof(int));

        for (int i = 0; i < count; i++)
                distance[i] = INF;

        distance[src]=0;

        for (int i = 0; i < count -1; i++)
        {
                for (int j = 0; j < count; j++)
                {
                        ListPtr head = G->dpHead[j];
                        while(head)
                        {
                                int newDistance = distance[j]+ head->weight;
                                if(distance[head->index] > newDistance)
                                {
                                        distance[head->index] = newDistance;
                                        path[head->index]=j;
                                }
                                head = head->next;
                        }
                }
        }
        for(int i=0;i<count;i++)
                printf("%d to %d weight %d \n", path[i], i , distance[i]);
}
```

All Pairs Shortest Paths

Given a weighted graph G(V, E), the all pair shortest path problem is to find the shortest path between all pairs of vertices u, v є V.

Execute n instances of single source shortest path algorithm for each vertex of the graph.
The complexity of this algorithm will be $O(n^3)$

303

1. In all the path finding algorithm we have created a path array which just store immediate parent of a node, print the complete path for it.

2. All the functions are implemented considering as if the graph is represented by adjacency list. To write all those functions for graph representation as adjacency matrix.

3. Given a start string, end string and a set of strings, find if there exists a path between the start string and end string via the set of strings.

    A path exists if we can get from start string to end the string by changing (no addition/removal) only one character at a time. The restriction is that the new string generated after changing one character has to be in the set.

    start: "cog"
    end: "bad"
    set: ["bag", "cag", "cat", "fag", "con", "rat", "sat", "fog"]
    one of the paths: "cog" -> "fog" -> "fag" -> "bag" -> "bad"

CHAPTER 14: STRING ALGORITHMS

Introduction

String in C language is an array of character. We use string algorithm in so many tasks, when we are using some copy-paste, some string replacement, and some string search. When we are using some dictionary program we are using string algorithms. When we are searching something in google we are passing some information which is also a string and that will further convert and processed by google.

Note: This chapter is very important for the interview point of view as many interview problems are from this chapter.

String Matching

Every word processing program has a search function in which you can search all occurrences of any particular word in a long text file. For this we need string matching algorithms.

Brute Force Search

We have a pattern which we want to search in the text. The pattern is of length m and the text is of length n. Where m < n.

The brute force search algorithm will check the pattern at all possible value of "i" in the text where the value of "i" range from 0 to n-m. The pattern is compared with the text, character by character from left to right. When a mismatch is detected, then pattern is compared by shifting the compare window by one character.

Example 14.1:

```
int BruteForceSearch(char *text, char *pattern)
{
        int i=0, j=0, count = 0;
        const int n = strlen(text);
        const int m = strlen(pattern);

        while (i<=n-m)
        {
                j=0;
                while (j<m && pattern[j]== text[i+j])
                        j++;
                if (j==m)
                        return(i);
                i++;
        }
        return -1;
}
```

Worst case *Time Complexity* of the algorithm is O(m*n), we got the pattern at the end of the text or we didn't get the pattern at all.

Best case *Time Complexity* of this algorithm is O(m)
The average *Time Complexity* of this algorithm is ***O(n)***

Robin-Karp algorithm

Robin-Karp algorithm is somewhat similar to the brute force algorithm. Because the pattern is compared to each textbox. But instead of pattern at each position a hash code is compared, only one comparison is performed. The hash code of the pattern is compared with the hash code of the text window. We try to keep the hash code as unique as possible.

The two features of good hash code are:
- The collision should be excluded as much as possible.
- The hash code of text must be calculated in constant time.

A collision occurs when hash code matches, but the pattern does not.
Calculation in constant time, one member leaves the window and a new number enters a window.

Multiplication by 2 is same as left shift operation. Multiplication by 2^{m-1} is same as left shift m-1 times. We want this multiple times so just store it in variable pow(m) = 2^{m-1}

We don't want to do big multiplication operations so modular operation with a prime number is used.

Example 14.2:

```
int RobinKarp(char *text, char *pattern)
{
        int n=strlen(text);
        int m=strlen(pattern);
        int i, j;
        int prime = 101;
        int powm=1;
        int TextHash=0, PatternHash=0;

        if(m==0 || m>n)
                return -1;

        for (i = 0; i < m-1; i++)
                powm = (powm << 1) % prime;

        for (i = 0; i < m; i++)
        {
                PatternHash = ((PatternHash << 1) + pattern[i]) % prime;
                TextHash = ((TextHash << 1) + text[i]) % prime;
        }

        for( i=0;i<=(n-m);i++)
        {
                if(TextHash == PatternHash)
                {
                        for (j = 0; j < m; j++)
                        {
```

```
                    if (text[i+j] != pattern[j])
                            break;
            }
            if (j == m)
                    return i;
        }
        TextHash  = (((TextHash  - text[i]*powm) << 1)   + text[i+m]) % prime;

        if (TextHash  < 0)
                    TextHash  = (TextHash  + prime);

    }
        return -1;
}
```

Knuth-Morris-Pratt algorithm

After a shift of the pattern, the brute force algorithm forgotten all the information about the previous matched symbols. This is because of which its worst case *Time Complexity* is O(mn).

The Knuth-Morris-Pratt algorithm make use of this information that is computed in the previous comparison. It never re compares the whole text.

It uses preprocessing of the pattern. The preprocessing takes O(m) time and whole algorithm is **O(n)**

Preprocessing step: we try to find the border of the pattern at a different prefix of the pattern.

A **prefix** is a string which comes at the start of a string.
A **proper prefix** is a prefix which is not the complete string. Its length is less than the length of the string.
A **suffix** is a string which comes at the end of a string.
A **proper suffix** is a suffix which is not the complete string. Its length is less than the length of the string.

A **border** is a string which is both proper prefix and a proper suffix.

Example 14.3:

```
void KMPPreprocess(char* pattern, int* ShiftArr)
{
        const int m = strlen(pattern);
        int i = 0, j = -1;
        ShiftArr[i] = -1;
        while(i < m)
        {
                while(j >= 0 && pattern[i] != pattern[j])
                        j = ShiftArr[j];
                i++;
                j++;
                ShiftArr[i] = j;
        }
}
```

We have to loop outer loop for the text and inner loop for the pattern when we have matched the text and pattern mismatch, we shift the text such that the widest border is considered and then the rest of the pattern matching is resumed after this shift. If again a mismatch happens then the next mismatch is taken.

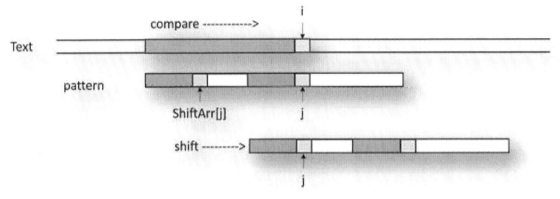

Example 14.4:

```
int KMP(char *text, char *pattern)
{
        int i=0, j=0, count = 0;
        const int n = strlen(text);
        const int m = strlen(pattern);

        int* ShiftArr = (int *)calloc(m+1, sizeof(int));

        KMPPreprocess(pattern,ShiftArr);

        while (i<n)
        {
                while (j>=0 && text[i]!=pattern[j])
                        j=ShiftArr[j];
                i++;
                j++;
```

```
                if (j==m)
                {
                        return (i - m);
                }
        }
        return -1;
}
```

Example 14.5: Use the same KMP algorithm to find the number of occurrences of the pattern in a text.

```
int KMPFindCount(char *text, char *pattern)
{
        int i=0, j=0, count = 0;
        const int n = strlen(text);
        const int m = strlen(pattern);
        int* ShiftArr = (int *)calloc(m+1, sizeof(int));

        KMPPreprocess(pattern,ShiftArr);
        while (i<n)
        {
                while (j>=0 && text[i]!=pattern[j])
                        j=ShiftArr[j];

                i++;
                j++;

                if (j==m)
                {
                        count++;
                        j=ShiftArr[j];
                }
        }
        return count;
}
```

Dictionary / Symbol Table

A symbol table is a mapping between a string (key) and a value which can be of any type. A value can be an *integer* such as occurrence count, dictionary meaning of a word and so on.

Binary Search Tree (BST) for Strings

Binary Search Tree (BST) is the simplest way to implement symbol table. Simple strcmp() function can be used to compare two strings. If all the keys are random, and the tree is balanced. Then on an average key lookup can be done in *O(logn)* time.

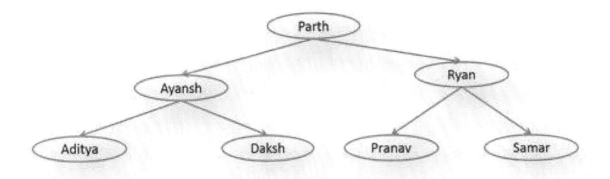

BINARY SEARCH TREE AS DICTIONARY

Below is an implementation of binary search tree to store string as key. This will keep track of the occurrence count of words in a text.

Example 14.6:

```
1.      #include<stdio.h>
2.      #include<stdlib.h>
3.      #include<string.h>
4.      #include<iostream>
5.      using namespace std;
6.
7.      struct treeNode_t{
8.          char* value;
9.          int count;
10.         treeNode_t* lChild;
11.         treeNode_t* rChild;
12.     };
13.
14.     typedef treeNode_t* treePtr;
```

```
1.      void printTree(treePtr root)/*   pre order  */
2.      {
3.          if(root)
4.          {
5.              cout<<" value is ::"<<root->value;
6.              cout<<" count is :: "<<root->count<<endl;
7.              printTree(root->lChild);
8.              printTree(root->rChild);
9.          }
10.}
```

```
1.      treePtr insertNode(char *value, treePtr root)
2.      {
3.              int compare;
4.              if(root==NULL)
5.              {
6.                      root=(treePtr)malloc(sizeof(treeNode_t));
7.                      if(root==NULL)
8.                      {
9.                              printf("fallel memory shortage ...");
10.                             return root;
11.                     }
12.                     root->value=(char*)malloc((1+strlen(value))*sizeof(char));
13.                     strcpy(root->value,value);
14.                     root->lChild=root->rChild=NULL;
15.                     root->count=1;
16.             }
17.             else
18.             {
19.                     compare=strcmp(root->value,value);
20.                     if(compare==0)
21.                     {
22.                             root->count++;
23.                     }
24.                     else if(compare==1)
25.                     {
26.                             root->lChild=insertNode(value,root->lChild);
27.                     }
28.                     else
29.                     {
30.                             root->rChild=insertNode(value,root->rChild);
31.                     }
32.             }
33.             return root;
34.     }
```

```
1.      void insertNode(char* value, treePtr * ptrRoot)
2.      {
3.              *ptrRoot = insertNode(value,*ptrRoot);
4.      }
```

```
1.      void freeTree(treePtr* rootPtr)
2.      {
3.              *rootPtr=freeTree(*rootPtr);
4.      }
```

```
1.      treePtr freeTree(treePtr root)
2.      {
3.              if(root)
4.              {
5.                      freeTree(root->lChild);
6.                      freeTree(root->rChild);
7.                      free(root->value);
8.                      free(root);
9.              }
10.             return NULL;
11.     }
```

```
1.      treePtr findNode(treePtr root, char* value)
2.      {
3.              int compare;
4.              if(!root)
5.                      return NULL;
6.              compare=strcmp(root->value,value);
7.              if(compare==0)
8.                      return root;
9.              else
10.             {
11.             if(compare==1)
12.                     return findNode(root->lChild,value);
13.             else
14.                     return findNode(root->rChild,value);
15.             }
16.     }
```

```
1.      int frequency(treePtr root, char* value)
2.      {
3.              int compare;
4.              if(!root)
5.                      return 0;
6.              compare=strcmp(root->value,value);
7.              if(compare==0)
8.                      return root->count;
9.              else
10.             {
11.                     if(compare==1)
12.                             return frequency(root->lChild,value);
13.                     else
14.                             return frequency(root->rChild,value);
15.             }
16.     }
```

```
1.       int getword(char* a, FILE* fp)
2.       {
3.              int i=0;
4.              while(1)
5.              {
6.                     a[i]=getc(fp);
7.                     if(a[i]==EOF)
8.                     {
9.                            a[i]='\0';
10.                           return 0;
11.                    }
12.                    else if(a[i]==' '||a[i]=='\t'||a[i]=='\n')
13.                    {
14.                           a[i]='\0';
15.                           return 1;
16.                    }
17.                    i++;
18.             }
19.      }
```

```
1.       int main()
2.       {
3.
4.              treePtr root=NULL;
5.              treePtr temp=NULL;
6.              FILE* fp=fopen("binaryString.cpp","r");
7.              char a[100];
8.              while(getword(a,fp))
9.              {
10.                    root=insertNode(a,root);
11.             }
12.             printTree(root);
13.             printf("\n");
14.             cout<<"quency returned :: "<<frequency(root,"&&");
15.             printf("\n");
16.      }
```

Hash-Table

The Hash-Table is another data structure which can be used for symbol table implementation. Below Hash-Table diagram, we can see the name of that person is taken as the key, and their meaning is the value of the search. The first key is converted into a hash code by passing it to appropriate hash function. Inside hash function the size of Hash-Table is also passed, which is used to find the actual index where values will be stored. Finally, the value which is meaning of name is stored in the Hash-Table, or you can store a reference to the string which store meaning can be stored into the Hash-Table.

Hash Function

String ----------------------------------> Index

Data	Hash Codes		Index
Parth	3		3
Ayansh	12		5
Aditya	50	%7	1
Daksh	91		0
Ryan	104	Modulo Table Size	6
Pranav	177		2
Samar	39		4

Hash Table

Index	String
0	Daksh meaning...
1	Aditya meaning...
2	Pranav meaning...
3	Parth meaning...
4	Samar meaning...
5	Ayansh meaning...
6	Ryan meaning...

Hash-Table has an excellent lookup of *O(1)*.

Let us suppose we want to implement autocomplete the box feature of Google search. When you type some string to search in google search it propose some complete string even before you have done typing. BST cannot solve this problem as related strings can be in both right and left subtree.

The Hash-Table is also not suited for this job. One cannot perform a partial match or range query on a Hash-Table. Hash function transforms string to a number. And also a good hash function will give a fairly distributed hash bode even for partial string and there is no way to relate two strings in a Hash-Table.

Trie and Ternary Search tree are a special kind of tree which solves partial match and range query problem well.

Trie

Trie is a tree, in which we store only one character at each node. This final key value pair is stored in the leaves. Each node has R children, one for each possible character. For simplicity purpose, let's consider that the character set is 26, corresponds to different characters of English alphabets.

Trie is an efficient data structure. Using Trie we can search the key in O(M) time. Where M is the maximum string length. Trie is also suitable for solving partial match and range query problems.

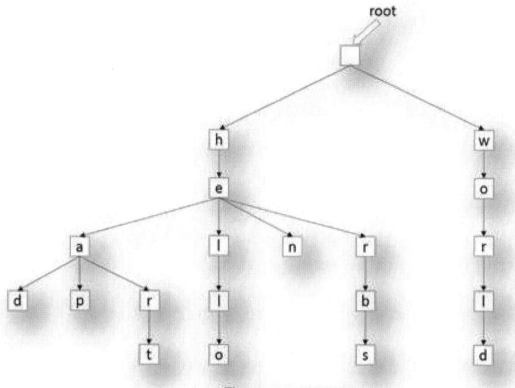

TRIE DICTIONARY

Example 14.7:

```
1.    #include<iostream>
2.    using namespace std;
3.    struct trieNode_t{
4.            int flag;
5.            char ch;
6.            trieNode_t* child[26];
7.    };
8.    typedef trieNode_t* triePtr;
```

```
1.    triePtr createNode()
2.    {
3.            triePtr   temp=(triePtr)malloc(sizeof(trieNode_t));
4.            for(int i=0;i<26;i++)
5.                    temp->child[i]==NULL;
6.            return temp;
7.    }
```

```
1.    void myToLower(char* str)
2.    {
3.            int length=strlen(str);
4.            for(int i=0;i<length;i++)
5.                    str[i]=tolower(str[i]);
6.    }
```

```
7.      void trie(triePtr root, char *str)
8.      {
9.              if(*(str+1)=='\0')
10.             {
11.                     if(root->child[*str-'a']==NULL)
12.                     {
13.                             root->child[*str-'a']=createNode();
14.                     }
15.                     root->child[*str-'a']->flag=1;
16.                     root->child[*str-'a']->ch=*str;
17.                     return;
18.             }
19.             else
20.             {
21.                     if(root->child[*str-'a']==NULL)
22.                     {
23.                             root->child[*str-'a']=createNode();
24.                             root->child[*str-'a']->flag=0;
25.                     }
26.                     root->child[*str-'a']->ch=*str;
27.                     trie(root->child[*str-'a'],(str + 1));
28.             }
29.     }
```

```
1.      triePtr trieInsert(triePtr root, char *str)
2.      {
3.              myToLower(str);
4.              if(str==NULL || *str=='\0')
5.                      return root;
6.              if(root==NULL)
7.              {
8.                      root=createNode();
9.                      trie(root,str);
10.             }
11.             else
12.             {
13.                     trie(root,str);
14.             }
15.             return root;
16.     }
```

```
1.    int findNode(triePtr root, char* str)
2.    {
3.            myToLower(str);
4.            if(str==NULL)
5.            {
6.                    cout <<"node found"<<endl;
7.                    return 0;
8.            }
9.            if(root==NULL)
10.           {
11.                   cout <<"node found"<<endl;
12.                   return 0;
13.           }
14.           while(root->child[*str - 'a']&& *(str+1)!='\0' && root->child[*str - 'a']->ch == *str )
15.           {
16.                   root=root->child[*str - 'a'];
17.                   str++;
18.           }
19.           //char does not match  or  char index child does not exist
20.           if( !root->child[*str - 'a'] || root->child[*str - 'a']->ch != *str)
21.           {
22.                   cout <<"node not found"<<endl;
23.                   return 0;
24.           }
25.           if( *(str+1)=='\0')
26.           {
27.                   if(root->child[*str - 'a']->ch == *str   && root->child[*str - 'a']->flag==1)
28.                   {
29.                           cout <<"node found"<<endl;
30.                           return 1;
31.                   }
32.           }
33.           cout <<"node not found"<<endl;
34.           return 0;
35.   }
```

```
1.    int main()
2.    {
3.            triePtr root=NULL;
4.            char a[]="hemant";
5.            char b[]="heman";
6.            char c[]="hemantjain";
7.            char d[]="jain";
8.            root = trieInsert(root,a);
9.            root = trieInsert(root,d);
10.           printf("%s",findNode(root,a));
11.           printf("%s",findNode(root,b));
12.           printf("%s",findNode(root,c));
13.           printf("%s",findNode(root,d));
14.   }
```

Tries have a very good search performance of O(M) where M is the maximum size of the search string. But tries have a very high space requirement. Every node Trie contains references to multiple nodes, each reference corresponds to possible characters of the key. To avoid this high space requirement Ternary Search Trie (TST) is used.

A TST avoid the heavy space requirement of the traditional Trie while still keeping many of its advantages. In a TST each node contains a character, an end of key indicator, and three pointers. The three pointers are corresponding to current char hold by the node (equal), characters less than and character greater than.

The *Time Complexity* of ternary search tree operation is proportional to the height of the ternary search tree. In the worst case we need to traverse up to 3 times that many links. However, this case is rare.

So TST is a very good solution for implementing Symbol Table, Partial match and range query.

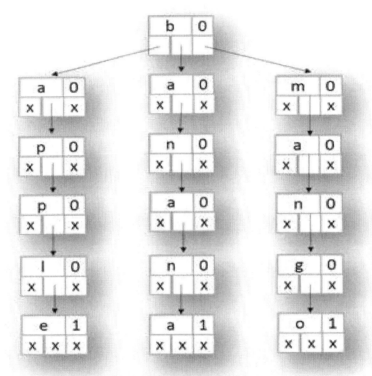

TERNARY Search Tree

Example 14.8:

```
struct Node
{
        char data;
        unsigned isLastChar : 1;
        struct Node *left, *equal, *right;
};
typedef Node* NodePtr;
```

```
NodePtr newNode(char data)
{
        NodePtr temp = (NodePtr)malloc(sizeof(struct Node));
        temp->data = data;
        temp->isLastChar = 0;
        temp->left = temp->equal = temp->right = NULL;
        return temp;
}
```

```
void insert( NodePtr* root, char *word)
{

        if (!(*root))
                *root = newNode(*word);

        if ((*word) < (*root)->data)
                insert(&((*root)->left), word);
        else if ((*word) > (*root)->data)
                insert(&((*root)->right), word);
        else
        {
                if (*(word + 1))
                        insert(&((*root)->equal), word + 1);
                else
                        (*root)->isLastChar = 1;
        }
}
```

```
int searchTST(NodePtr root, char *word)
{
        if (!root)
                return 0;

        if (*word < (root)->data)
                return searchTST(root->left, word);
        else if (*word >(root)->data)
                return searchTST(root->right, word);
        else
        {
                if (*(word + 1) == '\0')
                        return root->isLastChar;

                return searchTST(root->equal, word + 1);
        }
}
```

```
int searchTSTWrapper(NodePtr root, char *word)
{
        int ret = searchTST(root,word);
        printf(" %s : ", word);
        ret ? printf("Found\n") : printf("Not Found\n");
        return ret;
}
```

```
int main()
{
        NodePtr root = NULL;
        insert(&root, "banana");
        insert(&root, "apple");
        insert(&root, "mango");

        printf("\nSearch results for apple, banana, grapes and mango :\n");
        searchTSTWrapper(root, "apple");
        searchTSTWrapper(root, "banana");
        searchTSTWrapper(root, "grapes");
        searchTSTWrapper(root, "mango");

        return 0;
}
```

Problems in String

Regular Expression Matching

Implement regular expression matching with the support of '?' and '*' special character.
'?' Matches any single character.
'*' Matches zero or more of the preceding element.

Example 14.9:

```
int matchExpUtil(char* exp, char* str, int i, int j)
{
        if (i == strlen(exp) && j == strlen(str))
                return 1;

        if ((i == strlen(exp) && j != strlen(str))
                || (i != strlen(exp) && j == strlen(str)))
                return 0;

        if (exp[i] == '?' || exp[i] == str[j])
                return matchExpUtil(exp, str, i + 1, j + 1);

        if (exp[i] == '*')
                return matchExpUtil(exp, str, i + 1, j) || matchExpUtil(exp, str, i, j + 1)
                || matchExpUtil(exp, str, i + 1, j + 1);
        return 0;
}
```

```
int matchExp(char* exp, char* str)
{
        return matchExpUtil(exp, str, 0, 0);

}
```

Order Matching

Given a long text string and a pattern string. Find if the characters of pattern string are in the same order in text string. Eg. Text String: ABCDEFGHIJKLMNOPQRSTUVWXYZ
Pattern string: JOST

Example 14.10:

```
int match(char* source, char* pattern) {
        int iSource = 0;
        int iPattern = 0;
        int sourceLen = strlen(source);
        int patternLen = strlen(pattern);

        for (iSource = 0; iSource < sourceLen; iSource++) {
                if (source[iSource] == pattern[iPattern]) {
                        iPattern++;
                }
                if (iPattern == patternLen) {
                        return 1;
                }
        }
        return 0;
}
```

ASCII to Integer Conversion

Write a function that take *integer* as a char array and convert it into an int.

Example 14.11:

```
1.      int myAtoi(const char* str)
2.      {
3.              int value=0;
4.              while(*str)
5.              {
6.                      value=(value<<3)+(value<<1)+(*str - '0');
7.                      str++;
8.              }
9.              return value;
10.     }
```

Unique Characters

Write a function which will take a string as input and return 1 if it contain all unique characters else return 0.

Example 14.12:

```
int isUniqueChar(char* s)
{
        int bitarr = 0;
        int size= strlen(s);
        for (int i = 0; i < size; i++)
        {
                char c = s[i];
                if ('A' <= c && 'Z' >= c)
                {
                        c = c - 'A';
                }
                else if ('a' <= c && 'z' >= c)
                {
                        c = c - 'a';
                }
                else
                {
                        printf("Unknown Char!\n");
                        return 0;
                }

                if (bitarr & (1 << c))
                {
                        printf("Duplicate detected!\n");
                        return 0;
                }
                bitarr |= (1 << c);
        }
        printf("No duplicate detected!\n");
        return 1;
}
```

To Upper Case

Write a function that will convert all lower case letters in a string to upper case.

Example 14.13: ToUpper

```
1.      char ToUpper(char s)
2.      {
3.              if(s>=97 && s<=(97+25))
4.                      s=s-32;
5.              return s;
6.      }
```

To Lower Case

Write a function that will convert upper case letter in a string to lower case

Example 14.14: ToLower

```
1.      char ToLower(char s)
2.      {
3.              if(s>=65 && s<=(65+25))
4.                      s=s+32;
5.              return s;
6.      }
```

Permutation Check

Write a function to check if two strings are permutation of each other.

Example 14.15:

```
bool isPermutation(char* s1, char* s2)
{
        int count[256];

        int length = strlen(s1);
        if (strlen(s2) != length)
        {
                printf("is permutation return false\n");
                return false;
        }
        for (int i = 0; i < 256; i++)
        {
                count[i] = 0;
        }

        for (int i = 0; i < length; i++)
        {
                char ch = s1[i];
                count[ch]++;
                ch = s2[i];
                count[ch]--;
        }

        for (int i = 0; i < length; i++)
        {
                if (count[i])
                {
                        printf("is permutation return false\n");
                        return false;
                }
        }
        printf("is permutation return true\n");
        return true;
}
```

Palindrome Check

Given a string as an array of characters find if the string is a palindrome or not?

Example 14.16:

```
int isPalindrome(char* str)
{
        int i=0,j=strlen(str)-1;
        while(i<j && str[i] == str[j])
        {
                i++;
                j--;
        }
        if(i<j)
        {
                printf("String is not a Palindrome");
                return 0;
        }
        else
        {
                printf("String is a Palindrome");
                return 1;
        }
}
```

Time Complexity is **O(n)** and Space Complexity is **O(1)**

Integer to ASCII Conversion

Write a function that convert and *integer* into a char array.

Example 14.17:

```
1.      void myItoa(char* buffer, int value,)
2.      {
3.              static int index=-1;
4.              int     remender=value%10;
5.              value/=10;
6.              if(value)
7.                      myItoa(buffer, value);
8.              buffer[++index]='0'+ remender;
9.              buffer[index+1]='\0';
10.     }
```

ASCII to float Conversion

Write a function that take *float* as a char array and convert it into a *float*.

Example 14.18:

```
float MyAtof(char* str)
{
        float num = 0.0F;
        float fraction = 0.1F;
        int decimalStart = 0;
        int size = strlen(str);

        for (int i = 0; i < size; i++)
        {
                if (str[i] == '.')
                {
                        decimalStart = 1;
                        continue;
                }
                if (!decimalStart)
                {
                        num = (num * 10) + (str[i] - '0');
                }
                else
                {
                        num += (str[i] - '0') * fraction;
                        fraction *= 0.1F;
                }
        }
        return num;
}
```

Reverse Case function

Write a function that will convert Lower case letter in a string to upper case and upper case letter to lower case.

Example 14.19:

```
1.      /* lower to upper */
2.      using namespace std;
3.      char LowerUpper(char s)
4.      {
5.              if(s>=97 && s<=(97+25))
6.                      s=s-32;
7.              else if(s>=65 && s<=(65+25))
8.                      s=s+32;
9.              return s;
10.     }
```

String Copy function

Write a function to copy string provided as a source in the array provided as destination, including the terminating null character.

Example 14.20:

```
1.      char* myStrcpy(char* dst, char* src)
2.      {
3.              char* ptr=dst;
4.              while(*dst++=*src++);
5.                      return ptr;
6.      }
```

Power function

Write a function which will calculate x^n, Taking x and n as argument.

Example 14.21: Power function

```
1.      int pow(int x, int n)
2.      {
3.              int value;
4.              if(n==0)
5.                      return(1);
6.              else if(n%2==0)
7.              {
8.                      value=pow(x,n/2);
9.                      return(value*value);
10.             }
11.             else
12.             {
13.                     value=pow(x,n/2);
14.                     return(x*value*value);
15.             }
16.     }
```

String Compare function

Write a function strcmp() to compare two strings. The function return values should be:
The return value is 0 indicates that both first and second strings are equal.
The return value is negative indicates the first string is less than the second string.
The return value is positive indicates that the first string is greater than the second string.

Example 14.22:

```
1.      int myStrcmp(char *a, char* b)
2.      {
3.              while((*a)==(*b))
4.              {
5.                      if(*a=='\0')
6.                              return 0;
7.                      a++;
8.                      b++;
9.              }
10.             if(*a=='\0')
11.                     return -1;
12.             if(*b=='\0')
13.                     return 1;
14.             int value=(*a-*b);
15.             return value;
16.     }
```

Substring function

Write a C function that will copy first n character from a source string to the destination string.

Example 14.23:

```
1.      char* mySubstr(char* src, char* dst, int n)
2.      {
3.              int count=n;
4.              char* ptr=dst;
5.              do
6.              {
7.                      n--;
8.                      if(n==0)
9.                      {
10.                             ptr[count-1]='\0';
11.                             break;
12.                     }
13.                     else
14.                     {
15.                             dst++=src++;
16.                     }
17.             } while(src);
18.             return ptr;
19.     }
```

String duplicate function

Write a C function which will return a pointer to a new string which is a duplicate of the input string. Memory for the new string is obtained with malloc and freed with free.

Example 14.24:

```
1.      char* myStrdup(char *src)
2.      {
3.              char* dst=(char*)malloc((strlen(src)+1)* sizeof(char));
4.              char* ptr=dst;
5.              while(*dst++=*src++);
6.              return ptr;
7.      }
```

Memcpy Function

The function memcpy function copies n characters from the source array to destination array.

Example 14.25:

```
1.      void mymemcpy(void *destPtr, const void *srcPtr, int size)
2.      {
3.              char *destTemp=(char*)destPtr;
4.              const char *srcTemp=(char*)srcPtr;
5.              while(size--)
6.              {
7.                      *destTemp++=*srcTemp++;
8.              }
9.      }
```

Reverse N characters

Example 14.26: Reverse first N characters of a string

```
1.      void reverse (char *s, int N)
2.      {
3.              char *p, *q;
4.              char t;
5.              for (p = s, q = s+N-1; p < q; ++p, --q) {
6.                      t = *q;
7.                      *q = *p;
8.                      *p = t;
9.              }
10.     }
```

328

Memmove Function

The function Memmove function copies n characters from the source array to destination array. It also takes case if the source and destination memory arrays overlaps.

Example 14.27:

```
1.      void mymemmove(void *from, void *to, size_t size)
2.      {
3.              char *destTemp=(char*)to;
4.              char *srcTemp=(char*)from;
5.              size_t i;
6.              if(from == to)
7.              {
8.                      // Nothing to copy!
9.              }
10.             else if(from > to)
11.             {
12.                     for(i = 0; i < size; i++)
13.                             destTemp[i] = srcTemp[i];
14.             }
15.             else
16.             {
17.                     for(i = size-1; i >= 0; i--)
18.                             destTemp[i] = srcTemp[i];
19.             }
20.             #ifdef BIG_ENDIAN
21.             reverse (destTemp, size);
22.             #endif
23.     }
```

String Length function

Write a C function to find the length of the char array, string passed as argument.

Example 14.28:

```
1.      int myStrlen(char* src)
2.      {
3.              int length=0;
4.              while(*src!='\0')
5.              {
6.                      length++;
7.              }
8.              return length;
16.     }
```

String Concatenate function

Write a c function to concatenate two strings. Assuming that first string has enough space for the second string.

Example 14.29:

```
1.      char* strcat(char* s1, char* s2)
2.      {
3.              char* ptr=s1;
4.              while(*s1++);
5.              while(*s2!='\0')
6.                      *s1++=*s2++;
7.              return ptr;
8.      }
```

Reverse String

Example 14.30: Reverse all the characters of a string.

```
void reverseString(char *a,int lower,int upper)
{
        char tempChar;
        while(lower<upper)
        {
                tempChar=a[lower];
                a[lower]=a[upper];
                a[upper]=tempChar;
                lower++;
                upper--;
        }
}
```

Reverse Words

Example 14.31: Reverse order of words in a string sentence.

```
void reverseWords(char *a)
{
        int length= strlen(a);
        int lower,upper=-1;
        lower=0;
        for(int i=0;i<=length;i++)
        {
                if(a[i]==' '||a[i]=='\0')
                {
                        reverseString(a,lower,upper);
                        lower=i+1;
                        upper=i;
                }
                else
                {
                        upper++;
                }
        }
        reverseString(a,0,length-1); //-1 because we do not want to reverse '\0'
}
```

Print Anagram

Example 14.32: Given a string as character array, print all the anagram of the string.

```
void printAnagram (char *a)
{
        int n=strlen(a);
        printAnagram (a,n,n);
}
```

```
void printAnagram (char *a,int max, int n)
{
if(max==1)
        printString(a,n);

        for(int i=-1;i<max-1;i++)
        {
                if(i!=-1)
                        a[i]^=a[max-1]^=a[i]^=a[max-1];
                printAnagram(a,max-1,n);
                if(i!=-1)
                        a[i]^=a[max-1]^=a[i]^=a[max-1];
        }
}
```

Shuffle String

Example 14.33: Write a program to convert array ABCDE12345   to A1B2C3D4E5

```
void shuffle(char ar[],int n)
{
        int count=0;
        int k=1;
        char temp='\0';
        for(int i=1;i<n;i=i+2)
        {
                temp=ar[i];
                k=i;
                do{
                        k=(2*k)%(2*n-1);
                        temp^=ar[k]^=temp^=ar[k];
                        count++;
                }while(i!=k);

                if(count == (2*n-2))
                {
                        break;
                }
        }
}
```

Example 14.34: Given two binary string find the sum of these two binary strings.

```c
char* addBinary(char* first, char* second)
{
        int size1 = strlen(first);
        int size2 = strlen(second);
        int totalIndex;
        char* total;
        if(size1>size2)
        {
                total = (char*) malloc((size1+2)*sizeof(char));
                totalIndex = size1;
        }
        else
        {
                total = (char*) malloc((size2+2)*sizeof(char));
                totalIndex = size2;
        }
        total[totalIndex + 1] = '\0';
        int carry =0 ;
        int curr = 0;
        size1--;
        size2--;
        while(size1 >=0 || size2 >=0)
        {
                int firstValue = (size1 < 0) ? 0 : first[size1]-'0';
                int secondValue =  (size2 < 0)? 0: second[size2]-'0';
                int sum = firstValue + secondValue + carry;

                carry = sum >> 1;
                sum = sum & 1;

                total[totalIndex] = (sum==0) ? '0' : '1';

                totalIndex--;
                size1--;
                size2--;
        }
        total[totalIndex] = (carry==0) ? '0' : '1';
        return total;
}
```

Example 14.35: Write a C function to remove all spaces from a string.

```c
void removeSpaces(char* str)
{
        char* to = str;
        char* from = str;

        if (str == NULL)
                return;

        while (*from != '\0')
        {
                if (*from == ' ')
                {
                        from++;
                        continue;
                }

                *to = *from;
                from++;
                to++;
        }
        *to = '\0';
}
```

Exercise

1. Given a string find the longest substring without reputed characters.

2. The function memset() copies ch into the first 'n' characters of the string

3. Serialize a collection of string into a single string and de serializes the string into that collection of strings.

4. Write a smart input function which take 20 characters as input from the user. Without cutting some word.
   > User input: "Harry Potter must not go"
   > First 20 chars: "Harry Potter must no"
   > Smart input: "Harry Potter must"

5. Write a code that returns if a string is palindrome and it should return true for below inputs too.
   > Stella won no wallets.
   > No, it is open on one position.
   > Rise to vote, Sir.
   > Won't lovers revolt now?

6. Write an ASCII to *integer* function which ignore the non-integral character and give the *integer*. For example, if the input is "12AS5" it should return 125.

7. Write code that would parse a Bash brace expansion.
   example: the expression "(a,b,c)d,e" and would output all the possible strings: ad, bd, cd, e

8. Given a string write a function to return the length of the longest substring with only unique characters

9. Replace all occurrences of "a" with "the"

10. Replace all occurrences of %20 with ' '.
    E.g. Input: www.Hello%20World.com
    Output: www.Hello World. com

11. Write an expansion function that will take an input string like "1..5,8,11..14,18,20,26..30" and will print
    "1,2,3,4,5,8,11,12,13,14,18,20,26,27,28,29,30"

12. Suppose you have a string like "Thisisasentence". Write a function that would separate these words. And will print whole sentence with spaces.

13. Given three string str1, str2 and str3. Write a complement function to find the smallest sub-sequence in str1 which contains all the characters in str2 and but not those in str3.

14. Given two strings A and B, find whether any anagram of string A is a sub string of string B.
    For eg: If A = xyz and B = afdgzyxksldfm then the program should return true.

15. Given a string, find whether it contains any permutation of another string. For example, given "abcdefgh" and "ba", the function should return true, because "abcdefgh" has substring "ab", which is a permutation of the given string "ba".

16. Give an algorithm which removes the occurrence of "a" by "bc" from a string? The algorithm must be in-place.

17. Given a string "1010101010" in base2 convert it into string with base4. Do not use an extra space.

CHAPTER 15: ALGORITHM DESIGN TECHNIQUES

Introduction

In real life when we are asked to do some work we try to correlate it with our past experience and then try to solve it. Similarly, when we get a new problem to solve. We first try to find the similarity of the current problem with some problems for which we already know the solution. Then solve the current problem and get our desired result.

This method provides following benefits:
1) It provides a template for solving a wide range of problems.
2) It provides us the idea of the suitable data structure for the problem.
3) It helps us in analyzing, space and *Time Complexity* of algorithms.

In the previous chapters we have used various algorithms to solve different kind of problems. In this chapter, we will read about various techniques of solving algorithmic problems.

Various Algorithm design techniques are:
1) Brute Force
2) Greedy Algorithms
3) Divide-and-Conquer, Decrease-and-Conquer
4) Dynamic Programming
5) Reduction / Transform-and-Conquer
6) Backtracking and Branch-and-Bound

Brute Force Algorithm

Brute Force is a straight forward approach of solving a problem based on the problem statement. It is one of the easiest approaches to solve a particular problem. It is useful for solving small size dataset problem.

Some examples of brute force algorithms are:
- Bubble-Sort
- Selection-Sort
- Sequential search in an array
- Computing pow(a, n) by multiplying a, n times.
- Convex hull problem
- String matching
- Exhaustive search: Traveling salesman, Knapsack, and Assignment problems

Greedy Algorithm

In greedy algorithm solution is constructed through a sequence of steps. At each step choice is made which is locally optimal. Greedy algorithms are generally used to solve optimization problems. We always take the next data to be processed depending upon the dataset which we have already processed and then choose the next optimum data to be processed. Greedy algorithms does not always give optimum solution.

Some examples of brute force algorithms are:
- Minimal spanning tree: Prim's algorithm, Kruskal's algorithm
- Dijkstra's algorithm for single-source shortest path problem
- Greedy algorithm for the Knapsack problem
- The coin exchange problem
- Huffman trees for optimal encoding

Divide-and-Conquer, Decrease-and-Conquer

Divide-and-Conquer algorithms involve basic three steps, first split the problem into several smaller sub-problems, second solve each sub problem and then finally combine the sub problems results so as to produce the final result.

In divide-and-conquer the size of the problem is reduced by a factor (half, one-third, etc.), While in decrease-and-conquer the size of the problem is reduced by a constant.

Examples of divide-and-conquer algorithms:
- Merge-Sort algorithm (using recursion)
- Quicksort algorithm (using recursion)
- Computing the length of the longest path in a binary tree (using recursion)
- Computing Fibonacci numbers (using recursion)
- Quick-hull

Examples of decrease-and-conquer algorithms:
- Computing pow(a, n) by calculating pow(a, n/2) using recursion.
- Binary search in a sorted array (using recursion)
- Searching in BST
- Insertion-Sort
- Graph traversal algorithms (DFS and BFS)
- Topological sort
- Warshall's algorithm (using recursion)
- Permutations (Minimal change approach, Johnson-Trotter algorithm)
- Computing a median, Topological sorting, Fake-coin problem (Ternary search)

Consider the problem of exponentiation: Compute x^n

Brute Force:	n-1 multiplications
Divide and conquer:	$T(n) = 2*T(n/2) + 1 = n-1$
Decrease by one:	$T(n) = T(n-1) + 1 = n-1$
Decrease by constant factor:	$T(n) = T(n/a) + a-1$ $= (a-1) n$ $= n$ when $a = 2$

While solving problems using Divide-and-Conquer method, there may be a case when recursively sub-problems can result in the same computation being performed multiple times. This problem arises when there are identical sub-problems arise repeatedly in a recursion.

Dynamic programming is used to avoid the requirement of repeated calculation of same sub-problem. In this method we usually store the result of sub - problems in a table and refer that table to find if we have already calculated the solution of sub - problems before calculating it again.

Dynamic programming is a bottom up technique in which the smaller sub-problems are solved first and the result of these are sued to find the solution of the larger sub-problems.

Examples:
- Fibonacci numbers computed by iteration.
- Warshall's algorithm for transitive closure implemented by iterations
- Floyd's algorithms for all-pairs shortest paths

```
int fibonacci(int n)
{
        if (n <= 1)
                return n;
        return fibonacci(n - 1) + fibonacci(n - 2);
}
```

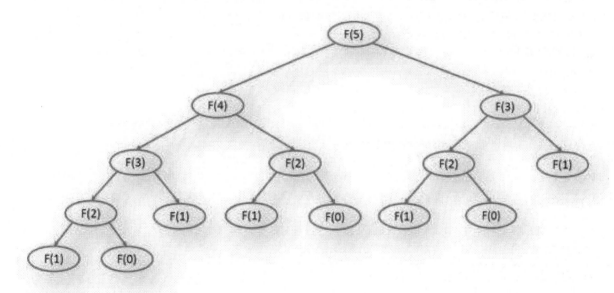

Using divide and conquer the same sub problem is solved again and again, which reduce the performance of the algorithm. This algorithm has an exponential *Time Complexity*. And linear *Space Complexity*.

```
int fibo(int n)
{
        int first = 0, second = 1;
        int temp, i;

        if (n == 0)
                return first;
        else if (n == 1)
                return second;

        for (i = 2; i <= n; i++)
        {
                temp = first + second;
                first = second;
                second = temp;
        }
        return temp;
}
```

Using this algorithm we will get Fibonacci in linear *Time Complexity* and constant *Space Complexity*.

Reduction / Transform-and-Conquer

These methods works as two-stage procedure. First, the problem is transformed into a known problem for which we know optimal solution. In the second stage the problem is solved.

The most common types of transformation are sort of an array.

For example: Given an array of numbers finds the two closest number.

The brute force solution for this problem will take distance between each element in the array and will try to keep the minimum distance pair, this approach will have a *Time Complexity* of $O(n^2)$

Transform and conquer solution, will be first sort the array in *O(nlogn)* time and then find the closest number by scanning the array in another *O(n)*. Which will give the total *Time Complexity* of *O(nlogn)*.

Examples:
- Gaussian elimination
- Heaps and Heapsort

Backtracking

In real life, let us suppose someone gave you a lock with a number (three digit lock, number range from 1 to 9). And you don't have the exact password key for the lock. You need to test each and every combination till you got the right one. Obviously you need to test starting from something like "111", then "112" and so on. And you will get your key before you reach "999". So basically what you are doing is backtracking.

Suppose the lock produce some sound "click" correct digit is selected for any level. If we can listen to this sound such intelligence/ heuristics will help you to reach your goal much faster. These functions are called Pruning function or bounding functions.

Backtracking is a method by which solution is found by exhaustively searching through large but finite number of states, with some pruning or bounding function which will narrow down our search. For all the problems like (NP hard problems) for which there does not exist any other method we use backtracking.

Backtracking problems have the following components:
1. Initial state
2. Target / Goal state
3. Intermediate states
4. Path from the initial state to the target / goal state
5. Operators to get from one state to another
6. Pruning function (optional)

The solving process of backtracking algorithm starts with the construction of state's tree, whose nodes represents the states. The root node is the initial state and one or more leaf node will be our target state. Each edge of the tree represents some operation. The solution is obtained by searching the tree until a Target state is found.

Backtracking uses depth-first search:
1) Store the initial state in a stack
2) While the stack is not empty, repeat:
3) Read a node from the stack.
4) While there are available operators, do:
   a. Apply an operator to generate a child
   b. If the child is a goal state – return solution
   c. If it is a new state, and pruning function does not discard it push the child into the stack.

There are three monks and three demons at one side of a river. We want to move all of them to the other side using a small boat. The boat can carry only two persons at a time. Given if on any shore the number of demons will be more than monks then they will eat the monks. How can we move all of these people to the other side of the river safely?

Same as the above problem there is a farmer who has a goat, a cabbage and a wolf. If the farmer leaves, goat with cabbage, goat will eat the cabbage. If the farmer leaves wolf alone with goat, wolf will kill the goat. How can the farmer move all his belongings to the other side of the river?

You are given two jugs, a 4-gallon one and a 3-gallon one. There are no measuring markers on jugs. There is a tap that can be used to fill the jugs with water. How can you get 2 gallons of water in the 4-gallon jug?

Branch-and-bound

Branch and bound method is used when we can evaluate cost of visiting each node by a utility functions. At each step we choose the node with lowest cost to proceed further. Branch-and bound algorithms are implemented using a priority queue. In branch and bound we traverse the nodes in breadth-first manner.

A* Algorithm

A* is sort of an elaboration on branch-and-bound. In branch-and-bound, at each iteration we expand the shortest path that we have found so far. In A*, instead of just picking the path with the shortest length so far, we pick the path with the shortest estimated total length from start to goal, where the total length is estimated as length traversed so far plus a heuristic estimate of the remaining distance from the goal.

Branch-and-bound will always find an optimal solution which is shortest path. A* will always find an optimal solution if the heuristic is correct. Choosing a good heuristic is the the most important part of A* algorithm.

Conclusion

Usually a given problem can be solved using a number of methods, however it is not wise to settle for the first method that comes to our mind. Some methods result in a much more efficient solutions than others.

For example the Fibonacci numbers calculated recursively (decrease-and-conquer approach), and computed by iterations (dynamic programming). In the first case the complexity is $O(2^n)$, and in the other case the complexity is $O(n)$.

Another example, consider sorting based on the Insertion-Sort and basic bubble sort. For almost sorted files Insertion-Sort will give almost linear complexity, while bubble sort sorting algorithms have quadratic complexity.

So the most important question is, how to choose the best method ?
First you should understand the problem statement.
Second by knowing various problems and there solutions.

CHAPTER 16: BRUTE FORCE ALGORITHM

Introduction

Brute Force is a straight forward approach of solving a problem based on the problem statement. It is one of the easiest approaches to solve a particular problem. It is useful for solving small size dataset problem.

Many times there are other algorithm techniques which can be used to get a better solution of the same problem.

Some examples of brute force algorithms are:
- Bubble-Sort
- Selection-Sort
- Sequential search in an array
- Computing pow (a, n) by multiplying a, n times.
- Convex hull problem
- String matching
- Exhaustive search
- Traveling salesman
- Knapsack
- Assignment problems

Problems in Brute Force Algorithm

Bubble-Sort

In Bubble-Sort, adjacent elements of the list are compared and are exchanged if they are out of order.

```
// Sorts a given array by Bubble Sort
// Input: An array A of orderable elements
// Output: Array A[0..n - 1] sorted in ascending order

Algorithm BubbleSort(A[0..n - 1])
        sorted = false
        while !sorted do
                sorted = true
                for j = 0 to n - 2 do
                        if A[j] > A[j + 1] then
                                swap A[j] and A[j + 1]
                                sorted = false
```

The *Time Complexity* of the algorithm is $\theta(n^2)$

Selection-Sort

The entire given list of N elements is traversed to find its smallest element and exchange it with the first element. Then, the list is traversed again to find the second element and exchanged it with the second element. After N-1 passes, the list will be fully sorted.

```
//Sorts a given array by selection sort
//Input: An array A[0..n-1] of orderable elements
//Output: Array A[0..n-1] sorted in ascending order

Algorithm SelectionSort (A[0..n-1])
        for i = 0 to n - 2 do
                min = i
                for j = i + 1 to n - 1 do
                        if A[j] < A[min]
                                min = j
                swap A[i] and A[min]
```

The *Time Complexity* of the algorithm is $\theta(n^2)$

Sequential Search

The algorithm compares consecutive elements of a given list with a given search keyword until either a match is found or the list is exhausted.

```
Algorithm SequentialSearch (A[0..n], K)
        i = 0
        While A [i] ≠ K do
                i = i + 1
        if  i < n
                return i
        else
                return -1
```

Worst case *Time Complexity* is $\Theta(n)$.

Computing pow (a, n)

Computing a^n (a > 0, and n is a nonnegative *integer*) based on the definition of exponentiation.
N-1 multiplications are required in brute force method.

```
// Input: A real number a and an integer n = 0
// Output: a power n

Algorithm Power(a, n)
        result = 1
        for i = 1 to n do
                result = result * a
        return result
```

The algorithm requires $\Theta(n)$

String matching

A brute force string matching algorithm takes two inputs, first text consists of n characters and a pattern consist of m character (m<=n). The algorithm starts by comparing the pattern with the beginning of the text. Each character of the patters is compared to the corresponding character of the text. Comparison starts from left to right until all the characters are matched or a mismatch is found. The same process is repeated until a match is found. Each time the comparison starts one position to the right.

```
//Input: An array T[0..n - 1] of n characters representing a text
// an array P[0..m - 1] of m characters representing a pattern
//Output: The position of the first character in the text that starts the first
// matching substring if the search is successful and -1 otherwise.

Algorithm BruteForceStringMatch (T[0..n - 1], P[0..m - 1])
        for i = 0 to n - m do
                j = 0
        while j < m and P[j] = T[i + j] do
                j = j + 1
        if j = m then
                return i
        return -1
```

In the worst case, the algorithm is O(mn).

Closest-Pair Brute-Force Algorithm

The closest-pair problem is to find the two closest points in a set of n points in a 2-dimensional space.
A brute force implementation of this problem computes the distance between each pair of distinct points and find the smallest distance pair.

```
// Finds two closest points by brute force
// Input: A list P of n >= 2 points
// Output: The closest pair
Algorithm BruteForceClosestPair(P)
dmin = infinite
for i = 1 to n - 1 do
        for j = i + 1 to n do
                d = (xi − xj)² + (yi − yj)²
                if d < dmin then
                        dmin = d
                        imin = i
                        jmin = j
return imin, jmin
```

In the *Time Complexity* of the algorithm is $\theta(n^2)$

Convex-Hull Problem

Convex-hull of a set of points is the smallest convex polygon containing all the points. All the points of the set will lie on the convex hull or inside the convex hull. Illustrate the rubber-band interpretation of the convex hull. The convex-hull of a set of points is a subset of points in the given sets.

How to find this subset?
Answer: The rest of the points of the set are all on one side.

Two points (x1, y1), (x2, y2) make the line ax + by = c
Where a = y2-y1, b = x1-x2, and c = x1y2 - y1x2

And divides the plane by ax + by - c < 0 and ax + by - c > 0
So we need to only check ax + by - c for the rest of the points

If we find all the points in the set lies one side of the line with either all have ax + by - c < 0 or all the points have ax + by - c > 0 then we will add these points to the desired convex hull point set.

For each of n (n -1) /2 pairs of distinct points, one needs to find the sign of ax + by - c in each of the other n - 2 points.
What is the worst case cost of the algorithm? O(n3)

```
for i=0 to n-1
  for j=0 to n-1
    if (xi,yi) !=(xj,yj)
        draw a line from (xi,yi) to (xj,yj)
        for k=0 to n-1
          if(i!=k and j!=k)
              if ( all other points lie on the same side of the line (xi,yi) and (xj,yj))
              add  (xi,yi) to (xj,yj) to the convex hull set
```

Exhaustive Search

Exhaustive search is a brute force approach applies to combinatorial problems.
In exhaustive search we generate all the possible combinations. See if the combinations satisfy the problem constraints and then finding the desired solution.
Examples of exhaustive search are:
- Traveling salesman problem
- Knapsack problem
- Assignment problem

Traveling Salesman Problem (TSP)

In the traveling salesman problem we need to find the shortest tour through a given set of N cities that salesman visits each city exactly once before returning to the city where he started.

Alternatively: Finding the shortest Hamiltonian circuit in a weighted connected graph. A cycle that passes through all the vertices of the graph exactly once.

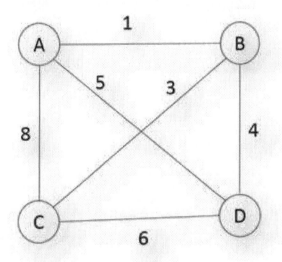

Tours where A is starting city:

Tour	Cost
A→B→C→D→A	1+3+6+5 = 15
A→B→D→C→A	1+4+6+8 = 19
A→C→B→D→A	8+3+4+5 = 20
A→C→D→B→A	8+6+4+1 = 19
A→D→B→C→A	5+4+3+8 = 20
A→D→C→B→A	5+6+3+1 = 15

```
Algorithm TSP
Select a city
MinTourCost = infinite
For ( All permutations of cities ) do
        If( LengthOfPathSinglePermutation < MinTourCost )
                MinTourCost = LengthOfPath
```

Total number of possible combinations = (n-1)!

Cost for calculating the path? $\Theta(n)$
So the total cost for finding the shortest path? $\Theta(n!)$

Knapsack Problem

Given an item with cost C1, C2,..., Cn, and volume V1, V2,..., Vn and knapsack of capacity Vmax, find the most valuable (max $\sum Cj$) that fit in the knapsack ($\sum Vj \leq$ Vmax).

The solution is one of all the subset of the set of object taking 1 to n objects at a time, so the *Time Complexity* will be O(2^n)

```
Algorithm KnapsackBruteForce
MaxProfit = 0
For ( All permutations of objects ) do
        CurrProfit = sum of objects selected
        If( MaxProfit < CurrProfit )
                MaxProfit = CurrProfit
                Store the current set of objects selected
```

Conclusion

Brute force is the first algorithm that comes into mind when we see some problem. They are the simplest algorithms which are very easy to understand. But these algorithms rarely provide an optimum solution. Many cases we will find other effective algorithm which is more efficient than the brute force method.
This is the most simple to understand the kind of problem solving technique.

CHAPTER 17: GREEDY ALGORITHM

Introduction

Greedy algorithms are generally used to solve optimization problems. To find the solution that minimizes or maximizes some value (cost/profit/count etc.).

In greedy algorithm solution is constructed through a sequence of steps. At each step choice is made which is locally optimal. We always take the next data to be processed depending upon the dataset which we have already processed and then choose the next optimum data to be processed.

Greedy algorithms does not always give optimum solution. For some problems, greedy algorithm gives an optimal solution. For most, they don't, but can be useful for fast approximations.

Greedy is a strategy that works well on optimization problems with the following characteristics:
1. Greedy choice: A global optimum can be arrived at by selecting a local optimum.
2. Optimal substructure: An optimal solution to the problem is made from optimal solutions of sub problems.

Some examples of brute force algorithms are:
Optimal solutions:
- Minimal spanning tree:
    - Prim's algorithm,
    - Kruskal's algorithm
- Dijkstra's algorithm for single-source shortest path
- Huffman trees for optimal encoding
- Scheduling problems

Approximate solutions:
- Greedy algorithm for the Knapsack problem
- Coin exchange problem

Problems on Greedy Algorithm

Coin exchange problem

How can a given amount of money N be made with the least number of coins of given denominations D= {d1... dn}?

The Indian coin system {5, 10, 20, 25, 50,100}

Suppose we want to give change of a certain amount of 40 paisa.

We can make a solution by repeatedly choosing a coin ≤ to the current amount, resulting in a new amount. The greedy solution is to always choose the largest coin value possible without exceeding the total amount.

For 40 paisa: {25, 10, and 5}
The optimal solution will be {20, 20}

The greedy algorithm did not give us optimal solution, but it gave a fair approximation.

```
Algorithm  MAKE-CHANGE (N)
C = {5, 20, 25, 50, 100} // constant.
S = {}                   // set that will hold the solution set.
Value = N
WHILE Value != 0
        x = largest item in set C such that x < Value
        IF no such item THEN
                RETURN   "No Solution"
        S = S + x
        Value = Value - x
RETURN S
```

Minimum Spanning Tree

A spanning tree of a connected graph is a tree containing all the vertices.
A minimum spanning tree of a weighted graph is a spanning tree with the smallest sum of the edge weights.

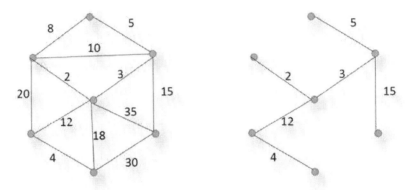

Prim's Algorithm

Prim's algorithm grows a single tree T, one edge at a time, until it becomes a spanning tree.
We initialize T with zero edges. And U with single node. Where T is spanning tree edges set and U is spanning tree vertex set.

At each step, Prim's algorithm adds the smallest value edge with one endpoint in U and other not in us.
Since each edge adds one new vertex to U, after n − 1 additions, U contain all the vertices of the spanning tree and T becomes a spanning tree.

```
// Returns the MST by Prim's Algorithm
// Input: A weighted connected graph G = (V, E)
// Output: Set of edges comprising a MST
Algorithm Prim(G)
        T = {}
        Let r be any vertex in G
        U = {r}
        for i = 1 to |V| - 1 do
                e = minimum-weight edge (u, v)
                        With u in U and v in V-U
                U = U + {v}
                T = T + {e}
        return T
```

Prim's Algorithm using a priority queue (min heap) to get the closest fringe vertex
Time Complexity will be O(m log n) where n vertices and m edges of the MST.

Kruskal's Algorithm

Kruskal's Algorithm is used to create minimum spanning tree. Spanning tree is created by choosing smallest weight edge that does not form a cycle. And repeating this process till all the edges from the original set is exhausted.

Sort the edges in non-decreasing order of cost: c (e1) ≤ c (e2) ≤ · · · ≤ c (em).
Set T to be the empty tree. Add edges to tree one by one if it does not create a cycle. (If the new edge form cycle then ignore that edge.)

```
// Returns the MST by Kruskal's Algorithm
// Input: A weighted connected graph G = (V, E)
// Output: Set of edges comprising a MST

Algorithm Kruskal(G)
        Sort the edges E by their weights
        T = {}
        while |T| + 1 < |V| do
                e = next edge in E
                if T + {e} does not have a cycle then
                        T = T + {e}
        return T
```

Kruskal's Algorithm is O(E log V) using efficient cycle detection.

Dijkstra's algorithm for single-source shortest path problem

Dijkstra's algorithm for single-source shortest path problem for weighted edges with no negative weight. It determine the length of the shortest path from the source to each of the other nodes of the graph.

Given a weighted graph G, we need to find shortest paths from the source vertex s to each of the other vertices.

 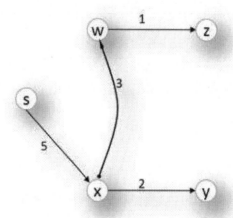

Single-Source shortest path

The algorithm starts by keeping track of the distance of each node and its parents. All the distance is set to infinite in the beginning as we don't know the actual path to the nodes and parents of all the vertices are set to null. All the vertices are added to a priority queue (min heap implementation)

At each step algorithm takes one vertex from the priority queue (which will be the source vertex in the beginning). Then update the distance array corresponding to all the adjacent vertices. When the queue is empty, then we will have the distance and parent array fully populated.

```
// Solves SSSP by Dijkstra's Algorithm
// Input: A weighted connected graph G = (V, E)
// with no negative weights, and source vertex v
// Output: The length and path from s to every v

Algorithm Dijkstra(G, s)
for each v in V do
            D[v] = infinite      // Unknown distance
            P[v] = null          //unknown previous node
            add v to PQ          //adding all nodes to priority queue

D[source] = 0 // Distance from source to source

while (Q is not empty)
            u = vertex from PQ with smallest D[u]
            remove u from PQ
                    for each v adjacent from u do
                            alt = D[u] + length ( u , v)
                            if  alt < D[v] then
                                    D[v] = alt
                                    P[v] = u
Return D[] , P[]
```

Time Complexity will be O(|E|log|V|).

Note: Dijkstra's algorithm does not work for graphs with negative edges weight.
Note: Dijkstra's algorithm is applicable to both undirected and directed graphs.

Huffman trees for optimal encoding

Coding is basically an assignment of bit strings of alphabet characters.

There are two types of encoding:
* Fixed-length encoding (eg., ASCII)
* Variable-length encoding (eg., Huffman code)

Variable length encoding can only work on prefix free encoding. Which means that no code word is a prefix of another code word.

Huffman codes are the best prefix free code. Any binary tree with edges labeled as 0 and 1 will produce a prefix free code of characters assigned to its leaf nodes.

Huffman's algorithm is used to construct a binary tree whose leaf value is assigned a code which is optimal for the compression of the whole text need to be processed. For example the most frequently occurring words will get the smallest code so that the final encoded text is compressed.

Initialize n one-node trees with words and the tree weights with their frequencies. Join the two binary tree with smallest weight into one and the weight of the new formed tree as the sum of weight of the two small trees. Repeat the above process N-1 times and when there is just one big tree left you are done.

Mark edges leading to left and right subtrees with 0's and 1's, respectively.

Word	Frequency
Apple	30
Banana	25
Mango	21
Orange	14
Pineapple	10

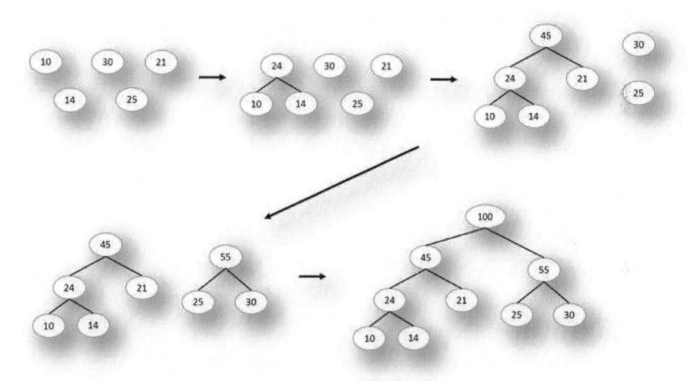

Word	Value	Code
Apple	30	11
Banana	25	10
Mango	21	01
Orange	14	001
Pineapple	10	000

It is clear that more frequency words gets smaller Huffman's code.

```
// Computes optimal prefix code.
// Input: Array W of character probabilities
// Output: The Huffman tree.

Algorithm Huffman(C[0..n - 1], W[0..n - 1])
        PQ = {} // priority queue
        for i = 0 to n - 1 do
                T.char = C[i]
                T.weight = W[i]
                add T to priority queue PQ

        for i = 0 to n - 2 do
                L = remove min from PQ
                R = remove min from PQ
                T = node with children L and R
                T.weight = L.weight + R.weight
                add T to priority queue PQ
        return T
```

The Time Complexity is **O(nlogn)**.

Activity Selection Problem

Suppose that activities require exclusive use of common resources, and you want to schedule as many activities as possible.

Let $S = \{a1,..., an\}$ be a set of n activities.

Each activity ai needs the resource during a time period starting at si and finishing before fi, i.e., during [si, fi). The optimization problem is to select the non-overlapping largest set of activities from S.

We assume that activities $S = \{a1,..., an\}$ are sorted in finish time $f1 \le f2 \le ...\ fn-1 \le fn$ (this can be done in $\Theta(n \lg n)$).

Example

Consider these activities:

i	1	2	3	4	5	6	7	8	9	10	11
S[i]	1	3	0	5	3	5	6	8	8	2	11
F[i]	4	5	6	7	8	9	10	11	12	13	14

Here is a graphic representation:

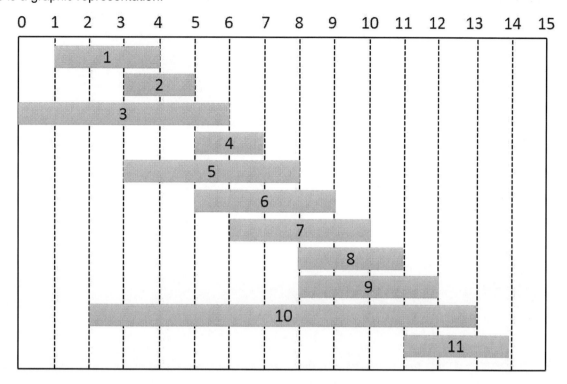

We chose an activities that start first, and then look for the next activity that starts after it is finished. This could result in {a4, a7, a8}, but this solution is not optimal.

An optimal solution is {a1, a3, a6, a8}. (It maximizes the objective function of a number of activities scheduled.)

Another one is {a2, a5, a7, a9}. (Optimal solutions are not necessarily unique.)

How do we find (one of) these optimal solutions? Let's consider it as a dynamic programming problem...

We are trying to optimize the number of activities. Let's be greedy!

- The more time left after running an activity, the more subsequent activities we can fit in.
- If we choose the first activity to finish, the more time will be left.
- Since activities are sorted by finish time, we will always start with a_1.
- Then we can solve the single sub problem of activity scheduling in this remaining time.

```
Algorithm ActivitySelection(S[], F[], N)
        Sort S[] and F [] in increasing order of finishing time
        A = {a1}
        K = 1
        For m = 2 to N do
                If S[m] >= F[k]
                        A = A + {am}
                        K = m
        Return A
```

Knapsack Problem

A thief enters a store and sees a number of items with their cost and weight mentioned. His Knapsack can hold a max weight. What should he steal to maximize profit?

A thief can take a fraction of an item (they are divisible substances, like gold powder).

The fractional knapsack problem has a greedy solution one should first sort the items in term of cost density against weight. Then fill up as much of the most valuable substance by weight as one can hold, then as much of the next most valuable substance, etc. Until W is reached.

Item	A	B	C
Cost	300	190	180
Weight	3	2	2
Cost/weight	100	95	90

For a knapsack of capacity of 4 kg.
The optimum solution of the above will take 3kg of A and 1 kg of B.

```
Algorithm FractionalKnapsack(W[], C[], Wk)
        For i = 1 to n do
                X[i] = 0
        Weight = 0
//Use Max heap
        H = BuildMaxHeap(C/W)
        While Weight < Wk do
                i = H.GetMax()
                If(Weight + W[i] <= Wk) do
                        X[i] = 1
                        Weight = Weight + W[i]
                Else
                        X[i] = (Wk – Weight)/W[i]
                        Weight = Wk
        Return X
```

A thief can only take or leave the item. He can't take a fraction.
A greedy strategy same as above could result in empty space, reducing the overall cost density of the knapsack.

In the above example, after choosing object A there is no place for B or C so there leaves empty space of 1kg. And the result of the greedy solution is not optimal.
The optimal solution will be when we take object B and C. This problem can be solved by dynamic programming which we will see in the coming chapter.

CHAPTER 18: DIVIDE-AND-CONQUER, DECREASE-AND-CONQUER

Introduction

Divide-and-Conquer algorithms works by recursively breaking down a problem into two or more sub-problems (divide), until these sub problems become simple enough so that can be solved directly (conquer). The solution of these sub problems is then combined to give a solution of the original problem.

Divide-and-Conquer algorithms involve basic three steps
1. Divide the problem into smaller problems.
2. Conquer by solving these problems.
3. Combine these results together.

In divide-and-conquer the size of the problem is reduced by a factor (half, one-third etc.), While in decrease-and-conquer the size of the problem is reduced by a constant.

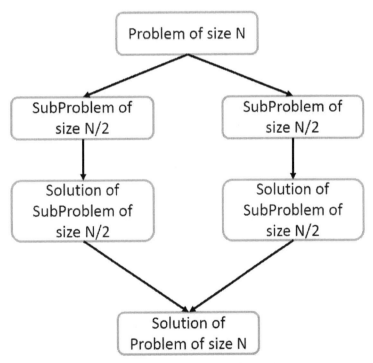

Divide-and-Conquer algorithms

Examples of divide-and-conquer algorithms:
- Merge-Sort algorithm (recursion)
- Quicksort algorithm (recursion)
- Computing the length of the longest path in a binary tree (recursion)
- Computing Fibonacci numbers (recursion)
- Convex Hull

Examples of decrease-and-conquer algorithms:
- Computing POW (a, n) by calculating POW (a, n/2) using recursion
- Binary search in a sorted array (recursion)
- Searching in BST
- Insertion-Sort
- Graph traversal algorithms (DFS and BFS)
- Topological sort
- Warshall's algorithm (recursion)
- Permutations (Minimal change approach, Johnson-Trotter algorithm)
- Fake-coin problem (Ternary search)
- Computing a median

General Divide-and-Conquer Recurrence

T(n) = aT(n/b) + f (n)
- Where a ≥ 1 and b > 1.
- "n" is the size of a problem.
- "a" is a number of sub-problem in the recursion.
- "n/b" is the size of each sub-problem.
- "f(n)" is the cost of the division of the problem into sub problem or merge of the results of sub-problem to get the final result.

Master Theorem

The master theorem solves recurrence relations of the form:
$T(n)$ = a T(n/b) + f(n)

It is possible to determine an asymptotic tight bound in these three cases:
Case 1: when f(n) =$O\ (n^{log_b\ a\ -\ \epsilon})$ and constant $\epsilon > 1$, than the final *Time Complexity* will be:
T(n) =$\Theta(n^{log_b\ a})$

Case 2: when f(n) = $\Theta(n^{log_b\ a}\ log^k\ n)$ and constant k ≥ 0, than the final *Time Complexity* will be:
T(n)= $\Theta(n^{log_b\ a}\ log^{k+1}\ n)$

Case 3: when f(n) = $\Omega(n^{log_b\ a+\epsilon})$ and constant $\epsilon > 1$, Then the final *Time Complexity* will be:
T(n) =$\Theta(f(n))$

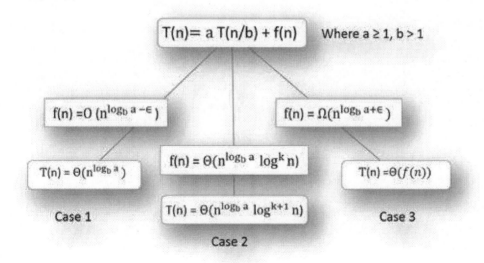

Modified Master theorem: This is a shortcut to solving the same problem easily and fast. If the recurrence relation is in the form of T(n)= a T(n/b) + dx^s

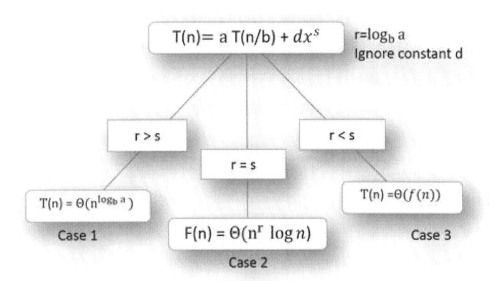

Example 1: Take an example of Merge-Sort, $T(n) = 2$ T(n/2) + n
Sol:-
$log_b a = log_2 2 = 1$
f(n) = n = $\Theta(n^{log_2 2} log^0 n)$
Case 2 applies and T(n)= $\Theta(n^{log_2 2} log^{0+1} n)$
T(n)= $\Theta(n\ log(n))$

Example 2: Binary Search $T(n) = $ T(n/2) $+O(1)$
$log_b a = log_2 1 = 0$
f(n) = 1 = $\Theta(n^{log_2 1} log^0 n)$
Case 2 applies and T(n)= $\Theta(n^{log_2 1} log^{0+1} n)$
T(n)= $\Theta(log(n))$

Example 3: Binary tree traversal $T(n) = $ 2T(n/2) $+O(1)$
$log_b a = log_2 2 = 1$
f(n) = 1 = $O(n^{log_2 2-1})$
Case 1 applies and T(n) =$\Theta(n^{log_2 2})$
T(n) =$\Theta(n)$

Merge-Sort algorithm

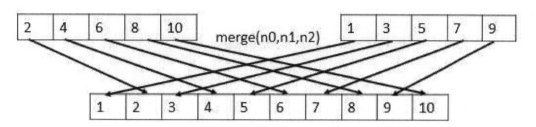

```
// Sorts a given array by mergesort
// Input: An array A of orderable elements
// Output: Array A[0..n − 1] in ascending order

Algorithm Mergesort(A[0..n − 1])
if n ≤ 1 then
return;
copy A[0..⌊n/2⌋ − 1] to B[0..⌊n/2⌋ − 1]
copy A[⌊n/2⌋..n − 1] to C[0..⌈n/2⌉ − 1]
Mergesort(B)
Mergesort(C)
Merge(B, C, A)
```

```
// Merges two sorted arrays into one array
// Input: Sorted arrays B and C
// Output: Sorted array A
Algorithm Merge(B[0..p − 1], C[0..q − 1], A[0..p + q − 1])
i = 0
j = 0
for k = 0 to p + q − 1 do
if i < p and (j = q or B[i] ≤ C[j]) then
A[k] = B[i]
i = i + 1
else
A[k] = C[j]
j = j + 1
```

Time Complexity: **O(nlogn)**
Space Complexity: **O(n)**
The *Time Complexity* of Merge-Sort is *O(nlogn)* in all 3 cases (worst, average and best) as Merge-Sort always divides the array into two halves and take linear time to merge two halves.

It requires the equal amount of additional space as the unsorted list. Hence, it's not at all recommended for searching large unsorted lists.

Quick-Sort

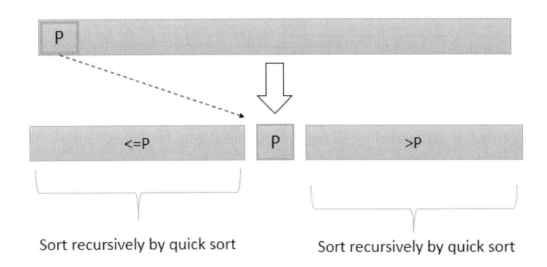

Sort recursively by quick sort   Sort recursively by quick sort

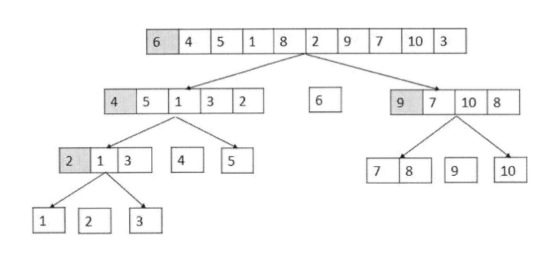

```
// Sorts a subarray by quicksort
// Input: An subarray of A
// Output: Array A[l..r] in ascending order

Algorithm Quicksort(A[l..r])
if l < r then
p ← Partition(A[l..r]) // p is index of pivot
Quicksort(A[l..p − 1])
Quicksort(A[p + 1..r])
```

```
// Partitions a subarray using A[..] as pivot
// Input: Subarray of A
// Output: Final position of pivot

Algorithm Partition(A[], left, right)
pivot = A[left]
lower = left
upper= right
while lower < upper
while A[lower] <= pivot
                lower = lower + 1
while A[upper] > pivot
upper = upper − 1
if lower < upper then
swap A[lower] and A[upper]
swap A[lower] and A[upper] //upper is the pivot position
return upper
```

Worst Case *Time Complexity:* $O(n^2)$
Best Case Time Complexity: **O(nlogn)**
Average Time Complexity: **O(nlogn)**
Space Complexity: **O(nlogn)**

The space required by Quick-Sort is very less, only **O(nlogn)** additional space is required.

Quicksort is not a stable sorting technique, so it might change the occurrence of two similar elements in the list while sorting.

External Sorting

External sorting is also done using divide and conquer algorithm.

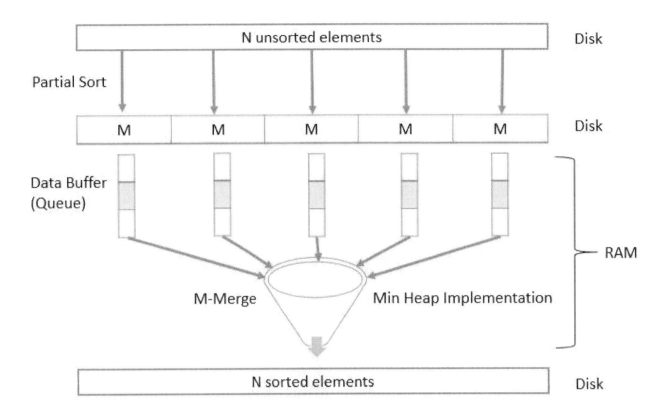

Binary Search

We get the middle point from the sorted array and start comparing with the desired value.
Note: Binary search requires the array to be sorted otherwise binary search cannot be applied.

```
// Searches a value in a  sorted array using binary search
// Input: An sorted array A and a key K
// Output: The index of K or −1

Algorithm BinarySearch(A[0..N − 1], N, K)
        low = 0
        high = N-1
        while low <= high do
                mid = ⌊ (low + high)/2⌋
                if K = A[mid] then
                        return mid
                else if A[mid] < K
                        low = mid + 1
                else
                        high = mid - 1
        return −1
```

```
// Searches a value in a  sorted array using binary search
// Input: An sorted array A and a key K
// Output: The index of K or −1

Algorithm BinarySearch(A[], low, high, K)
        If low > high
                return -1
        mid = ⌊ (low + high)/2⌋
        if K = A[mid] then
                return mid
        else if A[mid] < K
                return BinarySearch(A[],mid + 1, high, K)
        else
                return BinarySearch(A[],low, mid - 1, K)
```

Time Complexity: **O(logn)**. If you notice the above programs, you see that we always take half input and throwing out the other half. So the recurrence relation for binary search is $T(n) = T(n/2) + c$. Using a divide and conquer master theorem, we get $T(n) = $ **O(logn)**.
Space Complexity: **O(1)**

Power function

```
// Compute Nth power of X using divode and conquer using recursion
// Input: Value X and power N
// Output: Power( X, N)

Algorithm Power( X, N)
        If N = 0
                Return 1
        Else if N % 2 == 0
                Value = Power(X, N/2)
                Return Value * Value
        Else
                Value = Power(X, N/2)
                Return Value * Value * X
```

Convex Hull

Sort points by X-coordinates
Divide points into equal halves A and B
Recursively compute HA and HB
Merge HA and HB to obtain CH

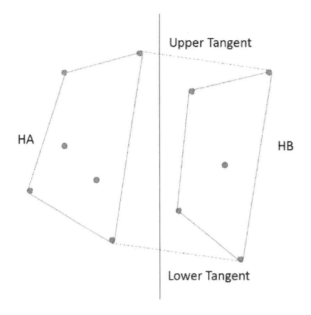

```
LowerTangent(HA, HB)
        A = rightmost point of HA
        B = leftmost point of HB
        While ab is not a lower tangent for HA and HB do
                While ab is not a lower tangent to HA do
                        a = a − 1 (move a clockwise)
                While ab is not a lower tangent to HB do
                        b = b + 1 (move b counterclockwise)
        Return ab
```

Similarly find upper tangent and combine the two hulls.

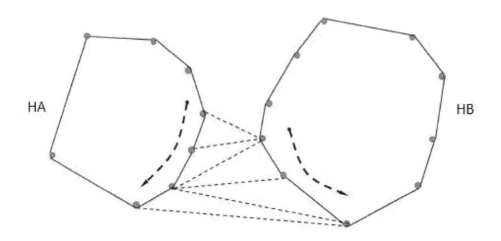

Initial sorting takes *O(nlogn)* time
Recurrence relation T (N) = 2T (N/2) + *O(N)*
Where, *O(N)* time for tangent computation inside merging
Final *Time Complexity* will be T (N) = *O(nlogn)*.

Closest Pair

Given N points in 2-dimensional plane, find two points whose mutual distance is smallest.

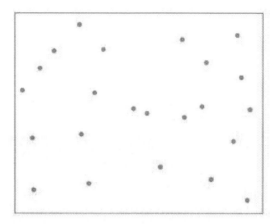

A brute force algorithm takes each and every point and find its distance with all the other points in the plane. And keep track of the minimum distance points and minimum distance. The closest pair will be found in $O(n^2)$ time.

Let us suppose there is a vertical line which divide the graph into two separate parts (let's call it left and right part). The brute force algorithm, we will notice that we are comparing all the points in the left half with the points in the right half. This is the point where we are doing some extra work.

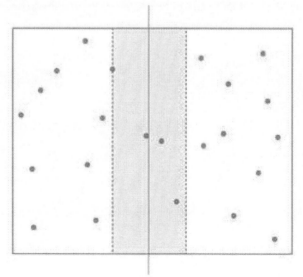

To find the minimum we need to consider only three cases:
1) Closest pair in the right half
2) Closest pair in the left half.
3) Closest pair in the boundary region of the two halves. (Gray)

Every time we will divide the space S into two parts S1 and S2 by a vertical line. Recursively we will compute the closest pair in both S1 and S2. Let's call minimum distance in space S1 as δ1 and minimum distance in space S2 as δ2.

We will find δ = min (δ1, δ2)

Now we will find the closest pair in the boundary region. By taking one point each from S1 and S2 in the boundary range of δ width on both sides.

The candidate pair of point (p, q) where p ∈ S1 and q ∈ S2.

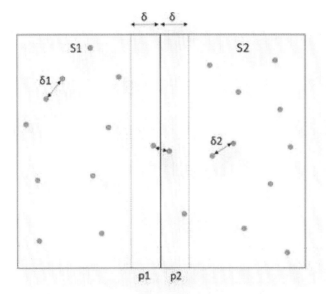

We can find the points which lie in this region in linear time **O(N)** by just scanning through all the points and finding which all points lie in this region.

Now we can sort them in increasing order in Y axis in just **O(nlogn)** time. And then scan through them and get the minimum in just one more linear pass. Closest pair can't be far apart from each other.

Let's look into the next figure.

Then the question is how many points we need to compare. We need to compare the points sorted in Y axis only in the range of δ. So the number of points will come down to only 6 points.

By doing this we are getting equation.

$T(N) = 2T(N/2) + N + N\log N + 6N = O(n(\log n)^2)$

Can we optimize this further?
Yes

Initially, when we are sorting the points in X coordinate we are sorting them in Y coordinate too. When we divide the problem, then we traverse through the Y coordinate list too, and construct the corresponding Y coordinate list for both S1 and S2. And pass that list to them.

Since we have the Y coordinate list passed to a function the δ region points can be found sorted in the Y coordinates in just one single pass in just *O(N)* time.

$T(N) = 2T(N/2) + N + N + 6N = $ ***O(nlogn)***

```
// Finds closest pair of points
// Input: A set of n points sorted by coordinates
// Output: Distance between closest pair

Algorithm ClosestPair(P)
        if n < 2 then
                   return ∞
        else if n = 2 then
                   return distance between pair
        else
                   m = median value for x coordinate
                   δ₁ = ClosestPair(points with x < m)
                   δ₂ = ClosestPair(points with x > m)
                   δ = min(δ₁, δ₂)
                   δ₃ = process points with m −δ < x < m + δ
                   return min(δ, δ₃)
```

First pre-process the points by sorting them in X and Y coordinates. Use two separate lists to keep this sorted points.

Before recursively solving sub-problem pass the sorted list for that sub-problem.

CHAPTER 19: DYNAMIC PROGRAMMING

Introduction

While solving problems using Divide-and-Conquer method, there may be a case when recursively sub-problems can result in the same computation being performed multiple times. This problem arises when there are identical sub-problems arise repeatedly in a recursion.

Dynamic programming is used to avoid the requirement of repeated calculation of same sub-problem. In this method we usually store the result of sub - problems in some data structure (like a table) and refer it to find if we have already calculated the solution of sub - problems before calculating it again.

Dynamic programming is applied to solve problems with the following properties:
1. Optimal Substructure: An optimal solution constructed from the optimal solutions of its sub-problems.
2. Overlapping Sub problems: While calculating the optimal solution of sub problems same computation is repeated again and again.

Examples:
- Fibonacci numbers computed by iteration.
- Assembly-line Scheduling
- Matrix-chain Multiplication
- 0/1 Knapsack Problem
- Longest Common Subsequence
- Optimal Binary Tree
- Warshall's algorithm for transitive closure implemented by iterations
- Floyd's algorithms for all-pairs shortest paths
- Optimal Polygon Triangulation
- Floyd-Warshall's Algorithm

Steps for solving / recognizing if DP applies.
1) Optimal Substructure: Try to find if there is a recursive relation between problem and sub-problem.
2) Write recursive relation of the problem. (Observe Overlapping Sub problems at this step.)
3) Compute the value of sub problems in a bottom up fashion and store this value in some table.
4) Construct the optimal solution from the value stored in step 3.
5) Repeat step 3 and 4 till you get your solution.

Problems on Dynamic programming Algorithm

Fibonacci numbers

```
int fibonacci(int n)
{
        if (n <= 1)
                return n;
        return fibonacci(n - 1) + fibonacci(n - 2);
}
```

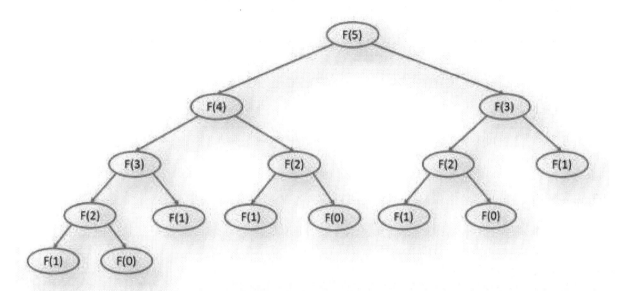

Using divide and conquer same sub-problem is solved again and again, which reduce the performance of the algorithm. This algorithm has an exponential *Time Complexity*.

Same problem of Fibonacci can be solved in linear time if we sort the results of sub problems.

```
int fibonacci (int n)
{
        int first = 0, second = 1;
        int temp, i;

        if (n == 0)
                return first;
        else if (n == 1)
                return second;

        for (i = 2; i <= n; i++)
        {
                temp = first + second;
                first = second;
                second = temp;
        }
        return temp;
}
```

Using this algorithm we will get Fibonacci in linear *Time Complexity* and constant *Space Complexity*.

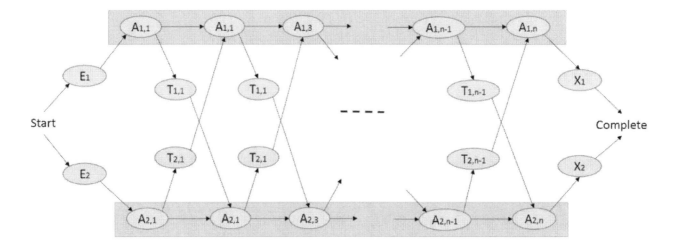

We consider the problem of calculating the least amount of time necessary to build a car when using a manufacturing chain with two assembling lines, as shown in the figure

The problem variables:

- e[i]: entry time in assembly line i
- x[i]: exit time from assembly line i
- a[i,j]: Time required at station S[i,j] (assembly line i, stage j)
- t[i,j]: Time required to transit from station S[i,j] to the other assembly line

Your program must calculate:

- The least amount of time needed to build a car
- The list of stations to traverse in order to assemble a car as fast as possible.

The manufacturing chain will have no more than 50 stations.

If we want to solve this problem in the brute force approach, there will be in total 2^n Different combinations so the *Time Complexity* will be $O(2^n)$

Step 1: Characterizing the structure of the optimal solution

To calculate the fastest assembly time, we only need to know the fastest time to S1;n and the fastest time to S2;n, including the assembly time for the nth part. Then we choose between the two exiting points by taking into consideration the extra time required, x1 and x2. To compute the fastest time to S1;n we only need to know the fastest time to S1;n1 and to S2;n1. Then there are only two choices...

Step 2: A recursive definition of the values to be computed

$$f1[j] = \begin{cases} e1 + a1,1 & if\ j = 1 \\ \min(f1[j - 1] + a1,j, & f2[j - 1] + t2,j - 1 + a1,j)\ if\ j \geq 2 \end{cases}$$

$$f2[j] = \begin{cases} e2 + a2,1 & if\ j = 1 \\ \min(f2[j - 1] + a2,j, & f1[j - 1] + t1,j - 1 + a2,j)\ if\ j \geq 2 \end{cases}$$

Step 3: Computing the fastest time finally, compute f* as

Step 4: Computing the fastest path compute as li[j] as the choice made for fi[j] (whether the first or the second term gives the minimum). Also, compute the choice for f* as l*.

```
FASTEST-WAY(a, t, e, x, n)
 1  f1[1] ← e1 + a1,1
 2  f2[1] ←e2 + a2,1
 3  for j ← 2 to n
 4      do if f1[j - 1] + a1,j ≤ f2[j - 1] + t2,j-1 + a1,j
 5          then f1[j] ← f1[j - 1] + a1, j
 6              l1[j] ← 1
 7          else f1[j] ← f2[j - 1] + t2,j-1 + a1,j
 8              l1[j] ← 2
 9      if f2[j - 1] + a2,j ≤ f1[j - 1] + t1,j-1 + a2,j
10          then f2[j] ← f2[j - 1] + a2,j
11              l2[j] ← 2
12          else f2[j] ∞ f1[j - 1] + t1,j-1 + a2,j
13              l2[j] ← 1
14  if f1[n] + x1 ≤ f2[n] + x2
15      then f* = f1[n] + x1
16          l* = 1
17      else f* = f2[n] + x2
18          l* = 2
```

Matrix chain multiplication

Same problem is also known as Matrix Chain Ordering Problem or Optimal-parenthesization of matrix problem.

Given a sequence of matrices, $M = M1,..., Mn$. The goal of this problem is to find the most efficient way to multiply these matrices. The guild is not to perform the actual multiplication, but to decide the sequence of the matrix multiplications, so that the result will be calculated in minimal operations.

To compute the product of two matrices of dimensions pXq and qXr, pqr number of operations will be required. Matrix multiplication operations are associative in nature. So matrix multiplication can be done in many ways. For example, M1, M2, M3 and M4, can be fully parenthesized as:

(M1· (M2· (M3·M4)))
(M1· ((M2·M3)· M4))
((M1·M2)· (M3·M4))
(((M1·M2)· M3)· M4)
((M1· (M2·M3))· M4)

For example,
Let M1 dimensions are 10 × 100, M2 dimensions are 100 × 10, and M3 dimensions are 10 × 50.
((M1·M2)· M3) = (10*100*10) + (10*10*50) = 15000
(M1· (M2·M3)) = (100*10*50) + (10*100*50) = 100000

So in this problem we need to parenthesize the matrix chain so that total multiplication cost is minimized.

Given a sequence of n matrices M1, M2,... Mn. And their dimensions are p0, p1, p2,..., pn.
Where matrix Ai has dimension $pi - 1 × pi$ for $1 \leq i \leq n$. Determine the order of multiplication that minimizes the total number of multiplications.

If you try to solve this problem using the brute - force method, then you will find all possible parenthesization. Then will compute the cost of multiplication. Then will pick the best solution. This approach will be exponential in nature.

There is an insufficiency in the brute force approach. Take an example of M1, M2,..., Mn. When you have calculated that ((M1·M2) · M3) is better than (M1· (M2·M3) so there is no point of calculating then combinations of (M1· (M2·M3) with (M4, M5.... Mn).

Optimal substructure:
Assume that M (1, N) is the optimum cost of production of the M1,..., Mn.

An array p [] to record the dimensions of the matrices.
P [0] = row of the M1
p[i] = col of Mi   1<=i<=N

For some k
M(1,N) = M(1,K) + M(K+1,N) + p0*pk*pn

If M (1, N) is minimal then both M (1, K) & M (K+1, N) are minimal.

Otherwise, if there is some M'(1, K) is there whose cost is less than M (1.. K), then M (1.. N) can't be minimal and there is a more optimal solution possible.

For some general i and j.
M(i,j) = M(i,K) + M(K+1,j) + pi-1*pk*pj

Recurrence relation:

$$M(i,j) = \begin{cases} 0 & \text{if } i = j \\ \min \{M(i,k) + M(k,j) + pi - 1 * pk * pj\} & i \le k < j \end{cases}$$

Overlapping Sub problems:

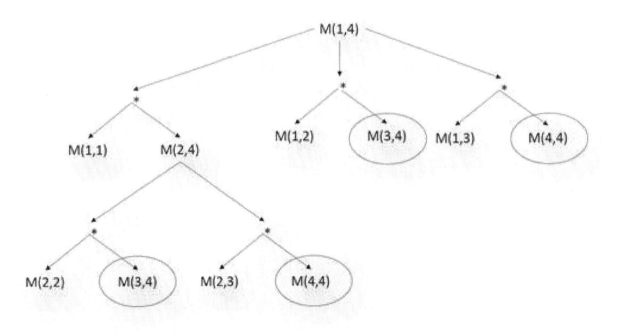

Directly calling recursive function will lead to calculation of same sub-problem multiple times. This will lead to exponential solution.

```
Algorithm MatrixChainMultiplication(p[])
   for i := 1 to n
      M[i, i] := 0;
      for l = 2 to n // l is the moving line
         for i = 1 to n − l +1
            j = i + l − 1;
            M[i, j] =  min {M(i, k) + M(k, j) + pi − 1 ∗ pk ∗ pj }
                         i ≤ k < j
```

Time Complexity will O(n^3)

Constructing optimal parenthesis Solution

Use another table s[1..n, 1..n]. Each entry s[i, j] records the value of k such that the optimal parenthesization of Mi Mi+1...Mj splits the product between Mk and Mk+1.

```
Algorithm MatrixChainMultiplication(p[])
for i := 1 to n
M[i, i] := 0;
for l = 2 to n // l is the moving line
for i = 1 to n − l +1
j = i + l − 1;
M[i, j] =  min {M(i, k) + M(k, j) + pi − 1 ∗ pk ∗ pj }
             i ≤ k < j
S[i, j] = k for  min {M(i, k) + M(k, j) + pi − 1 ∗ pk ∗ pj }
                   i ≤ k < j
```

```
Algorithm MatrixChainMultiplication(p[])
   for i := 1 to n
   M[i, i] := 0;
   for l = 2 to n // l is the moving line
      for i = 1 to n − l +1
         j = i + l − 1;
         for k = i to j
            if( (M(i, k) + M(k, j) + pi − 1 ∗ pk ∗ pj ) <  M[i, j]
               M[i, j] =  (M(i, k) + M(k, j) + pi − 1 ∗ pk ∗ pj )
               S[i, j] =  k
```

```
Algorithm PrintOptimalParenthesis(s[], i, j)
   If i = j
      Print Ai
   Else
      Print "("
      PrintOptimalParenthesis(s[], i,s[i, j])
      PrintOptimalParenthesis(s[], s[i, j],j)
      Print ")"
```

Longest Common Subsequence

Let X = {x1, x2,...., xm} is a sequence of characters. And Y = {y1, y2,..., yn} is another sequence. Z is a subsequence of X if it can be driven by deleting some elements of X. Z is a subsequence of Y if it can be driven by deleting some elements form Y. Z is LCS of it is subsequence to both X and Y, and there is no subsequence whose length is greater than Z.

Optimal Substructure:

Let X = < x1, x2, ..., xm > and Y = < y1, y2, ..., yn > be two sequences, and let Z = < z1, z2, ..., zk > be a LCS of X and Y.

- If xm = yn, then zk = xm = yn ⇒ Zk−1 is a LCS of Xm−1 and Yn−1
- If xm != yn, then:
    ○ zk != xm ⇒ Z is an LCS of Xm−1 and Y.
    ○ zk != yn ⇒ Z is an LCS of X and Yn−1.

Recurrence relation
Let c[i, j] be the length of the longest common subsequence between X = {x1, x2,...., xi} and Y = {y1, y2,..., yj}. Then c[n, m] contains the length of an LCS of X and Y

$$c[i,j] = \begin{cases} 0 & if\ i = 0\ or\ j = 0 \\ c[i-1, j-1] + 1 & if\ i, j > 0\ and\ x_i = y_j \\ \max(c[i-1,j], c[i,j-1] & otherwise \end{cases}$$

```
Algorithm LCS(X[], m, Y[], n)
for i = 1 to m
        c[i,0] = 0
for j = 1 to n
        c[0,j] = 0;
for i = 1 to m
        for j = 1 to n
                if X[i] == Y[j]
                        c[i,j] = c[i-1,j-1] + 1
                        b[i,j] = ↖
                else
                        if c[i-1,j] ≥ c[i,j-1]
                                c[i,j] = c[i-1,j]
                                b[i,j] = ↑
                        else
                                c[i,j] = c[i,j-1]
                                b[i,j] = ←
```

```
Algorithm PrintLCS(b[],X[], i, j)
if i = 0
        return
if j = 0
        return
if b[i, j] = ↖
        PrintLCS (b[],X[], i – 1, j – 1)
        print X[i]
else if b[i, j] = ↑
        PrintLCS (b[],X[], i – 1, j)
else
        PrintLCS (b[],X[], i, j – 1)
```

Coin Exchanging problem

How can a given amount of money N be made with the least number of coins of given denominations D= {d1… dn}?

For example, Indian coin system {5, 10, 20, 25, 50,100}. Suppose we want to give change of a certain amount of 40 paisa.

We can make a solution by repeatedly choosing a coin ≤ to the current amount, resulting in a new amount. The greedy solution is to always choose the largest coin value possible.
For 40 paisa: {25, 10, and 5}

This is how billions of people around the globe do change every day. That is an approximate solution of the problem. But this is not the optimal way, the optimal solution for the above problem is {20, 20}

Step (I): Characterize the structure of a coin-change solution.
Define C [j] to be the minimum number of coins we need to make a change for j cents.

If we knew that an optimal solution for the problem of making change for j cents used a coin of denomination di, we would have:
C[j] = 1+C[j – di]

Strep (II): Recursively defines the value of an optimal solution.

$$c[j] = \begin{cases} \text{infinite} & \text{if } j < 0 \\ 0 & \text{if } j = 0 \\ 1 + \min(c[j - di]) \ 1 \le i \le k & \text{if } j \ge 1 \end{cases}$$

Step (III): Compute values in a bottom-up fashion.

```
Algorithm CoinExchange(n, d[], k)
C[0] = 0
for j = 1 to n do
        C[j] = infinite
for i = 1 to k do
        if j < di and 1+C[j − di] < C[j] then
                C[j] = 1+C[j − di]
return C
```

Complexity: O(nk)

Step (iv): Construct an optimal solution
We use an additional array Deno[1.. n], where Deno[j] is the denomination of a coin used in an optimal solution.

```
Algorithm CoinExchange(n, d[], k)
C[0] = 0
for j = 1 to n do
        C[j] = infinite
for i = 1 to k do
        if j < di and 1+C[j − di] < C[j] then
                C[j] = 1+C[j − di]
        Deno[j] = di
return C
```

```
Algorithm PrintCoins( Deno[], j)
        if j > 0
                PrintCoins (Deno, j −Deno[j])
print Deno[j]
```

CHAPTER 20: BACKTRACKING AND BRANCH-AND-BOUND

Introduction

Suppose the lock produce some sound "click" correct digit is selected for any level. You just will find the first digit, then find the second digit, then find the third digit and done. This will be a greedy algorithm and you will find the solution very quickly.

But let us suppose the lock is some old one and it creates same sound not only at the correct digit but at some other digits also. So when you are trying to find the digit of the first ring, then it may product sound at multiple instances. So at this point you are not directly going straight to the solution, but you need to test various states and in case those states are not the solution you are looking for, then you need to backtrack one step at a time and find the next solution. But sure this intelligence/ heuristics of click sound will help you to reach your goal much faster. These functions are called Pruning function or bounding functions.

Problems on Backtracking Algorithm

N Queens Problem

```c
void print(int *Q, int n)
{
        for ( int i = 0; i< n; i++)
                printf(" %d ",Q[i]);
}
```

```c
int Feasible(int *Q, int k)
{
        for ( int i = 0; i< k; i++)
        {
                if(Q[k] == Q[i] || abs(Q[i] - Q[k]) == abs(i-k))
                        return 0;
        }
        return 1;
}
```

```
void NQueens(int* Q, int k, int n)
{
        if( k == n)
        {
                print( Q, n);
                return;
        }
        for ( int i = 0; i< n; i++)
        {
                Q[k]=i;
                if(Feasible(Q, k))
                        NQueens(Q, k+1, n);
        }
}
```

```
int main()
{
        int Q[8];
        NQueens(Q,0,8);
        return 0;
}
```

Tower of Hanoi

The Tower of Hanoi puzzle, disks need to be moved from one piller to another such that any large disk cannot rest above any small disk.

This is a famous puzzle in the programming world, its origins can be tracked back to India.
"There is a story about an Indian temple in Kashi Viswanathan which contains a large room with three timeworn posts in it surrounded by 64 golden disks. Brahmin priests, acting out the command of an ancient hindu prophecy, have been moving these disks, in accordance with the immutable rules of the Brahma the creator of universe, since the beginning of time. The puzzle is therefore also known as the Tower of Brahma puzzle. According to the prophecy, when the last move of the puzzle will be completed, the world will end." ;) ;) ;)

```
void towers(int num, char from, char to, char temp)
{
    if (num < 1)
        return;

    towers(num - 1, from, temp, to);
    printf("\n Move disk %d from peg %c to peg %c", num, from, to);
    towers(num - 1, temp, to, from);
}
```

```
int main()
{
    int num=10;
    printf("The sequence of moves involved in the Tower of Hanoi are :\n");
    towers(num, 'A', 'C', 'B');
    return 0;
}
```

CHAPTER 21: COMPLEXITY THEORY AND NP COMPLETENESS

Introduction

Computational complexity is the measurement of how much resources are required to solve some problem.

There are two types of resources:
1. Time: how many steps it takes to solve a problem
2. Space: how much memory it takes to solve a problem.

Decision problem

Much of Complexity theory deals with decision problems. A decision problem always has a yes or no answer.

Many problems can be converted to a decision problem which have answered as yes or no. For example:
1. Searching: The problem of searching element can be a decision problem if we ask to find if a particular number is there in the list?

2. Sorting of list and to find if the list is sorted you can make a decision problem is the list is sorted in increasing order or not?

3. Graph coloring algorithms: this is also can be converted to a decision problem. Can we do the graph coloring by using X number of colors?

4. Hamiltonian cycle: Is there is a path from all the nodes, each node is visited exactly once and come back to the starting node without breaking?

Complexity Classes

Problems are divided into many classes such that how difficult to solve them or how difficult to find if the given solution is correct or not.

Class P problems

The class P consists of a set of problems that can be solved in polynomial time. The complexity of a P problem is $O(n^k)$ Where n is input size and k is some constant (it can't depend on n).

Class P Definition: The class P contains all decision problems for which there exists a Turing machine algorithm that leads to the "yes/no" answer in a definite number of steps bounded by a polynomial function.

For example:
Given a sequence a1, a2, a3…. an. Find if a number X is in this array.
We can search, the number X in this array in linear time (polynomial time)

Another example:
Given a sequence a1, a2, a3…. an. If we are asked to sort the sequence.
We can sort and array in polynomial time using Bubble-Sort, this is also linear time.

Note: $O(logn)$ is also polynomial. Any algorithm which has complexity less than some $O(n^k)$ is also polynomial.

Some problem of P class is:
1. Shortest path
2. Minimum spanning tree
3. Maximum problem.
4. Max flow graph problem.
5. Convex hull

Class NP problems

Set of problems for which there is a polynomial time checking algorithm. Given a solution if we can check in a polynomial time if that solution is correct or not then the problem is NP problem.

Class NP Definition: The class NP contains all decision problems for which, given a solution, there exists a polynomial time "proof" or "certificate" that can verify if the solution is the right "yes/no" answer

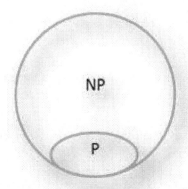

Note: There is no guarantee that you will be able to solve this problem in polynomial time. But if a problem is an NP problem, then you can verify an answer in polynomial time.

NP does not mean non polynomial. Actually, it is Non-Deterministic polynomial type of problem. They are the kind of problems which can be solved in polynomial time by a Non-Deterministic Turing machine. At each point all the possibilities are executed in parallel. If there are n possible choices, then all n cases will be executed in parallel. We don't have non deterministic computers. Don't confuse it with parallel computing because the number of CPU is limited in parallel computing it may be 16 core or 32 core but it can't be N-Core.

In short NP problems are those problems for which, if a solution is given. We can verify that solution (if it is correct or not) in polynomial time.

Boolean Satisfiability problem

A Boolean formula is satisfied if there exist some assignment of the values 0 and 1 to its variables that causes it to evaluate to 1.

$(A1 \lor A2 …) \land (A2 \lor A4..) ….\land (..\lor AN)$

There are in total N Different Boolean Variables A1, A2... AN. There are an M number of brackets. Each bracket has K variables.

There is N variable so the number of solutions will be 2^n
And to verify if the solutions really evaluate the equation to 1 will take total $2^n * km$ steps
Given solution of this problem you can find if the formula satisfies or not in KM steps.

Hamiltonian cycle

Hamiltonian cycle is a path from all the nodes of a graph, each node is visited exactly once and come back to the starting node without breaking.
Is an NP problem, if you have a solution to it, then you just need to see if all the nodes are there in the path and you came back to where you started and you are done? The checking is done in linear time and you are done.

Determining whether a directed graph has a Hamiltonian cycle doesn't have a polynomial time algorithm. O(n!)

However, if someone have given you a sequence of vertices, determining whether or not that sequence forms a Hamiltonian cycle can be done in polynomial time (Linear time).
Hamiltonian cycles are in NP

Clique Problem

In a graph given is there is a clique of size K or more. A clique is a subset of nodes which are fully connected to each other.
This problem is NP problem. Given a set of nodes you can very easily find out whether it is a clique or not.
For example:

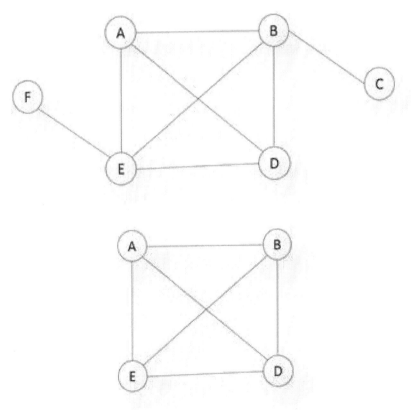

Clique of size 4

Prime Number

Finding Prime number is NP. Given a solution, it is easy to find if it is a Prime or not in polynomial time. Finding prime numbers is important as cryptography heavily uses prime numbers.

```
int isPrime(int n){
    int answer = (n>1)? 1: 0;

    for(int i = 2; i*i <= n; ++i)
    {
        if(n%i == 0)
        {
            answer = 1;
            break;
        }
    }
    return answer;
}
```

Checking will happen till the square root of number so the *Time Complexity* will be $O(\sqrt{n})$. Hence prime number finding is an NP problem as we can verify the solution in polynomial time.

Graph theory have wonderful set of problems
- Shortest path algorithms?
- Longest path is NP complete.
- Eulerian tours is a polynomial time problem.
- Hamiltonian tours is a NP complete

Class co-NP

Set of problems for which there is a polynomial time checking algorithm. Given a solution if we can check in a polynomial time if that solution is incorrect the problem is co-NP problem.

Class co-NP Definition: The class co-NP contains all decision problems such that there exists a polynomial time proof that can verify if the problem does not have the right "yes/no" answer.

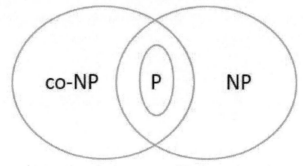

Relationship between P, NP and co-NP

Class P is Subset of Class NP

All problems which are P also are NP ($P \subseteq NP$). Problem set P is a subset of problem set NP.

Searching
If we have some number sequence a1, a2, a3.... an. We already know that searching a number X inside this array is of type P.
If it is given that number X is inside this sequence, then we can verify by looking into each and every entry again and find if the answer is correct in polynomial time (linear time.)

Sorting
Another example of sorting a number sequence, if it is given that the array b1, b2, b3.. bn is a sorted then we can loop through this given array and find if the list is really sorted in polynomial time (linear time again.)

NP–Hard:

A problem is NP-Hard if all the problems in NP can be reduced to it in polynomial time.

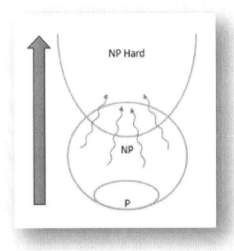

NP–Complete Problems

Set of problem is NP-Complete if it is an NP problem and also an NP-Hard problem.
It should follow both the properties:
1) Its solutions can be verified in a polynomial time.
2) All problems of NP are reduced to NP complete problems in polynomial time.

You can always reduce any NP problem into an NP-Complete in polynomial time. And when you get the answer to the problem, then you can verify this solution in polynomial time.

Any NP problem is polynomial reduced to NP-Complete problem, if we can find a solution to a single NP-Complete problem in polynomial time, then we can solve all the NP problems in polynomial time. But so far no one is able to find any solution of NP-Complete problem in polynomial time.

$P \neq NP$

Reduction

It is a process of transformation of one problem into another problem. The transformation time should be polynomial. If a problem A is transformed into B and we know the solution of B in polynomial time, then A can also be solved in polynomial time.

For example

Quadratic Equation Solver: We have a Quadratic Equation Solver, which solves equation of the form $ax^2 + bx + c = 0$. It takes Input a, b, c and generate output r1, r2.

Now try to solve a linear equation 2x+4=0. Using reduction second equation can be transformed to the first equation.

$2x+4 = 0x^2 + 2x + 4 = 0$

ATLAS: We have an atlas and we need to color maps so that no two countries have the same color. Let us suppose below is the various countries. And different pattern represents different color.

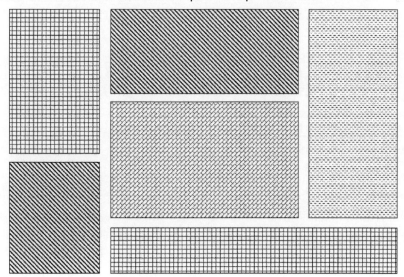

We can see that same problem of atlas coloring can be reduced to graph coloring and if we know the solution of graph coloring then same solution can work for atlas coloring too. Where each node of the graph represents one country and the adjacent country relation is represented by the edges between nodes.

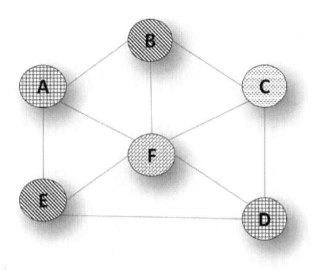

The sorting problem reduces (≤) to Convex Hull problem.

SAT reduces (≤) to 3SAT

Traveling Salesman Problem (TSP)

The traveling salesman problem tries to find the shortest tour through a given set of n cities that visits each city exactly once before returning to the city where it started.
Alternatively: Finding the shortest Hamiltonian circuit in a weighted connected graph. A cycle that passes through all the vertices of the graph exactly once.

```
Algorithm TSP
Select a city
MinTourCost = infinite
For ( All permutations of cities ) do
        If( LengthOfPathSinglePermutation < MinTourCost )
                MinTourCost = LengthOfPath
```

Total number of possible combinations = (n-1)!
Cost for calculating the path? $\Theta(n)$
So the total cost for finding the shortest path? $\Theta(n!)$

It is an NP-Hard problem there is no efficient algorithm to find its solution. Even if some solution is given, it is equally hard to verify that this is a correct solution or not. But there are some approximate algorithms which can be used to find a fairly good solution. We will not always get the best solution but will get a fairly good solution.

Our approximate algorithm is based on the minimum spanning tree problem. In which we have to construct a tree from a graph such that every node is connected by edges of the graph and the total sum of the cost of all the edges it minimum.

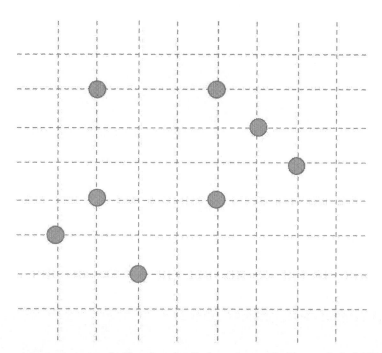

In the above diagram, we have a group of cities (each city is represented by a circle.) Which are located in the grid and the distance between the cities is same as per the actual distance. And there is a path from each city to another city which is a straight path from one to another.

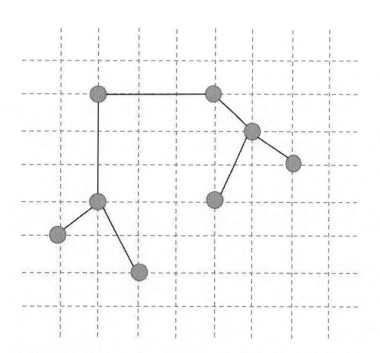

We have made a minimum spanning tree for the above city graph.

What we want to prove that the shortest path in a TSP will always be greater than the length of MST. Since all nodes are connected to the next node which is the minimum distance from the group of node so some node is removed and new nodes will be added to make it a path so TSP path will always be greater than MST.

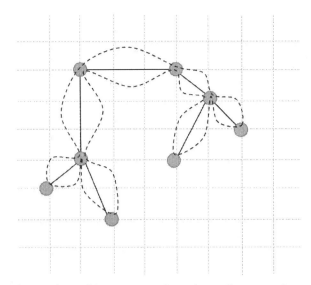

Now let's take a path from starting node and traverse each node on the way given above and then come back to the starting node. The total cost of the path is 2MST. The only difference is that we are visiting many nodes multiple times.

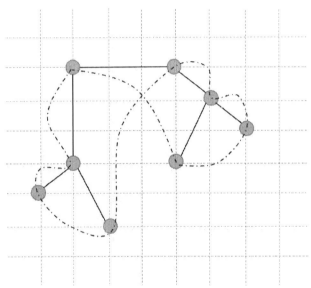

Now let's change our traversal algorithm so that it will become TSP in our traversal, we didn't visit an already visited node we will skip them and will visit the next unvisited node. In this way we will reach the next node by as shorter path. (The sum of the length of all the edges of a polygon is always greater than a single edge.) Ultimately we will get the TSP and its path length is no more than twice the optimal solution. So the proposed algorithm gives fairly good results.

End Note

Nobody has come up with such a polynomial-time algorithm to solve a NP-Complete problem. Many important algorithms depends upon it. But at the same time nobody has proven that no polynomial time algorithm is possible. There's a million US dollars for anyone who can do either solve any NP Complete problem in polynomial time. The whole economy of the world will fall as most of the banks depends on public key encryption will be easy to break if P=NP solution is found.

CHAPTER 22: INTERVIEW STRATEGY

Introduction

Success in tech interview depends on so many factors, your non-technical skills, your technical skills, etc. But above all the interviewers should be convinced that they would enjoy working with you.

Resume

The best resumes are those that communicate your skills and accomplishments in a clear and effective way.

A good resume format has the following attributes:
1. Multiple Columns: Multiple columns make it easier for someone to quickly skim your company name, positions, collage, and other key facts.
2. Short and Sweet: Interviewer is going to spend about 30 Sec reading your resume. You should just focus on the highlights. One page is all you need, but if you are 10+ years of experience, then you can justify two pages.
3. No Junk: No objective, No oath, Summary section/Key skills section may be fine, if your resume is short and concise then you don't need a summary section.
4. Use Tables: You can use tables, but it should not waste space.
5. Highlights: highlights should be short. Keep your highlights to one liner.
6. Neat: Keep your resume neat and clean. Use appropriate Fonts and Formatting. Bold to represent highlights and maybe italics in some places.

Nontechnical questions

Prepare for various non-technical questions. The first thing to do is to prepare answers of any question that is related to your resume. The interviewer is going to look into it and ask a few questions to get an idea about you. So go through all the past/current job and projects and make sure you know what they were about and your role.

These questions may be like:
1. What was the most challenging activity you have done in project ABC?
2. What did you learn from project ABC?
3. What are your responsibilities in the current job?
4. What was the most interesting thing you have done in your current job?
5. Which course in university did you like most and why?

Technical questions

Solving a technical question is not just about knowing the algorithms and designing a good software system. The interviewer wants to know you approach towards any given problem.

Many people make mistakes like they don't ask clarifying questions about a given problem? They assume a lot of things and begin working with that. Well the truth is the interviewer to actually expect you to ask constraints questions. There are a lot of data that is missing that you need to collect from your interviewer before beginning to solve a problem.

For example: Let us suppose the interviewer ask you to give a best sorting algorithm.
Some interviewee will directly jump to Quick-Sort *O(nlogn)*. Oops, mistake you need to ask many questions before beginning to solve this problem.

Questions:
1. What kind of data we are talking about? Are they *integer* s?
2. How much data are we going to sort?
3. What exactly is this data about?
4. What kind of data-structure used to hold this data?
5. Can we modify the given data-structure? And many, many more...?

Answer:
1. Yes, they are *integer* s.
2. May be thousands.
3. They store a person's age.
4. Data are given in the form of some array.
5. No you can't modify the data structure provided.

Ok from the first answer we will deduce that the data is *integer* . The data is not so big it just contains a few thousand entries. The third answer is interesting from this we deduce that the range of data is 1-150. Data is provided in an array. From fifths answer we deduce that we have to create our own data structure and we cannot modify the array provided. So finally we conclude, we can just use bucket sort to sort the data. The range is just 1-150 so we need just 151 capacity integral array. Data is under thousands so we don't have to worry about data overflow and we get the solution in linear time *O(N)*.

CHAPTER 23: SYSTEM DESIGN

System Design

The section we will look into questions in which interviewer asks to design a high-level architecture of any software system.

Note: - This is an advance chapter It may be that the user is not able to understand it completely. I would suggest that give it some time read the chapter and try to read online. The more time you give to this chapter the better understanding you will get. It may also help if you give multiple rounds of reading.

There are two kinds of questions in this and which will be asked depends on the type of companies. The first kind of questions is to design some kind of elevator system, valet parking system, etc. In this, the interviewer just wants to test how well you are able to design a system, especially how well your classes are interacting.

The Second kind of system design problems is more interesting, in which the interviewer asks you to design some kind of website or some kind of service or some API interface. For example, design google search engine or design some feature of Facebook like how friends mapping is done on Facebook, design a web-based game that allows 4 people play poker etc. They are interesting one and in this, the interviewer can ask about scalability aspect.

Now comes a question to our mind, how would you design google search engine in 10-15 minutes? Well, the answer is you can't. It took many days if not years by a group of a smart engineer to design google search engine. The interviewer is expecting a Higher-level architecture of the system that can address the given Use-Cases and Constraints of the problem in hand. There is no single right solution. The same problem can be solved in a number of ways. The most important thing is that you should be able to justify your solution.

System Design Process

Let's look into a 5 Steps approach for solving system design problems:
1. Use Cases Generation
2. Constraints and Analysis
3. Basic Design
4. Bottlenecks
5. Scalability

Use Cases

Just like algorithm design problems, the system design questions are also most likely weakly defined. There is so much information that is missing and without them the design is impossible. So first thing in the design process is that you should gather all the possible use cases. You should ask questions to the interviewer to find the use case of the system. The interviewer wants to see your **requirement gathering capability**. Same as algorithm questions never assume things, which are not stated.

Constraints and Analysis

This is the step in which you will define various constraints of the system and then analyse them. Your system design will depend on the analysis that you do in this step. In this step, you need to find answers to questions like. How many users will be using the system? What kind of data that we are going to store? Etc.

Basic Design

In this step, you will design the most basic design of the system. Draw your main components and make connections between them. In this step, you need to design a system with the supposition that there is no memory limitation and all data can fit in one single machine. You should be able to justify your idea. In this step, you need to handle all the use-cases.

Bottlenecks Analysis

In this step, you will find the one or more bottlenecks on the basic design you had proposed. The "Scalability Theory" given below will help to identify the bottlenecks. You need to know the below theory which experts had developed over time. In this step, you will consider how much data your proposed system can handle, memory limitations etc.

Scalability

In this step, you will remove all the bottlenecks of the system and you are done. There may be multiple iterations between "Bottlenecks analysis" and "Scalability" until we reach our final solution. We will be reading various concepts like Vertical scaling, Horizontal scaling, Load-Balancer, Redundancy and Caching in this chapter. "Scalability Theory" given below will help you to understand these concepts.

Scalability Theory

In this section, we will be designing a generic web server, which will be handling a large number of requests. You can imagine it as some sort of website like Facebook in which large number of users are accessing it.

Vertical scaling

Vertical scaling means that you scale by adding more resources (Higher speed CPU, More RAM etc.) To your existing machine.

Vertical scaling has its own limit it can help you to handle more load, but until its limit is reached, then we have to go for horizontal scaling.

Horizontal scaling

Horizontal scaling means that you scale by adding more machines to your pool of resources.

Distribute the request by distributing the request among more than one web server. In doing this we need to have a load balancer, which will distribute the request among the servers.

Load Balancer (Application layer)

Load balancer has to decide which server should serve the next request. So distributing the load can be made using different strategies:

1) **Round Robbin**: Round robin is the way of distributing requests in a sequential fashion. The request is sent to the server 1 then the next request is sent to server 2 and so on till we reach the end of the server list. Then when we reach the end, it is sent again to server 1. Round robin has a problem that a server, which is already busy, may get another request. Round robin also has a problem with sticky sessions. We want that a request to be sent to the same server the next time.

2) Another approach is to select server corresponds to the hash value of the data. Find the hash value of the data, mod the hash value by the number of servers. Assign the job to a machine whose value we got after mod. Stick session problem is already solved in hash value approach. However, the problem of uneven load distribution is there, there is possible to have a more load sent to a server, which is already busy.

3) May be the load balancer know, how much load each server has or how busy each the server is. Moreover, will send the next request to the least busy server.

4) The server can be a specialized one serving image some serving video and some serving other data.

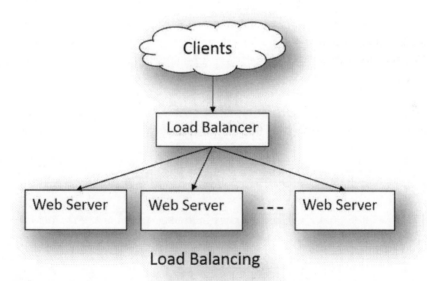

Load Balancing

Problems of load Balancing

Consider a customer who had selected some items in his buy cart on Amazon. When he selects another item then it should be added to the same cart so it should be sent to the same server. Also, the user profile which is saved to one server and if the user request reaches the other server his profile will be empty this is also not a good idea.

This problem can be solved by making the load balancer decide that a particular user request would always go to the same server. The user profile and cart details should be saved in some database.

Stick session: same sessions should lend to the same server. How to get this done. The first approach is that we store the IP address returned by load balancing into a cookie and then use this IP address in the subsequent requests. However, this reveals the IP address of the server to the world that we do not want. Therefore, another solution is that we use some session id that is a number that the load balancer knows that belongs to which server. By this, we are preventing our servers being exposed to the outer world and prevent it from being attacked.

Load Balancer (Database layer)

1. The most basic approach is **Round Robin**. Data is distributed in a circular fashion. First, data go to the first database, the second will go to the second database and so one. Each database server had an equal load. However, it has a disadvantage that the data lookup is complex. And need a large lookup table.

2. Another approach is to divide the data in such a way that all the data will go to the first machine until it reaches its maximum capacity. When maximum capacity is reached, then data goes to the second machine and so on. This approach has an advantage that only the required number of machines is used. However, it has a disadvantage that the data lookup is complex. And need a large lookup table.

3. Another approach is to select database corresponds to the hash value of the data. Find the hash value of the data. Mod the hash value by the number of databases. The data are then stored in the database value we got after modulus. For has a value approach we do not require any lookup table. We can find the database, which is storing the data, by finding the hash value. However, the problem of uneven distribution of data is there, there is possible to have a more data sent to a database, which has already reached its maximum capacity. In this case, we need to find a better load-balancing key or split the data from the database into a number of databases.

4. In the hash value, based distribution of data there is no relation between the data that is stored in a particular database. Information about the data can be used to make the database accessible faster. For example, in social networking like Facebook, if someone who lives in India is more likely to have friends from India. And someone who lives in the USA is more likely to have friends in the USA.

5. Perhaps location aware (approach 4) and the hash value based (approach 3) distribution of data may be the best approach to keep the data so that it can take advantage of both the approaches. Country code and user ID can be used to get the location of the database.

Redundancy

There is one problem in our system, there is a redundancy in the servers but our load balancer is now our single point of failure. We add a secondary load balancer in case the primary load balancer dies, then secondary load balancer becomes primary and then all the requests will be handled by it.

Load Balancing

Raid (Redundant Array of Inexpensive Disk): Raid is a technology to create redundancy in the databases. Multiple hard drives are used to replicate data, thereby proving redundancy.

Caching

A cache is a simple key-value store and it should reside as a buffering layer between your application and your data storage. Whenever your application wants to read, it first tries to retrieve the data from your cache. Only if data is not present in the cache, then only it tries to get the data from the main database.

Caching improves application performance by storing portion of data in memory for low-latency access. We need databases and access to the database is slow, so we use multiple types of caching to make our system faster. Database servers itself does caching so do the other entities in between the user and the database.

Memcached: It is a server software, what it does is it kept whatever you access in memory. It can run on the same server as the webserver or it can run on a separate machine all together.

Redis: It is a data structure server based on **"NoSQL"** which is a key-value data store. Data is stored as the value with respect to corresponding key. This data is later retrieved by the use of the key. Redis is used for caching it is best to store the whole object as one instance so that the data can be accessed in parallel and data expiration will flush out the whole object.

There is a problem since ram is finite, then the cache will get full. The expired object will be removed so everything that is accessed then its expiry will be reset and if there is an object that is not used for some time then it was deleted. Cache is more important when the website that we are designing is more read heavier than a write.

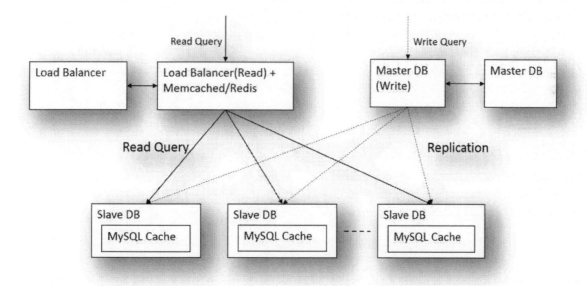

A complete web server implementation

The summary of the above system.
1. The Web-Servers of scalable web service is hidden behind a load balancer. The load balancer evenly distributes load across all the servers.
2. The user should get the same result from web-server regardless which server is actually serving the request. Therefore, every server should be identical to each other. Servers should not contain any data like session information or user profile.

3. Session need to be stored in a centralized data store (DB) which is accessible to all the servers. Data can be stored in some external database. Redundancy in the database is provided by raid technology.
4. The database is slow, so we need a cache. In-memory based cache like Redis or Memcached.
5. However, the cache has a problem of expiring. When a table changes, then the cache is outdated.
6. For Memcached there are two options:
a. We can save queries to the DB
b. We can save the whole object that will keep us close to web-server.
7. CDN (Content delivery networks) can be used to provide a pre-processed web page.
Below diagram will give you a complete picture of the whole system.

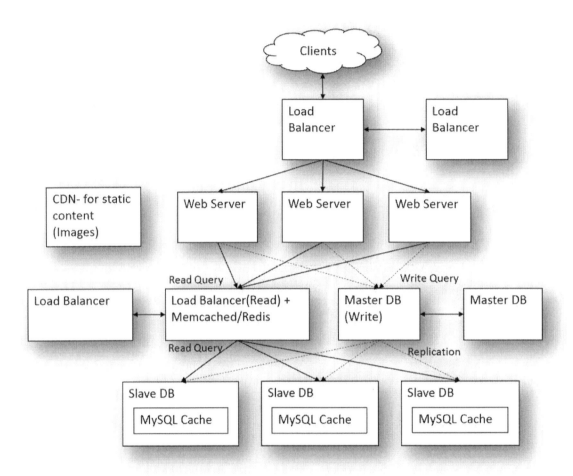

Design simplified Facebook

Design simplified Facebook where people can add other people as friends. In addition, where people can post messages and that messages are visible on their friend's page. The design should be such that it can handle 10 million of people. There may be, on an average 100 friends each person has. Every day each person posts some 10 messages on an average.

Use Case

1. A user can create their own profile.
2. A user can add other users to his friend list.
3. Users can post messages to their timeline.
4. The system should display posts of friends to the display board/timeline.
5. People can like a post.
6. People can share their friends post to their own display board/timeline.

396

Constraints

1. Consider a whole network of people as represented by a graph. Each person is a node and each friend relationship is an edge of the graph.
2. Total number of distinct users / nodes: 10 million
3. Total number of distinct friend's relationship / edges in the graph: 100 * 10 million
4. Number of messages posted by a single user per day: 10
5. Total number of messages posted by the whole network per day: 10 * 10 million

Basic Design

Our system architecture is divided into two parts:
1. First, the web server which will handle all the incoming requests.
2. The second database, which will store the entire person's profile, their friend relations and posts.

First, three requirements creating a profile, adding friends, posting messages are written some information to the database. While the last operation is reading data from the database.

The system will look like this:
1. Each user will have a profile.
2. There will be a list of friends in each user profile.
3. Each user will have their own homepage where his posts will be visible.

A user can like any post of their friend and that likes will reflect on the actual message shared by his friend.
If a user shares some post, then this post will be added to the user home page and all the other friends of the user will see this post as a new post.

Bottleneck

A number of requests posted per day is 100 million. Approximate some 1000 request are posted per second. There will be an uneven distribution of load so the system that we will design should be able to handle a few thousand requests per seconds.

Scalability

Since there is, a heavy load we need horizontal scaling many web servers will be handling the requests. In doing this we need to have a load balancer, which will distribute the request among the servers.

Load Balancing

This approach gives us a flexibility that when the load increases, we can add more web servers to handle the increased load.

These web servers are responsible for handling new post added by the user. They are responsible for generating various user homepage and timeline pages. In our diagram, the client is the web browser, which is rendering the page for the user.

We need to store data about user profile, Users friend list, User-generated posts, User like statues to the posts.

Let us find out how much storage we need to store all this data. The total number of users 10 million. Let us suppose each user is using Facebook for 5 to 6 years, so the total number of posts that a user had produced in this whole time is approximately 20,000 million or 20 billion. Let us suppose each message consists of 100 words or 500 characters. Let us assume each character take 2 bytes.

Total memory required = 20 * 500 * 2 billion bytes.
= 20,000 billion bytes
= 20, 000 GB
= 20 TB

1 gigabyte (GB) = 1 billion bytes
1000 gigabytes (GB) = 1 Terabytes

Most of the memory is taken from the posts and the user profile and friend list will take nominal as compared with the posts. We can use a relational database like SQL to store this data. Facebook and twitter are using a relational database to store their data.

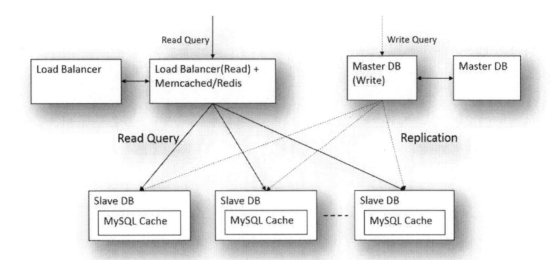

Responsiveness is key for social networking site. Databases have their own cache to increase their performance. Still database access is slow as databases are stored on hard drives and they are slower than RAM. Database performance can be increased by replication of the database. Requests can be distributed between the various copies of the databases.

Also, there will be more reads then writes in the database so there can be multiple slave DB which are used for reading and there can be few master DB for writing. Still database access is slow to we will use some caching mechanism like Memcached in between application server and database. Highly popular users and their home page will always remain in the cache.

There may be the case when the replication no longer solves the performance problem. In addition, we need to do some Geo-location based optimization in our solution.

Again, look for a complete diagram in the scalability theory section.

If it were asked in the interview how you would store the data in the database. The schema of the database can look like:

Table Users	Table Posts
<ul><li>User Id</li><li>First Name</li><li>Last Name</li><li>Email</li><li>Password</li><li>Gender</li><li>Birthday</li><li>Relationship</li></ul>	<ul><li>Post Id</li><li>Author Id</li><li>Date of Creation</li><li>Content</li></ul>
Table Friends	Table Likes
<ul><li>Relation Id</li><li>First Friend Id</li><li>Second Friend Id</li></ul>	<ul><li>Id</li><li>Post Id</li><li>User Id</li></ul>

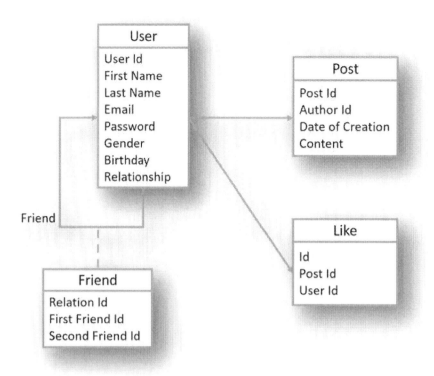

Design Facebook Friends suggestion function

Design a system to implement a friend suggestion functionality of Facebook, with millions of users. The algorithm should suggest all the friends of the immediate friends as a proposed list to add as friends.

Use Case

The system should suggest friends of the friends as suggested new friends.

Constraint

Millions of user's lot of data with billions of relations.

Basic Design

Forget about millions of users. Just consider there are only a few persons and they are connected with each other as friends.

Consider that people are represented by vertices of graphs and their friendship relation is represented by edges.

Since there are only a few people, then we can keep everything in memory and find the friend suggestion using Breadth First Traversal.
We just need to find the nodes, which are just 2 degrees apart from the starting node.

Bottleneck

Since there are millions of users, we cannot have everything in memory. Since there are millions of users, we cannot keep the data on one machine. One friends' profiles may lie on many different machines.

Scalability

Since there are millions of users, their user profile is distributed among many different database servers. User profiles can be distributed depending upon Geo-Location. The Indian users profile will lie in a server located in India and US citizen's profile lie in the server located in the US.

Each user will have corresponding User Id associated with them. Some portion of ID can be used to get Geo location of the user. Another portion of user id can find the user profile on that server.

The user profile is not that frequently updated so there is more read than write. So single master writer - multiple slave reader architecture is most suitable for this application.

The application server can process the data; it can do the optimization to query less from the database by accumulating user list to be processed.

```
class system {
        map<int, int> personIdToMachineIdMap;
        map<int, Machine> machineIdToMachineMap;

        Machine getMachine(int machineId);
        Person getPerson(int personId)
        {
                int machienId = personIdToMachienIdMap[personId];
                Machine m = machineIdToMachineMap[machienId];
                return m.getPersonWithId(personId);
        }
}
```

Optimization: Reduced the number of jumps by first finding the list of friends whose profile is on the same machine. Then send the find next degree friends query which will return the list of next level friends. By doing, this work is distributed among various machines. Finally, the result of the various queries will be merged and then suggested the friends list.

Better result: You can calculate the degree of the friends with the friend list. The person who is a friend of many of my friends is more likely to be my friend than the person who is just a friend of one of my friends. We need to keep track of the friend reference counts by keeping Hash-Table for the friend list and make the count 1 whenever we find a new person otherwise increase the count by 1.

If we want to take advantage of caching, then we need to add some database cache in between.

There can be multiple web servers, which will be querying the databases, and there will be multiple users who are accessing their Facebook profile and each one of them is proposed with new friends list so the final architecture is again same as the one proposed in the complete web server implemented in scalability theory.

Design a shortening service like Bitly

Use Case

Basic use case:
1. Shortening takes a URL and returns a short URL.
2. Redirection takes a short URL and redirects to the original URL.
3. Custom URL.
4. High availability of the system.

Additional use cases:
1. Analytics
2. Automatic link expiration.
3. Manual link removal.
4. Specific company URL.
5. UI or just API

Requirement Analysis/ Math
Firs we need to find the usage pattern.
You can directly ask this data from the interviewer or you can derive it using some data that the interviewer provides. Let us suppose that the interviewer tells that there will be 1 billion requests per month. In addition, out of these 10% times, it is a new request and 90% of the time, it is a redirection of the already shortened URL. Let us write down the data that we get.
1. 1BN requests per month
2. 10% are for new URL/shortening and 90% are for redirection.
3. New URLs per month is 100MLN
4. Requests per second 1BN/ (30*24*3600) = 385. Roughly, you can assume it 400 requests per seconds.
5. Total number of URLs stored in 5 years.
5* 12* 100 MLN = 6BN URLs in 5 years.
6. Let us suppose the spase required by each URL is 500bytes.
7. Let us suppose the spase required by each Hash code for corresponding URLs is 6byte long.

402

8. Total data we need to store in five years. 3TBs for all the URLs and 36gb for hashes
6,000,000,000 * 500 bytes = 3 terabytes
6,000,000,000 * 6 bytes = 36 gigabytes
9. New data write requests per second: 40 * (500+6): 20k

Basic design

Web server: provide the website for the Bitly service where users can generate the short URL.
Application Server: provides the following services:
1. Shortening service
2. Redirection service
3. Key = Hash Function (URL)
Database Server:
1. Keep track of hash to URL mapping.
2. Works like a huge Hash-Table stores the new mapping and retrieves old mapping given key.
Bottleneck
1. Traffic is not much
2. Data storage can be a problem.

Scalability

Application Server:
1. Start with the single machine.
2. Test how far it takes up.
3. Do a vertical scaling for some time?
4. Add load balancer and a cluster of machines to handle spikes and to increase availability.

Data Storage:
1. Billions of objects
2. Each object is fairly small
3. There is no relationship between objects
4. Reads are more than write.
5. 3TBs of URLs and 36GB of hash.

MySQL:
1. Widely used
2. A mature technology
3. Clean scaling paradigms (master/slave, master/ master)
4. Used by Facebook, google, twitter etc.
5. Index lookup is very fast.

Mappings: <Hash, URL>
1. Use only MySQL table with two fields.
2. Create a unique index on the hash we want to hold it in memory to speed up lookups.
3. Vertical scaling of MySQL for a while
4. Partition of data into many partitions
5. Master-slave (read from slave and write to master.)
6. Eventually, partition the data by taking the first character of the hash mod the number of partitions.

Stock Query Server

Implement a stock query service that can provide an interface to get stock price information like open price, close price, highest price, lowest price etc. You should provide an interface that will be used to enter these data and interface to read this data.

Use Case

There will be two interfaces to this system.
1) First interface to add daily stock price information to the system.
2) Second interface to read stock price information giving the date and stock id as input.

Constraints

Let us suppose the system will be used by thousands of users.
For each stock, there will be only one write operation per day. However, there will be any number of read operations that can happen per stock so the application is more read heavy then write heavy.
The solution should be flexible enough so that if new data fields need to be added to the stock they can easily be added to the system.
The solution provided should be secure.

Basic Design

We can use a database like SQL to store stock data. Client can access the database using the web server interface. Below diagram will show the basic architecture.

In the above architecture, the user can access the database using web service. Any number of flexibility can be provided for the use. For example, what is the max price of some stock in 6 months etc. At the same time, the user does not have access to the data they should not have. We can provide different access of read and write depending on the normal users or administrator. Well-defined rolling back, backing up data and security features are provided by the SQL database. The above architecture is easily extendable to use with a website or some mobile application.

Scalability

Since we have 1000's of users, then having a single web server and a single database is not extendable. We need to distribute data among N number of Databases, which sit behind some load balancer. In addition, multiple N number of web server which will sit behind some load balancer. Each of the load balancers needs to be provided with some redundancy as they will be a single point of failure. Finally, the solution will look like below diagram. (For details, see scalability theory explained earlier in this chapter)

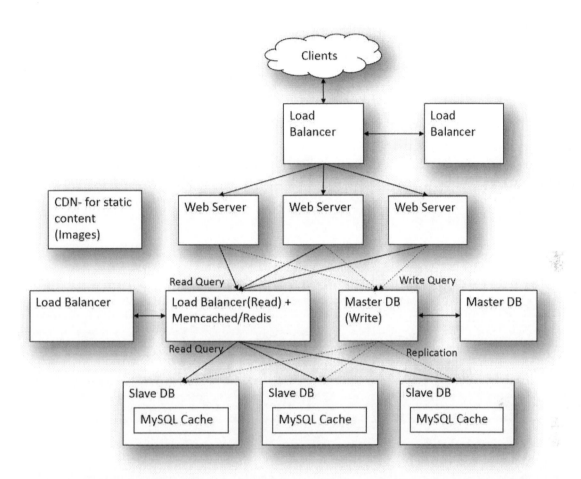

Design a basic search engine Database

You are given millions of URLs; how would you create your database. So that given a query string of words, how to find the URLs, which contain all the words of the query string. The words can come in any order.

Use Case

1) We are given a list of millions of URLs.
2) The user of the system will provide query string. And we need to return the URLs, which contain all the words of the query string.
3) It is some kind of search engine so we can pre-process the data and make our database.

Requirement Analysis

In the requirement step, you need to find out how many users are going to use this search engine. In our case, let us suppose there are not many users who are going to use our system so the sour main concern is a database.

Maybe we have N number of machines that can be used to fast our data pre-processing.

Basic Design

In this step, we will make the basic design so let us make a working system with just a few URLs. How would you find the required URL from the given URLs, which contains all the words of the input query string?
We can make a Hash-Table in which words are the keys and document ids are values.
"Hello" -> {url1, url2, url3}
"World" -> {url2, url4, url5}
To search the document, which contains "hello world", we can find the intersection of the two lists. In addition, url2 is the result.

Bottleneck

In this step, we will look back to our original problem in which there are millions of URLs that we need to pre-process. There may be a number of different words so it may not be possible to keep the whole Hash-Table on a single machine. Therefore, we need to divide the Hash-Table and keep it on a separate machine.
We need to retrieve the URLs that match a given word efficiently. So that we can find the intersection.
Pre-processing all the millions, URLs by single machine will be slow. We need to find a way to parallel process pre-processing step.

Scalability

Let us look into the problem of keeping the Hash-Table in different databases. One solution is to divide the words alphabetically. We can make tables corresponding to each word. Each database contains tables of words under some range. For example, DB1 contains all the words, which start with alphabet "a", and DB2 contains all the words, which starts with the alphabets "b" and so on. Data is stored in the database and when a database reaches its maximum capacity, then the data is stored to next machine and a tree kind of structure can be made. Finding the list of URLs corresponding to some word is easy, we can go to the corresponding database and find the table and get all the data of that table. Finally, we can take the intersection of the result of various words. In addition, the result will be given as output.

Processing of the millions of URLs with a single machine is slow. Therefore, we can divide a bunch of URL processing among an N number of machines, each URL processing is independent of each other and the final Hash-Table of the URLs can be finally combined. This approach of processing independent data and finally combining their result is used in MapReduce.

MapReduce: A MapReduce divides the input dataset into independent chunks, which are processed in parallel. Then their output is combined to get the result.

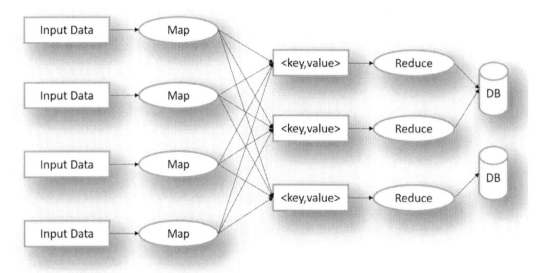

Duplicate integer in millions of documents

Given millions of documents with all distinct numbers, find the number, which occurs multiple times.

Basic Design

Consider there are just a few numbers, and we want to find the duplicate numbers.

The first approach is to find keep a sorted list of the numbers and see if the next read number matches with some number in the list.

Another better approach is to find a hash value corresponding to number and add that the number to a Hash-Table.

Constraint

Millions of documents and there is no range of number so we cannot keep everything in memory.

Scalability

We can find the hash value for all the integers and then add that integer to its corresponding hash value file or database. If there is some duplicate, then they will fall in the same file. In the first pass, various files are created and integers are distributed.

In the second pass all, the data of the individual files can be loaded into memory and sorted to find if there is some duplicate value.

We can use the same technique explained above to process the various documents of integer in parallel by different machines and then combine their output to get our result faster.

Design a basic search engine Caching

Given a search engine database implementation which supports QuerySearch() function which will return the best list of URLs based on the words of the query. This time you need to design the web server implementation of this such that there are N number of the web servers which are responding to the user queries. Any web server can be picked at random. QuerySearch() is a heavy operation so you need to design, caching for this system so that database access is reduced.

Use Case

1)   The user of the system will provide query string and system will respond with the proper list of URLs corresponding to his request.
2)   Given that, the database operations are very heavy we need to minimize them by caching the queries at the web server.
3)   We need to keep the frequent queries in the cache and stale queries need to be removed from the cache.
4)   We need to have some proper refresh mechanism for each query.

Basic Design

Let us lust forget about an N number of machines and assume that QuerySearch() operation happens on a single machine. Now we would like to cache queries. Each query will consist of some string. And the result of a query is a list of URLs.

We need to have a quick cache lookup so that we can get the result of the Query from the cache if it is present there. Also, need to have some proper refresh mechanism for each query.

The Hash-Table is most effective to keep the cache. By using a hash, a table lookup is fast. However, if the cache is filled how you would remove the least used data from the cache.

A linked list can be used to remove the old data. You can keep a double linked list to manage the old data removal. Whenever a data is accessed, it can be moved to the front of the linked list and the removal can happen from the end of the linked list.

Taking advantage of both the solutions, we can keep the cache in a linked list and add its reference to the Hash-Table.

Now the last problem of how to remove the data upon the expiry of it. For example, most frequently accessed query result will always remain in the linked list even though that result is changed and if it is accessed again from the database then it will give some updated result. For this, we need to have some TTL (time to live) associated with each query depending upon the result of URLs we get from each query. For example, some weather or current news related queries should have a TTL of days, on the other hand, some historic data should have a long TTL. The TTL can be derived from how frequently the URLs are changing in the query result.

Bottleneck

There are N different web servers. And any particular query can be served by any server.
Data access should be fast.

Scalability

The various solutions that we can think about are:

Approach 1:
Servers can have their own cache. If some query is sent to Machine1 it will catch it in its cache when the same query is sent to it again it will return it from its cache. However, if some query is sent to Machine1 first, it will cache it and if the same query is sent to Machine2, it will again do a database lookup and cache it to its own cache. This implementation is suboptimal as it is doing more number of database lookups than what is actually required.

Approach 2:
Another approach is that each machine stores identical cache. Whenever some database access happened then the same cache is updated by all the web server. This approach has a drawback that whenever a data is updated in cache same cache update is fired to all the N web servers. Another disadvantage is that all the cache stores the same data so we are wasting precious cache space.

Approach 3:
In this approach, we will divide our cache such that each web server holds a different part of the cache. When a query reach to some web server it knows which webserver actually holds the cache for this query or at least knows that which server is supposed to keep a cache of the particular query.
To do this we need a hash-based approach. We find the server, which serves the query, by just finding the hash (query) percentage N.

When a query request come to some web server, it will find the webserver corresponding to this query by applying the formula. It will ask the QuerySearch() function to that particular server. That server will in turn will query the database if required or provide the result from its own cache.

Now, regarding the cache expiration and old cache removal. We are keeping the TTL corresponding to each query so there can be a thread running which looks for the expired data and remove it from the cache.

In addition, combination of linked list and Hash-Table is used to keep the cache to get rid of less accessed data when the cache is almost full.

As a further improvement, we can think of some sort of Geo location aware webserver selection and cache policy so that query related to India is more supposed to be done in India and query related to china is supposed to come more from china.

Zomato

Use Case

1. Given a location, the list of hotels in that locality needs to be displayed.
2. Given a hotel name that hotel's rating, review, and menu need to be displayed
3. There should be some option to find if a delivery option is there in the hotel.
4. There should be some option to select a hotel on veg/non-veg category.
5. There should be some option to select hotels, which serve alcohol.
6. The user should be able to add reviews, add personal ratings to the hotels.
7. The user has some account or can access as guest.
8. Users/Admin should be able to add a new hotel to the system.

Constraints

1. A number of queries per second, suppose 100 queries per second.
2. There are more reads than writes.
3. 90% of the time there is read operation and only 10% of the time there is a write operation.
4. 100 * 60 * 60 * 24 = 8,640,000

Basic Design

The scalability will be same as that of the examples explained above in the case of basic Facebook. Same concept of redundancy, load balancing, scalability etc.

Abstract Design

Each hotel has some hotel id associated with it.
1. Data of the hotel can be Name, Address, Rating, Review List, Veg-Nonveg, and Alcohol etc.
2. The region is a field in the address.
3. Search: When a user does a region based query all the entries of the hotels in that region need to be displayed to the user.
4. Search: User should be able to search specific hotel.
5. Add Review/ Rating: When users assess a hotel, then he should be able to add reviews and rating for the hotel.
6. Obviously the images are stored in CDN

Application Service layer
1. Start with fewer machines
2. All load balancer + a cluster of machines over time.
3. Traffic spike handling.
4. High availability.

Data Storage Layer:
1. Thousands of hotels.
2. There are no relationships between the object.
3. Reads are more than writing.
4. Relational database option is MySQL
5. Widely used.
6. Clear scaling paradigms. (Master-Master replication, Master-Slave replication)
7. Index lookups are very fast.

One optimization that we can assign an id to hotels the id can be derived from the locality so that it would be easy to find hotels in that locality.

YouTube

Scenarios

1. Users have some profile according to which content is shown.
2. Content thumbnails are shown when the user opens the YouTube web page.
3. When the user clicks on some thumbnail, then that video is played on flash player.

Constraints

1. Millions of users are going to use this service.
2. 200 million video requests served per day.
3. More reads than writes.

Design

1. YouTube is supposed to serve huge number of videos for which it has video serving clusters. A single video can be served from multiple servers in clusters and from multiple clusters thereby distributing the disk read which increases the performance of the system.
2. The most popular videos are served from CDN, CDN is more close to the user which reduce the response time. And reduce the load to the video serving clusters.

3. The rest of the metadata of the video is served from other servers as the user is not much interested in the metadata.
4. The rest of the application will be same as it will have an application server, database servers, load balancer, caching etc.
5. There is more read than write so the master server topology will be used. Therefore, there can be a single master for writing and multiple slaves for reading.
6. Master data is replicated to slaves. Since slaves are same as master then the master is down, then slaves can be promoted to make as master.
7. Page to be displayed to the user depends on his subscribed pages, History etc.
8. Information can be cached in the Memcached implemented near the database load balancer.

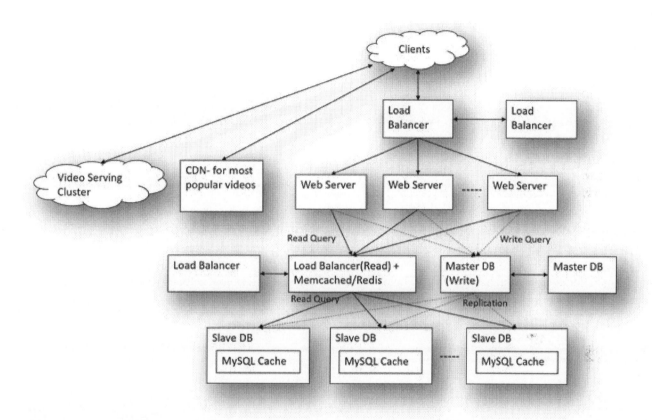

Design IRCTC

Scenario

1. The user should be able to query trains between two stations.
2. The query should be based on the date, quota, from and to the station.
3. The user should be able to see the availability in the train list retrieved from the above query.
4. The user should be able to book tickets for the available seats.

Constraints

1. There will be a huge number of people requesting the service. Let us suppose 0.01 percent of the population use the service daily once.
2. Geo-Redundancy should be provided.
3. More read query/ request then writes requests.

Design

1. The basic architecture from the scalability theory topic can be used here too.
2. There should be a huge number of servers which are serving the users.
3. There should be multiple servers at multiple geo locations to provide geo-redundancy. The database should be replicated at these multiple geo locations. There may be multiple servers in one particular zone too.
4. There is a huge number of read query, the user generally does a large number of query to find the seat he wants to book. There will be more reads then write so master-slave.
5. Queries can be cached; little old data is ok.
6. All the search will be served by slave servers.
7. When we book a ticket then transaction goes directly to the master server. Locks on train number can be taken to prevent race conditions. Once a lock is acquired then only you can book a ticket. Some counts can be used to avoid unnecessary locking and some counter can be used for this.
8. Each station has a quota in train and seats are allocated from that quota.
9. Each physical train will have two train ids one when trans go from source to destination station and one when it comes back. So in the system, there will be two train ids. Keeping these two separate ids will make the query easier to implement.
10. When final charting is done then each seat is swapped for the empty slots and we try to find the request from source station whose destination is also in that slot. The first fit is allotted that seat.
11. A load balancer is used to distribute traffic.
12. There may be multiple booking servers which ask for a booking token to the master server. Master server allocate a token for that server and reserve it for some time. When all the user information is filled and payment is done then only it allocates real seat depending upon user preference.
13. Slave server will handle user request till the end. Final booking request with the user payment and his complete information will go to the master server and the corresponding ticket will be booked.

Object Oriented Class Diagram

There are four kind of relationships between two classes in UML: Using, Composition, Aggregation, and Inheritance. These four relationships are depicted in the following diagram:

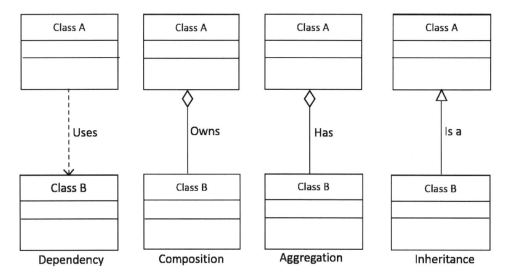

The above relation are as follows:

1. **Dependency**: class A uses class B
2. **Composition**: class A owns a class B
3. **Aggregation**: class A has a class B
4. **Inheritance**: class B is a sub class of Class A (or class A is extended by class B)

Relationship Description

Dependency
Objects of one class use objects of another class temporarily. When a class create an instance of another class inside its member function and use it and when the function exits then the instance of the other class is deleted.

Association
Objects of one class work with objects of another class for some prolonged amount of time

Aggregation
One class owns but share a reference to objects of other class. When a class stores the reference of another class inside it. Just a reference(pointer) is kept inside the class.

Composition
One class contains objects of another class. In Composition, the containing object is responsible for the creation and deletion of the contained object.

Generalization / Inheritance
One class is a sub-type of another class. Inheritance is a fairly straightforward relationship to explain the parent-child relationship.

Alarm Clock

How would you design an alarm clock?

Use Case

Alarm clock should have all the functions of clock. Should be able to show time.
The User can set the alarm time
The User can reset the alarm.
The User can set the alarm.

Constrains

The Granularity of alarm can be 15 min.

Test Case

Set the alarm at some time 6:00AM and set it.
The Alarm should work at 6:00AM
Stop the alarm, then alarm should stop ringing.

Design

There can be a clock class, which manages time and shoe time to the screen.
It has functions getTime() and setTime()

Alarm Clock extends Clock, and have some more function like startAlarm(), stopAlarm(), setAlarmTime(), ring()

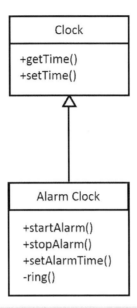

Implementation

A timer entry will run for granularity of 15 min. Or one min depends on customer requirement.
It will check if current time == alarm time if true then ring. And the alarm is on,
If start Alarm is called, it will set alarm on
If stop alarm is called, it will set alarm off.

Design for Elevator of a building

Scenarios

A typical lift has buttons (Elevator buttons) inside the cabin to let the user who got the lift to select his/her desired floor. Similarly, each floor has buttons (Floor buttons) to call the lift to go floors above and a floor below respectively. The buttons illuminate indicating the request is accepted. In addition, the button stops illuminating when the lift reaches the requested floor.

Use cases:
User
- Presses the floor button to call the lift
- Presses the elevator button to move to the desired floor
Floor Button & Elevator Button
- Illuminates when pressed by user
- Places an elevator request when pressed
Elevator
- Moves up/down as per instruction
- Opens/closes the door

Each button press results in an elevator request which has to be served. Each of these requests is tracked at a centralized place. Elevator Requests, the class that stores, elevator requests can use different algo to schedule the elevator requests. The elevator is managed by a controller class, which we call Elevator Controller. Elevator controller class provide instructions to the the elevator. Elevator controller reads the next elevator request to be processed and served.

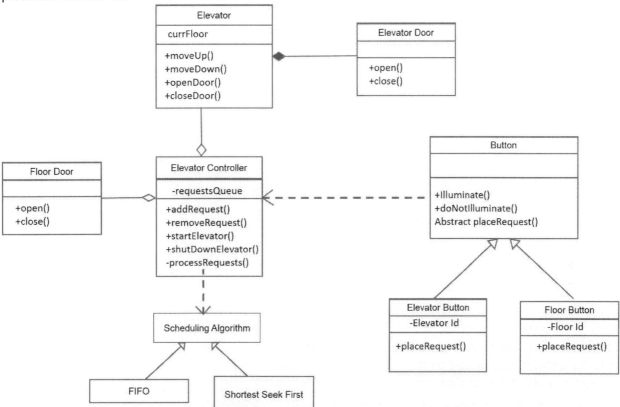

The button is an abstract class defining common behaviour like illuminate, doNotIlluminate. FloorButton, Elevator Button extends Button type and define placeRequest () method which is invoked when a button is pressed. When a floor button or elevator button is presses a requests is added to a common queue. ElevatorController reads the next request and instruct next action to the elevator.

How can we extend this to multiple elevators?

In the single elevator scenario, there is a single elevator and an elevator controller and a common server where the floor requests and the elevator button request are stored. Which are processed as per the scheduling algorithm.

To extend this to multiple elevator scenarios there will still be single elevator controller. Floor based requests can be served by any elevator whereas elevator button requests will be served only by the elevator to whome the button belongs.

FloorButton's placeRequest() adds a request to the common queue, which is accessed by the elevator controller thereby assigning the request to one of the elevators. ElevatorButton's placeRequest adds a request to the elevator directly as it is supposed to serve it. Elevator controller will be running various algorithms like shortest seek etc. to decide which lift is supposed to handle which request.

Valet parking system

Design a valet parking system.

Use Case

The requirements of the valet parking system should be:
1. Given a Parking lot having a fixed number of slots
2. Where a car can enter the slot if there is a free slot and then it will be given the direction of the free slot.
3. When exiting the car has to pay the fees for the duration of the time the car is in the slot.

Constraints

1. Parking slots come in multiple sizes- small, mid and large
2. Three types of vehicles, small, mid, large
3. A small vehicle can park in a small, medium, or large spot
4. A medium vehicle can park in a medium or large spot
5. A large vehicle can park only in a large spot

Design & Implementation

The parking lot will have the interface to

```
Class parkingLot{
        Public:
        Bool reserveSpace(Space);
        int unreserveSpace(Space);
        Private:
        Map<int,Space*> unreservedMap;
        Map<int,Space*> reservedMap;
};
```

```
Bool reserveSpace(Space)
{
// It will find if there is space in the unreserved map
// If yes, then we will pick that element and put into the reserved map with the current time value.
}
```

```
int unreserveSpace(Space)
{
// It will find the entry in reserve map if yes then we will pick that
// Element and put into the unreserved map. And return the charge units with the current time value.
}
```

OO design for a McDonalds shop

Let's start with the description of how the McDonalds shop works.
1. In a McDonalds shop, the Customer selects the burger and directly places the order with the cashier.
2. In a McDonalds shop, the Customer waits for the order ready notification. Customer upon being notified that the order is ready collects the burger himself.

There are three different actors in our scenario and below is the list of actions they do.
Customer
1. Pays the cash to the cashier and places his order, get a token number and receipt
2. Waits for the intimation that order for his token is ready
3. Upon intimation/ notification, he collects the burger and enjoys his drink

Cashier
1. Takes an order and payment from the customer
2. Upon payment, creates an order and places it into the order queue
3. Provide token and receipt to the customer

Cook
1. Gets the next order from the queue
2. Prepares the burger
3. Places the burger in the completed order queue
4. Places a notification that order for token is ready

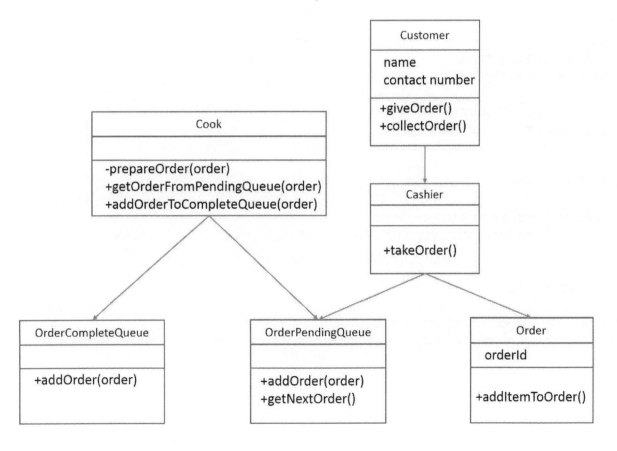

Object oriented design for a Restaurant

Let's describe how the restaurant works.
1. In a restaurant, the waiter takes order from the customer.
2. The waiter waits for the order to be ready and once ready serves the dishes to the customer.

These are the different actors in the model and I have listed the different actions against each actor
Customer
1. Selects the dish from the menu and call upon a waiter
2. Places the order
3. Enjoys his meal once the dish is served on his plate
4. Ask for the bill
5. Pays for the services

Waiter
1. Responds to the customers call on the tables he is waiting
2. Takes the customer's order
3. Places the order in the pending order queue
4. Waits for the order ready notifications
5. Once notification is received, collects the dish and serves the dish to the corresponding customer
6. Receives the bill request from customer
7. Asks the Cashier to prepare the bill
8. Gives the bill to the customer and accepts the payment

Cashier
1. Accepts the prepared bill request from the waiter for the given order details
2. Prepares the bills and hands it over to the waiter
3. Accepts the cash from the waiter towards the order

Cook
1. Gets the next order from the pending order queue
2. Prepares the dish and push the order to finished order queue
3. Sends a notification that the order is ready

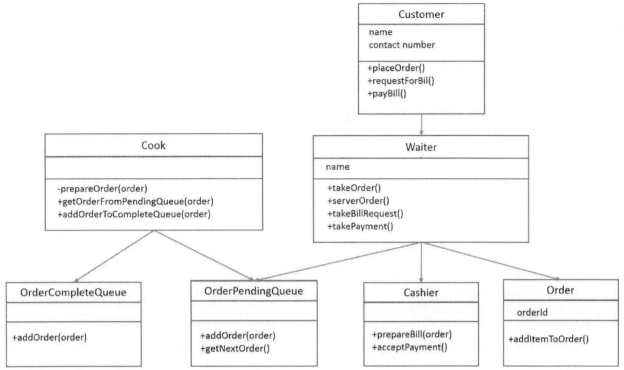

Class diagram for the Restaurant.

Object oriented design for a Library system

A library has a set of books, which the users can borrow for a certain period of time and return back. Users may choose to renew the return date if they feel they need more time to read the book.

The typical user actions with this online library would be
- Sign in/register
- Search books
- Borrow books
- Renew books
- Return books
- View his profile

The online library must keep track of the different books in the library currently available for users to borrow and the books already borrowed by users. Put it simply the inventory should be managed.

The various components of the system:
1. User
2. Librarian
3. Library
4. Book
5. Transection
6. Event Manager

The below class diagram, which depicts how these components inter-operates.

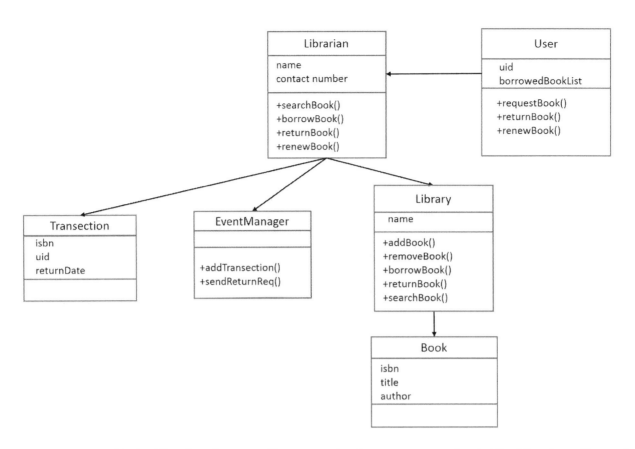

The User interacts with the Librarian, the user either request, return or renews a book. The Librarian will search for the book if the book is available in the Library then issue it to the user. A Transection will be created and added to the Event Manager. Event Manager will support add transaction and send return request interface. Once the book is overdue then the event manager will send an indication to the student that the book needs to be returned. When the book is renewed then the library state is not changed but the Transection detail is renewed at the Event Manager.

Suggest a shortest path

Use Case

The user had some coordinate by searching the coordinate from the name.
Show the whole map considering the coordinate as its centre.
Suggest the shortest path between two points.

Constraints

All paths are positive in cost.
For simplicity, I am considering all paths are for vehicle only, no pedestrian (pedestrian can walk in either direction even in one-way road.)

Design

The whole city map is stored as a graph in google.
We need to find the map by looking into the objects, which are in the distance shown by the browser.
The same path is stored as directed graph. And the graph that needs to be rendered depends on the zoom level.
The preferred algorithm is a* for this application to get the shortest path.
Weight = h(x, y) + g(x, y)

1. Design a system to implement social networking like Facebook, with millions of users? How would you find the connection between two people?

2. Autocomplete in www.booking.com. Design autocomplete feature for www.booking.com.

3. Instagram, Instagram is an online mobile-based photo sharing, video sharing service, which enables users to take pictures, and video upload them to the server and share them on social networking sites like Facebook or Twitter.
Note: - CDN is used to store active images.

4. Monolithic Website, assume you have a monolithic website and you are asked to rearchitect the website
Hint: - Discuss whole scalability theory section here.

5. Trip Advisor
URL's are parsed; content is collected from various services, and then applied to a template.

6. Cinchcast
Live audio streaming for business to do conferences.

7. BlogTalkRadio
Audio social network

8. Client based recommendation feature
How would you design a client based recommendation feature (based on customer history) on the product detail page? Design Customers who viewed item A also view item B and item C in an online shopping portal.

9. Car renting system
Design a car renting system, including reserving a car, checking in and checking out. Consider all the cases: reserve a car, then check out successfully; reserve a car, but the car is sold out before you check out...
Test Cases:
1. Try to reserve a car for more than one person
2. Try to reserve a car that is sold out
3. Verify the checkout process. After checking out a particular, you should be able to reserve it for another customer.
4. Try to reserve the same car for different customers in different dates

10. Online cab booking system (like Uber)
Admin Module
1. Admin should be able to add new driver / taxi details.
2. Should be able to calculate the amount that needs to be paid to the drivers. Monthly, weekly or daily.
User Module
1. Should be able to choose from and to location.
2. Available Taxies type, along with fare details.
3. Select a Taxi type
4. Book the taxi.
5. A confirmation message for the booking.

Driver Module

1. A driver should be able to register as a driver to Uber.
2. When a job is displayed to the driver he should be able to accept the job.
3. When the driver reaches to the customer then he should be able to start a trip.
4. When the driver had taken the customer to the desired location then he should stop the trip.
5. The driver should collect the fare based on the amount displayed in the app.
6. The driver should be able to give customer feedback.

Note: Just assume 2 minutes is equal to 1 KM.

11. Online teaching system

In an online teaching system, there are n number of teachers and each one teaches only one subject to any number of students.

And a student can join to any number of teachers to learn those subjects.

And each student can give one preference through which he can get updates about the subject or class timings etc.

Those preferences can be through SMS or Twitter/Facebook or Email etc.

Design above system and draw the diagram for above.

12. Customer Order Booking System

Admin Module

1. Should be able to add/edit/delete item, along with quantity, price, and unit.
2. Should be able to see all orders.

Customer Module

1. Should be able to enter his/her details for shipping, along will basic information like name, email, contact etc.
2. Can choose item, quantity
3. automatically payable price should be generated as per selected item and quantity.
4. Should be able to confirm the order.
5. After confirmation can see order confirmation report along with order number, which will be, system generated.

13. Online Movie Booking System

Admin Module

1. Should be able to enter all movies, which have been released, and about to release in next week with all possible details like theatre location, price, show timings and seats.
2. Should be able to delete movies, which are no longer in the theatre.
3. Can see a number of booked tickets and remaining tickets for single theatre or for all theatre.

User Module

1. User should be able to check all ongoing movies in theatre along with locations, availability of seats, price, and show timings
2. The user should be able to check all upcoming movies for next week too.
3. All movies those are running on theatre should be available for booking (one ticket or more than one ticket can be booked).
4. After booking user should see the confirmation message of booking.

14. Design an online Auction system (similar to e-bay)

Functionalities include enlisting a product for auction by bid owner, placing the bid for a product by bidders, Bid winner selection, Notification of bid winner etc.).

APPENDIX

Algorithms	Time Complexity
Binary Search in a sorted array of N elements	$O(logN)$
Reversing a string of N elements	$O(N)$
Linear search in an unsorted array of N elements	$O(N)$
Compare two strings with lengths L1 and L2	$O(min(L1, L2))$
Computing the Nth Fibonacci number using dynamic programming	$O(N)$
Checking if a string of N characters is a palindrome	$O(N)$
Finding a string in another string using the Aho-Corasick algorithm	$O(N)$
Sorting an array of N elements using Merge-Sort/Quick-Sort/Heap-Sort	$O(N * logN)$
Sorting an array of N elements using Bubble-Sort	$O(N!)$
Two nested loops from 1 to N	$O(N!)$
The Knapsack problem of N elements with capacity M	$O(N * M)$
Finding a string in another string – the naive approach	$O(L1 * L2)$
Three nested loops from 1 to N	$O(N^3)$
Twenty-eight nested loops … you get the idea	$O(N^{28})$
Stack	
Adding a value to the top of a stack	$O(1)$
Removing the value at the top of a stack	$O(1)$
Reversing a stack	$O(N)$
Queue	
Adding a value to end of the queue	$O(1)$
Removing the value at the front of the queue	$O(1)$
Reversing a queue	$O(N)$
Heap	
Adding a value to the heap	$O\ logN$
Removing the value at the top of the heap	$O(logN)$
Hash	
Adding a value to a hash	$O(1)$
Checking if a value is in a hash	$O(1)$

INDEX

A

Abstract data type (ADT) 55
Adjacency List 289
Adjacency Matrix 288
Algorithm 38
All Pairs Shortest Paths 303
Array 18, 56
Array ADT Operations 56
Array Interview Questions...................................21
Asymptotic analysis...................................38

B

Backtracking...................................338, 377
Balanced Binary search tree 60
Bellman Ford Shortest Path 303
Big-O Notation 38
Binary Search 22, 70
Binary Search Tree (BST) for Strings...................................63
Binary Search Tree ADT Operations 60
Binary Search Trees (BST) 60
Binary Tree...................................59, 203
Breadth First Traversal 293
Breadth-First Search (BFS) 67
Brute Force Algorithm 335, 341
Bubble-Sort 101, 341
Bucket Sort...................................113

C

Caching 395
Call by Reference...................................30
Call by value 29
Calloc 26
Circular Linked List 120, 154
Class co-NP 383
Class NP problems 381
Class P problems 380
Collision Resolution Techniques 274
Collisions...................................274
Comparisons of the various sorting algorithms...................................116
Complete binary tree 205
Constant Time 41
Counting Sort 67

D

Data-Structure 55
Decision problem 380
Depth First Traversal 291
Depth-First Search (DFS)...................................66
Dictionary 63
Digraph 286
Dijkstra's algorithm 300, 349
Directed Acyclic Graph 296
Divide-and-Conquer 336, 356
Doubly Circular list 162
Doubly Linked list...................................119
Doubly Linked List 144
Dynamic Memory Allocation 26
Dynamic Programming 337, 368

E

External Sort 115

F

Fibonacci Number 34
Forest...................................287
Free...................................26
Function 27

G

Graph Algorithms 66
Graphs 65, 286
Greatest common divisor 34
Greedy Algorithm...................................335, 347

H

Hash Function 273
Hashing and Symbol Tables 71
Hashing with Open Addressing...................................274
Hashing with Separate chaining...................................278
Hash-Table 62, 63, 273, 313
Hash-Table Abstract Data Type...................................62, 273
Heap ADT Operations 61, 250
Heap-Sort 114, 260
Height-balanced Binary Tree 207

I

Insertion-Sort 104

K

Knuth-Morris-Pratt algorithm 307
Kruskal's Algorithm 299, 349

L

Left skewed binary tree 206
Linear Probing 274
Linear Search 69
Linear Time 41
Linked List 57, 119
Linked List ADT Operations 57
Load Balancer 393
Load Factor 273
Logarithmic Time 41

M

Malloc 26
Master Theorem 46
Max Heap 249
Merge-Sort 107, 359
Min Heap 249
Minimum Spanning Trees (MST) 297

N

N-LogN Time 41
NP–Complete Problems 384
NP–Hard: 384

O

Omega-Ω Notation 39

P

Perfect binary tree 205
Pointer to structure 25
Pointers 17
Preparation Plans 13
Prim's Algorithm 297, 348
Priority Queue 61, 248

Q

Quadratic Probing 274
Quadratic Time 42
Queue 58

Queue Abstract Data Type 191
Queue ADT Operations 59
Queue Using Array 192
Queue Using linked list 194
Quick Select 111
Quick-Sort 109, 360

R

Realloc 26
Recursive Function 31
Redundancy 394
Right skewed binary tree 206
Robin-Karp algorithm 306

S

Selection of Best Sorting Algorithm 116
Selection-Sort 105, 342
Sequential Search 22, 342
Single Source Shortest Path 299
Singly Linked List 119, 120
Sorting Algorithms 67
Spanning tree 288
Stack 27, 58
Stack Abstract Data Type 169
Stack ADT Operations 58
Stack using Array 171
Stack using linked list 176
Strictly binary tree 205
Structure 24
Symbol Table 63, 309
System stack and Function Calls 28

T

Ternary Search Tree 64, 318
Ternary Search Trie 64, 318
Theta-Θ Notation 40
Time Complexity Order 41
Topological Sort 296
Tower of Hanoi 33
Tree Sorting 115
Trees 59
Trie 64, 314

U

Uses of Heap 264

V

Variable 17

Printed in Great Britain
by Amazon